D1560150

LEFT ON BASE IN THE BUSH LEAGUES

LEFT ON BASE IN THE BUSH LEAGUES

Legends, Near Greats, and Unknowns in the Minors

Gaylon H. White

ROWMAN & LITTLEFIELD
Lanham • Boulder • New York • London

Published by Rowman & Littlefield
An imprint of The Rowman & Littlefield Publishing Group, Inc.
4501 Forbes Boulevard, Suite 200, Lanham, Maryland 20706
www.rowman.com

6 Tinworth Street, London SE11 5AL, United Kingdom

British Library Cataloguing in Publication Information Available

Library of Congress Cataloging-in-Publication Data

Name: White, Gaylon H., 1946–, author.
Title: Left on base in the bushes : minor league legends, near greats, and unknowns / Gaylon H.
   White.
Description: Lanham : Rowman & Littlefield, [2019] | Includes bibliographical references and index.
Identifiers: LCCN 2018046859 (print) | LCCN 2019002460 (ebook) | ISBN 9781538123669 (elec-
   tronic) | ISBN 9781538123652 (cloth : alk. paper)
Subjects: LCSH: Baseball players—United States—Biography. | Minor league baseball—United
   States—History.
Classification: LCC GV865.A1 (ebook) | LCC GV865.A1 W48 2019 (print) | DDC 796.3570922
   [B]—dc23
LC record available at https://lccn.loc.gov/2018046859

♾ ™ The paper used in this publication meets the minimum requirements of
American National Standard for Information Sciences Permanence of Paper for
Printed Library Materials, ANSI/NISO Z39.48-1992.

Printed in the United States of America

To my understanding and patient wife,
Mary Lynn Joette Gilkey White, and our children,
Shane Andrew, Erin Lynn, and Rory Patrick Graham.
Thanks for your support and encouragement.

CONTENTS

FOREWORD

Wes Parker

Carlos Bernier played for the Hollywood Stars, one of eight teams in the Pacific Coast League, which from 1946 to 1957 many considered to be a third major league. My father first took me to see the Stars play at Gilmore Field on the West Side of Los Angeles in 1948, when I was eight years old, and I quickly became an avid fan.

The grass was as green, the sky as blue, the crack of the bat as sharp and clean as today, even sharper because Gilmore Field held slightly less than 13,000 paying customers, making it very much a sensory experience. Bernier, along with Frankie Kelleher and Chuck Stevens, were my favorite players. He could hit, throw, run, hit for power, and run. Lord, could he run. Back then they had pregame activities in which players would race one another around the bases. Bernier never lost. One time he circled the bases home to home, a straight-line run of 360 feet, in less than 14 seconds. That is how he came to be known as the "Cuban Comet" (even though he was Puerto Rican).

Players were not analyzed, dissected, and interviewed to nearly the extent that they are today. They played, then disappeared, returning to the mysterious life from which they came. They were like gods—majestic, young, supremely skilled, beautiful in those white uniforms with the red-and-blue highlights, the exact same color and shade Superman wore.

When games were sold out, they roped off the outfield and allowed us to sit on the outfield grass behind the ropes, close to our gods, so close we were within 10 feet of them. We could sense them, hear them, feel their energy. It got so that while driving to the games I prayed for a sellout so I could share the same grass with them and watch them from close range.

As an adult I looked back and wondered who Carlos Bernier really was, what kind of a life he lived, what happened to him after the Dodgers forced the Stars to relocate to Salt Lake City in 1958. I knew he played briefly in the big leagues with Pittsburgh but nothing more. Was he happy? Sad? Regretful? Pleased with himself and his career? What kind of man was he? What happened to him after his career ended?

This man and the 1950s era he played in remain among my most treasured memories, an era when the entire world seemed more alive and beautiful and civilized than it does today. And now, because of this book, I get to relive it and learn what Carlos Bernier and the other men I so admired during that wonderful time were really like.

Thank you, Gaylon White.

* * *

Wes Parker grew up in the Brentwood section of Los Angeles, graduated from the University of Southern California, and played first base for the hometown Dodgers from 1964–1972, winning six consecutive Gold Glove Awards while batting .264, with 64 homers. In 1974, he played in Japan for the Nankai Hawks, earning another award for outstanding defense and hitting .301. Jim Murray, legendary *Los Angeles Times* sports columnist, called Wes the "most graceful athlete I think I ever saw," adding, "Parker plays the game with such effortless ease he makes a ballerina look as if she had corns."[1]

PREFACE

If you were a kid baseball junkie in the 1950s and 1960s, the best fix was the annual baseball guide published by the *Sporting News*. It was chock full of stories and statistics from the lowest of the minors to the majors. Most of the minor leaguers were unknown and would remain that way. A few stepped out of the back pages of the guide and into the national limelight.

A photo in the 1954 edition introduced a young black player named Henry Aaron, batting champion of the Class A South Atlantic League (Sally) the previous season. He went on to hammer 755 home runs in a Hall of Fame career.

The following year, 1955, another black, Al Pinkston, led the Sally League in hitting. He's pictured wearing a baseball cap with the letter "A" for Athletics inscribed on it. The same photo of Pinkston, minus the letter on the cap, showed up in the guides for 1960, 1961, 1962, and 1963. He was the Class AA Mexican League batting king each year with averages ranging from .369 to .397.

It was a select group of minor leaguers pictured in the guides, as they featured only the top hitter and pitcher with the best earned run average from Class A leagues and above.

Pinkston's name continued to appear among the Mexican League's top batsmen until he retired after the 1965 season, a month shy of his 48th birthday. He never made it to the majors.

Who was this guy smiling from the pages of the baseball guide for almost a decade? Why didn't he make it to the big leagues? What happened to him?

In June 1975, I traveled to New Orleans, Louisiana, to meet Pinkston and get answers to my questions. The year before, I interviewed Joe Bauman in Roswell, New Mexico, and Bob Crues in Amarillo, Texas.

In the 1955 guide, at the end of a lengthy review of the 1954 season, Bauman is credited with the "top feat of the year in the minors," for pounding a record 72 home runs at Roswell. He broke the mark of 69, set by Joe Hauser of Minneapolis in 1933, and tied by Amarillo's Crues in 1948.[1]

The closest Bauman got to the majors was the one game he played at the Triple-A level of the minors. Crues didn't make it past Class A. Why?

I was asking the same question about the star players I saw play in the Pacific Coast League (PCL) growing up in Los Angeles—Carlos Bernier, Joe Brovia, Bob Dillinger, and Joe Taylor.

Prior to the arrival of the Dodgers in 1958, the PCL was as big league as you could get in Los Angeles. It was the only minor league with open classification status. Many of the former big-leaguers in the PCL didn't want to go back.

One of them was Bernier. He got a shot with the Pittsburgh Pirates in 1953 and, unhappy with his playing time, decided to remain in the PCL with the Hollywood Stars, where he was as big a celebrity as the movie stars who came out to see him play. Why?

Brovia wanted to play in the majors and deserved to go after slamming 71 homers and driving in 247 runs at Portland in 1950–1951. He had to wait four years until he got a chance at age 33. Why?

Dillinger posted a .306 batting average in six big-league seasons but was exiled to Sacramento in the PCL, where he won the batting title in 1953, with an average of .366. No team in the majors wanted him. Why?

In his PCL debut for the Portland Beavers in 1955, Taylor belted three of the longest home runs ever seen at the Beavers' 52-year-old ballpark. A teammate thought Taylor would be the "black Babe Ruth," but instead he spent most of the next eight seasons shuttling back-and-forth between the PCL and the majors. Why?

Ron Necciai pitched three games for Hollywood in 1955, and then retired from baseball at the age of 23. Three years earlier, at Bristol, Virginia, in the Class D Appalachian League, he became the first and only pitcher in baseball history to strike out 27 batters in a nine-inning game. He finished the 1952 season in the majors with a 1-6 record for the Pirates.

The catcher in Necciai's historic game was Harry Dunlop. He also was the player-manager at Stockton in 1964, when the Baltimore Orioles decided to give Steve Dalkowski, a hard-throwing-and-drinking pitcher called the "Living Legend," one last chance. Dunlop is uniquely qualified to discuss the minor-league pitching sensations that left us wondering, What if?

The best way to answer these questions was to talk to the players themselves—as many as possible. I met with Necciai in Monongahela, Pennsylvania, and Dunlop in Elk Grove, California. Twice I visited Brovia in Santa Cruz, California, and Taylor in Pittsburgh. After a two-year search for Bernier, I spent an entire day with him at his home in Paterson, New Jersey.

Over time the original concept for the book morphed to include chapters on Walter Buckel, Pat Stasey, and Tom Jordan Sr., as well as Jordan's son Tommy—lesser-known players with stories well worth telling.

I became fascinated with the marriage of convenience between Bobo Newsom, a legend in his own mind, and Joe Engel, colorful owner of the Chattanooga Lookouts. Bobo pitched two years for the Lookouts to prove he belonged back in the majors, where he had won 205 games earlier in his career.

It all started with the baseball guides that got me curious about minor-league greats that never made it to the majors or struggled if they did. I found out that the difference between success in the minors and failure in the majors can be razor thin and have less to do with a player's ability than the circumstances.

Forrest "Frosty" Kennedy never had his picture in one of the guides. Yet, he crushed 228 homers in his 10-year career, including 60 at Plainview, Texas, in 1956. Frosty never made it above Class AA. "I had a couple chances to go up, but what was the point?" he said.[2]

Frosty made more money in the minors, plus he was treated to dinner and drinks everywhere he played. "I was a king in the minor leagues. Why go up to the majors and be just a spear-carrier?"[3]

Sometimes a player's rise or fall came down to luck. "I've always said I'd rather be lucky than good," Bob Dillinger said. "Because as far as I'm concerned, a lot of baseball has to do with inches. And inches, to me, can be luck, too."

ACKNOWLEDGMENTS

When I began researching *Left on Base in the Bush Leagues* in 1974, President Richard Nixon was about to be forced out of office by the Watergate scandal, George Brett was a rookie third baseman for the Kansas City Royals on his way to the Hall of Fame, and the star of David Clyde, a teenage pitching phenom for the Texas Rangers, already was fading. By the time I finished, a friend chided, Clyde could qualify for the book. He was right.

Half of my life has passed since I sat in the Kansas City Royals dugout at Royals Stadium listening to Royals coach Harry Dunlop tell me about catching three no-hitters in his first 14 days in pro baseball, one of them a 27-strikeout game by Ron Necciai.

There's a bunch of folks to thank, starting with my wife, Mary, and our three children, Shane, Erin, and Rory, for staying the course with me. Jim Ladesich, a longtime family friend, hung in there until his death in 2015. Bill Swank provided research assistance and encouragement.

Bob Wirz, publicity director for the Royals at the time, paved the way early on by giving me access to his collection of *Sporting News* baseball guides and a press pass that made it possible to interview Joe Garagiola, Birdie Tebbetts, and other baseball people passing through Kansas City.

I wound up interviewing more than 200 players, managers, coaches, umpires, and sportswriters. They reached into their memory banks to share everything they could remember. My biggest regret is that most of the players featured in this book are no longer around.

Still living in 2018 were Tom Jordan Sr. and his son, Tom Jr.; Steve Dalkowski; Tito Arencibia; Dunlop; and Necciai. At age 99, Tom Sr. ended the year as the oldest living Major League Baseball player. I had the pleasure of watching the first two games of the 2016 World Series on TV with Tom Sr. and Tommy at their home in Roswell, New Mexico.

To all of the players who welcomed me into their homes and talked with me on the telephone, thank you for trusting me with your stories.

The manuscript was almost complete when Jim McConnell volunteered to review it. The author of a superb book about Bobo Newsom, *Baseball's Traveling Man*, I couldn't send chapters to him fast enough. Jim made everything better and contributed anecdotes from stories he did as a sports columnist for the *San Gabriel Valley Tribune*.

Bob Rives shared the transcript of an interview he did with Joe Bauman that was the basis for a biography about Joe he wrote for the Society of American Baseball Research website.

A native of Elk City, Oklahoma, Royse Parr filled in the gaps for the three years Bauman played for the Elk City Elks semipro team.

Jim Waldrip, a fellow graduate of the University of Oklahoma, provided a wealth of information on Bauman's later years. They were so close that they are buried next to one another in a cemetary across from Joe Bauman Stadium in Roswell.

I heard that the batboys for the Artesia Drillers had some interesting stories to tell about Bauman's two years in the small New Mexico town. So, I tracked down Ralph "Skip" Nix in Artesia; Mike Currier in nearby Carlsbad; and Lin Patterson in Broken Arrow, Oklahoma. They provided insight as valuable as Buck Lanier and Jerry Brown, the sportswriters who teamed up on the coverage of Bauman's record-breaking homers at Artesia the last day of the 1954 season.

Ferrell Dunham, Harold Hobson, and Blaine Stribling relived the dream of the summer of 1956, when their Roswell team, led by Tom Jordan Jr., captured the Little League World Series championship.

John-William Greenbaum, a walking encyclopedia on Dalkowski, guided me around the myths that surround the legendary pitcher.

Al Pinkston Jr. and Néstor Bernier both shed light on their fathers, Al Pinkston Sr. and Carlos Bernier. Pinkston was unknown to most baseball fans in the United States and the controversial Bernier widely misunderstood.

Patricia Stasey Aylor wrote a book, *Stealing Home*, about her father, Pat, and invited me to the annual Stasey family reunion celebrated at Stasey Field, the family's own field of dreams deep in the sticks of Texas.

Quoted throughout *Left on Base* is Chuck Stevens, the oldest living major-league player when he died on May 28, 2018, at the age of 99. He was best friends with Bob Dillinger and his wife Eleanor, who hit the century mark Chuck just missed.

I'm not sure when I first saw the April 5, 1948, issue of *Life* magazine with the same cover photograph as this book. But I knew immediately that it summed up the story I was trying to tell about Minor League Baseball after World War II and before the majors began expanding in 1961. Thanks to Joe Chaillot for putting a name to one of the faces by identifying his father, Emile Chaillot, a star for the Crowley, Louisiana, Millers in 1950. Emile is the olive-skinned guy fourth row up from the bottom of the photo and second from the right. A huge thanks as well to Christen Karniski and her team at Rowman & Littlefield for making the cover design possible.

The photos of Bauman were taken by Kenyon Cobane, a Roswell-based freelancer who got the attention of *Life* magazine with the series of images he captured the night Joe became pro baseball's new home run king. Cobane's collection is being preserved by the Institute of Historical Survey Foundation (IHSF) in Las Cruces, New Mexico. The Bauman pics are truly historical and should be on display at Cooperstown so more people can enjoy them.

Doug McWilliams and David Eskenazi came through in the clutch with other pictures needed.

The photos of Al Pinkston were given to me by Big Al himself in 1975. This enabled me to give his son copies after Hurricane Katrina destroyed Big Al's home and all of his memorabilia in 2005.

There are several images from the *Los Angeles Times* Photographic Archive, and the master sleuth who found them was Simon Elliott of the special collections department at UCLA's Charles E. Young Library.

Barry McMahon of Ladysmith, British Columbia, graciously shared gems from questionnaires he has sent to hundreds of Pacific Coast League players over the years.

It took a while for Brittany Wollman of the Angelo State University library in San Angelo, Texas, to find the date of a key newspaper story about Pat Stasey, but she tracked it down. Bob Hamilton of the Hobbs, New Mexico, library, helped locate another important article.

With the deadline for the manuscript fast approaching, my wife Mary asked me, "What would you do without Leann?"

She was referring to Leann DeBord, my helper extraordinaire on all my books. She proofreads every page; prepares the index; sorts out dreaded technology headaches; and handles the minutiae that drive me batty.

I didn't answer my wife because I don't even want to think about doing a book without Leann.

INTRODUCTION

Baseball once defined whether a city in America was major or minor league.

There was a time, wrote Atlanta sports columnist Furman Bisher, "when every town big enough to have a bank also had a professional baseball team, and the peak of excitement was reached when the bank was robbed or the baseball team won a pennant."[1]

No town was too small to field a pro team.

Snow Hill, North Carolina, population 940, had a team in the Class D Coastal Plain League, and its moniker, which was combined with the name of the town, was a classic—the Snow Hill Billies. "There was a wealthy merchant in Snow Hill who loved baseball," Bisher recalled, "and he intended to have a team if he were the only patron in the stands."

Bisher could've been thinking about Tito Arencibia and other Cubans who played at Big Spring, Texas, in the late 1940s and early 1950s when he penned, "Players with foreign names of many syllables came to a town, married a local belle, and never left."[2]

There were 52 minor leagues in 1948, when *Life* magazine published the compelling photograph on the cover of this book. Looking up at photographer George Silk's camera was a sea of "550 fresh-faced young Americans, supercharged with ambition to play baseball for the Brooklyn Dodgers."[3]

They were rookies from throughout the United States at the Dodgers' new spring training camp in Vero Beach, Florida. Most of those who made the cut wound up on one of the Dodgers' 25 farm clubs scattered throughout the country in places like Nashua, New Hampshire; Idaho Falls, Idaho; Ponca City, Oklahoma; and Valdosta, Georgia, at the bottom of the minor-league ladder, which ranged from Class D to Class AAA.

These were the leagues that came to be known as the bushes. They were made up primarily of players who remained unknown outside the towns where they played. But there were also players who achieved hero status and enthralled local fans as much as the stars in the majors.

Jim Reeves was born in 1946, in Carlsbad, New Mexico. The local team was called the Potashers, a member of three different leagues from 1953 through 1961. Reeves went on to become a baseball writer and sports columnist for the *Fort Worth Star-Telegram*.

"I covered 28 World Series," he said. "I saw some great players and great games and great World Series. But I still harken back to those days watching the Potashers play out at Montgomery Field in Carlsbad."

The Potashers were in the same league as the Roswell Rockets, and, in 1954, the Rockets had mighty Joe Bauman. He was on his way to slugging 72 homers, the most in baseball history, and folks came out to see if he could plop a ball into the Pecos River beyond the right-field fence.

"It was kind of an idyllic type thing to grow up in a small town watching a very small minor-league team," Reeves said. "It was grassroots professional baseball at its best. The games were intense. You wanted your team to not only win but to get to the playoffs, to win the championship."

Reeves was 13 in 1959, when the Potashers' Gil Carter, a former Negro Leaguer and heavyweight boxer, "out-Mantled Mickey" with a blast that landed in the yard of a house 733 feet from home plate. The distance was measured using aerial photographs taken by the local newspaper, the *Current-Argus*.[4]

"I didn't have a major-league team that I could identify with," Reeves said. "The team that I identified with was the Carlsbad Potashers, and they were my heroes."

Reeves wasn't alone.

The Pacific Coast League (PCL) was part of the minors, but for many West Coast fans it was their own major league until the Brooklyn Dodgers relocated to Los Angeles and the New York Giants to San Francisco in 1958.

The biggest PCL star in the mid-1950s was Stout Steve Bilko of the Los Angeles Angels, also called the Sergeant of Swat. He was so popular that his manager, Bob Scheffing, once boasted, "More people in L.A. today know Bilko than Marilyn Monroe."[5]

Stout Steve won the PCL Triple Crown in 1956, with a .360 batting average, 55 home runs, and 164 runs batted in.

Novelist Harry Turtledove, seven years old at the time, can tell you what Stout Steve did, but he doesn't remember Mickey Mantle winning the American League Triple Crown the same year. "The majors were a voice from another room," he said. "The PCL was in my room, if you know what I mean."

Turtledove eventually let Bauman into his room, and that got him to thinking about Roswell, the place where Joe belted most of his homers in 1954, and the site of the UFO incident seven years earlier. Could there be a connection? Turtledove makes you think so in a story he wrote about Bauman.

The minor leagues were filled with players that stirred and stretched the imagination, arousing curiosity.

Wade Cline was 18 years old in 1953, when Bob Dillinger won the PCL batting title with a .366 average. He recalled Dillinger starring for the St. Louis Browns. "He was one of the few good players the Browns had," Cline said. "He led the league in stolen bases three years. I thought that it was ironic that Dillinger the base thief had the same name as Dillinger the famous bank robber. A good question is why he left the major leagues?"

Why was Bobo Newsom, winner of 205 games in the majors at the time, back in the minors in 1949, pitching for the Chattanooga Lookouts, a Southern Association team run by Joe Engel, known as the "P. T. Barnum of the Bushes"? Because of the zany stunts he pulled? Was this another one?

By the end of the 1963 season, the minors were down to 18 leagues.

"They deleted all the classes but AAA, AA, and A, attempting to create a delusion of quality that isn't there," Bisher lamented. "They took something away from baseball when they took away the 'bush league' designations, the Ds, Cs, and Bs."[6]

Gone was the excitement of watching a player make the rare jump from Class D to the majors in the same season. Bristol's "Rocket" Ron Necciai did it in 1952, after becoming the first and only pitcher in history to strike out 27 batters in a nine-inning game. Rocket Ron was in Bristol less than a month before the Pittsburgh Pirates moved him up to Class B and then put him in their starting rotation.

"He has given us the kind of terrific baseball stories you dream about," *Bristol Herald Courier* sports editor Gene Thompson wrote. "It matters little that Ron began his baseball career in Salisbury, NC, and that he will eventually wear a Pittsburgh uniform. To us who follow the Twins he'll always belong to Bristol."[7]

That's what made the minor leagues of the 1950s so special. The players belonged to the towns where they played, and their accomplishments and fame were a source of great civic pride long after they left.

Bristol has made sure future generations remember the amazing performance of Rocket Ron the night of May 13, 1952. Outside the city's ballpark, DeVault Stadium, there's a plaque that reads, "In over one million professional baseball games played since Organized Baseball began in 1869, no one has ever matched Rocket Ron's feat that special evening. It remains one of baseball's greatest individual accomplishments."

Roswell has named its ballpark Joe Bauman Stadium, but the other players featured in this book are forgotten heroes.

Left on Base in the Bush Leaues puts you in the front row, on the field, and in the locker room with these players through interviews with them and their teammates, managers, and opponents. It's important to preserve and share their remarkable stories because they make the lore of Minor League Baseball richer and more fascinating. And they leave us with a sense of wonder of what might've been.

I

BUSHES AND BUSHERS

Three Bush League Legends and Two Unknowns

Philip K. Wrigley, longtime owner of the Chicago Cubs, knew a lot more about chewing gum than baseball. But he was onto something in 1953, when he called for baseball to eliminate the terms "major" and "minor," and sell the sport similarly to how General Motors sold cars.

GM was the gorilla of the car world at the time, each of its five divisions with a well-defined persona: Chevrolet, Buick, Pontiac, Oldsmobile, and Cadillac. None of the cars were subordinated to the other, Wrigley reasoned, selling each model on its own merits. Baseball needed to do the same, designating leagues in a way "that would give a true picture of varying ability and experience."[1]

No one paid any attention to Wrigley, and baseball continues to use the terms "major" and "minor" to market its product. The distinction between the two is greater in baseball than any other sport. In fact, baseball is the only major sport to have minor leagues that were once referred to as "bushes" and its players as "bushers."

A headline in the *Sporting News*, the self-proclaimed bible of baseball, used "bushes" in a headline as early as 1898.[2]

The term "busher" was indelibly written into the baseball lexicon with the publication, in 1916, of Ring Lardner's *You Know Me Al*, a novel consisting of letters by Jack Keefe, a fictional bush-league pitcher struggling to stick with the Chicago White Sox, to a friend, Al Blanchard. All six chapters have the word in their titles.

Lardner blurred the line between reality and imaginary by weaving such baseball characters as Ping Bodie, a stocky, swashbuckling outfielder, into busher Keefe's letters to Al back home in Bedford, Indiana: "Tonight at supper Bodie says, 'How did I look to-day Kid?' Gleason [William "Kid" Gleason] says, 'Just like you always do in the spring. You looked like a cow.'"[3]

Bodie's 52-ounce bat came close to making up for lead feet that inspired one of baseball's classic lines when he was thrown out trying to steal a base: "Ping had larceny in his heart, but his feet were honest."

In 1910, Bodie belted a record 30 home runs for the San Francisco Seals of the Pacific Coast League (PCL) to become a local hero and earn a shot in the majors with the White Sox.

"To kids on the sandlots of San Francisco, there were three great names in baseball—[Ty] Cobb, Babe Ruth, and Ping Bodie," said Joe Cronin, another San Francisco native who went on to become a Hall of Fame shortstop and top baseball executive.[4]

A fence-buster in the minors, the White Sox expected great things of Bodie. After hitting five homers in 1911 and four in 1912, the headlines of one newspaper proclaimed, "PING BODIE TO THE MINORS" and "FENCE BUSTER HAS OUTLIVED HIS USEFULNESS."

"Ping lived up to his reputation earned on the Coast for one season," the story noted. "Then he went back to the Coast and acted as a beer agent during the winter, came back fat as a pig, and the fences were comparatively safe."[5]

Bodie lasted another two years with the White Sox, returned to the Seals in the Coast League for two years, and then went back to the majors for five seasons before playing six more years in the minors. Overall, he had a respectable .275 batting average in the big leagues. But his 43 homers didn't come close to the 203 he blasted in the bushes.

Ping is best remembered for a remark he made while with the New York Yankees on what it was like rooming with the gallivanting Ruth. "I don't room with Ruth," he said. "I room with his suitcase."[6]

It was the kind of quote you'd expect from Lardner's Keefe, and it fueled speculation that Bodie was the inspiration for the famous busher. He denied this in a 1942 interview with J. G. Taylor Spink, publisher of *Sporting News*, but admitted to providing material to Lardner.

Ring was writing short stories and plays on other topics in 1928, when the 40-year-old Bodie ended his pro career in San Francisco, where it had started two decades earlier. On the same team was another brash, hard-hitting outfielder with an equally unusual name and all the idiosyncrasies of a Lardner creation—Smead Jolley.

The tall, lanky, lefty slugger from the Arkansas Ozarks believed each bat had a certain number of hits in it. So he'd take a new bat, stand it on the ground, and rub it down from the handle to the barrel, forcing all the hits into the barrel so it was easier for them to come out.

No one laughed at the results. He hit .367 in 16 minor-league seasons, winning a record-tying six batting titles. Four of them came in the rugged Coast League at a time it was producing major-league stars in assembly line fashion. He was a pretty fair country hitter in the majors, batting over .300 in three of the four seasons he split between the White Sox and Boston Red Sox for a career .305 average.

"I swing at anything I can reach," Smead said.[7]

This troubled White Sox manager Donie Bush, who mumbled, "If I could only get that Jolley to stop chasin' bad balls, he'd hit .400."[8]

A far greater concern was Jolley's clumsiness catching fly balls, which one teammate likened to a "kid chasing soap bubbles."[9]

Missed fly balls were made more memorable by Jolley one-liners: "There's a bad sky today—not an angel in the clouds."[10]

The misplay that ensured Jolley's legendary status as the worst out-fielder in baseball history took place at Boston's Fenway Park when there was a 10-foot incline called "Duffy's Cliff" in front of the left-field wall. "When the ball is hit, turn, run up the hill, and stand there," Bush instructed Jolley, peppering him in practice with fly balls to make sure he remembered. "Do that and you'll make the catch easy."

Jolley speared three hard-hit balls. "I've got that hill licked now," he said triumphantly.

The next inning, Jolley ran up the hill again to catch a high fly ball. "When I turned around, the ball wasn't there. It was going to fall short of the ramp. I took one step down, then another, walked right off into space, and fell flat on my face."

Jolley explained what happened to teammate Willie Kamm in the dugout later: "Willie, Bush told me how to get UP that hill. BUT HE NEVER SAID A WORD ABOUT HOW TO GET DOWN IT."[11]

Such stories made Jolley a cult hero. His inability to catch a ball and ability to hit one had people talking about him long after he quit the game in 1941.

For sheer color and entertainment, few can match "The Mad Russian," the nickname for Lou Novikoff, a socking, singing outfielder who was the world's best softball player before joining the Los Angeles Angels of the PCL near the end of the 1939 season and batting .452 in 36 games. He continued his torrid hitting in 1940, with a .363 average and 41 home runs.

Novikoff went on to hit a respectable .282 in the majors with the Chicago Cubs and Philadelphia Phillies. But he never fulfilled the promise showed in winning four minor-league batting titles. "Now I know why they call you the Mad Russian," one opposing manager taunted Novikoff. "If I couldn't hit any better than that, I'd be mad, too."

After misplaying a few balls in the outfield, he said, "I can't play in Wrigley Field because the left-field foul line isn't straight like in the other parks . . . it's crooked."[12]

He also claimed to be allergic to the ivy covering the walls at Wrigley Field. None of this mattered to Cubs fans. They loved the Mad Russian and his zany ways.

When Cubs manager Jim Wilson pinch-hit for him, fans howled their disapproval. "Never since Dizzy Dean have I seen the fans go so goo-goo over a guy as they have the Russian."[13]

The Mad Russian's charm didn't stop with the fans. "He's given me a lot of laughs, and I can't stay mad at him," Wilson explained.

One evening in Pittsburgh, Wilson went looking for the Mad Russian after he left the team's hotel past midnight. "Where do you suppose I found him? In one of those small night clubs, sitting on top of the piano singing at the top of his voice. How he loves to sing. If he could only hit as well as he sings, he'd be a .350 slugger."[14]

Like Jolley, the Mad Russian ended his career on the West Coast in the lower minors, the Class B Western International League. They could still hit, Jolley batting .345 and Novikoff .326. But they were never able to overcome the good-hit, no-field label and the eccentricities the media focused on to depict them as clowns. To Edgar Munzel of the *Chicago Sun-Times*, for example, Novikoff was just another "player with a minor-league complex."[15]

"People knocking the minor leagues, I hear that stuff all the time," Forrest "Frosty" Kennedy told sports columnist Jim McConnell in 1997.[16]

Frosty is one of 14 players to hit 60 or more home runs in a season. He did it in 1956, for Plainview, Texas, in the Class B Southwestern League. Hitting 60 homers in the minors was harder than in the majors, he insisted:

> A shorter season, rotten lights at rotten little ballparks, rotten pitchers who couldn't or wouldn't throw me a pitch to hit, freezing weather in the spring, hot as hell in the summer. Don't let anyone ever tell you there was anything cheap about my getting 60 home runs. I was there, Charlie. [17]

Outfielder Ben Howard "Rosie" Cantrell had his own reasons for spending his entire 16-year career in the minors, where he had a lifetime batting average of .315 and was widely known for hitting the bottle as hard as the ball.

When Rosie played for Little Rock in the Southern Association in 1947, he kept a bottle of Four Roses bourbon stashed inside the ballpark's hand-operated scoreboard in center field. If he made the last out in an inning, he'd take a swig or two. "If he wasn't going to hit during that inning, he didn't come in," recalled Little Rock catcher Marland "Duke" Doolittle. "The more intoxicated he became the better hitter he was."

"How do you do it?" some younger teammates asked Rosie after he smashed four line-drive hits in a game.

"You fellows have a problem that I don't have," he said. "When you go to the plate and you're sober, you only see one ball. You have to hit what you see. When I go to the plate and I'm feeling good or high, I see three or four. I always pick out the one I like the best."

Shagging fly balls in the outfield prior to one game in Little Rock, Duke sidled up to Rosie and said, "You're such a good hitter that you'd go to the big leagues in nothing flat if they knew you weren't messing around with liquor anymore."

Rosie thought about the question for a moment and asked, "Why would I want to do that? Where can you go from there?"

Rosie was content in Little Rock. He wasn't paid all that much but most big-league players made about the minimum annual salary of $6,000. The cost of living was a lot less in Little Rock than New York City, Philadelphia, Boston, Chicago, or St. Louis, where 11 of the 16 major-league teams were located at the time. "There were a lot of minor-

A star for the Little Rock Travelers in the 1940s, Rosie Cantrell had big-league potential but no interest in moving up. "Where do you go from there?" he once asked teammate Duke Doolittle. Duke's wife, Norma Jean, took this photo of Rosie when she was a photographer for a Little Rock newspaper. *Photo by Norma Jean Hyatt Doolittle, courtesy of Sandy Doolittle.*

league ballplayers, but there were very few major-league teams," Duke said. "Competition was keen."

In no other professional sport is success on one level so overshadowed by the lack of success on another. A minor-league star that doesn't make it to the big leagues or live up to expectations while there is a flop. Rarely is there an in-between.

In 1978, 20-year-old Clint Hurdle was pictured on the cover of *Sports Illustrated*, wearing a Kansas City Royals uniform and a big smile, symbolic of the promising career ahead of him. The headline emphasized this point in bright yellow letters: "THIS YEAR'S PHENOM."[18]

Hurdle's rookie numbers weren't all that bad—.264 batting average, 7 homers, and 56 runs batted in. But he was no phenom and never achieved star status in the big leagues until he became a manager. "If I'd done everything I was supposed to," Hurdle said halfway through his first year, "I'd be leading the league in homers, have the highest batting average, have given $100,000 to the Cancer Fund, and be married to Marie Osmond."[19]

Joe Garagiola was a big-league catcher for nine years before moving into the broadcast booth. "Big-league baseball is a tough grind. I hit .356 one year in the minors; I never hit .300 in the big leagues."

Actually, he hit .318 in 34 games for the St. Louis Cardinals in 1950. But his name is on a plaque at the National Baseball Hall of Fame in Cooperstown, New York, because he was better poking fun at himself than hits on the field.

In early 1946, Joe was sitting in a U.S. Army tent in Manila, Philippines, listening to a sports report on Armed Forces Radio. The announcer raved about "this new phenom" who's going to take over catching duties for the Cardinals: "This kid can hit, the ball explodes from the bat, and oh, he can throw, gotta gun for an arm."

Garagiola was thinking to himself, "Christ, if this guy is for real, when we get out of here and I go back to baseball, I'm gonna be in the minors for 120 years. Who is this guy?"[20]

The announcer finally named the catcher—Joe Garagiola.

"Unfortunately, people think a guy is going to be as great in the major leagues as he was in the minor leagues," Garagiola said. "That isn't necessarily the case at all. I can't explain it. I can only go with what Mr. Rickey would say: 'The difference between a minor leaguer and a major leaguer is the strike zone.'"

Branch Rickey was the architect of extensive minor-league systems for the Cardinals, Brooklyn Dodgers, and Pittsburgh Pirates, which produced World Series titles for each organization. He stockpiled players so if one went down, another was up and ready to go.

"You take fellows that have big, big years in the minor leagues, keep in mind that they don't see great pitching every day," Garagiola said.

Rickey's mantra became his own: "If a hitter can control the strike zone in the major leagues, he's going to hit. If a pitcher can control the strike zone, he's going to win."

* * *

David "Gus" Bell played 15 years in the majors, starting with the Pittsburgh Pirates before moving to the Cincinnati Reds, where he was a four-time National League All-Star in the 1950s. His son, Buddy, and two grandsons, David and Mike, combined to play 31 years in the big leagues.

"Ever hear of a guy by the name of Bill Pierro?" Gus asked. "That would have to be the most fascinating story ever told."

Standing 6-foot-1 and weighing 155 pounds, William "Wild Bill" Pierro looked like a harmless beanpole until he unleashed one of the sidearm fastballs that catapulted him from the bottom of the minors to the majors. "I pitched sidearm—right from the hip like Ewell Blackwell," he said.

Called "The Whip," Blackwell was the most feared pitcher in baseball at the time, winning 22 games for Cincinnati in 1947. That was the same year the cocky, fast-talking Pierro persuaded the Pirates to give him a tryout and whiffed 180 batters in 134 innings at Bartlesville, Oklahoma, in Class D. His second season at Bartlesville, in 1948, he amassed 300 strikeouts in 230 innings, followed by 311 in 285 innings, including postseason playoff games, in 1949, at Waco, Texas, a Class B team. Altogether, that's an average of almost 11 strikeouts per nine-inning game.

The right-handed Pierro walked 304 batters and plunked 28 more in 364 innings in his two seasons at Bartlesville. He cut down on the free passes at Waco but still hit a league-high 16 batters.

"Pierro was death on right-handers," said Waco manager Morris "Buddy" Hancken. "One day he was pitching against Texarkana, I believe, and one of their right-handers came back to the bench moaning, 'If you left-handers don't knock him out soon, he's gonna kill all of us right-handers.'"[21]

Because of an amazing 755 strikeouts in 619 innings, the Brooklyn-born Pierro was being hailed as a "Flatbush version of Bob Feller" in 1950, when he moved up to Indianapolis in the American Association. By mid-July he had pitched a one-hitter, the eighth of his career; won eight games to improve his overall record to 51-31; and was leading the Triple-A loop in strikeouts. "He was one of the hottest prospects coming up to Pittsburgh," said Bell, also a Pirates rookie in 1950.

Wild Bill lived up to his nickname with the Pirates, walking 28, hitting two more, and throwing three wild pitches in 29 innings. Pitches thrown near the plate didn't fool anyone, producing 33 hits, 34 runs, 2 losses, and a 10.55 earned run average. "I had a rough half-season up there because I couldn't find the plate," Bill admitted.

When Rickey became general manager of the Pirates in November 1950, he set out to change Pierro. "He wanted me to throw overhand, and I refused to do it," Pierro said.

Rickey threatened to send Bill back to the minors if he didn't follow orders.

"Fine, send me back to the minors," Bill fired back. "I've been throwing sidearm ever since I've been throwing a ball, and I'm not going to change it for anybody."

Pierro didn't need to be told he was good, but baseball greats Joe DiMaggio and Paul Waner did anyway, urging him to stick with the sidearm delivery that got him to the majors. "Learn how to put the ball over the plate and nobody is going to beat you," they advised.

While Rickey raved about Pierro's fastball, he wanted him to throw overhand to improve his control and develop a curveball.

"We could readily see that a pitcher with his delivery would have a tough time against left-hand hitters," said Bill Posedel, the Pirates' pitching coach. "He didn't have the breaking ball to offset the one pitch he had."

Rickey even offered Pierro special coaching, arranging to meet him at 8:30 one morning with Posedel and another instructor. When Bill showed up 40 minutes late, Rickey ordered him to pack his bags for reassignment in the minors.

"Right now, I don't care where that boy pitches this season," Rickey said. "He doesn't have the attitude to play on this ballclub."[22]

"There are some guys you can help and a lot of guys you can't help," Posedel said. "I always felt that if you could do the job, it's great to be cocky. But to be cocky and not do the job, that's different."

"Posedel used to get a little disgusted with me, but I listened to him," Bill said. "He thought he'd make a helluva pitcher out of me as soon as 'you get the wild hairs out of your butt.' I tried to throw overhand, but they started hitting long balls off of me. I mean, they were tagging me pretty good. I gave that up after one or two games."

The Pirates sent Pierro back to Indianapolis. He never made it. "I had what I thought was the flu during spring training. I traveled north with the ballclub, playing exhibition games. I couldn't seem to shake this flu."

Bill was hospitalized briefly in Cincinnati. "The team was in Pittsburgh, and I wanted the hell out of there or else I was going to wind up back in the minors. Nobody can hold you against your will. I signed myself out against the doctor's advice."

Bill rejoined the Pirates in Pittsburgh, checking into the Webster Hall Hotel, where the other players were staying.

Gus Bell and his wife had a room on the same floor as Pierro. "We were walking down the hall to go to the ballpark and hear some noises," Bell recalled. "This door is open. The maid comes out and says, 'Oh, that guy is really drunk in there.'"

Upon arriving at the ballpark, Bell overheard Pierro's roommate, veteran third baseman Bob Dillinger. "Pierro is sick," Dillinger said. "He's out of his head."

The team's physician suggested that a taxi be sent to the hotel to get Pierro and take him to the hospital. "You send an ambulance for that boy," the normally soft-spoken Dillinger shouted. "He's sick."

On April 15, 1951, his 25th birthday, Pierro was rushed to Pittsburgh's Presbyterian Hospital in a cab. A headline in the *Terre Haute Star* best captured the situation: "BUCS' BILL PIERRO NEAR DEATH FROM DISEASE OF BRAIN."

Bill had either encephalitis (inflammation of the brain) or meningitis (inflammation of the brain lining) and was in critical condition. "Only yesterday," the story noted, "Pierro had been assigned to Indianapolis on a 24-hour option."[23]

The Pirates quickly called off the deal.

It took a team of doctors several days to establish Pierro had encephalitis. "It's akin to polio and meningitis," Bill said. "They couldn't give me any medication. If I had meningitis, medication for polio would have killed me."

Bill was in a coma for two weeks. "The ballclub saw that I had the best. They did everything in the world that was possible. They weren't worried whether I ever pitched major-league ball again. They wanted to save my life. I was close to death."

Bill had joined the U.S. Marines out of high school and saw action in Guam during World War II. He believed that's where he contracted the disease and it remained dormant until 1951.

"When I got out of the hospital, the first thing I did was go to the ballpark."

Ironically, Bill's uniform number with the Pirates was 13.

"I didn't put a ball suit on. I walked out on the field and stood on the mound. Nobody was there. I started winding up like I was going to throw the ball. I staggered all over the place. I said, 'That's it! Might as well forget it.' So I packed it up and lived with it ever since."

The next time Bell saw Pierro was at Ebbets Field when Bill came from his home in Brooklyn to see the Pirates play the Dodgers. They talked in the clubhouse before the game.

"Where you sitting?" Bell asked.

"Second deck—in the bleachers."

"Isn't that something?" Bell thought to himself.

A couple of months earlier they had been teammates, on the field and in the dugout together, and now Bill was sitting in the bleachers.

"I think he was too embarrassed to come to the ballpark after that," Bell said.

Pierro stopped following baseball. "I'm not bitter. It's just that if I can't play, I get bugged. I start feeling sorry for myself. I don't need that, so I stayed away from it. I love the game."

Encephalitis is a rare disease caused by a virus, affecting mostly children and the elderly. Bill lost all coordination in his legs so when he walked, it appeared he was drunk. He got a job finishing furniture. It was something he could do as he got older, and the effects of encephalitis required him to use a cane and, eventually, a wheelchair.

"That's the way the cookie crumbles," Bill said. "One thing I've always said: 'Thank God I made it to the big leagues—that this didn't happen to me in Triple-A and for the rest of my life I would've wondered if I could've pitched in the big leagues.' I know I did. That's the consolation I take in what happened to me. I have no regrets."

Bell blamed the Pirates, particularly Rickey, for treating Bill unfairly before he became ill. "They really crapped on this guy."

Pierro didn't feel that way. "Mostly, it was my fault. I was a very cocky kid."

Bill praised Rickey, recalling the time the Pirates boss told him, "You know something, young man, you're good! You and every other ballplayer that's here is good. Every player that's sitting on this bench in the bullpen is good. You wouldn't be sitting here in the big leagues if you weren't good. Don't ever feel bad about that."

On another occasion, Rickey encouraged Bill and other Pirates youngsters with a pep talk: "You can give me the best college team in baseball and I'll put any Class D ballclub on the field with them. The college team may beat them in five games. But put this college team with a Class D ballclub for 154 games and the Class D team is going to shellac them."

Pierro paused to emphasize a point he was about to make. "Bush League to a ballplayer is very low. I've always felt the minor leagues were not bush leagues. They are still professional baseball."

Pierro died April 1, 2006, at the age of 79—almost 55 years after encephalitis ended his promising baseball career. "If I knew I was going to get encephalitis, I'd still do it again," he said. "Believe me I would. That's how much I enjoyed it—minor leagues and all."

2

FOLLOWING A DREAM

Walter Buckel and the "Biggest Little Baseball City
in the United States"

U.S. Highway 80 once was the "Broadway of America," connecting San Diego on the West Coast to Georgia's Tybee Island on the East Coast. The young man hitchhiking on the stretch of highway passing through his hometown of Holtville, California, in the spring of 1941 was on his way to another small city on U.S. 80 a thousand miles to the east—Big Spring, Texas. Walter Buckel was following his dream of being a professional baseball player.

The year before, Big Spring was home to the Barons before they moved mid-season to Odessa and became the Oilers. The Barons/Oilers had the worst record (45-95) in pro baseball. The team was back in Big Spring for the 1941 season, under new ownership, a new manager, Jodie Tate, and a new nickname, the Bombers. The 19-year-old Buckel figured Big Spring needed new players, too.

Three car rides later he was in El Paso, where he hooked up with a truck driver on his way to Big Spring. "That's the ballpark over there," Buckel said excitedly as they rolled into town.

He grabbed a black tin suitcase carrying his glove, spikes, khaki pants, and t-shirts, and jumped off the truck. "Good luck, kid," the truck driver said.

At the ballpark, Buckel introduced himself to Tate.

"Kid, I can't use you," the manager said. "I've got a working agreement with Brooklyn. And they're going to send me all the ballplayers I can use. But if you'll hang around, I'll take you over to the highway and point you up toward Lamesa, a little town up the road about 40 miles. They can use some ballplayers."

That's how Buckel got to Lamesa, Texas, a cattle-ranching and cotton-farming community of about 10,000 people 60 miles south of Lubbock.

He signed a $75 a month contract to play third base for the Lamesa Loboes of the West Texas–New Mexico (WT–NM) League in 1941, and then returned in 1947, as a shortstop for two more seasons. He played briefly in 1949, before becoming the team's business manager, a position he held through 1950. "I could field, but I couldn't hit," Buckel said. A career batting average of .226 attests to that.

Buckel was good at organizing things. He rallied public support for a new 3,500-seat ballpark and arranged for new uniforms without the "e" in the nickname Loboes, saying it stood for error "and no ballclub wants an error anywhere. We have a brand new ballpark, a lineup dotted with new players—now we have a brand new name," Buckel explained.[1]

In 1950, Lamesa lived up to the claim on the club's letterhead: "THE BIGGEST LITTLE BASEBALL CITY IN THE UNITED STATES."

"Regardless where a person might perambulate," sports editor "Irish" Matthews wrote in the *Lamesa Daily Reporter*, "we don't think they will find more baseball enthusiast(s), grandstand umpires, and managers, or just plain old peanut crunching baseball fans, than right here in Lamesa."[2]

Lamesa's total attendance of 100,000 was 10 times its population and more than Amarillo and Albuquerque, the largest cities in the league. "We drew 87,000 during the season and 13,000 more in the playoffs," Buckel bragged.

Even when Lamesa went on the road in the playoffs, almost 1,500 fans showed up at Lobo Park to sit in the grandstands and cars nearby to listen to Buckel enliven telephone reports from the game sites with a colorful play-by-play account over the loudspeaker system.

Buckel wound up living in Lamesa for 66 years. He continued to broadcast local sports events while wearing a variety of hats, ranging from transportation and cafeteria manager for city schools to county clerk to insurance agency owner to radio station manager.

In 1967, townsfolk persuaded him to purchase a small weekly newspaper, the *Dawson County Free Press*, and compete against the *Lamesa Reporter*, an absentee-owned semiweekly. "I knew nothing about newspapers," he said.

It didn't matter because eight months later consummate newspaper publisher James Roberts of Andrews, Texas, hatched a plan to form the Roberts Publishing Company, buy out Buckel's competitor, and establish the *Lamesa Press-Reporter*, with Buckel as president and publisher.

"It opened up a whole new world because Mr. Roberts had his mind set on building a group of community newspapers in county seat towns," Buckel said. "He was the visionary and the dreamer; I was the detail man. Every paper we acquired I was on the board and the secretary on most of them."

Halfway between Lamesa and Andrews, a distance of 55 miles, there's a huge elm tree on the side of the road. "He'd pick up the phone and say, 'Walter, meet me at the tree.' We did a lot of business under that tree."

They teamed to gobble up 15 daily and weekly newspapers in West Texas. "We found papers that had problems with the publishers," Buckel said.

New publishers were given strong incentives to get involved in the community and provide leadership. "We don't cover the moon shots; we write local news and that's all."

Pro baseball was long gone by 1978, when Buckel wrote a series of 48 articles about his experiences in the WT–NM League. A compilation of the stories titled *SportScrapbook* was published in 1990, to give readers a glimpse of what baseball was like in Lamesa before and after World War II. The anecdote-packed stories also offer a snapshot of life in one of baseball's most colorful minor leagues.

The WT–NM loop was classified as a "D" league in 1941, and "C" after the war.

The windswept plains produced plenty of jokes: "Stand in any one place and you can see five miles; stand on a tuna fish can and you can see 10."

Balls soared over the short fences of the ballparks, aided by prevailing winds and the dry, thin air in the league's cities. Amarillo's Bob "Round Trip" Crues belted 69 in 1948, breaking the league mark of 57 set the year before by Lubbock's Bill Serena and tying pro baseball's single-season high. In 1949, Lamesa's D. C. "T-Bone" Miller swatted 52.

"The West Texas–New Mexico League thinks nothing of 90 to 100 tallies in an evening," a wire-service correspondent reported.[3]

High-scoring games in the WT–NM and Longhorn leagues produced unusual headlines, like the one when the Odessa, Texas, Oilers lost, 27-25: "ODESSA FAILS IN FINAL QUARTER." The story began, "It was fourth down, one to go, and Odessa needed two points to tie the game when the whistle blew."[4]

A game scheduled the following night was postponed by wind gusts as high as 55 miles per hour, reducing visibility to near zero and flattening the center-field fence. This little ditty summed up things nicely:

> The wind she blew and the base hits flew
> And our pitchers lasted an inning or two.[5]

It was a golden era for baseball in West Texas, one that Buckel wanted to chronicle for future generations.

"Before television, before air conditioning, before backyard barbecue—the best place you could go on a summer night was the ballpark," Buckel recalled. "It was an era of Minor League Baseball where communities adopted the team. They adored their baseball players. They'd take you into their homes and restaurants. It was just beautiful. You were a celebrity in the town."

Buckel was sitting in the living room of his daughter's home in Lubbock, where he and his wife, Rubye, moved in 2010, to be closer to health care facilities. He was 91. "If I live to 90," Buckel told a former teammate, "I'm going to be a .400 hitter. Everybody else is dead. They can't refute it anymore."

He laughed at the thought of being another Ted Williams, the last big-leaguer to hit .400 in a season.

On a nearby table was a spiral binder with his *SportScrapbook* stories. He picked it up and started talking about Grover Seitz, longtime manager of the Pampa Oilers. He was called "Wild Bull of the Pampans" because he was always mixing it up with opposing players, umpires, and fans.

"Grover was a showman and could fill ballparks with displays of emotion that would have won him Oscars and Emmys had he been in motion pictures," Buckel wrote.

One night in Lamesa, Grover was the target of a highly vocal fan named Sid sitting behind home plate. They taunted one another throughout the game until Grover "raced to the screen with a terrible scowl on his face, reached into his pocket, and pulled a pistol while Sid scrambled to get out of the seat."[6]

Grover soaked Sid with a water pistol purchased in town that morning.

Walter "Lefty" Condon, an easygoing pitcher for Lamesa in 1947, didn't fit baseball's stereotype of left-handers as temperamental and eccentric, but his wife, Phyllis, did. "She wore a leopard skin coat winter and summer, whatever the weather was," Buckel said. "She roamed the stands and could cuss like a Barbary Coast sailor at umpires and everybody else."

Phyllis pestered manager George Sturdivant to ride the team bus on road trips, something that was taboo for any player's wife. "No women going to ride our bus," Sturdivant huffed.

So, Phyllis, wearing her leopard skin coat, hitchhiked to games hundreds of miles away. "We would be breezing down the road and pass Phyllis heading for the same destination," Buckel reported. "Lefty would merely stick his head out, wave, and holler, 'See you in Borger, hon,' and we'd keep on rolling. Oftentimes she would beat us to our destination and be waiting for ol' Lefty when he crawled off the bus."[7]

Traveling in old, rickety buses at night in the wide, open spaces of West Texas and eastern New Mexico was an adventure even if nothing went wrong. When something did, well, it made for a harrowing experience.

Two Lamesa players almost didn't survive a trip home from Albuquerque in 1951. Seated in the rear of the team bus directly over the motor, the players got sick from carbon monoxide gas fumes. One of them collapsed. Both wound up in the hospital.

Buckel related his favorite bus story.

The Lobos were on their way to Abilene, 140 miles southeast of Lamesa. Just outside Abilene is Merkel, home of a town marshal who took particular pleasure in pulling over speeding motorists in his old, dilapidated, unmarked car. Veteran pitcher Eulis Rosson knew this; kid pitcher John Fetzer did not.

Fetzer was driving the bus when Rosson noticed the marshal following close behind. "Fetzer, step on it!" Rosson urged. "There's an old guy driving that car. Don't let him beat us to Abilene."

Fetzer stepped on the gas; the marshal did the same. As Buckel described it, "The old car and the old bus raced side-by-side down the highway while the players hooped and hollered, egging Fetzer on."[8]

When Fetzer finally pulled over, he discovered he had been racing the town marshal. "I didn't know you wanted to stop us," he said.

"I ought to throw the whole ball club in jail," the marshal yelled. Instead, he gave Fetzer a "severe tongue-lashing" and let the team go on to Abilene, where they played that night.

Fetzer was one of several Lobos to marry a local girl. A number of other players, like Rosson, nicknamed the "Arkansas Hummingbird" after his home state, remained in Lamesa after quitting baseball.

Detroit-born pitcher Stan Grzywacz settled in Lubbock after winning 46 games in three seasons with the Lobos. "He didn't have an overpowering fastball or curve," Buckel said. "He made up for it with a fiercely competitive attitude that was a joy to watch. He thought he could beat anybody any day. Just let him pitch."

Or run the bases.

Gryz, as he was called, was on first base when a teammate doubled to right field. He rounded second and was racing for third when he stumbled and flopped to the ground. He got up, only to fall again halfway between third and home plate. Exhausted, he was crawling toward home when he was tagged out. "You started your slide too soon, Gryz," one of the Lobos hollered as he returned to the dugout. "You're supposed to wait until you're closer to home."

Buckel recalled Stan taking "about all the ribbing he could and then announced to the world: 'If you bums could hit the ball hard enough to get a pitcher around to third base more than once a month we wouldn't be so unfamiliar with that bag and could handle it better.'"[9]

Throughout the years, Buckel described Stan's "early slide" dozens of times. "You played for the fun of the game," he said, "and hoped you had the opportunity to move up the line some place."

Few players in the WT–NM League made it to the higher minors or majors. One of them was Bill Serena, a stocky shortstop for the Lubbock Hubbers in 1947, and the starting third baseman for the Chicago Cubs three years later.

"He had a beautiful upper-cut swing," Buckel said of Serena. "He seldom hit a ground ball. Everything was swinging up. And in the light air out here, he lofted them over a lot of fences."

Serena slugged 70 homers for the Hubbers—57 during the regular season and 13 in the playoffs. He clouted 50 more for Double-A and Triple-A teams before the Cubs tabbed him to start at third base in 1950. He belted 17 homers as a rookie but finished his big-league career with only 48 spread across six seasons.

At age 22, Serena was younger than the league's other top fence-busters—Bob Crues, D. C. Miller, and Joe Bauman—who led the league in 1946, with 48 homers. "They could hit 75 home runs, and they weren't going any place because they were old-timers finishing up in this league," Buckel said. "Serena was in the league only one year. Had he stayed out here with his upper-cut swing, he would've set a bunch of records."

One of those records would've been the amount of money collected through a ritual called "picking the screen" or "picking lettuce." When a hometown player hit a home run, fans poked cash through the screen separating the grandstands and the playing field. "They had chicken wire around the backstops all the way—down the third-base and first-base lines," Buckel said. "Normally, it was one-inch chicken wire. You could stick a dollar bill, a five, or 10 in there; maybe a 20. It all depended on the euphoria of the game and how it was going."

The tradition was particularly strong in the WT–NM League, where fans had more money than entertainment to spend it on. "Lamesa was one of the most generous of all places to play," Buckel said, "simply because the fans were right on top of the action and felt a closer relationship with the players than those in the bigger cities in the league."[10]

Some players made more in screen money than they did on their monthly salary.

The prospect of making bigger money than he could back home in Hickory, North Carolina, is what attracted D. C. Miller to Lamesa in 1949.

D. C. was known as T-Bone in Lamesa because, as Buckel explained, "He was beefed-up like Barry Bonds." Elsewhere he was called Pud.

"To say that Pud is a big man is no understatement, friend," columnist George Webb wrote in Miller's hometown newspaper, the *Hickory Daily Record*. "Two hundred and thirty-five pounds muscled out on a six-foot-plus frame can strain most any bedspring that Pud decides to put to the test. Five pounds of lard sprinkled in with the lean push him slightly past his best playing weight."[11]

Words like hefty, huge, mammoth, massive, and bruising were used to describe Miller, who butchered pitchers in the Class B Big State League for 57 homers in 1947, and 29 in 1948, despite an injured finger that sidelined him for a month.

The Lobos had only four homers in 27 games when player-manager James "Jay" Haney shuffled the roster in late May, bringing in Miller and releasing Buckel so he could be the team's business manager.

Miller started the 1949 season at Gladewater, Texas, in the East Texas League, where he was hitting .333, with three home runs. He was as widely traveled as a Greyhound bus. Stops included Mooresville, North Carolina; Lafayette, Louisiana; St. Joseph and Carthage in Missouri; Bristol and Petersburg in Virginia; Elmira, New York; Spartanburg, South Carolina; and the Texas cities of Wichita Falls, Texarkana, Dallas, and Gladewater—11 ballclubs in 10 leagues. And he was only 26 years old.

The closest D. C. got to the majors was a spring trial in 1948, with the San Francisco Seals of the Pacific Coast League, a Triple-A circuit. "His fielding is questionable, but clubbing is not," one sportswriter reported just prior to his sale and demotion to Dallas in Double-A. [12]

From there he went to Texarkana in Class B and eventually Gladewater and Lamesa in Class C.

"I'm not trying to go up to the majors so what's the use of me going crazy out there in the field?" D. C. dismissed his defensive shortcomings. "No sir, I won't worry about the fielding, just give me that bat. You know how it is. People pay to see me hit so that's what I'll be in there trying to do." [13]

The Lobos needed help on the field and at the gate. In 1948, they placed last, winning only 44 games. Attendance plunged to a league-worst 34,303, almost half of the year before. Buckel finished the year as manager. "They came to me and said, 'Buckel, will you take the club for the last month of the season? And, then, we'll cut the roster down to 12 players and try to get by'—bad year, 1948."

T-Bone became the scourge of the league, batting .404 and swatting one shot after another over the left-field fence—52 in 109 games.

"Miller's home run clouting is all the more outstanding due to the fact that he didn't join the Lobos until six weeks of the season had already elapsed," Warren Hasse wrote in the *Pampa Daily News*. "Had he spent the entire season there he might well have eclipsed the 69 circuit-blow record of Bob Crues."[14]

Fans filled the seats, boosting attendance to a then-franchise record of 76,627. "He liked the altitude (2,992 feet) out here, and he liked picking the screen," Buckel said. "He gave the fans a real thrill for their money."

In one game, he slammed four-straight homers, filling his pockets after each shot. "He started looking for the money to be sticking through the backstop screen when rounding second base and reaped $149 for the night's effort," Buckel wrote.

That is the equivalent of approximately $1,000 today. But T-Bone wasn't happy. "Four home runs and yet I averaged less than $50 a shot," he complained.

"Who won the game was of no consequence," Buckel concluded his *Press-Reporter* story on T-Bone. "He was in Lamesa to make what he could from the ownership of the club and the fans who stuck their cash through the screen for his prodigious home runs into the West Texas skies."[15]

T-Bone was a hired gun, off to a higher bidder in the next town after a few months. Buckel was a company man, all about the team, the fans, and the community.

"He dressed like a bum, acted like a bum, and hit like a major leaguer," Buckel said, picking up where he had left off in his story on T-Bone.

> He went to the plate with one thing in mind—hit the ball out of the ballpark. He was big, and he was sloppy in his work and in his talk and everything else. You'd see him walking around town in his open shower shoes, long shirt hanging out, and bumming meals. "I'll hit two home runs tonight if you'll give me a beer," he probably told people. I vividly remember the night he hit four home runs and got $149 picking the screen.

The next morning, T-Bone walked into the team's office under the stands. Buckel was there, along with the president of the club, Horace Duke. "He was a mild-mannered farmer who loved baseball."

Duke was excited to see Miller and shook his hand as he congratulated him on hitting four homers. He was shocked to hear T-Bone call the fans cheapskates and demand, "You give me $100 cash or I'm going home."

"I don't have $100 cash," Duke said.

"Well, you get it before the end of the day or I'm gone."

Duke went to a nearby bank, got a $100 bill, and gave it to T-Bone, who hit two more home runs that night.

"He blackmailed the president of the club," Buckel said in disbelief. "He was that kind of a guy."

Miller was sold for an estimated $1,500 to his hometown team, the Hickory Rebels of the Class D North Carolina State League.

"Miller informed Lobo officials that he had no desire to return to Lamesa, and, in fact, would not play here again," columnist Perry Roberts wrote in the *Lamesa Daily Reporter*. "Miller seemed to feel that he did not get what he termed 'a fair deal at the end of the season.' It seems he desired a bonus, over and above the one paid him for being in the playoffs, and Lobo officials refused to give it to him because they could not give one to every player."[16]

Roberts noted that no team tried to draft Miller at baseball's winter meetings, requiring Lamesa to make a deal afterward.

Back in Hickory, D. C. was praising Lamesa fans for their generosity. "Why, I'm sure going to miss those folks out in Texas," he said. "You know, I never got less than $35 for a home run out there. On three occasions I can remember I got as much as $150."

Knowing that much money never changed hands at Hickory's ballpark in an entire year, let alone a single night, D. C. offered this handy hint: "Did they pass around the hat? I should say not. They'd just come up and stick it through the wire."[17]

D. C. was one of those baseball characters you remember long after they're gone. "Folks in Lamesa still ask me whatever happened to D. C. Miller?" Buckel said. "I tell them he's either back home in North Carolina or he's in jail someplace."

D. C. settled in Hickory, spending most of his last four seasons with the Rebels and, then, working 25 years as a salesman for the Anchor Supply Company in Hickory.

In 1950, his first year in Hickory, Miller batted .369, with 29 homers, taking over as Rebel manager midway through the season. He continued as player-manager in 1951, swatting 40 round-trippers, while hitting a whopping .425 to earn Hillerich & Bradsby's Louisville Slugger Silver Bat award for the highest batting average in the minors.

"The Miller stance, the nonchalant way he tossed his bat from one hand to the other, handling it like a toothpick, was enough to worry any pitcher," the *Hickory Daily Record* gushed after D. C. won the national batting crown. "And Pud Miller singles were really singles. They cut across the grass like an electric mower, knocking gloves off of outstretched hands and smashing against the fences."[18]

A sportswriter in nearby High Point, North Carolina, was less charitable, writing that D. C. "was far more interested in his batting average than in his team's standings."[19]

Rebel officials obviously agreed, refusing D. C.'s demands for more money by explaining "they were much impressed with Miller's batting prowess but inclined to doubt his managerial ability."[20]

D. C. packed up and headed off to Owensboro, Kentucky, in the Kentucky–Illinois–Tennessee (KITTY) League, where he was player-manager until half-way through the 1952 season when "he gave up because of the attitude of Owensboro fans."[21]

D. C. claimed he quit so he could return to Lamesa as player-manager. He never made it. Forever the mercenary, he accepted a better offer from Hickory to rejoin the Rebels as a player only. He remained in Hickory until late in the 1953 season, when he moved to Shelby, North Carolina, his birthplace. D. C. ended up with a lifetime batting average of .350 and 268 homers.

Upon Miller's death in 1978, at age 55, the *Daily Record* aptly summed up his career with a story headlined, "'PUD' MILLER COULD HIT THE BALL."[22]

"He could hit the ball," Buckel agreed. "In Lamesa, it was about 330 feet down the left-field line. He hit the ball over the fence and over the road and into the park next door. He gave the fans a real run for their money."

But Buckel was shocked to hear Miller became a manager. "He did? He was probably a better guy than I give him credit for," he said, chuckling.

Buckel was working for the Lamesa school system in February 1951, when Haney, the Lobos' feisty manager, revealed plans to make Lamesa the first Texas team in Organized Baseball to use black players.

As early as April 1950, there were rumors that Haney was looking to sign a "stellar Negro first baseman."[23]

Haney denied knowing anything about the player, leading Matthews of the *Daily Reporter* to conclude "this mythical performer was a product of the grapevine."

The grapevine also produced a "café poll" that, according to Matthews, showed "more people than was expected accepted the idea and was ready to bring a Negro performer here if he could aid in giving the outfit a winning club."[24]

Jackie Robinson broke Organized Baseball's color barrier in 1946. By 1951, Robinson had three black teammates on the Brooklyn Dodgers: Roy Campanella, Don Newcombe, and Dan Bankhead. Larry Doby and Luke Easter were starring for the Cleveland Indians; Satchel Paige was pitching for the St. Louis Browns; Sam Jethroe of the Boston Braves was fresh from winning the National League's Rookie of the Year award; and a kid phenom named Willie Mays was primed to join the New York Giants and their black sluggers, Monte Irvin and Hank Thompson.

Haney was born in Dallas, married a Lamesa girl, and operated a Humble gas station in Lamesa. He spent most of his 15 years in baseball managing and playing for teams in Texas. He knew using black players in a small Texas town was risky business. But it was a risk worth taking. The Korean War was syphoning off young prospects, and salaries for veteran or so-called "class" players were rising and making it difficult for teams to be both competitive and financially stable.

The Longhorn League team in nearby Big Spring, the Broncs, was made up entirely of light-skinned Cuban players with the exception of Pat Stasey, the white player-manager-owner who was winning and smiling all the way to the bank. Why not, Haney reasoned, mix in a few black Cubans?

Buckel never wrote about this, probably because it exposed the racism of the times and the bigotry of some of his friends and neighbors. West Texans don't take kindly to criticism from outsiders, and he was a transplanted Californian.

He made this point in a story about Joe Kelly, the New York–born sports editor of the *Lubbock Avalanche-Journal* who "wrote in the style of upstate New York" and "bathed in hot water most of the time" with the players, owners, and fans. "Kelly epitomized the New Yorker—haughty, cocky, and everything," Buckel noted.

Kelly "never quite understood the fans' reaction when he took a pot shot at some opposing player or city," Buckel said, adding, "West Texas and eastern New Mexico sports fans are different. They were in 1948; they still are in 1978."[25]

If Kelly's column, "Between the Lines," crossed the lines, Haney was trying to blur and erase them with black players in what had always been a snow-white league. Kelly broke the story about Lamesa using "Cuban Negroes" after a telephone conversation with Haney. "I'm willing to try an experiment," Haney said.[26]

Kelly was the son of a Presbyterian minister and his column the perfect pulpit for Haney to spread his message.

"I'm a Southern boy myself," Haney told Kelly. "I dropped any resentment to Negro ball players in the service when I played with them and against them. They're good ball players, and that's what matters to me. I won't take them unless they're good players, but if they are, they'll play on my team."[27]

In December 1949, Buckel and Haney attended baseball's winter meeting in Baltimore, Maryland, "looking for an outfielder and a pitcher to bolster the fortunes" of the Lobos. They acquired two Puerto Rican players—center fielder Pedro Santiago and pitcher Israel Ten.

The 5-foot-5, 150-pound Santiago "set the league afire and captured the imagination of Lamesa fans" by batting .356 in 1950, and .324 in 1951. He opened the 1950 season with a 30-game hitting streak that included a string of 11 consecutive hits. Ten compiled a won–loss record of 8-7 in 1950.

Buckel called the purchase of Santiago and Ten the "best $750 Lobo management ever spent in trying to build a baseball winner."[28]

Harry Gilstrap, a columnist for the *Amarillo Daily News*, piggybacked on Kelly's story about Haney using Cubans by asking in his sports column,

> Why is the Lamesa club chancing this, with the certain knowledge that it will arouse violent objection, even bitterness, among some baseball fans?
>
> The answer is simple. The Cubans are draft-exempt. Also, they come cheap, and a cheap ballplayer is a rara avis in the West Texas–New Mexico League, as indeed in most other leagues, these years.[29]

In announcing his plans to sign Cubans, Haney cited a player shortage due to the U.S. military drafting men for the escalating war in Korea. "We have our quota of $200 players. What we need now is some good material. And the veterans are all sticking us up, knowing that it will be hard to get players."[30]

Haney made his case in an open letter published by the *Lamesa Daily Reporter*:

> Personally, I feel if we are able to obtain two very "above average" Negro men who can really play ball, it should be a credit to the league as well as to our own town.
>
> Baseball is strictly a business just like any other business with employees. In any other business we choose the worker who can do the job best and at the most reasonable price. We are all aware of the fact that there is a definite shortage of ballplayers due to the drafting of our younger and most promising talent into the armed services.[31]

Haney received several threatening letters, all of them anonymous. One, penned by a man from Big Spring, was printed by the *Daily Reporter*: "Jay, I personally know you and I wish you well in your baseball career, but you had better take a fan's advice and not try to cram a Jackie Robinson deal down a bunch of red-blooded West Texans' throat. They won't go for it at the gate."[32]

Haney was not to be deterred. He scheduled a one-day all-Negro tryout camp, believed to be the first for professional players in the United States, and invited blacks from throughout the country.

"The announcement of the tryout camp brings a sudden realization that not only Cuban Negroes—as previously reported—will be considered by the Lobo club," the *Daily Reporter* informed readers.[33]

Twenty hopefuls showed up.

"Nearly everyone in Lamesa was out at one time or another during the day to see what was taking place," Marvin Veal wrote in his *Daily Reporter* column. "When the tryouts ended, there were probably 250 or 300 persons in the grandstand."[34]

Haney singled out two Texans, shortstop J. W. Wingate from Beaumont and outfielder Connie Heard from Texas City, as "pretty good prospects and they would have the same chance as the rest of the players to make the team in spring training."[35]

By Opening Day, Haney had decided they "fell short of the rigid standards he had set for the first Negro players in Organized Ball in Texas only on ability."[36]

He quickly changed his mind about Wingate, calling him back to join pitcher Roberto Leyva and catcher Douglas McBean, described by one sportswriter as "Cuban Negroes fresh from the cane-breaks, and quite capable ballplayers."

After winning a game, the Cuban combo was "fired" suddenly by Haney "because he couldn't speak Cuban and they couldn't talk English and the signals got mixed."[37]

Haney's dismissal of the Cubans left the 23-year-old Wingate as the lone black on the team. He hit safely in his first six games, including three doubles. "The crowd cheers lustily when he makes a play afield or gets a hit, and his appearance in the lineup has packed the Negro bleachers every night," one wire service reported after the Lobos' first homestand.[38]

A week later in Abilene, Wingate socked a home run and two singles, prompting Collier Parris, sports editor of the *Abilene Reporter-News*, to write, "A better than average crowd of about 1,650 gave the colored player a big hand for the homer and applause for some sparkling work at shortstop."[39]

Parris became Wingate's biggest and most outspoken supporter and let his disgust be known when Wingate was released after 27 games because, as Haney put it, "fans might be staying away from the games on account of his presence in the lineup."[40]

Wingate was batting .250 at the time.

"We understand he was erratic and flouncy on other fields, including that of his home team," Parris said. "But Abilene fans are surprised by his departure. Lamesa fans, being sturdy, southern home-towners to whom Negroes mean cotton pickers, shine boys, and car-washers, never did give Wingate a chance."[41]

Parris confronted Haney about the decision to release Wingate.

"We weren't drawing many fans," Haney said. "So we let him go. We still ain't drawing many fans."[42]

West Texas is known for its extreme heat, extreme wind, extreme cold, and extreme attitudes.

Buckel recalled a conversation with a local farmer named Dan who was one of the Lobos' biggest fans.

"Is Haney going to play that black boy?" Dan asked.

"Yeah," Buckel replied.

"I'll never come to another game," Dan said.

Dan wasn't alone, as attendance dropped 32 percent, to 59,283, even though the Lobos won 81 games and placed third, both franchise bests.

Crowds were shrinking throughout the minor leagues, this *Sporting News* headline summing it up best: "MINORS' GATE TOBAGGONED 20 PERCENT IN '51."[43]

Lamesa and the rest of the minors were on a slippery slope, television and increased competition for the entertainment dollar dropping attendance from the all-time high of almost 42 million in 1949 to slightly less than 28 million in 1952.

The '52 season was the end for Haney as Lobos manager and Lamesa's last in the WT–NM League.

Haney was attending a league meeting in Clovis, New Mexico, when he received a telegram from the directors of the Lamesa Baseball Club informing him he had resigned. "We think the less publicity, especially to sportswriters, given this matter, will be best for you and the ballclub," the message ended. The telegram was great fodder for columnist Kelly.

"I was fired," Haney told his comrade in arms. "I never replied to the telegram. I never have resigned as manager at Lamesa."[44]

The Lobos also announced the return of D. C. Miller, but that didn't materialize because D. C. got more money to stay home in Hickory.

Buckel hardly mentioned Haney in his retrospective of the Lobos.

"Haney was a very unusual guy," he said. "I had a difficult time understanding him; he was rather distant. He made moves that I never did know about and I was the business manager. He'd just come in and tell you he was going to do this and that was it. If you liked it, okay. If not, you could lump it."

Haney, of course, defied the racial segregation laws entrenched in Texas at the time.

"He was trying to push the envelope with J. W. Wingate," Buckel said. "It turned the fans off, and it was probably one of the things that led to the demise of baseball in Lamesa."

Haney also recruited such power hitters as Miller, Glenn Burns, and Forrest "Frosty" Kennedy, a muscular infielder who smacked 25 homers in 1952, a precursor of the 60 he would blast four years later at Plainview, Texas. "Haney made some bold moves, but I don't know that the ownership could afford some of those guys," Buckel said. "He made some comments that I didn't approve of, but we won't get into that."

A losing record (69-73) and a major drought combined to cut attendance in 1952 to 41,541—less than half of what it had been two years earlier. The Lamesa franchise, players, and equipment were sold to Plainview.

"A drought effects the club perhaps as it hurts no other team in this area in that many of its fans have farming interests or are dependent upon people who do," the *Big Spring Herald* observed.[45]

The drought lasted until September 1953, when a front-page story in the *Daily Reporter* described how "farmers looked out across their breakfast tables, past their wives, and outside to wet fields for the first time in three years."[46]

It looked like pro baseball was dead in Lamesa until the Longhorn League persuaded Harold Webb to take over a franchise that in a six-month span bounced like a double-play ball from the Texas towns of Sweetwater to Pecos to Lamesa.

Webb was owner-manager of a team in Midland, Texas, from 1947–1951, before retiring to his farm to raise Jersey cattle. He was a "roly-poly, cheerful, umpire-baiting guy" who rallied the fans by promising a young, hustling team that should finish in the first division. Approximately 1,800 fans showed up on Opening Day.

"It was a good turnout," according to Art Gatts of the *Lubbock Morning Avalanche*. Buckel, newly elected Dawson County clerk, received kudos for his work as public address announcer. "The county clerk did just what a PA man should do, announce the batters, subs and that's all. None of that monotonous and usually bad play-by-play stuff."[47]

Dust storms caused four games to be postponed, and "cold weather cut deeply into attendance on many other games." By mid-May, the Lobos were averaging 270 fans per game, and Webb was looking to take the team elsewhere.[48]

For Ben Peeler, a columnist for the *Odessa American*, this stirred memories of the Lobos' glory days. He recalled when Lamesa was the "toast of the baseball world" and "pulling people into its park like gangbusters."[49]

On May 29—38 days after the gala home opener—Webb announced that the "club will have to fold or move after Saturday night's game due to weather and lack of attendance."[50]

It was fitting that the last game was on Memorial Day. Only 350 fans showed up to see the Lobos buried, a 25-10 drubbing that was a "grim reminder that baseball has left the city."[51]

Webb gave his team a new nickname, Eagles, and flew the coop to Winters and Ballinger, Texas, cities 16 miles apart. "We personally feel sorry for the Winters–Ballinger people, and we ain't gonna say no differently," Peeler said. "It is a team that can't draw flies at the gate, nor catch the same in the outfield."[52]

The new Eagles, dubbed the "Harold Webb Express," lost all three games before Webb called it quits, leaving the Longhorn League with seven teams.

Things were so desperate that another Longhorn League team, Big Spring, was trying to sign a local boy so they could attract more fans. "All I'd draw would be my mother," the boy quipped. "And she'd be on a pass probably."[53]

Leagues were folding like an accordion. The WT–NM League shut down after the 1955 season. The Longhorn ceased operating at the same time, replaced by the Southwestern League, which lasted two years (1956–1957).

By 1957, Southwestern teams were playing musical chairs. Clovis and Plainview pulled out in June, followed by El Paso and San Angelo in July. Midland shifted to Lamesa in August—the "answer to a five-year-long dream." It didn't matter that the new team, the Indians, was in the cellar of the four-team league, 17½ games out of first. Pro baseball was back in Lamesa.[54]

Lobo Park was reported to be in tip-top condition, but that's not what Hobbs pitcher Jim Waldrip remembered. "It was like sand dunes. The restroom was like a kitty litter box. They didn't have time to get the field in shape. Whoever lined the field not only did the batter's box, they put straight lines from first to second and second to third. It was rather interesting."

Some 800 fans turned out for the home opener, but few of them found the Indians interesting enough to come back for the remaining 14 games at Lobo Park. It was the last hurrah for the "biggest little baseball city in the United States."

In the Lobos' heyday, fans would be at home and hear "Take Me Out to the Ballgame," the theme song of Buckel's radio show, stop what they were doing, and head to the ballpark. "Many ol' farmers came through the gate and said, 'Buck, I wasn't coming tonight but I heard you on the radio and here I am.' It was an era of great excitement that will never happen again."

Buckel was wearing khaki pants and a dark green, black, and gold shirt with black shoes—much like he was dressed when he hitched the ride to Texas that shaped the rest of his life.

When he stepped down as county clerk in 1957, to go into the insurance business, Buckel was sports director of the local radio station. If a community project needed funding, he raised the money. He organized and led the Lamesa Little League, and served as president of the Chamber of Commerce and the Kiwanis Club—all the things he would later expect publishers in his newspaper group to do.

"Baseball was a catalyst," Buckel said. "Baseball helped me get elected county clerk. Everybody in town knew me as a baseball player and, then, broadcasting on the radio for so many years. I was a natural to go into the newspaper business. And baseball gave me that start."

Buckel even met his wife, Rubye, through baseball.

Bill Serena introduced them in 1946, when he and Buckel played for Montgomery, Alabama, of the Southeastern League. Serena belted 22 homers and Buckel had a .209 batting average, a preview of what both would do in West Texas.

"Bill was an entertainer playing baseball," Buckel said. "No matter where we were on a road trip, if anybody wanted a song-and-dance man, Bill would entertain them. He could play the piano and the accordion, tap dance, and tell jokes. He was a showman."

Serena was playing third base for the Cubs when Walter and Rubye attended a game at Sportsman's Park in St. Louis.

"Bill!" Walter hollered from his seat behind the Cubs dugout. "Bill!"

Serena ran to the dugout, jumped on top of it, and rushed into the stands to greet his former teammate.

"I'll never forget what Bill said: 'Buck, you ought to be up here. It's still 60 feet, six inches from the mound. It's still 90 feet around the bases. It's still three strikes, four balls. Baseball is no different here than it was in Montgomery, Buck. You could play up here.'"

Walter and Rubye returned to Lamesa, where they would raise their two children, Barbara and Bob, and follow James Roberts into the newspaper business. "Come along with me, Buckel, we'll get us a string of community newspapers," Roberts told his handpicked protégé.

Walter Buckel was 19 when he hitchhiked from California to Texas and hooked up with a team in Lamesa—the "biggest little baseball city in the United States." He wound up becoming publisher of the local newspaper, the *Press-Reporter*, and living 66 years in Lamesa. *Photo by the author.*

"All of them have done well," Buckel noted. "We're thriving in a dying business."

The population of Lamesa today is 9,422, down slightly from 1950. The ornate cast iron and wood benches dotting the square around the Dawson County Courthouse are usually empty. If you stand in the middle of one of the wide, red brick streets downtown, you can listen to country music coming from speakers atop one of the buildings without worrying about getting hit by a car.

At first glance, the newly painted Tower Theater, on the east side of the courthouse square, looks like it is open for business just as it was in the 1950s. On closer inspection you see blue sky through the window openings on the second floor and a poster announcing the coming of the 2008 film *Indiana Jones and the Kingdom of the Crystal Skull*. It's all a façade.

You can still watch a movie at the Sky-Vue Drive-In Theatre, where rock and roll legend Buddy Holly once performed on the roof of the projector building.

On Highway 87, the road Buckel traveled from Big Spring to Lamesa in 1941, there's a time-tested, 20-foot-tall fiberglass "Uniroyal Gal" statue made in the 1960s by Uniroyal Tire Company to promote its products. Her bouffant hairdo and clunky high heels aren't as up to date as the Lamesa High School Golden Tornadoes cheerleader outfit she's wearing.

Lobo Park is long gone, like the cannon shots D. C. Miller propelled over the left-field fence. Weeds and sand reclaimed the playing field soon after pro baseball left town in 1957. The grandstand and backstop were torn down later, leaving no sign that a ballpark was ever there.

Buckel is gone, too. He died on November 27, 2013, at the age of 92.

He is buried about two miles from his beloved Lobo Park at Lamesa Memorial Park Perpetual Care Cemetery under a large headstone decorated with a baseball bat and the *Lamesa Press-Reporter* masthead depicting a cotton boll and oil derrick. "The guy that sold me the stone and prepared it is an old preacher and a close friend. He said, 'When you think of Walter Buckel, you're going to think of baseball, and then you're going to think of the *Press-Reporter* publisher.'"

The headstone reads, "A CALIFORNIA BOY & AN ALABAMA GIRL WHO FOUND A HOME IN TEXAS."

3

ROUND TRIP TO NOWHERE

Bob "Round Trip" Crues

Bob Crues was nicknamed "Round Trip" because of all the home runs he hit for the Amarillo Gold Sox in 1948. But the round-tripper that mattered most was the one that landed him on baseball's equivalent of the moon— 70. Nobody had been there before. One more circuit blast and a picture of the free-swinging Crues would grace the front of Wheaties cereal boxes on millions of breakfast tables throughout the United States.

With two games to play, Crues had 69 homers and a share of the single-season record for Organized Baseball set by Joe Hauser of the Minneapolis Millers in 1933.

The 6-foot-3, 185-pound Texan already owned the all-time mark for runs batted in with 254, 32 more than the previous minor-league high of 222. "It was absolutely phenomenal," recalled Robert "Buck" Fausett, the Gold Sox manager, who played briefly in the majors. "Actually, it was unbelievable."

He was referring to Crues's RBI total. The big-league mark is 191, set by Hack Wilson in 1930. Since World War II, the closest anyone has come in the majors is 165, by Manny Ramirez of the Cleveland Indians in 1999.

Eight of Crues's homers were grand slams; 12 came with two runners on base; and 26 with one aboard. His home runs alone produced 143 runs.

"He was a cut and slasher," Fausett said of the right-handed Crues. "He left the bench swinging. He was a bad-ball hitter. I've seen him hit balls over his head—slash them over the right-field fence."

Almost any pitch in the same zip code, Crues sent flying over the fence in 1948. "It didn't make any difference to me where they threw—my ankles or knees or belt high or up at my shoulders," Crues explained. "I hit a home run one night off of one that bounced in front of the plate. That son of a gun looked like it was going to come in there knee-high. It hit in front of the plate, and I swung. I swung at anything I could reach."

Through 35 games—one-fourth of the 140-game schedule—Crues had 50 runs, 58 hits, 21 homers, 131 total bases, and 70 runs batted in. *Amarillo News-Globe* sports editor Harry Gilstrap did the math: "Multiply these figures by four and see what you get: 200 runs, 232 hits, 84 home runs, 524 total bases, 280 runs batted in."[1]

Crues was up to 31 homers by mid-June and still on track to top 80. That number dropped to 77 in late July, as he had 53 homers with 44 games to play.

Gilstrap penned a story for *Sporting News*, the national baseball weekly that had paid scant attention to Crues's pursuit of the all-time record. The headline above a photo of Crues read, "RUTH OF WEST TEXAS."[2]

It was Crues's coming-out party in the baseball world, and it coincided with the death of Babe Ruth, the original Sultan of Swat.

On August 17, the day the Babe died after a long battle with cancer, Crues twice cleared the center-field fence at Gold Sox Field to hike his total to 59. He needed 11 in the next 22 games to reach the magic mark of 70. "He will have to average a home run every other game to do it, which is exactly his pace for the first 118 games," Gilstrap wrote.[3]

The latest homers made it appear that Crues had no lingering effects from pulling a groin muscle during the first game of a Sunday doubleheader at Pampa, Texas, two days earlier. The opener was scheduled for the afternoon, with the finale that evening. Rain delayed the games five hours. "The field was a loblolly of gumbo throughout the day and still sticky and in terrible condition when the teams finally got together in the nocturnal twinner," Gilstrap reported.[4]

Chasing a fly ball, Crues slipped on the wet outfield grass, aggravating a childhood back injury. He struck out four times in the twin bill.

Crues played the rest of the season with his left side swathed in tape. "Half of me was wrapped like a mummy. Had sponge rubber from my navel down to my crotch. Tied it as tight as they could tape it. What good it was doing I don't know."

"He'd have spasms," Fausett said. "Maybe for two or three days he didn't swing hard at the plate. He wouldn't lay out a game. He'd keep on playing."

Visibly bothered by the pain, Crues left one game early after straining his back while striking out.

Gold Sox owner Bob Seeds goaded Crues, telling him he couldn't break Hauser's record.

"Seeds was always throwing out that challenge to him," Fausett said. "Crues was a very fierce competitor. He loved challenges."

Crues hit only three homers the last two weeks of August. After a two-homer performance to begin September, he was up to 64. The next two games were at Albuquerque's Tingley Field, the largest ballpark in the league.

"The fans were riding him—that he couldn't hit a home run in a big ballpark," Fausett said. "So he walked up to bat, looked around at the fans, and said, 'Just wait!' The second pitch he hit about a mile over the left-field fence."

Crues returned to Amarillo with 65 homers and four games to reach the jackpot. The odds were against him. But they meant nothing if the wind was blowing out at Gold Sox Field.

With the wind at his back, he belted a pair in two straight games to tie Hauser's record going into a season-ending doubleheader against the Lubbock Hubbers. Fausett moved him into the leadoff spot to give his masher more swings in the two seven-inning games.

The *Globe-Times* published a blow-by-blow account of Crues's homers, including the opposing pitcher's last name and team. He was averaging a home run every second game—69 in 138 games. The last line of the list read, "70. ? ? ? ? ? ?"[5]

A Labor Day crowd of 4,851 showed up, the largest to see a baseball game in Amarillo and almost 10 percent of the city's population. To the fans' dismay, a stiff wind was blowing in toward home plate. "He knew how to play that wind," Fausett said. "If the wind was blowing to right, he'd try to slash it that way. If it was blowing to left, he'd go right with it."

First time up, Crues lined a shot to left field that looked like it would clear the fence until the wind knocked it down and off the top of the barrier for a long single.

Crues was easygoing and amiable, popular with fans and players alike. The Hubbers wanted him to break the record, too. The second game meant nothing in the standings, so in the seventh and last inning, they sent catcher-outfielder Don Moore to the mound. "They were trying to let me hit the 70th home run," Crues acknowledged. "They were just lobbing the ball in there."

Moore grooved pitch after pitch, as he often did in batting practice. "I was pulling the ball, and the wind would catch it and pull the danged thing foul. Hit 15 foul balls out of sight. That don't make any difference."

Finally, Crues singled. It was his fourth single in eight at-bats. He also walked, struck out, grounded out, and popped out. "The way I always looked at it, either I do or I don't. That night I didn't. I hit the ball good. As long as a man hits the ball good, he doesn't have a gripe coming."

Gilstrap conducted a postmortem in his sports column.

"If baseball were like politics, we could demand a recount on Bob Crues's home run record and maybe get it allowed," he began. "There seems to be little doubt that Bob actually did hit 70 this season but was defrauded one."[6]

It was the home run that didn't count. And it gnawed at Crues as long as he lived. "The night that tore me up was in Abilene when I hit that 70th home run—it hit the scoreboard."

The base umpire was Frank Secory, who wound up becoming a highly respected arbiter in the majors. He ruled the ball hit the fence and caromed back onto the playing field. Crues was credited with a triple. "It was definitely a home run," Fausett said. "I don't doubt his honesty in what he called, but he was wrong. In fact, the Abilene left fielder (Al Stone) told some of our boys after the game that it hit high enough on the scoreboard to be a home run."

Crues was even more adamant. "Anybody with two eyes could see that it hit the top of the scoreboard. It went completely over the fence. It was a low-hit ball—on a line. Highest it ever got was when it hit that scoreboard."

One news account had the ball denting the left-center-field fence, approximately 384 feet from home plate at Blue Sox Stadium in Abilene.

Bill Chick, a sportswriter for the *Abilene Reporter-News*, said the ball couldn't be followed clearly from the press box but noted, "There were many fans in the park who believed the ninth-inning blow really hit a signboard atop the fence. That would make it a home run according to Sox Stadium ground rules."

Chick was the official scorer for Abilene home games, as well as the statistician for the West Texas–New Mexico (WT-NM) League. "It would be tough for Beltin' Bob to fall one short of the league standard," he admitted.[7]

With 34 homers halfway through the season, Crues was virtually a cinch to break the league record of 57, set the previous year by Bill Serena. When he passed Serena in mid-August, Chick worried the ruling in Abilene might prevent him from getting his 70th.

He wrote a letter to Gilstrap saying, "Won't it be awful, if he fails to get it when I'll always believe he should have had one here in our park . . . I, too, thought it hit the scoreboard and should have been an automatic homer. I've been afraid ever since that home run might play a big part in breaking or not breaking the record."[8]

The wind always lords over the Texas Panhandle. It giveth and taketh away. In the span of 24 hours, the wind helped Crues hit two home runs to tie the all-time record and, then, stopped him from breaking it.

"If I had of hit that 70th one out that night, boy it would have been something else," he said wistfully.

"He wanted that homer bad, real bad," Bob's wife, Billie, said years later. "Wheaties was there. If he had hit that homer, we'd have been eating Wheaties the rest of our lives."[9]

* * *

The wind, it blew, and the homers, they flew out of the ballparks in the WT-NM League, called the "happy home of the home run" by *Sporting News*.[10]

A league record 1,217 were hit in 1948, Amarillo leading the way with 214. At 69, Crues was tops, followed by Lubbock's Virgil Richardson, with 38. Altogether, 17 players had 20-plus homers.

"Hardest hitting circuit in all professional baseball," proclaimed Harold Ratliff, sports editor of the Associated Press wire service.[11]

In 1948, six of the eight clubs had team batting averages over .300. Crues was one of four players to hit .400-plus, but his batting average of .404 was only third best in the league.

Teams combined to score 9,090 runs, or an average of 16 runs per game. Someone suggested paying official scorers by the run.

A typical evening of run-making was the 83 produced in four games the night before Ratliff's story appeared in newspapers nationally. Amarillo walloped Lamesa, 22-3; Abilene outslugged Borger, 17-9; Pampa pummeled Clovis, 13-4; and Albuquerque axed Lubbock, 10-5.

Pitchers deserved combat pay and medals for valour.

The best pitcher in 1948 was Albuquerque's Frank Shone, a hard-drinking left-hander who won 21 games and led the league with a 3.84 earned run average. On road trips, Shone sat in a folding chair next to the bus driver so he had easy access to a six-pack of beer stashed in the glove compartment.

The strange thing about the league, Ratliff observed, was the "fact that each season it's the pitchers that move up and go places in higher classifications."

The league was, in effect, the school of hard knocks for kid pitchers. Their teachers were the grizzled hitters who kicked around baseball's bushes as long as they could kick. "They're not going anywhere, but they can still hit that ball," Ratliff wrote. [12]

Crues was one of those guys. So were Albuquerque's Hershel Martin and Borger's Eddie Carnett, the top two hitters, with batting averages of .425 and .409, respectively. Martin spent six years in the majors, Carnett three.

"Ballplayers like to hit, and it was a hitter's league," explained Howard Green, co-owner of the Abilene Blue Sox from 1946–1948. "A guy who wasn't going to the major leagues that could be a star out here, why would he want to go to the Texas League or the Southern League and be just another ballplayer? They got good salaries—A and Double-A salaries. They were treated like kings."

In addition to their monthly paycheck, Crues and the league's other sluggers received "fence" money, stuck through the chicken-wire screen by fans after they hit a home run. "It was the Texas way of doing things—an expansive way of doing things," Green said. "Right after World War II, prices were low and we had a real era of prosperity."

Crues needed help collecting the money the night he tied Hauser's record of 69 home runs. "There were five or six people in the stands with two-gallon buckets."

They collected almost $300 in change. Add another $400 in bills shoved through the screen and Crues went home with $700—almost double his monthly salary of $375.

Young pitchers had to watch hitters rake in the dough at their own expense, and it could be humiliating.

"You could count the good pitchers in the league on one hand," Lamesa infielder Walter Buckel said. "The rest of them would be so-so pitchers that were maybe over the hump or youngsters coming into the league. And Crues would just feast on those guys."

Toughened by the veteran hitters, the best of the young pitchers advanced to the big leagues.

In 1946, 21-year-old Warren Hacker won 20 games for the Pampa Oilers. He went on to win 62 in the majors, mostly for bad Chicago Cubs teams.

The following year, Lubbock's Paul Hinrichs, also 21, fashioned an 18-5 record and 3.34 earned run average. He had a four-game stint with the Boston Red Sox in 1951.

The ultimate babe-in-the-woods survival story is Don Ferrarese, a raw 19-year-old talent when he joined the Albuquerque Dukes in 1949.

Two years earlier, the smallish southpaw was awarded the Lou Gehrig Memorial Trophy as the outstanding player of the Hearst Sandlot Classic, a game featuring the best high school players in the country. He pitched three hitless innings, striking out six and walking three. The legendary Ty Cobb was so impressed he tipped off Casey Stengel, then-manager of the Oakland Oaks, a minor-league team near Ferrarese's hometown of Lafayette, California. Stengel signed him.

Ferrarese won 14 games for the Dukes, whiffing 216. He also walked 184 batters—almost one for each of the 188 innings he pitched. "They used to have guys warming up in the bullpen when I started the game," he said.

The oldsters were more disciplined and didn't swing at a lot of bad pitches. "You got the ball over, and they pounded that damn thing."

He was struggling three weeks into the season when his parents arrived in Albuquerque to watch him pitch. "I walked, I don't know, two, three guys, four guys, whatever the hell that it was."

He gave up four runs on five walks and a hit, leaving the game with no outs in the second inning. "I blamed it on my parents being there because they made me nervous."

Martin, the Dukes' player-manager, decided to make the incident a teaching point. He pulled the Ferrareses aside and said, "Don doesn't know this but he's starting the game tomorrow night. You stay but hide from him and, then, come to the game."

The next night, Don tossed a seven-hitter and hit a home run to win, 7-5. He walked 10 batters and fanned nine before Martin took him out in the ninth inning.

"That was sort of a turning point," Don said. "All that bad experience that I had—bases loaded and nobody out and walking the guys in—hardened me. I was fortunate that they stuck with me. I could've been shipped to a D league and never got any farther."

Ferrarese lasted eight years in the majors. He won 19 games, the highlight a two-hit shutout for the Baltimore Orioles against the New York Yankees in 1956, which earned him an appearance on Ed Sullivan's popular television show.

None of the league's young pitchers in 1948 got close to the majors. Only six had earned run averages under five, sort of a demarcation line for pitchers hoping to stay employed.

"My earned run average I felt was pretty good when I came out with a four something," said Jerry Folkman, an infielder-turned-pitcher.

The inexperience of the pitchers was one reason for the lofty number of hits and runs in the league.

Some blamed a lively ball, the short outfield fences, the thin air in the league's cities, ranging in elevation from 1,719 feet in Abilene to 5,112 in Albuquerque, and, of course, the prevailing wind.

The elevation in Amarillo is 3,605 feet. Gold Sox Field measured 324 feet down both foul lines and 360 feet to center.

Lamesa pitcher Stanley Grzywacz appeared three times on the list of Crues's victims. "If you were going to try and get sick anywhere, you tried to get sick in Amarillo. You could fool a man and it'd be a home run. The wind always blew from up behind home plate. You got a ball up in the air and it was out."

Crues hit 41 of his 69 homers at Gold Sox Field. "Bob was perfect for that park," Buckel said. "He'd poke them out of there like shooting beans."

The wind obviously helped Crues, but how much is debatable.

"Some of the balls he hit were out of any ballpark," said Amarillo catcher Ted Clawitter. "They weren't any humpty-dumpty home runs. A lot of these parks, the wind was blowing in as much as it was blowing out. Same way in Amarillo."

Gold Sox Field was the easiest place to hit a home run, according to Grzywacz, but Crues could've done the same thing in a larger ballpark. "He could hit the ball a country mile. I'm sure some of them were cheap home runs, but he was strong."

"It was a pretty big factor," Fausett said. "In fact, I doubt—well, I know—if it hadn't been for the wind he wouldn't have hit that many home runs. He might've hit 45 or 50, but that wind blowing for him— that's the reason he hit 69."

In the playoffs at the end of the 1948 season, Amarillo played Tyler, Texas, of the Lone Star League. The sports editor of the Tyler newspaper suggested that the winds in Amarillo unfairly favored Gold Sox hitters.

Gilstrap responded by writing that the Amarillo Chamber of Commerce was using the winds for propaganda purposes.

> They have such intense civic pride that whenever an Amarillo player strides to the plate at Gold Sox Field, they blow outward in order to help him hit a home run. Conversely, when an East Texas player is at bat, the wind maliciously shifts and blows in to limit him to a single if he could meet the ball squarely. [13]

This tongue-in-cheek explanation was as good as any for all the home runs at Gold Sox Field. The only problem is someone from the Chamber of Commerce messed up the night the wind blew the wrong way, denying Crues his 70th home run and Amarillo a lot of good publicity.

* * *

The story goes that Crues was a "chicken picker" in 1939, when Amarillo owner "Suitcase" Bob Seeds signed him as a pitcher for $125.

Tipped off by a doctor friend, Seeds paid Crues a visit in Plainview. "I found him in a small chicken-picking outfit. He was one of the foremen. They were hanging these chickens up and killing them, and throwing them in a barrel. I called him a chicken picker."

"There was no more truth in that," Crues protested. "I worked for a wholesale grocery."

Seeds was a jokester, and most likely he was teasing Crues.

"Seeds used to rib him all the time," said Joe Bauman, who played for the Gold Sox in 1946–1947.

Sometimes the humor was self-effacing. "I could go out and take a look at the biggest, darkest clouds and they'd just disintegrate," Seeds said.

Upon meeting Crues, Seeds noticed he was missing the forefinger on his right throwing hand. The finger was cut off in a windmill accident when he was three years old.

"Hell, can you throw a curve?" Seeds asked.

"Danged right," Crues said.

Later on, Seeds kidded Crues about the missing finger, demanding back part of what he paid for Crues because he didn't get a whole man.

"I liked him, I really did," Seeds admitted. "He was kind of my pet, if I had any."

"We were good friends—laughing and cutting up," Crues said. "He was always nagging at me. In fact, Seeds was that way with all the players. That's why guys on the club got along so well—friendship. Nobody didn't like Bob Seeds as a man."

Crues had a good curveball, but Seeds didn't think his fastball had enough zip. "He had a good fastball for that league but not for any future. I always tried to judge a kid on a big league. If he couldn't go on up there, I always kind of discouraged him."

Seeds was in his second season with the New York Giants in 1939, his fifth major-league team, when he became owner and president of the Gold Sox. He's the only big-leaguer to own a team in the minors while he was still active. His wife, Nona, was vice president and business manager, purportedly the first woman executive in Organized Baseball.

"I didn't think he was good enough to make it as a pitcher, so I let him go to Lamesa," Seeds said.

Crues began the 1940 season at Lamesa, losing four of five decisions, before he was released and picked up by the Borger Gassers, another team in the WT–NM League, a Class D loop before World War II.

By the end of the year, he was known as "Three Finger" Crues, after Mordecai "Three Fingers" Brown, legendary Hall of Fame pitcher. He wound up winning 23 games, including three in the playoffs. "It never affected me at all," Crues said of the missing finger. "I was just as used to that as if I had it."

The Boston Red Sox bought Crues's contract and sent him to Scranton, Pennsylvania, in the Class A Eastern League. Sitting in the dugout during a spring exhibition game in Greenville, South Carolina, he was hit on the shoulder of his throwing arm by a wild pitch. "That finished my pitching career," Crues lamented.

The Red Sox didn't give up on Crues immediately, assigning him to their farm club in Canton, Ohio. He lasted three and one-third innings in his first start for Canton, giving up 10 of the 25 runs scored by the opposing team and prompting his catcher to propose pitchers wear chest protectors.

Crues rebounded to win his next two starts, taking a shutout into the seventh inning of the second game by throwing nothing but knuckleballs. "I couldn't throw a fastball. That's just how bad it hurt."

From Canton he went to Oneonta, New York, and finally back to Borger, where he had a 3-4 record. Crues was at Borger on July 4, 1942, when most of the minor leagues shut down because of World War II. There were 31 leagues to begin the year and only nine in 1943, the smallest number in history.

He worked at an ordnance plant near Amarillo that produced bombs and shells for the armed forces prior to serving in the U.S. Army at North Camp Hood in Texas, from January 1944 to April 1946. "I stayed in the same place the entire time," he said. "All I did was play baseball and basketball, and drive a danged bus."

Crues played first base and the outfield for the North Camp Hood baseball team, managed by Ed Head, a pitcher for the Brooklyn Dodgers. Like Crues, Head had overcome physical adversity, learning to throw right-handed as a teenager when his left arm was mangled in a bus accident that killed his girlfriend. Of his 27 big-league victories, one was a no-hitter.

"I learned to hit in the military," Crues said. "I did it myself."

Playing three games a week against big-leaguers on other military service teams, Crues hit around .600 his last year at North Camp Hood.

"I got him back after the war was over," Seeds said. "He was a pretty good hitter. He really could hit a long ball."

Crues didn't go directly to Amarillo out of the army. He stopped first at Lamesa. After 19 days, he called Seeds and pleaded, "Get me out of here."

Seeds already had the slugging Bauman at first base. He didn't need outfielders until one of his starters shattered an ankle sliding into home plate.

"I was ready to get Crues anyway," Seeds said. "I'd already talked to Lamesa about him. They said, 'You can have him. We'll send his release to you.' And they did."

Crues had 11 hits in a five-day trial. Two weeks later, he slammed three straight home runs in a 32-0 rout of Lamesa. That evening an ebullient Crues was bragging about the homers to his bunkmate, who just happened to be Seeds, now player-manager, as well as owner.

Seeds casually mentioned he belted seven homers in back-to-back games in 1938, for the Newark Bears of the International League. This was news to Crues, and he didn't know what to say at first. Suddenly, he blurted out, "Just think of it—10 homers in three games, right here in this bed!"

The biggest bopper for the Gold Sox in 1946 was Joe Bauman, a behemoth facetiously called "Little Joe" by local sportswriters. He was fresh out of the U.S. Navy and mopping up on pitchers like they were the deck of a ship.

The war was behind the players, their baseball careers no longer on hold.

"Man, you're going to see something!" Seeds announced at the start of spring drills. "The war has changed the attitude of baseball players. These boys who have been in the service are working as players never did before, and it's going to be rough going this year for the deadheads who don't want to put out, believe me."[14]

Bauman blasted a league-record 48 homers.

Crues batted .341 and amassed 29 round-trippers, 46 doubles, 12 triples, and 120 RBIs.

Sportswriters selected Crues to the league's all-star team but snubbed Bauman, one of the few times he was passed over in favor of Crues. "We had a pretty good two-chop wallop," Bauman said.

Someone else localized the situation: "Those two men probably frightened more pitchers than a cage of rattlesnakes."[15]

"When a pitcher figures out a way to stop Bob Crues, Joe Bauman goes on a tear," wrote Frank Godsoe, Jr., of the *Globe-Times*. "Sometimes they both explode at the same contest. When that happens, it's plain murder."[16]

In 1947, Crues hit 14 more homers than Bauman (52 to 38) and batted in 51 more runs (178 to 127), and his batting average was 30 points higher (.380 to .350). Still, he remained in Bauman's shadow.

"When Bauman hit a home run, it went so far it took the life out of another team," Amarillo sportswriter Putt Powell said. "He looked terrible striking out."

It was all or nothing with Bauman, and that's what made him a fan favorite.

"I never hit any high home runs," Crues said. "Mine was all on a line."

Bauman batted fourth in the lineup, the cleanup spot, and Crues fifth.

In a tie game with runners on second and third, Lubbock intentionally walked Bauman to load the bases and pitch to Crues, who had gone 10 games without a homer. As he waited in the on-deck circle, Bill Southworth, a car dealer in Amarillo, waved a $100 bill and hollered, "Bob, if you hit it over my sign out there, I'll give you this hundred dollars."

Crues ripped the first pitch 340 feet over the Southworth Motor Company sign in right field. "I came around and started picking the fence. And he tore that $100 bill in two."

"Next one you hit, the other $50 is yours," Southworth said.

The following night, the Gold Sox trailed by a run when Bauman led off the ninth inning with a single. Crues followed by lofting the ball over the 360-foot center-field fence. Bob made a beeline toward Southworth to collect the other half of the $100 bill.

Crues went 6-for-6 in another game, lashing two homers, two singles, and a triple and a double to drive in three runs. A headline over the box score in the *Daily News* read, "CAN YOU COOK TOO, BOB?"[17]

The box score heading for the next game read, "COPY-CAT BAUMAN."[18]

Joe was 5-for-5—two homers, two singles, and a double to knock in four runs.

"They all hated to see Joe walk to the plate, and they hated to see me," Crues said. "I ain't bragging just because it was me, but they hated to see us walk up there one right behind the other."

"We were good friends, and we just played to win," Joe said. "There was never any jealousy or anything like that at all."

Even though he broke Bauman's home run record, Crues was second banana in 1947, to Lubbock's Serena, who totaled 57.

"Crues didn't blossom until Bauman left," Powell added. "I never pictured him as a home run hitter . . . always pictured him as a good, solid hitter."

Bauman moved up the ladder in 1948, going as high as Triple-A before spending most of the season in the Class A Eastern League.

Crues had center stage in Amarillo to himself. People were calling him "Round Trip" and expecting him to hit home runs like clockwork. Could he do it?

* * *

There were five games left in the 1948 season, and Crues had 65 home runs. Except for a wire-service story and a *Sporting News* article, the national media ignored Crues and his pursuit of the minor-league home run record.

Even in the tiny Texas Panhandle town of Gruver near the Oklahoma border, folks didn't know much about Crues.

"We would like to know who this great BOB CRUES IS?" two readers asked in a letter Gilstrap published verbatim in his *Daily News* column. "How come he's not up with some other team. Class C is not the best we hope. I understand this boy has tried out at some other place called Little Rock. Amarillo must be paying a mighty good salary to take a player away from a Class A club."

"Who is Bob Crues?" Gilstrap responded, adding,

> Only a Panhandle boy who has accomplished greater batting feats than any other player in the history of the WT–NM League; who has broken three league hitting records this year and may break two more; who has hit more home runs than any other player in Organized Baseball has done in one regular season since 1933.[19]

At the end of the 1947 season, Seeds sold Crues to the Little Rock Travelers of the Class AA Southern Association. The sale was conditional, meaning Crues would be returned to the Gold Sox if he didn't make the grade. Crues was back in Amarillo the following April. "I got homesick, and a homesick ballplayer is no good to anyone," Gilstrap quoted him as saying.[20]

Actually, Crues left the Travelers because of a contract dispute. "They had nerve enough to send me a contract for $300 a month. I was making $350 here. I told them I wasn't going to play."

The Travelers were headed to Dallas for an exhibition game.

"When we get to Dallas," Crues said to Travelers manager Jack Saltz-gaver, "if they haven't raised my salary from $300 to $450, I'm not going to stay."

Saltzgaver called Travelers owner Ray Winder to pass on Crues's ultimatum.

"No way," Winder said.

Crues hopped on a bus in Dallas and returned to Amarillo. He went immediately to Seeds's hardware and sporting goods store, which also served as his baseball office. "Walked into the store and that son of a gun stood back there with a grin on his face about a foot wide."

"I knew you'd be back," Seeds said.

The Gold Sox owned his contract, and Crues insisted they option him to either Little Rock or Jackson, Mississippi, at the end of the season to prevent other teams from taking him in baseball's annual winter draft. The Jackson Senators were in the Class B Southeastern League and regularly did business with Seeds and Winder.

"It was a damned cover-up to keep someone from drafting him," Bauman said. "He wasn't going to make the damned ballclub if he went down there and hit one thousand."

"Yeah, they could conspire to keep him down there in that way," Abilene's Howard Green said.

Crues claimed a scout for the Kansas City Blues, a top affiliate of the New York Yankees in the American Association, offered $7,500 for his contract at the end of the 1947 season. "Seeds wouldn't take it," he declared.

Crues was in Seeds's store at the time and overheard the conversation. "Big-mouth Seeds, you could hear them all over the store."

Seeds denied any wrongdoing, however. "All ballplayers think they're the victim of a raw deal. I've been on both sides of it. He didn't get any raw deal."

Seeds said Little Rock couldn't use Crues and wanted to send him to Jackson. "Of course, he didn't want to go. I was for that all the way. I guess he knew that."

Crues complained Seeds "was so tight he squeaked when he walked," but he also knew that he could make more money in Amarillo. "Every time he hit a home run he got $100 or more," Seeds said, referring to the fence money.

In 1948, WT–NM League teams could carry 16 players and pay up to the monthly team salary limit of $3,200, slightly more than $213 per player. Seeds gave Crues a $25 raise, to $375 a month.

"There was widespread cheating," Green confirmed. "Everybody knew about it, but nobody would do anything."

Star players were given cash, in addition to a monthly check for their official salary. Bauman was under contract to Little Rock the two years he played in Amarillo. "I was making more money than the salary limit would allow. I'd get two checks—one from Little Rock and one from Seeds."

Bauman didn't know what Crues made, but he knew he was worth twice the amount.

"Crues was shrewd enough, he was a self-educated man," Bauman said. "But I don't think he knew what his own worth was to that ballclub. He could just as easily have gone into Seeds and said, 'I want $500 or $600 and that's minimum!' He would have probably got it after the damn wrestling was over."

Robert Fulton Crues was born December 31, 1918, in Celina, Texas, north of Dallas. He soon moved with his family to a farm in the Texas Panhandle.

He was three when the index finger of his right hand was cut off by a windmill. At age 11, he was thrown off a plow and landed on a tree stump, tearing muscles in his back. "As you get older, it'll bother you more," doctors predicted.

Back problems plagued him the last month of the 1948 season and eventually forced him to quit baseball.

Bob left high school six months before he was to graduate so he could help his ailing father on the farm. He found time to pitch for a semipro team. "I had a fastball, curveball, a fair change," he said.

Living near a railroad growing up, he used the glass insulators on telephone and telegraph poles along the track for target practice. "I must've broken ten thousand. Threw rocks at 'em."

This is how he learned to throw hard and accurately with three fingers.

He taught himself how to hit, too.

Soon after joining the Gold Sox in 1946, Crues went into a slump that dropped his batting average to well under .300. He asked Seeds for help.

"There ain't nobody can help you but yourself," Seeds said. "Just get up there and do it."

He took Seeds's advice. "It wasn't no time til I was hitting that curve-ball."

Crues socked 150 homers in his three years at Amarillo.

In addition to the 69 he hit during the regular season in 1948, Crues crushed three more in 17 postseason games to finish with 72. The 70th came in the first playoff game at Amarillo. Crues notched his 71st in the 11th game of the playoffs, smacking a first-inning homer over the center-field wall at Pampa to win the WT–NM League title and face the Kilgore Drillers, the Lone Star League champs, in the Little Dixie Series to deter-mine the best Class C team in Texas. Number 72 was a three-run shot at Gold Sox Field in the third contest of the series, won by Amarillo in five. Crues added 13 RBIs to end up with a mind-boggling 267 for the season.

But RBIs seldom made headlines. They didn't fill screens with dollar bills or keep the refrigerator stocked with food and ice-cold beer. What mattered most to Crues was his homers, and, unfortunately, they were the subject of widespread cynicism.

"How come you get so many home runs down there?" Gilstrap was asked repeatedly by other writers covering the 1948 World Series be-tween the Cleveland Indians and Boston Braves. [21]

When Seeds showed up at Travelers Field in Little Rock, a pop fly during batting practice inevitably caused someone to shout, "That's a homer in Amarillo." [22]

Crues couldn't satisfy the skeptics or Gold Sox fans. "It got to the point that they expected a home run every time I walked up there," he said.

No one expected Crues back in Amarillo. "The Class B clubs aren't going to pass up such a wonderful opportunity," Gilstrap wrote, predict-ing he would go quickly in the upcoming baseball draft. [23]

The Jackson Senators plucked him for the standard price of $1,000.

Jackson was managed by Seeds's friend and former teammate, Willis Hudlin, and linked closely with the Travelers, the team Crues walked out on the previous year. Combined, the three teams formed what he per-ceived as a "Bermuda Triangle" that doomed any hopes he had of playing in the majors.

"In my mind I could hit major-league pitching a dang sight better than the rest of 'em," said Crues. "I never had a chance. I didn't give up until the end of the '48 season when they sent me to Class B—Jackson. That's when I got teed off."

A banner headline in the *Jackson Clarion-Ledger* heralded Crues as the Babe Ruth of the minors. Gilstrap contributed the story, writing, "Skeptical Jackson folk at once will ask: 'What's wrong with him? How come the Senators got him for the paltry $1,000 draft price?'"

As Gilstrap saw it, the only thing wrong with Crues was his age—30. "That's the reason the Amarillo club couldn't find anyone who would buy him for what he's worth, though it was a foregone conclusion that he would be snapped up in the draft."

Gilstrap concluded by mentioning Crues "jumped" the Little Rock club to return to Amarillo. "If he can be persuaded to stay around, he ought to help the Senators plenty."[24]

Crues opted to play semipro ball in Elk City, Oklahoma. He moved his family to Elk City, 150 miles from Amarillo, and worked at a meat-packing plant there during the winter.

Then he got a call from Roswell, New Mexico. The city had a new baseball team, the Rockets, in the Class D Longhorn League, and was looking for a player-manager. It was a step down, but they offered $600 a month—the amount he was demanding from Jackson and $225 more than Seeds ever paid him at Amarillo.

"I could have kept him from going to Roswell," Seeds said. "But, hell, I let him go."

In late July, the Rockets were in fifth place, with a 41-49 record, when Crues was relieved of his managerial duties and replaced by the team's business manager, J. R. "Potsy" Allen.

Crues continued playing first base, ending up with 28 homers and 129 RBIs, both second-best in the league, and a .365 batting average.

The Rockets won only 16 of their last 49 games under Allen to finish in the cellar. They tried to get Crues to take the reins again, but he declined.

Crues didn't reject a deal for 1950 with the San Angelo Colts, another Longhorn League team. "They signed me before the end of the 1949 season. I got a bonus of $2,500 and $50 more a month in salary. Nobody knew anything about it. If they'd found that out, they'd shot both of us."

The eyes of San Angelo were on him. A wire-service report on Crues stepping up to the plate for the first time at spring training reads like a passage out of the classic baseball poem "Casey at the Bat."

"They all held their breath," the story began, as Crues "took a mighty roundhouse swing. A dullish pop sounded, and the ball rolled a couple of feet. But his bat was shattered and splintered."[25]

This happened in 1951—his second year with the Colts. Crues was wearing a steel back brace. "I wore it all year in 1950. It affected my swing. You can look at the record and see that."

The record for 1950 shows that Crues had 32 homers, 99 RBIs, and a .251 batting average.

"It was '51 when I really went down," he conceded.

Perhaps the splintered bat at spring training was an omen.

Crues was hitting .290, with 10 homers, in August when he was released by the Colts and picked up by the Lubbock Hubbers of the WT–NM League. He played in part of one game for the Hubbers, striking out twice and blasting a homer over the center-field fence before he was hit on the arm by a pitched ball. The next day, Lubbock let him go, citing the lame back that had plagued him in San Angelo.

Crues claimed he was healthy enough to play. A week later, the *Amarillo Daily News* announced in a headline, "'HOME RUN' CRUES IS BACK."[26]

Gilstrap reminded readers of the homers and RBIs he piled up three years earlier. "Baseball never before had seen, nor has it seen since, anything like the manner in which lean-faced Robert attacked league pitching."[27]

Crues was a shadow of what he used to be. Batting eighth in the lineup, he didn't lift a ball over the fence until his seventh game back in a Gold Sox uniform. He hit four more to wind up with 16 for the season, a career low. "My back was in such terrible shape, I just gave it up."

He was out of baseball all of 1952 and half of 1953. He had just been laid off by the Amarillo munitions plant where he worked during World War II when the Borger Gassers came to his rescue. They provided his first big chance in 1940 and 13 years later they were giving him his last.

Crues downplayed expectations, saying he was filling in until the end of the season. A comeback depended on his back and it was in sorry shape.

In his first game, he struck out three times, walked once, and botched one of three chances he had in left field. He made three errors in another game.

But there was one moment when he was, in the words of one observer, "the old master himself."[28]

The Gassers were at the Abilene ballpark, scene of the homer that wasn't in 1948. With two runners on base and his team trailing, 3-0, he took a lusty cut. This time there was no doubt, the ball soaring high over the left-field fence to tie the score. Later, he singled in the winning run. It was vintage Crues.

He homered the next day and again two days later. In 11 games, he had four homers and 12 RBIs. And, then, his aching back forced him out of the lineup and into retirement.

After baseball, Crues drifted from job to job trying to support his wife and four boys. "I tried to go into business for myself. Competition was too dang crazy," he said. "I was in the car polishing business. Then I went to Panhandle and got a service station. Before that I was selling cars. I came back to Amarillo and got in the beer business. Then I began driving a truck."

He lived in Albuquerque for several years and, then, Roswell, where he had a gas station near one operated by Bauman. "We had two guys running gas stations on the same street that hit more minor-league home runs than anybody else—72 and 69," one Roswell resident recalled. "That's a few taters."

By 1974, he was back in Amarillo, managing an ATEX station. He had the job long enough to recognize customers by their cars. "Here comes two dollars' worth of regular," he said upon seeing a battered two-tone 1959 Chevrolet pull into the station.

"Two bucks of regular," the driver confirmed.

The ATEX station was on the way to the local speedway, and cars going to the Fourth of July races were lined up for gas. "Pumped nearly 3,000 gallons a day," Crues said proudly. "Run as high as 180,000 gallons a month."

In 1975, he was inducted into the Panhandle Hall of Fame as its 35th member. He had been selected several years earlier, but no one could find him to let him know.

Crues's entry into the Panhandle Hall of Fame coincided with pro baseball leaving Amarillo.

"All successful operations in sports are based on personalities," Powell wrote late in the 1974 season, when it was apparent the Amarillo Giants of the Class AA Texas League were moving to Lafayette, Louisia-

Bob Crues never got his photo on the front of a Wheaties cereal box, but this shot of him is in the National Baseball Hall of Fame Library in Cooperstown, New York. The single-season home run mark that Crues tied at Amarillo in 1948 was broken six years later. His record of 254 runs batted in still stands. *National Baseball Hall of Fame Library, Cooperstown, NY.*

na. "Fans used to rush to the park to see such personalities as Bob Crues and Joe Bauman . . . the fans knew about them."[29]

Crues was ancient history. Powell resurrected his 1948 achievements: 228 hits, including 38 doubles and 3 triples, in 565 times at bat, for a .404 batting average and record-setting 479 total bases in 140 games. "Baseball followers marvel more at the 254 runs batted in than the 69 home runs," he said.[30]

The RBI mark always was a consolation prize.

The Associated Press story reporting Crues's death in 1987, at the age of 67, mentioned his home run record in the lead paragraph and three times overall. The lone reference to the RBI mark was buried in the fifth paragraph.

"I'm most proud of the home runs, but I've got an RBI record that I don't think will ever be touched," Crues said. "What do you think?"

The wind will stop blowing in Texas before the record is broken. It has lasted 70 years and counting. It ensures Crues a permanent place in the record book, one that eluded him in baseball and life.

4

THE MAN WHO WORE
THE TEXACO STAR

Joe Bauman

Joe Bauman is the most famous baseball player never to set foot on a big-league diamond. The bulk of his fame came late in life when steroid-clouded home runs soared out of ballparks, threatening the all-time record of 72 he slugged in the bushes of eastern New Mexico and West Texas in 1954.

Joe's death in 2005, at the age of 83, was national news, the *New York Times* reporting he "never envisioned reaching the bleachers at Yankee Stadium, figuring he would make out just fine running a gas station in the years to come."[1]

During the summer of 1954, Joe's day job was pumping gas at his Texaco service station in Roswell, New Mexico. On the last day of the regular season, he pumped three balls over the fence to become the first in history to top 70. At 6-foot-5 and 245 pounds, he was the physical embodiment of Texaco's "Tower of Power" tagline and its advertising jingle, "You can trust your car to the man who wears the star."

Wire-service stories spread the news of Joe's historic homers through-out the United States. They echoed a classic line written three days earlier by Buck Lanier of the *Roswell Daily Record* when he tied the mark: "It couldn't happen to a nicer guy."[2]

Life magazine published a half-page photo of Joe filling his fists with money pushed at him through a chicken-wire screen by adoring fans. The picture was taken by freelancer Kenyon Cobane of Roswell. Ironically, it marked the end of Joe's one season of fame, while paving the way for Cobane to photograph U.S. presidents Lyndon B. Johnson and Richard Nixon, Queen Elizabeth, and other famous people.

Joe played another year and part of a second until the lone star was the one on his Texaco uniform. He quit baseball midway through the 1956 season to devote himself to his businesses on a full-time basis.

No one challenged Joe's record until Mark McGwire belted 70 in 1998. Three years later, Barry Bonds left McGwire and Bauman in the dust with a barrage of 73 home runs, which Lanier called "steroid induced" because of substance abuse charges that tarnished the achievements of both Bonds and McGwire.

Life magazine photographer Kenyon Cobane captured this shot of Roswell's Joe Bauman "picking the screen" of money after whacking his record-breaking 70th homer. Joe clouted two more in the second game of the doubleheader at Artesia to end up with 72. Joe estimated the three homers yielded $500 in "fence money," while others, not concerned about the tax implications, put the amount at $800. *Kenyon Cobane Collection/IHSF.org.*

"I'm a Hall of Fame voter and have been for many, many, many years," said Jim Reeves, retired sports columnist for the *Fort Worth Star-Telegram*. "I won't vote for Barry Bonds ever for the Hall of Fame. Or Mark McGwire. Or anybody that I'm certain cheated at the time or used steroids at the time."

It took McGwire and Bonds to make Bauman famous again. For the better part of four decades, Bauman was a forgotten man. He liked it that way.

"I don't think of those days anymore," he said in 1961, to a writer asking about the challenges Roger Maris and Mickey Mantle faced in their pursuit of Babe Ruth's record of 60. "It was nice when I did it, but I don't remember them now."[3]

That didn't stop the media from calling Bauman every now and then.

He was easy to find. His name was in the Roswell phone book. And he was cordial to all who called. If you traveled to Roswell, he took time to visit and show you around town. One of the stops was the baseball field, Fair Park, at the Eastern New Mexico State Fairgrounds. It was renamed Joe Bauman Stadium in 2005.

In a Longhorn League playoff game in 1954, Joe clubbed a ball more than 500 feet over the right-field fence and into the middle of the adjacent rodeo grounds. "They stopped the rodeo, and the cowboys stood up and were throwing their hats," said Tom Brookshier, a Roswell pitcher who went on to become a star defensive back for the Philadelphia Eagles in the National Football League. "They knew who hit it."[4]

With the passage of time, Joe's home runs have become almost mythical.

"Joe didn't just hit 'em over the fence, he hit 'em over the lights," said Floyd "Greek" Economides, a catcher for the Artesia NuMexers in 1954.

Ralph "Skippy" Nix Jr. was a batboy for Artesia in 1952, when a Bauman blast just missed the lights at the team's ballpark. "Have you ever hit the lights?" Skippy asked.

Joe smiled, patted Ralph on his right shoulder, and said nothing. A couple of weeks later Joe hit the lights, causing a glass-popping explosion that fans rewarded with dollar bills stuck through the backstop screen. After harvesting the cash crop, he walked straight to Skippy in the dugout and said with a big, loud laugh, "Now I have."

In another game, the home plate umpire was blinded by the lights and didn't see a ball Joe rocketed over the center-field fence. He had already circled the bases and sat down in the dugout when the umpire confessed, "I don't know where the damned ball went. I never saw it. You're going to have to hit over."

Joe did all his clouting in the minors, where he was home run king four times: 1946, 1952, 1953, and 1954. A half-century later, Minor League Baseball established the Joe Bauman Award to honor the top home run hitter each season. Ryan Howard was the first recipient in 2004; Kris Bryant won in 2014.

Joe totaled 337 round-trippers in nine seasons, 238 coming the last five years after he turned 30. He was out of pro baseball for eight years during his 20s. These are the so-called lost years, when Joe played for the U.S. Navy or such semipro teams as the Elk City Elks.

Joe joined the Elks in 1949, after a miserable season at Hartford, Connecticut, a Boston Braves farm team in the Class A Eastern League. In 98 games, he batted .275 and hit 10 homers, far below the 86 he mashed the previous two seasons for Amarillo of the Class C West Texas–New Mexico (WT-NM) League.

"It was really a lost season for me," Joe said. "It seemed like a perpetual winter. "The grass stayed sopping wet at night. You ran up the aisle into a cold clubhouse and back to a stove to stay warm between innings. I felt like hell all the time."

The Braves offered Joe a $400-per-month contract, a $200 cut and less than what he made at Amarillo. "I told them I could make more money selling shoestrings on the street than that."

It was a favorite one-liner that Joe embellished, making the shoelaces 27 inches long and peddling them on the streets of Oklahoma City, where he grew up.

Joe was born on April 17, 1922, in Welch, Oklahoma, a town of 700 people in the northeast corner of the state. His family moved to Oklahoma City when he was one.

Joe was a natural right-hander and played first base. Upon hearing the advantages of being a lefty, he started throwing and hitting left-handed.

Chet Bryan, a highly successful baseball coach at Oklahoma State University from 1965–1977, played with Joe in the navy. "He'd work out left-handed one time and right-handed the next. He could throw just as good with either arm. It didn't matter."

Joe was 19 in 1941, when he signed to play professionally for the Little Rock Travelers of the Southern Association, a Class A-1 league at the time. The Travelers were independently owned and provided a chance to move up faster because they made money selling players to teams in the higher minors. In fact, Joe's contract entitled him to 25 percent of the selling price.

Joe went hitless in 10 at-bats for the Travelers and was immediately sent to the bottom of the minors—Newport, Arkansas, of the Class D Northeast Arkansas League. He batted .215, with just three homers, and didn't play pro ball again until four years later.

In 1942, Joe worked for Beech Aircraft in Wichita, Kansas, and played for its baseball team, the Beechcraft Flyers. By the end of the year, he was in the navy and back in Oklahoma working in the athletic department at the naval air station in Norman. "My main job was playing first base," he said.

The Navy Skyjackets were dubbed the "Little Yankees." Five of the players in 1943 were seasoned big-league veterans, and two more went on to play briefly in the majors. "Joe was as good as any of them," said Bryan, a second baseman on the team. "He'd hit tape-measure shots."

"Every time we left the base we had to have our liberty card," recalled Bennie Warren, a catcher for the Philadelphia Phillies before entering the navy. "Joe could hit the ball a good ways. So, during batting practice, he'd say, 'If any of y'all don't have your liberty card, just get on this one here.'"

"I was probably the sorriest damn player on the team when I started, but by the third year I was holding my own and doing just as good a job as a lot of them," Joe said. "I came out of there a pretty decent ballplayer. I was 24 years old and ready to go."

So were hundreds of other players discharged from the military at the end of World War II.

Joe still belonged to Little Rock. A scout for the St. Louis Cardinals urged him to buy back his contract so they could work out their own deal. "I figured they were out a thousand dollars on me," Joe said. "I was willing to give them their cost-plus just to give me a release. But, no, they wouldn't do it."

Little Rock rejected Joe's offer of $2,000.

Approximately 130 players flooded the Travelers spring training camp in 1946. Joe related,

Hell, you'd work out in shifts. They tried to look at these guys and evaluate them, but they couldn't see enough of them. They'd ship him out to Jackson or Amarillo or someplace. It was a hell of a mix of good players that should've been playing better baseball than those lower minor leagues.

Joe preferred the Amarillo Gold Sox even though they were in a league one notch below Jackson, Mississippi, in Class B. Amarillo was a straight shot on U.S. Route 66 from his home in Oklahoma City. The owner-manager of the Gold Sox was Bob Seeds, a former big-leaguer who also ran a combination hardware and sporting goods store. He could buy base-balls at wholesale prices, so the more Joe launched out of bandbox-sized Gold Sox Field, the better for business. He slugged 12 the first month and a league record 48 for the season.

"Go get your money up there," a teammate said to Joe as he stepped into the dugout after hitting his first homer for the Gold Sox.

"What money?" Joe asked.

The teammate pointed to the dollar bills sticking through the screen separating the grandstand from the field. "Go on, you fool, that's customary."

Joe made the rounds, jamming his pockets and cap full. "That was the first time I ever saw fans pay off in money for a home run. It didn't take me long to learn the custom."

Joe went to spring training with Little Rock in 1947, but he didn't want to stay. The ballpark was Death Valley for long-ball hitters, 380 feet from home to the right-field fence and 500 feet to center. "A power hitter was at a disadvantage. I don't care who it was—Ted Williams, Babe Ruth, or whoever. You play in that ballpark and it was a handicap."

Seeds had a working agreement with Little Rock and tried changing Joe's mind, telling him he could make it with the Travelers and in the majors as well. "If you get to the big leagues, everything will be twice as good," Seeds argued. "You don't have to ride many buses and station wagons. It's great."

"I don't care," Joe said.

"He didn't want to play for Little Rock," Seeds explained. "He didn't like the town for one thing. He wanted to come back to Amarillo."

At Amarillo, Joe upped his batting average from .301 to .350, hitting 38 homers. This produced enough screen money to buy a used Buick.

Near the end of the 1947 season, Little Rock sold Joe to the Milwaukee Brewers of the American Association, a Triple-A team owned by the Braves. The Brewers already had a first baseman, Heinz Becker, the league's defending batting champion. Joe batted once and then moved on to Hartford. If Joe had his druthers, he would've stayed in Amarillo all along.

"Joe never did care for publicity or all the fanfare," Seeds said. "He didn't like for people to make a fuss over him."

One exception, of course, was the custom of fans showering him with dollar bills after a home run. "Amarillo was the best," Joe said. "Any time you hit a home run in Amarillo, it was worth $50. Didn't matter whether you were ahead or behind."

Meanwhile, the Braves refused to budge on their "shoestring" offer to Joe, prompting a meeting with Seeds in Amarillo to discuss a deal that would enable his return to the Gold Sox in 1949.

Two weeks later, Harry Gilstrap of the *Amarillo Daily News* reported that Seeds had failed to land Joe, as the Braves "wanted a lot more money than any Class C baseball owner is going to pay for any player less than a Ted Williams, Joe DiMaggio, Stan Musial, Gene Bearden, or Johnny Sain."[5]

One of Joe's teammates with the Beechcraft Flyers at Wichita in 1942 was Dwight "Rip" Collins. They were both Oklahomans and lifelong friends. "He had everything," Collins said. "When I played with him in Wichita I didn't see how they could keep him out of the big leagues. He was so powerful."

Collins was building a team for Elk City, about halfway between Oklahoma City and Amarillo on U.S. Route 66. The town of 8,000 people was enjoying an oil boom, and its leaders wanted to entertain the growing population with a team that would win the National Baseball Congress (NBC) tournament, semipro baseball's version of the World Series.

"I was one of 'em footing the bill," said Donnie McClain, the team's manager before Collins took over. "Money didn't mean anything really. To have a winning team, that's all people wanted."

Joe was the ticket to winning, and Collins found him and his wife, Dorothy, fishing at a lake near Oklahoma City. "What are you going to do?" Collins inquired after Joe said he wasn't going back to Hartford.

"I don't know. Maybe play a little semipro down in the city or work for some company here."

Joe agreed to play at Elk City for $500 a month, a rent-free house, and a car. The owner of a mattress factory donated a custom-made bed, one foot wider and one and a half feet longer than a standard-sized bed. "I didn't do a damn thing. Played baseball three days a week and fished the rest of the time," Joe said.

Collins filled the roster with such talented minor leaguers as third baseman Tony Range, a consistent .300 hitter; Les Mulcahy, a power-hitting catcher; and pitchers Mitch Chetkovich and Dee Sanders, who had cups of coffee in the majors.

"I could go downtown and holler a couple of times we were going to try and import a pitcher," McClain said. "I'd have the money before I moved. Whatever it cost, we'd always get."

Joe ended up staying three years in Elk City. "We had a hell of a ballclub. With the opposition that we played, we could just have a ball and win. Everybody we played didn't have a bearing on anything. What we were looking forward to was that national tournament."

Playing mostly against other Oklahoma Semipro League teams, Elk City posted a 72-14 record in 1949, placing third in the NBC tourney. Joe batted .347 and accounted for 27 of the Elks' 52 home runs.

There were no cheapies at Ackley Park. The distance from home plate to the outfield walls was 335 feet down the foul lines, 375 in the power alleys, and 473 to center.

Royse Parr was a "pop boy" the three years Joe played there, selling bottles of Dr. Pepper, Orange Crush, and Grapette soft drinks. "Sold them for a dime and got two cents out of it," Parr said. "I never sold pop when he was up. The whole crowd was like me. We were there mainly to see Joe."

There were moments when Elk City fans could swear they were watching Babe Ruth or at least a reenactment of his home run shot in the 1932 World Series.

McClain was in the dugout when Joe announced he would hit one over a signboard. "He pointed to where he was going to hit it. We were behind and there were a couple of men on base."

Joe took a Ruthian cut at the first pitch. BAM!

"Hit it right over the signboard," McClain said. "He laughed when he did it."

"The rest of the team was nice, but he was head and shoulders above them all," said Parr, 13 years old when Joe first put on an Elks uniform and, with teammate Jack Riley, began operating a Texaco station on busy Route 66.

"It's the second Texaco station as you come into Elk City," Harry Gilstrap informed readers. "I am sorry I can't tell you anything about the operator of the first Texaco station. Chances are he is a nice guy, too."[6]

On Sunday mornings, Joe was usually there, looking sharp in his Texaco uniform.

Parr would sneak over to the station from church, buy a soda pop for a nickel, and sit silently in awe of his hero.

Joe Bauman pumped baseballs out of ballparks at night and gas at his Texaco service station during the day. Joe co-owned with teammate Jack Riley a Texaco station on Route 66 in Elk City, Oklahoma. His Roswell station was on the highway to a popular horse-racing track in Ruidoso, New Mexico. At one time, former Amarillo teammate Bob Crues operated a gas station on the same road. *Kenyon Cobane Collection/IHSF.org.*

A half-century later, Parr, a retired attorney living in Tulsa, was reading an article about Joe's home run record. He said, "That's the first time I realized I'd seen greatness and didn't even know it."

Parr wanted to find out more about his boyhood idol, so he telephoned him in Roswell. "I wished I talked to him in the Texaco station. He was an easy guy to talk to on the phone."

Joe hiked his batting average to .403 and poked 29 homers in 1950, to lead the Elks to a 60-11 mark and a heartbreaking second-place finish in the NBC. Some 600 people from Elk City traveled 275 miles to Wichita to cheer their Elks to six-straight wins before they lost the last two games. "It just about broke everybody," McClain said. "They put up so darn much money. They all went up to Wichita—anybody who could get off and go spend the whole week there."

In 1951, Joe hit .368, with 22 homers, to lead the Elks to a 44-12 record and a third-straight state championship. But the oil money had dried up, and the league shut down before the season ended. "That last year baseball just went down into nothing, and it stopped being interesting," Joe said. "We weren't playing enough ballgames to keep paying everybody like they did. They got tired of continually having to put money in the till."

Parr calculated that Joe's 78 home runs in 786 official at-bats with the Elks averaged out to 59 in a 162-game season for a grand total of 177—amazingly close to the 175 he would hit in pro ball the next three seasons.

In 2001, Joe was invited back to Elk City for an event celebrating the 100th anniversary of its incorporation as a city and the first local team since 1951 to qualify for the NBC tournament. Parr phoned Joe to advise a private aircraft was lined up to fly him and Dorothy from Roswell to Elk City.

Joe thanked him and then declined. "I want them to remember me the way I was."

* * *

The eye doctor could envision the man-mountain wearing the Texaco uniform batting cleanup for his baseball team in Artesia, New Mexico.

Dr. Marshall Dyke was on his way to the national baseball meeting in Columbus, Ohio, in early December 1951, when he pulled into the driveway of the most popular gas station in Elk City. He was part-owner and general manager of the Artesia Drillers, and looking for a power hitter, not gas. "If we got a hold of your contract from Boston, would you come to Artesia and play ball?" Dr. Dyke asked Joe.

"My God, this is a bolt out of the blue," Joe said. "I don't know."

The Elks were history, and he figured his baseball career was, too. "As far as trying to get anywhere, I quit when I was in Elk City. For all practical purposes, that finished me for trying to go up in Major League and Minor League Baseball, and I knew it."

The Texaco station he ran with Riley was his bread and butter. "At that time baseball was just extra income because, man, our living was right there in the station. We made our money from the business, and whatever we made off of baseball was just damn gravy."

The doctor's question got Joe thinking about playing pro ball again. He checked one of the maps sold in the station to find out where Artesia was located.

The Boston Braves still owned his contract, and he was skeptical Dr. Dyke would fare any better buying it than Amarillo's Seeds had in 1949. "The Braves punished him," Gilstrap insisted, "by setting so high a price on his contract that clubs outside their organization wouldn't buy him."[7]

Joe was almost 30. "A baseball player is better at 30, 31, and 32 than he is at any time," he said. "Those are really any ballplayer's best years as a hitter."

He discussed the opportunity with Riley, who agreed to run the station until Joe returned in the fall.

Dr. Dyke was a wheeler-dealer, buying and selling baseball teams in Roswell and the Texas cities of Borger and Ballinger. He moved the Ballinger team to Artesia at the end of the 1950 season and eventually sold his one-third interest to Artesia Baseball Club, Inc., a corporate entity with stock owned by townsfolk. He convinced the Braves that this was their last chance to get anything out of their investment in Joe and offered $1,500—a "whacking outlay for one player by a struggling Class C franchise," Gilstrap said, "but likely will get it back at the gate."[8]

The optometrist returned to Elk City to deliver the good news and offer Joe a signing bonus, the salary he wanted plus the option of buying back his contract for $250 at the end of the 1952 season. "That's what enticed me to go there," Joe said of the opportunity to control his own destiny.

Artesia had a new business and field manager—Earl Perry. He also was from Oklahoma and knew all about Joe from playing with and against him in the military.

Perry was charged with resurrecting a team that was buried at the bottom of the Class C Longhorn League standings with a 45-95 record. Joe was just what the doctor ordered to put the "drill" in Drillers, as they hit only 48 homers in 140 games.

Perry ordered Joe to burn off a couple of six-packs. He hit 11 homers in his first 22 games and finished with 50, the most in pro baseball, while hitting .375 and driving in 157 runs. "He had such power," Perry said. "You can't teach power. You just watch it, amazed, and hope your teeth don't fall out."[9]

Pitchers worked around Joe, walking him a league-high 148 times. In one game, he was walked five times by the same pitcher, twice intentionally with the bases empty.

Joe was, as one sportswriter aptly described, the "Man with the Bat."[10]

"I can remember him scraping his bats with beer bottle openers and, then, boning and sanding them," said Lin Patterson, a Drillers batboy. "He wanted the handle to be thinner, but he wanted a big barrel."

Joe held the knob of the Louisville Slugger in the palm of his calloused right hand, so he could get under the ball and lift it higher.

"That's the thing I remember most—how fast the ball left the ballpark so high and so far," Patterson said. "There's nobody who hit the ball with more force. It was pure power. Every once in a while, he'd get a hold of one, and it would be a line-drive sort of a thing—like watching headlights finally dim. The dad-gum thing would just clear the fence by 10, 12, 15 feet."

Patterson was 11 years old when Joe arrived in Artesia. He grew up to play center field for the University of New Mexico baseball team and then became a highly respected attorney in the oil and gas industry. Joe made such a lasting impression on Patterson as a kid that 60 years later, he could still paint a vivid word picture of him.

"He had an absolutely fabulous swing, and his bat speed was tremendous," said Patterson. "On the other hand, he had a very unusual finish, not unlike Babe Ruth, when he missed the ball. He wound up and came spinning around, and you'd think he would lose his balance."

Joe never batted right-handed in a game, but in batting practice he sometimes hit from the right side. "He hit the crap out of the ball right-handed," Patterson said. "He did it basically to hone his skills. He said it improved his eyesight."

A baseball group in Oklahoma recognized Joe as the outstanding minor-league player of 1952, and Mickey Mantle, a rising star with the New York Yankees, for bringing the most distinction to the state.

Joe decided to focus solely on baseball in 1953. He sold his half of the Texaco station in Elk City to his partner, Riley, and purchased his contract from the Drillers who told him, "Go make a deal and come back and tell us what the deal is and we'll see if we can match it."

He remained in Artesia after the Drillers matched a Roswell offer of $500 per month and a $1,500 cash bonus. This was big money for a small-town team struggling to survive financially.

Longhorn League teams ignored the monthly salary cap of $3,400, Artesia claiming its payroll was "next to the lowest at $6,000."[11]

Perry loaded the Drillers with such costly musclemen as Les Mulcahy, a sidekick of Joe's in Elk City. Mulcahy cracked 34 homers and Joe 53, once again tops in all of baseball. "If you travel in fast company, there is a certain price you must pay for the ride," Perry said after stepping down as field manager mid-season to concentrate on the business side. "But let's face it. We can't really afford what we have."[12]

Joe was Perry's handpicked successor. He guided the Drillers to a second-straight fourth-place finish, but he didn't like managing and regretted accepting the job. In late October, he told Artesia fans there was "pessimism up and down Main Street about baseball in 1954," warning, "There's no way if there's no will."[13]

Joe had already bought his contract from the Drillers. He also made a deal for a Texaco station in Roswell on the main highway to the mountain resort town of Ruidoso and its popular racetrack, Ruidoso Downs. The next week, the *Roswell Daily Record* announced in a banner headline, "MIGHTY JOE BAUMAN SIGNS WITH ROCKETS FOR 1954."[14]

Joe soon returned to Artesia in a Rockets uniform to launch the mightiest home run of his career.

Mike Currier, another Artesia batboy, would be there to see it. "I could strut up and down the street as a 12-year-old and tell everybody that I knew Joe Bauman and that I probably played catch with him one day," said Currier. "Heaven knows whether I did or not, but it sure makes for a good story."

* * *

Roswell's player-manager in 1954 was Frank "Pat" Stasey, the driving force in the Cubanization of baseball in Texas and New Mexico.

Stasey also was co-owner with another minor-league fixture, the hard-hitting Hayden "Stubby" Greer. They signed Tom Brookshier, a local boy and future NFL star, and filled the roster with Cubans. Three of them advanced to the majors—shortstop Ossie Alvarez and pitchers Evelio Hernandez and Oliverio "Baby" Ortiz. Another pitcher, José Gallardo, never made it, but he was the most famous of the bunch at the end of the season.

Stopping in town long enough to win one game was Vallie Eaves, a hard-drinking 43-year-old pitcher with 227 victories in the minors, described by one former manager as "part Indian by birth and part Scotch by midnight."[15]

Roswell was 40 miles north of Artesia and, with its population of 26,000, roughly three times bigger. Nearby was Walker Air Force Base, the largest in the Strategic Air Command at the time.

"I tried to go into business in Artesia, but I couldn't find anything that was suitable," Joe said. "Roswell was my next pick. It's not real small like Artesia and it's not big. I bought me a service station and said, 'This is gonna be it!'"

Moving to Roswell at about the same time was Buck Lanier, new sports editor of the local newspaper, the *Daily Record*. "I was there about a week and Joe Bauman got dropped on me and away we went."

By the end of the summer, Buck was the eyes and ears of the national media as Joe chased Organized Baseball's home run mark of 69, set by Joe Hauser in 1933, and tied by Bob Crues in 1948. "You don't have to do much talking in journalism and reporting," said Buck. "Keep listening. Never can tell what you're going to hear."

In mid-July, Buck was at a barber shop in Roswell's Nickson Hotel getting his crew cut trimmed and listening to a "renowned area gambler" expand on a letter to the editor he had written about the odds favoring Joe breaking the record. He had 45 homers at the time.

The gambler got Buck to thinking about Joe's chances. He got a second opinion from the grizzled Greer. A couple of days later, he got a telephone call from Robert Green, the man he had replaced on the *Daily Record*. Green was now New Mexico bureau chief for the Associated Press wire service, based in Albuquerque. He was working on a national story about Joe. It began with the question that was the hot topic in the barber shop: Will Joe break the record?

"Good God!" Joe said. "I'm having my best year. But a big part of that is because I haven't been hurt any—no bad ankles or shoulders or anything. I've been able to play every inning of every game—and that counts a lot. The park helps, too."[16]

Roswell's Fair Park was grossly unfair to visiting pitchers, measuring 329 feet down the right-field line and 387 feet to dead center. Factor in the altitude of 3,573 feet and Joe had plenty of help.

"If he didn't have to hit against anything but right-handers, he'd hit 150 homers this season," Greer said. "He sees all the left-handed pitching in the league, and when some team doesn't have a lefty ready to throw, they'll bring in a left-handed outfielder or first baseman to pitch to Joe."[17]

Joe was on track to hit 71 homers. "The first part of August is when we started doing some serious counting," Buck said.

On August 4, Joe had 51 homers with 35 games to play. He was at 54 when Buck wrote that the cash-starved Rockets might sell him to the Clovis Pioneers in the WT–NM League for $2,500 and four players. Greer quickly ended the speculation, saying, "The idea of selling the Roswell 'meal ticket' was absurd."[18]

"I haven't seen anything but junk for the past month," Joe groaned in mid-August.[19]

On August 22, Joe slugged three homers in a doubleheader to match Babe Ruth's big-league record of 60, but the United Press wire service reported, "It is doubtful if the feat will grab many headlines."[20]

The weather got more attention. Rain washed out three-straight games, then in the next six he knocked eight out of the park, including four in a single game. "Two to go!" Buck declared.

"The eyes of the United States are on Roswell at present," Buck wrote in his "Riding Herd" column. "If he does break it, pictures of Joe will be on the sports pages of every paper in the United States."[21]

There were six games left, two each against Midland, Big Spring, and Artesia.

Joe moved up in the batting order from fourth to first, so he'd get more chances. Pitchers walked him 150 times—or roughly every fourth at-bat. He seldom saw a fastball and rarely a pitch in the strike zone.

Joe had two near misses in the first game against Midland at Fair Park. Both were doubles, one coming within six inches of clearing the top of the right-centerfield wall.

If Joe was going to tie or break the record at home, he had to do it against Midland's Ralph Atkinson, a junk-balling lefty who had already blanked the Rockets twice, causing one writer to suggest they were cousins. "I hadn't had too much luck with him," Joe said.

Atkinson used his trash to get Joe out on a grounder and two fly balls. Then he plunked him with a pitch the crowd vehemently protested with boos and insults that got louder the next time Joe batted, with two runners on base. "He was trying to make damned sure he got the ball over the plate," Joe said.

He swung at the first pitch. POW! The ball soared 375 feet over the right-center-field wall to equal the all-time record of 69.

The game was delayed several minutes so Joe could collect the money fans stuck through the screen. Midland manager Rudy Briner, an ex-teammate, asked for a dollar bill. Joe handed him one.

Buck wrote exactly what most people were thinking: "It couldn't have happened to a nicer guy."

"He was one of the world's nicest people," Buck added, citing the time Joe gave screen money to a group of destitute kids. "He didn't want me writing about it."

Stasey, the Rockets manager, immediately turned his attention to the next two games, scheduled for Big Spring, 215 miles from Roswell. He had a better idea—switch them to Roswell, where a full ballpark was guaranteed. He pitched the idea to Bob "Pepper" Martin, Big Spring owner and player-manager, in a late-night teleconference that lasted two hours.

Martin was not related to the Pepper Martin of the St. Louis Cardinals' famous "Gashouse Gang" of the 1930s, but he was just as feisty. He once tried to distract Joe by doing calisthenics behind the pitcher.

Pepper rescued baseball in Big Spring, using his own money to buy and rebuild the team after it had folded the previous summer. His Broncs were fighting to survive, but he rejected Stasey's offer, "in four figures," to move the games to Roswell, reasoning, "Local fans, who had stuck by him all season, were entitled to sit in on any possible record-breaking."[22]

At Big Spring, Joe was held to a lone single in nine at-bats. He walked once. "I'd have walked 12 times if I'd batted normally," adding three extra at-bats for emphasis. "They didn't throw strikes. Strikes are hard enough to hit, let alone hit bad balls."

It was fitting that Joe's last and best chance to set the record would come in Artesia, the city that gave him his chance to get back into pro baseball.

The Artesia team had a different nickname, NuMexers, after the local NuMex refinery that bailed it out financially. The roster was revamped with young prospects supplied by the Dallas Eagles, a Class AA team. And Jimmy Adair, a former coach with the Chicago White Sox, was the new manager. The two constants were the ballpark, Brainard Park, and the fans' loyalty to Big Joe.

"We wanted to make him earn it, but we wanted him to get it," said John Goodell, the NuMexers' first baseman.

Artesia had first place wrapped up and was saving its best pitchers for the Longhorn League playoffs beginning the following day. It was a possibility that Joe might face John Goodell but not his brother Wayne, the team's ace, with 18 wins.

"It isn't natural for a pitcher to want to get the homers hit off him, but whoever it does happen to will be on the receiving end of as much publicity as Bauman himself," one writer pointed out. "All the books will then say, '70th home run hit off so and so.'"[23]

Approximately 1,000 people from Roswell traveled to Artesia for the Sunday night doubleheader. "If Brooklyn turned out in similar proportion, it would mean 105,000 people making the trip," Buck explained.[24]

Some 1,600 Artesia residents attended—almost one of five in the city of 8,500.

Skippy Nix, the Artesia batboy who asked Joe if he'd ever hit the lights, was in the grandstand. "You're going to see a record broken that will stand a long time," his father predicted.

Fans stood atop cars and the beds of pickup trucks behind the right-field fence so they could catch the record-setting ball with such home-made contraptions as cardboard funnels attached to the ends of long sticks. One man dangled a pole with a large fishing net from the roof of an old school bus parked parallel to the fence.

"If anybody deserves it, Joe does," Adair told his players. "We don't want to pitch batting practice to him. We want to make him earn it."

He delivered the same message to Joe during batting practice. "Joe, they're not going to walk you. You're going to have your chance."

This meant Joe would have six, possibly eight, chances in the two seven-inning games. "Naturally I walked to the plate looking for that ball in the strike zone," he said.

Buck was ready. So was Jerry Brown, sports editor of the *Carlsbad Current-Argus*. "We all agreed that this had great potential for being a historical evening in Organized Baseball," Jerry said. "We were not in the least bit competitive among ourselves."

Brainard Park had one pay telephone attached to a post. "I hired a teenage kid to get on that phone to the AP bureau in Albuquerque and just keep the line tied up so we could use it," Jerry said. "He just made a pretense of talking into it."

"My concern was Joe getting a home run on the first at-bat," Buck said. "I wanted it on the opening first pitch of the game. Get it out of the way."

Joe was the leadoff hitter. The crowd was loud and boisterous as he stepped to the plate. On the mound for Artesia was José Gallardo, a pitcher released by Roswell in late July.

The count was two balls and two strikes after Joe fouled off three-straight pitches. Every swing triggered annoying flashbulbs from the cameras of photographers seeking to capture the moment for national magazines. José reared back and fired a fastball. Joe hammered it 375 feet over the right-center-field wall.

"The people went absolutely dead-solid berserk," said Mike Currier, another batboy.

"The sound alone was enough to let you know it was going over the fence," Nix said.

Jerry already was on the phone to the Associated Press when Buck signaled from his position behind home plate that the ball was out of the park. The guy on top of the school bus with the fishing net was there to snare the ball and give it to Joe later.

The record-breaking homer was "just like having a piano lifted off your shoulders," Joe said. [25]

Players from both teams lined up to shake Joe's hand as he trotted around third base toward home plate.

Fans jockeyed for position behind the backstop screen, which looked more like a lettuce garden. Dorothy had a kiss for Joe, puckering to squeeze it through the screen.

Joe Bauman is greeted by Roswell teammates after slamming his record-breaking 70th homer, which he described as "just like having a piano lifted off your shoulders." Joe was the minors' home run king four times: 1946, 1952, 1953, and 1954. Today, the top home run blaster in the minors receives the Joe Bauman Award. *Kenyon Cobane Collection/IHSF.org.*

"Everybody tried to get up there and poke a dollar bill through the chicken wire for Joe," Currier said. "It seemed like forever before they threw another pitch."

Joe picked the screen clean from first base to third. He estimated the total at $500. One eyewitness, not worried about the tax implications, put it closer to $800.

Joe often gave some of his home run dollars to Cuban teammates making one-third of his salary. He shared with Rockets players and even umpires the half-ton of freshly cut smoked ham he received from the

Glover Packing Plant for the four-baggers he had hit at home. "We are the best-fed team in baseball," he joked.

Joe's generosity extended to the pitcher who made history with him. "Between games he came into our clubhouse and gave José $50 that he had collected from the fans," said Bobby Boyd, Artesia's backup catcher.

There was one more game to play and the opportunity for Joe to add a homer or two.

John Goodell was the first of three position players who pitched for the NuMexers in the nightcap. "We were all just throwing it up there, saying, 'Hit it if you can.'"

Number 71 came in the first inning against John. "I just threw the ball down the middle and let him hit it. Joe was a heckuva nice guy. Nobody minded that he had the record. We were glad that he did it."

In the seventh and last inning, Joe slammed his 72nd off of Frank Gallardo, an infielder and uncle of José.

Each time the Associated Press got a phone call updating the story, already being spread nationally by the wire service. "He hit another one!" Jerry shouted so he could be heard over the jubilant crowd.

Sports Illustrated called Joe's 72 home runs the "statistic of the year" and his other numbers "something out of Paul Bunyan"—224 runs batted in, 188 runs scored, a .400 batting average. He did all this in 138 games. [26]

Joe had 29 more homers than anyone else in the league. Ten of his dingers came in the last nine games, three on closing day.

The *Daily Record* wasn't published the next day, Labor Day, so Buck's story didn't make it into print until two days later, when "everybody in the damn world knew about it."

Jerry didn't have to wait. "Someday, perhaps, there will be a new home run record for professional baseball and a new record holder," he began his story in the *Current-Argus*, noting that Joe is the "champion who will be remembered" by those who saw his "three tremendous smashes." [27]

"It was electric," Buck said. "This is the pinnacle of my baseball memories. And it's the pinnacle of my 60 years as a newspaperman—that, covering the Vietnam War, and two trips to Antarctica."

"It was just a thrill to be there and see it happening," Jerry said. "It was the best professional sports story I ever covered."

José Gallardo, a 22-year-old Cuban pitcher, congratulated Joe Bauman on his 70th homer, which put both of them in the record books. The 5-foot-8, 149-pound right-hander started the season at Roswell and moved to Artesia mid-season. He had a combined 4-0 won–loss record and 6.90 earned run average for the season, his only one in the United States. *Kenyon Cobane Collection/IHSF.org.*

The story bonded the two journalists for life. Every five years, Buck would call Jerry on the anniversary of the historic homers and ask, "Where were you the evening of September 5, 1954?"

* * *

The first thing one notices entering the Chatsworth, California, house is a bookshelf with books titled *Alien Contact* and *The Best of the Weird.* "You'll see some pretty weird stuff," warned Harry Turtledove, the award-winning novelist who lives there.

Harry specializes in science fiction and alternate history. Imagine the South winning the Civil War in the United States and the Japanese occupying Hawaii after bombing Pearl Harbor in 1941. He has written about both, plus a science fiction piece about Bauman. "Think of Roswell, you think of UFOs. Think of baseball in Roswell, you think of Joe Bauman. There's got to be a connection."

Harry linked the two in *The Star and the Rockets*, a tale that blends fact and fiction, and elevates Joe's home run mark to a higher, otherworldly level. "The idea of connecting the Roswell UFO incident with Bauman's record was in the air in the 90s. It was a matter for discussion among the many science-fiction writers who hung out on the old GEnie message board."

Harry came across a *Sports Illustrated* story, "One for the X-Files," written by Keith Olbermann in 1998. It briefly chronicled Joe and eight other minor leaguers who slugged 60 or more homers in a single season. Upon learning Joe hadn't been to the Roswell museum where his record-setting ball was on display, Olbermann concluded, "Wait a minute. The museum is in Roswell, N. Mex.? Near the site of the alleged UFO crash in 1947? You don't suppose . . ."[28]

That got Harry to supposing. He never has been to Roswell. He never met Joe. The *Life* magazine photo of Joe picking the screen in Artesia after hitting his 70th homer told Harry what he needed to know about that tradition. He took it from there.

The story begins with an Olds Rocket 88 rolling into the driveway of Joe's Texaco station, much as the doctor had in Elk City. Except this was Roswell.

Joe had never seen this car before nor any of its three occupants. They looked exactly alike—bald guys in white shirts, jackets with lapels, fedoras, and sunglasses. The driver had a "funny voice, half rasp, half squeak." His hand was tiny, and it had "only three fingers to go with the thumb." At one point he took off the shades, revealing enormous eyes that "reflect[ed] light like a cat."

They talked and discovered one thing they had in common: Joe was a "man of the star and the Rockets" and so were they. "What a pleasant coincidence," the driver said before hurrying off without waiting for change.

This happened in January. Joe wouldn't see the trio again until the last day of the season in Artesia. They were sitting behind first base. He was gathering money after his record-breaking homer and saw a $100 bill shoved through the screen by a small hand with three fingers. A strange voice said, "Well done, man of the star."[29]

The *X-Files* television series mixed baseball and extraterrestrial life in "The Unnatural," an episode that aired in 1999. The alien character, Josh Exley, is part Joe and part Josh Gibson, the Negro League great.

A long-ball-hitting hulk for the Roswell Grays, Exley was content to play in the bushes, just like Joe. "It's nice and quiet," he said, adding, "I don't want to be no famous man."

There's an exchange between two kids that could easily pass for a debate on the merits of Joe's 72 home runs:

"If Ex hits a couple of dingers, that'll be 60," one boy said. "It ties the Babe."

"That ball's worth nothing," scoffed the other. "Ex ain't a major leaguer so the record don't count."

In his quest to learn more about Exley, FBI special agent Fox Mulder questioned Arthur Dales, the brother of a FBI agent by the same name and a Roswell policeman in 1947, when he discovered Exley was an alien. "They're all aliens," Dales said of baseball greats.

"Babe Ruth was an alien?" asked Mulder.

Ruth was an alien along with Joe DiMaggio, Willie Mays, Mickey Mantle, Sandy Koufax, and Bob and Kirk Gibson. "See, none of the great ones fit in," Dales said. "Not in this world. Not in any other world. They're all aliens, Mulder, until they step between the white chalk lines, until they step onto the outfield grass."[30]

Maybe that explains Joe's extraordinary season. He was a "man of the star and the Rockets," and his hitting was out of this world.

* * *

What do you do after doing something nobody in baseball history has done before?

Joe wanted to hang up his spikes and pump gas for his customers, clean the front windshields of their cars, check the level of the engine oil and air pressure of the tires—all the stuff that earned service stations their name.

"I was ready to quit after that," Joe said. "In fact, I went to the people of the ballclub and said this is it. They wanted me to come back and play another year to help them in the box office."

In late January 1955, Joe was in Tulsa, Oklahoma, to accept his latest minor-league player of the year award. With him was Stubby Greer, the Rockets' new owner-manager. On their way back to Roswell, they stopped in Comanche, Oklahoma, to see Jim Waldrip, a pitcher Joe had faced in the Oklahoma Semipro League.

"I didn't know him personally, but I knew who he was and he knew who I was," Waldrip said.

Joe knew Waldrip had starred for the University of Oklahoma team that won the 1951 NCAA baseball championship and pitched two years in the minors. He also knew Waldrip left baseball to teach and coach at a high school in Comanche, a town too small for a traffic light.

The only place open at night was a café and bar better known for its fights than its food. Wearing business suits, Joe and Stubby were inviting targets for cowboys and oilfield workers looking for trouble. "Hey, Big Man!" a well-lubricated roughneck hollered at Joe. Waldrip quickly ushered his guests to the back of the café.

"Come out to Roswell," Stubby said. "We'll give you 300 to sign and 350 bucks a month."

That was double what he got to pitch for two New York Giants farm clubs and a lot more than he was making as a teacher. Jim and his wife, Jo Anne, and their Siamese cat, Stubby, packed up for Roswell. There to greet them were Joe, Dorothy, and their Pekinese dog, Tojo.

Jim joined the Rockets as they were leaving on a 10-day road trip. Jo Anne was going to stay in a motel while he was gone. "Jo Anne, you bring your cat and stay with me," Dorothy said.

Joe and Jim sat next to one another on the bus ride to Big Spring. "Watch that big first baseman—Jim Zapp," Joe cautioned. "He has a lot of power. Man, don't hang something to him."

In the ninth inning, Jim threw a "dinky half-baked curve" that Zapp zipped over the fence. He won anyway—his only victory in three decisions before the Rockets released him.

"Jim, you work here at the service station," Joe said.

And he did for $1 an hour. "If I needed some money, I could take a Texaco card and buy a tire that never saw my car. Joe would give me the cash. He was that kind of person," Jim said.

Jim went on to compile an impressive resume as a high school teacher, coach, and school administrator in Roswell. He even returned to pro baseball in 1957, to win 18 games. "I didn't have much of a record," he recalled. "I had dreams."

He also had Joe. They became best friends. "I was with Joe when he decided to quit in 1956."

As he often did, Jim accompanied Joe to a game in Carlsbad in early June. He watched as Carlsbad's Richard "Steeple" Jack fired fastballs into Joe's wheelhouse. "His power was anywhere from his belt to his knees. If you were a right-hander, you could kiss it goodbye."

The 6-foot-9 Jack was a right-hander, and he struck out Joe twice. Driving back to Roswell after the game, Joe said, "Jim, I'm gonna hang 'em up. He threw right in my power. I can't see the ball anymore."

Joe had acquired another Texaco station and a tire distributorship. Business was thriving. "I just had all I wanted to do. In fact, baseball was getting in the way. I would work in the daytime, go home and lay down about an hour, and then go to the ballpark about 4:30. I just got wore out. No incentive to go to the ballpark."

In 1955, Joe's batting average, home run tally, and RBI production plummeted back to earth—.336, 46, and 132, respectively.

During the offseason, he slipped and fell in the snow, badly injuring an ankle and making it difficult to run. He wanted to quit, but Earl Perry, a friend and former boss, had purchased the Rockets and asked him to tough it out one more year. "He could barely get around," said Tom Jordan, the Rockets' manager.

Joe had 17 homers when he said farewell to fans at Fair Park in mid-June.

Roswell said goodbye to pro baseball in 1957, then hello again in mid-June 1959 when the Pittsburgh Pirates moved their Sophomore League team from San Angelo, Texas. Joe headed the group of business leaders that raised $10,000 to land the Pirates, but after two months, they were gone.

Joe faded further into baseball history and even away from Roswell for a while. The closing of the local air base forced him to sell his gas stations and tire distributorship. For the next five years, Joe ran a liquor store in Hobbs, New Mexico, with his father-in-law. He returned to Roswell in 1970 to work for the Pecos Sales Company and keep southern New Mexico flowing in Schlitz beer.

"You only go around once in life," Schlitz reminded folks in television commercials. "So grab for all the gusto you can."

Some of Joe's teammates with the Navy Skyjackets and the Beechcraft Flyers believed he had the talent to play in the majors but questioned whether he had the gusto.

"All of us thought Joe had a good chance of going to the big leagues," said Bennie Warren, the Skyjackets' catcher who toiled seven years for 11 different teams in the minors before playing in the majors for the Phillies and Giants. "I couldn't figure out why after he hit all those home runs some major-league ballclub didn't take him. That many home runs is phenomenal. Maybe Joe didn't have as much desire to play as I did. Joe's attitude was, 'Heck if I can't make any money playing ball, I'll just get out of it.'"

Some claimed he had too many weaknesses as a hitter. "My weakness was an all-American weakness—high and inside; low and outside," he said.

Others questioned Joe's fielding ability. "I wasn't a bad fielder at all," Joe insisted. "I'd either lead the league or be right next to it all the time."

Everyone, including Joe, agreed he was too slow. "I never could run worth a damn. After I got to first, I could get to second real good, but getting out of that damned batter's box and getting to first base was something else."

This self-assessment caused Joe to conclude, "It was probably lack of speed, maybe not getting the opportunity to prove that I could play in that class of baseball."

Joe had a chance to play for a Class AA team, the Atlanta Crackers, soon after joining Elk City in 1949, but he didn't want to break a promise he had made to stay the entire season. In 1955, the San Francisco Seals of the Pacific Coast League, an open-classification league, made Joe an offer he dismissed as a publicity stunt to exploit his newfound fame.

Joe remained in Roswell and mostly out of the spotlight, except for occasional calls from journalists.

In 1996, he recalled for the *Philadelphia Daily News* how a lot of pitchers in the Longhorn League "threw hard but had no idea where it would go." It didn't matter because he "was just on fire that season"—the ball "appeared as big as a cantaloupe."[31]

The home run derby between Mark McGwire and Sammy Sosa in 1998 had Joe's phone ringing constantly. "It got so bad for a while that I started taking the phone off the hook around 10 p.m. They were calling from coast-to-coast, even Canada."[32]

McGwire had 55 homers when Joe said the St. Louis Cardinals muscleman could hit as many as 67.

"How about 73?" he was asked.

"The more the merrier. It wouldn't bother me a bit."[33]

Joe attributed the rash of home runs during this period to a lively ball, bad pitching, and bigger, stronger hitters who pumped iron in the weight room. He never owned a set of dumbbells. His strength came from a steady diet of T-bone steaks and potatoes, washed down by ice cold

The ball looked like a cantaloupe to Joe Bauman in 1954. Two years later, the ball was more like a pea, and Joe retired mid-year. Joe totaled 337 round-trippers in nine seasons, 238 coming the last five years after he turned 30. *Kenyon Cobane Collection/IHSF.org.*

Miller High Life. "I didn't drink Schlitz until after I went to work for them," he confessed.[34]

McGwire smacked 70 and Sosa 66, to eclipse Maris's big-league mark of 61. Joe knew his record was next. "Nothing lasts forever," he said. "This one has gone on longer than I thought it would. Someday it will fall."[35]

That day was the last of the 2001 season. Barry Bonds of the San Francisco Giants bashed number 73 to become baseball's new home run king. Joe was sitting in his recliner at home and watching on TV. "It didn't bother me or anything. I just thought, 'There goes my record.'"[36]

Buck Lanier was so upset he labeled Bonds's homers "steroid induced" in a story he wrote for the *Long Beach Press-Telegram*. Said Lanier, "I was the only one that used steroid induced."

After leaving Roswell at the end of the 1954 season, Buck went to Carlsbad, El Paso, and eventually Long Beach, California, where he worked 37½ years for the *Press-Telegram*. He remained in contact with Joe. "Cheaters didn't have any business breaking Joe's record," Buck said. "Joe thought Bonds was a great athlete. And Bonds was a great athlete. I don't think he needed that much extra help."

The names of Bauman and Bonds will be forever linked in baseball history. They are etched on a bronze plaque unveiled on August 10, 2005—Joe Bauman Day—at old Fair Park in Roswell. The ballpark was renamed Joe Bauman Stadium on the same day.

Joe had to be talked into attending the dedication ceremony. "He didn't toot his own horn," Jim Waldrip said.

There were health reasons, too. He was unsteady on his feet from a stroke two years earlier and needed a walker to get around.

The Roswell mayor and city council members were going to revive the tradition of shoving dollar bills through the backstop screen when Joe stepped to the podium to speak. But seconds after getting up from his chair, he tumbled to the ground. "You could hear his pelvis break," Jim said. "But he wouldn't let them take him to the hospital."

He waved off paramedics with a bloodied right hand, got back up, said a few words, and uncovered the plaque. He even stuck around afterward to sign autographs for the kids at the event. "CAN'T KEEP A GOOD MAN DOWN," the *Roswell Daily Record* declared in a headline.[37]

Jim drove Joe home, but he was in so much pain when they got there, an ambulance was called to take him to the hospital. Six weeks later, Joe died of pneumonia, a complication of the fall. Jim was at his bedside. "If it hadn't been for Joe Bauman, I would've never come to Roswell. He was my hero."

Newspapers throughout the United States reported Joe's death, the *New York Times* treating him like a big-league star in an obituary that also mentioned Bonds.

On the day Joe died, Bonds hit his 706th career home run en route to 762, breaking the hallowed records of Ruth and Henry Aaron. He marked the occasion by telling the U.S. Congress it was wasting time probing steroids use in sports.

That was in stark contrast to how Joe celebrated his record-setting homers in 1954, quaffing a couple of Miller High Life's at Homer Glover's Honky Tonk. Homer also owned the packing plant that supplied Joe and his mates with performance-enhancing hams for hitting home runs at Fair Park.

Joe and Dorothy Bauman are buried at South Park Cemetery, across the Roswell–Artesia highway from Joe Bauman Stadium. Dorothy died in

2011. They share a headstone. Alongside Joe's name there is an engraving of a batter taking a home run swing.

Eight feet away is another headstone marked WALDRIP in capital letters, above the names Jim and Jo Anne, who died in 2009. Prominently displayed is a right-handed pitcher in the middle of his windup. "My kids picked out the stone, and they said, 'Dad, you need to be pitching to Joe.'"

Never mind that the artist made the left-handed-hitting Joe a right-hander. A pitcher facing Joe for eternity needs all the breaks he can get. "I wasn't even 1 percent of the pitcher as Joe was a hitter," Jim said. "Man, he was something else."

From the cemetery you can see the ballpark.

In 1974, Joe was showing a visitor where one of his blasts had rocketed over the right-field wall and fallen like a meteorite into the middle of the nearby rodeo grounds. "They say it went over the performers there," Joe said modestly.

The home run was his 73rd of the 1954 season, but it's not included in his total because it came in a playoff game.

Joe was pro baseball's undisputed home run king for 47 years. He still reigns over the minor leagues.

"Any regrets?" he was asked.

"Oh, I wouldn't take a million dollars for it, but I wouldn't want it to do over again either. I'd do a hell of a lot different than what I did."

His biggest mistake was signing out of high school with Little Rock, a minor-league team. "I could've signed with three or four major-league clubs, and I wish to hell I had of. I got in the worst camp in the world."

Joe laughed. "It's damn experience. I don't feel bitter about it. I think I've had my share."

He motioned toward the fence. "I can pee up there higher on the wall than some of them. It's no big-league record or anything, but it's something nobody else has ever done. So I'm satisfied with it."

5

FATHER, SON, AND LITTLE LEAGUE

Tom and Tommy Jordan

The blue 1953 Ford convertible was parked at a picnic area alongside the main highway connecting the southeastern New Mexico cities of Carlsbad and Roswell. It was a picture-perfect late summer day, but the couple in the car, Tom and Lorene Jordan, didn't travel 15 miles north from Carlsbad for the view. They were there to pick up a stronger signal for a baseball game being broadcast by a radio station in Roswell, another 60 miles up the road.

The game was the 1956 Little League World Series championship in Williamsport, Pennsylvania, between the Lions Club Hondo team of Roswell and Delaware Township, New Jersey. Pitching for Roswell was Tom and Lorene's son, Tom Jr.—Tommy.

The elder Tom was a catcher for the Carlsbad Potashers of the Class B Southwestern League. He was nearing the end of an 18-year career spanning three decades and producing eye-popping numbers in the minor leagues: 2,197 hits, 267 home runs, and a lifetime batting average of .338, including a .407 mark in 1955.

Tom started the 1956 season as player-manager of the Roswell Rockets. He quit in mid-July, went to Nuevo Laredo, Mexico, in the Mexican League for two games, then returned to New Mexico to play for Carlsbad so he could spend more time at his Roswell farm.

On the way to Carlsbad one afternoon Tom stopped by the Lions Hondo Little League field in Roswell to see Tommy play. It was the last game of the regular season and the only time he would see his son play that year. He didn't like what he saw. "Every time Tommy came up, they walked him intentionally. That sort of pissed me off. They didn't give him a chance to hit."

The catcher on the opposing team was Blaine Stribling, who said, "Tommy could hit it over the fence about any time he wanted to."

The pitcher was Ferrell Dunham. "I never wanted to walk anybody intentionally. We were little, but we had our little egos, too. We thought we could strike everybody out."

The manager was Dick St. John. "Ferrell wanted to pitch to me, but St. John wouldn't let him," Tommy said. "He had good enough stuff I wasn't going to hit him all the time."

St. John also was going to manage the Lions Hondo All-Stars in the upcoming Little League area tournament. That got Tom's dander up even more.

"I wouldn't play, the way they do you, walk you every time," he told Tommy. "Come on, go with me to Carlsbad, we're going on a week-long road trip."

Tommy frequently traveled with his father.

"No, Dad," he said, "we're going to the World Series."

"Ah, bullshit!" Tom blurted out. "You haven't got a chance of going to the World Series."

The Lions Hondo league had only four teams. They played on a wind-swept dirt field commonly referred to as the "Dust Bowl." Before games players tossed tumbleweeds over the outfield fence, but there was little they could do about the clumps of salt grass that thrive on arid land. And then there were the rocks that made fielding ground balls dangerous and reflexes better. "You never knew which way the ball was going to bounce," said Harold Hobson, an outfielder on a team that didn't win a single game during the regular season.

The dugouts were two wooden benches, and the backstop was made of chicken wire. There were no chalk lines on the field, no lights, and no bleachers.

Lions Hondo was the "other" Little League in town, as the Optimist league on the North Side boasted a grass field and supposedly better players. "That was upper class over there," said Blaine, the son of a health inspector.

"I don't remember any of us having a father with a professional job, a business, or a college degree," said Harold, a farmer's son.

No team from New Mexico had ever made it to the Little League World Series in its nine-year history. Lions Hondo had to win nine straight games just to get there and 12 to win it all. One loss in the single-elimination tournament and it was back to Roswell.

The previous year, Lions Hondo lost to Optimist in the first game. In a consolation contest, 11-year-old Tommy pitched a no-hitter. That's when he started thinking Roswell could win the Little League World Series. "I guess it was pretty naive of me. I just felt real confident."

Tommy was not your ordinary Little Leaguer. He started at age eight in Austin, Texas, played two years in Albuquerque, and two more in Roswell. "He had been carrying a baseball since he was born," Harold said.

When Tommy wasn't on a Little League diamond, he was at the ballpark with his father. "I got to take batting and infield practice, shag fly balls in the outfield, and throw to professional ballplayers all the time," Tommy recalled.

"He'd usually sit out in the bullpen," Tom added. "He picked up a lot of savvy from the pitchers in the bullpen."

Tommy had an "assortment of pitches that would do credit to a major leaguer—a teasing curve, a terrific fastball, a changeup," according to a *New York Times* sportswriter. [1]

"I had good stuff, and I just didn't think any Little League kid could hit me," Tommy said.

He also didn't think anyone could beat Ferrell, who pitched when Tommy played second base.

"If you had two good pitchers, you had a pretty good shot," Tommy said. "We had two good pitchers. And we hit home runs most every game. I just thought that us two were good enough to win the whole thing."

"Tommy and I would talk about that," Ferrell said. "We'd say, 'I don't think anybody can beat us.' We weren't cocky kids, but we were pretty confident."

The duo teamed up to pitch three shutouts and belt six home runs as Lions Hondo breezed through the state's Area playoffs in Carlsbad, crushing opponents, 17-0. Tommy struck out 29 of a possible 36 batters in the two games he pitched. He beat Optimist, 10-0, in the title game, fanning 15 and poking his third homer, a two-run blast.

An Optimist player was puzzled how Lions Hondo pounded his team 10-0. "We had all the good players," he said.

"I'll tell you why we got beat," a teammate replied. "Lions Hondo had Tommy Jordan, and he stuck that bat right up our asses."

"One of the classiest Little League ballclubs your agent has seen in many a moon," sports columnist Roy Hall gushed in the *Carlsbad Current-Argus*. "This club has all the qualifications to go a long way in tournament play and will do just that if it hits, fields, and pitches the way it did in the Area playoffs."[2]

"Carlsbad was supposed to have the premier boys—the big home run hitters and everything," Ferrell said. "We went there and just beat the socks off of them. In my mind, that's when I thought we were going all the way."

The one–two punch of Ferrell and Tommy sparked Lions Hondo to the state championship at Los Alamos.

In the first inning of a game against Los Alamos, Tommy smashed a home run over the regulation outfield fence, plus one used by Babe Ruth Leaguers 13 to 15 years old. The score was tied, 1-1, in the fourth when he came to bat. The Los Alamos pitcher, Butch Smith, had a blazing fastball and was in total control. "He just overmatched Ferrell," Tommy said. "And that was hard to do. Ferrell could hit anybody."

The distance between the pitcher's mound and home plate in Little League is 46 feet. Tommy scorched a line drive that ricocheted off Smith's stomach like it was a pinball machine, knocking him out of the game and into a hospital for examination. Roswell went on to win, 4-1.

A steady, cold drizzle fell throughout the title game with Hobbs. Tommy allowed two runs and six hits, and was unusually wild, walking five batters and throwing two wild pitches. "It was by far my worst game," he conceded.

It didn't matter, as Ferrell and Tommy each had three hits to pace a 9-2 romp. Tommy homered again, his fifth in as many games.

Next stop was Lubbock, Texas, and the Southwest regional district playoffs.

Ferrell tossed a one-hitter and homered twice to win the first game and set up a showdown between Tommy and a team from Albany, Texas, that hadn't been scored on in almost five games.

Tommy appeared 30 minutes before the start of the game, drinking a big strawberry milkshake.

"Where have you been?" someone asked.

"Riding the elevator," he mumbled. "They've got a three-story building with an elevator here in Lubbock."

Tommy doesn't remember any of this.

"For me, it was sort of symbolic of the whole trip," Harold said in relating the story. "The opposing team had been practicing for two or three hours before the game. They were all uptight."

Tommy, as cool as his milkshake and perhaps inspired by the elevator ride, gave Albany batters the shaft, allowing only one hit while whiffing 12. In the bottom of the sixth and last inning, Harold singled to drive in the only run of the game.

The regional finals, in San Antonio, Texas, were more of the same.

In the opener, Ferrell pitched a three-hitter and homered, while Blaine smashed two of his own for five runs in a 7-3 victory over Beaumont.

In the championship game against Houston West End, Tommy fired a three-hitter and struck out 16, as Lions Hondo third baseman Dave Sherrod slugged a tiebreaking homer in the extra seventh inning to win, 3-1.

The following morning, a police escort, with sirens screaming, whisked the players to a hotel in downtown San Antonio for a breakfast honoring their latest achievement. They were on their way to the Little League World Series in Williamsport.

"I didn't know where Williamsport was," Harold said.

Most people in Williamsport didn't know where Roswell was either.

They were about to find out.

∗ ∗ ∗

Tommy Jordan was the proverbial chip off the old block. In fact, his father and namesake, Thomas Jefferson Jordan, had a chiseled physique almost as striking as the Mount Rushmore sculpture of another Thomas Jefferson, the third president of the United States. "Tall and straight, and without an ounce of fat," one writer described the 6-foot-1, 195-pound Jordan.[3]

Tom had huge hands and a bone-crushing handshake. One player-turned-scout called him the strongest man he'd seen in 25 years of pro baseball. His muscles were honed on his 500-acre Roswell farm and two smaller family farms in nearby Dexter, which he operated with his older brother, Jerry. The primary crop was cotton, but they also raised cattle

Tom Jordan Sr. looked like he was chiseled out of rock. One scout called him the strongest man he'd seen in 25 years of pro baseball. Tom had brief flings with the St. Louis Browns, Cleveland Indians, and Chicago White Sox but preferred playing in the lower minors, closer to his ranch in Roswell. *Courtesy of Tom Jordan Sr.*

and grew corn, alfalfa, cantaloupes, watermelons, tomatoes, squash, and cucumbers. "I just love to watch stuff grow," Tom said.

Owners of big-league teams had never seen this side of Tom. They couldn't understand what made him tick or why he walked away from the majors three times.

In 1944, Tom appeared in 14 games for the Chicago White Sox and then quit the following year to work on the farms. He returned to the majors in 1946, to play 24 games for the White Sox and Cleveland Indians. In the spring of 1947, he retired after the Indians made him an offer he could easily refuse—$1,000 a month.

Tom ended his brief retirement three months later when the St. Louis Browns offered him $1,200 a month to play for San Antonio, their farm club in the Texas League. After Tom batted .309 in 69 games, Browns president Bill DeWitt sent him a contract for $800 a month to play for the Browns in 1948. "I hit over .300," he said. "I'm not gonna take no cut."

DeWitt upped the offer to $1,200 a month, and Tom agreed to join the Browns.

"I kinda had DeWitt over a barrel," Tom recalled. "His number-one catcher hadn't hit a lick the year before [Les Moss hit .157 with the 1947 Browns], and his number-two guy [Roy Partee] was threatening to quit. So he gave me the dough, but I could tell he really resented it."[4]

The *St. Louis Post-Dispatch* introduced Tom to Browns fans as a "rugged individualist." On the field, the story continued, "He knocks in a lot of runs, no matter what the club or league." But if Tom hears the call of his farms, "he just stays there and lets baseball magnates sweat it out."[5]

Tom had a sensational spring for the Browns, hitting almost .400, far better than the team's other catchers—Moss and Partee. But he batted only once during the regular season. "I never got a chance really," he said. "Zack Taylor was the manager, and he didn't like me very well. It was sort of mutual. I didn't like him very well."

Partee was incredulous when DeWitt asked him to tell Tom he was being demoted to the Browns' affiliate in Toledo, Ohio. "Tell him yourself, Bill," Partee balked, "but take a whip and chair with you!"[6]

Zack wound up delivering the news while the Browns were in New York City. "Zack," Tom said, "you ain't sendin' me nowhere."

Instead of flying to Toledo, Tom headed for St. Louis to meet with DeWitt. "Plans are to send him to Toledo if he agrees, but he doesn't always do as told," the *Star and Times* reported.[7]

"I'm not going to Toledo," Tom persisted. He was sent back to San Antonio.

In 39 big-league games, Tom stepped to the plate exactly 100 times, batting .240, with 1 home run.

Back-to-back games in 1946, against the New York Yankees at Yankee Stadium, showcased Tom's hitting potential and throwing problems as a sore-armed catcher.

In the first game, Tom flexed his muscles, belting a triple and two doubles. Seven of his 23 hits in the majors were for extra bases. Against the mighty Yankees, he hit .421 (8-for-19). "The one thing I could do was hit. There wasn't very many catchers that were outstanding hitters."

The next game, the Yankees ran wild on the bases, stealing second three times and third twice. "My arm was so sore I couldn't even throw it back to the pitcher. It was like somebody sticking a knife in your shoulder. I think I had a rotator cuff tear. But they didn't know what that was at the time."

Tom was happy to go back to San Antonio and spend the rest of his career playing mostly in the lower minors for teams in Texas and New Mexico. "I didn't enjoy my time in the major leagues," he lamented. "I was sort of a country boy, and after the game, everybody scattered, and you didn't see nobody until the next day at the ballpark. Man, some of them big cities was a pretty lonesome place. I had a bad arm most of the time. Never made no money much. Didn't have much fun."

Tom talked country, but he was as shrewd as any city slicker.

"I had something to fall back on," he said. "I had my ranch and farm, and I really didn't have no business playing baseball. It was a liability actually. If I hadn't enjoyed it so much, I probably wouldn't have been playing."

The price of cotton tripled from almost 10 cents a pound in 1940 to about 32 cents in 1947, and hovered there until peaking at 40 cents in 1950.

He made the same amount of money in San Antonio as he did in St. Louis, and the cost of living was lower. The warmer weather had a soothing effect on his sore arm, and, most importantly, he was closer to his farm in Roswell.

When the Browns sold his contract to Sacramento, California, in the Pacific Coast League in 1949, he refused to report and had the contract transferred to the Roswell Rockets in the Longhorn League. "I could make more money staying at home in Roswell than I could in the Coast League or any other league."

That was true until a wealthy cattle rancher named Herbert Kokernot Jr. came along and gave Tom $750 to play on weekends for his semipro team, the Cowboys, in Alpine, Texas, a little more than an hour away from Big Bend National Park.

Kokernot practically owned the town of Alpine and some 500,000 acres surrounding it. Two years earlier, in 1947, he poured $1 million into building Kokernot Field, once praised by *Sports Illustrated* as "quite possibly the world's most beautiful ballpark," with theater-style seats that gave fans a spectacular view of the majestic Twin Peaks in the Davis Mountains off in the distance.

Kokernot wanted a team to match the vista, so he recruited the best college players around and old pros like Tom and his brother, Jerry, a switch-hitting third baseman who played six seasons in the minors. Tom was hitting a torrid .440 for Roswell through 29 games, averaging almost two hits per game.

In his Alpine debut, he went 5-for-5, including a triple and three doubles. He swatted a home run the next game. "Say, you're only making $750 a month," Kokernot told Tom afterward. "You're way underpaid. I'm going to pay you a thousand dollars a month from now on."

That was almost double what he made at Roswell. "That's pretty good pay to just go down there on weekends, play a couple of games and come back home," Tom said. "It was sort of like a vacation. They furnished a room, all the beer you could drink, and big steaks. Everything was paid for."

One blast over the center-field fence in Alpine led to a congratulatory handshake from Kokernot. "He had a hundred-dollar bill in his hand," Tom recalled.

Kokernot spent an estimated $100,000 on the team, a huge sum in 1949. "Mr. Kokernot comes close to being the number-one club owner in this country," wrote Bob Ingram of the *El Paso Herald-Post*.[8]

The vacation ended when the Cowboys were eliminated early in the 1949 national semipro tournament.

Tom returned to the Roswell Rockets in 1950, this time as player-manager. He was a one-man wrecking crew with the bat, leading the league in five offensive categories: batting average (.391), home runs (44), runs batted in (181), runs scored (147), and hits (216). The Rockets finished second and attendance almost doubled to 82,671, an all-time high for pro baseball in Roswell. "I made more money hittin' home runs than I probably did my salary," Tom said. "I hit a home run one time with the bases loaded and won the game. I got nearly $200. The least I ever got was $37."

Tom did double duty the next six seasons. He was player-manager two years each at Austin (1951–1952) and Albuquerque (1953–1954), one at Artesia (1955), and approximately half of the 1956 season at Roswell. Four of his teams had winning records. With the bat, he averaged 22 home runs a year, while batting .354 in 1951, .346 in 1952, .332 in 1953, .338 in 1954, .407 in 1955, and .357 in 1956.

Tom was managing the last-place Rockets in mid-June 1956, when a fan wrote the *Roswell Daily Record* to complain that his handling of players "leaves much to be desired for a manager of even the lowest classification of Organized Baseball."[9]

The tobacco-chewing Tom didn't take anything off anybody according to Lin Patterson, a batboy at Artesia who went on to play baseball for the University of New Mexico and the United States in the Pan American Games. "Tom Jordan was, without a doubt, the meanest, toughest individual that I've ever seen on a baseball field," Patterson said. "You never sat next to Tom Jordan because he would spit tobacco juice all over your shoes."

Tom marched into the newspaper's office. "I want you to put something in your paper for me," he told sports editor Max Odendahl. "Tell that fan that wrote that letter in the paper the other day this: If he's got one gut in his body, he'll come out here to the ballpark. I'll issue him a uniform and he can manage the team for two nights. Maybe he can give us some pointers on how to play ball if he's so smart."[10]

The fan was a no-show.

"Tom let people do what they did best," said Bobby Boyd, a catcher for Artesia. "He got as much out of his players as anyone could."

Tom was player-manager of the Austin Pioneers in 1951, when Joe DiMaggio and the Yankees came to town for an exhibition game.

In the first inning, DiMaggio was flattened twice by a kid pitcher. The second time he got up in disgust and hollered at Tom behind the plate, "I'm not going to hit against that wild son of a bitch. I'm going back to the hotel."

Joe took himself out of the game after trickling a grounder for an infield single.

Tommy, then seven and a batboy for the Pioneers, carried Joe's glove as he left the ballpark. "I never said a word to him; he never said a word to me."

Almost 4,000 fans showed up to see DiMaggio or rookie sensation Mickey Mantle knock one out of the park. Instead, Tom hit the game's only homer. He always could hit Yankees pitching. "I think I could've been maybe a star in the major leagues if I hadn't hurt my arm," he professed.

In high school, Tom was asked to put down his ambition in life. "To play in the major leagues," he wrote.

"I played in every minor league—D, C, B, A, Double-A, Triple-A— and the major leagues," he said proudly. "I played in all of 'em."

When Tommy said he was going to the Little League World Series, Tom laughed because he thought it was so far-fetched.

But sitting in the car parked alongside the Carlsbad–Roswell highway and listening to a play-by-play account of the championship game in Williamsport, Tom realized Tommy was just like him and his son's seemingly impossible goal of winning it all might actually come true.

* * *

One of the pitchers Tommy rubbed shoulders with in the bullpen at Artesia in 1955 was Eddie Locke. "There are one-man gangs, then there is Eddie Locke," one writer wrote. "He'll beat you either pitching or hitting—or both."[11]

The 5-foot-11, 181-pound African American threw right and batted left. "He's probably the best player that ever played for me—really," Tom said. "He was one of the pitchers that I know could've won in the major leagues, if he'd just got a chance."

Locke bounced around the Negro and Mexican Leagues for five years and sat out two more before breaking into Organized Baseball in 1950, at the age of 27. He never got higher than Triple-A, and that was his final season in 1967.

From 1953 through 1959, Locke won 20-plus games four times. Altogether, he had a 161-134 record in the minors.

"He kept you off-balance with the way he turned his back on the batter before he threw the ball," said Boyd, the Artesia catcher. It was a slightly less exaggerated version of the windup Luis Tiant used two decades later to become a 4-time 20-game winner in the majors.

"I had as much trouble hittin' him as I did anybody," Tom said, comparing Eddie with Mariano Rivera, the outstanding relief pitcher for the New York Yankees. "Man, he had a cut fastball that would come up there to the plate and break about six or eight inches outside. Even if you hit it, you didn't hit it good."

Before managing Eddie in 1955, Tom played against him in 1953–1954. Tom was with the Albuquerque Dukes while Eddie strutted his stuff for the Amarillo Gold Sox in the West Texas–New Mexico League. "I'm gonna ask to be traded if you don't play me more," Eddie told Gold Sox manager Jim Matthews upon joining the team in early June. "I came here to play. I don't wanta play one day and rest three."[12]

Eddie won four games his first week, including both seven-inning games of a doubleheader. He successfully pulled off this iron-man feat four times, tossing one-hit and three-hit shutouts in one of them. "It is believed that no other pitcher in Organized Baseball during recent years has equaled this achievement," Harry Gilstrap wrote in the *Amarillo Daily News*.[13]

Eddie had a flair for the dramatic with the bat as well. In one game, he crushed two homers in the same inning, including a grand slam. He topped that by slugging two grand slammers and driving in 10 runs in a single game.

He had a batting average of .384, with eight homers and 42 RBIs in only 37 games, when a reporter and photographer from *Life* magazine arrived in Amarillo in late July. *Life* was a popular national publication that typically featured world leaders, movie celebrities, and such big-league stars as Joe DiMaggio, Ted Williams, and Roy Campanella, who had appeared on the cover the month before. Eddie was an obscure pitcher in a league baseball people didn't take all that seriously because of the inflated batting statistics.

"It didn't matter how many home runs or what your battin' average was, they just didn't pay any attention to it," Tom said. "It was really a hitter's league. You didn't have any strategy. You just tried to outscore the other team."

The *Life* team was hoping to see Eddie pitch his fourth-straight shutout and pop another grand slam. He won his 13th game in pitching his 14th complete game in as many starts, but he "seemed somewhat nervous and hardly up to usual form" in giving up four runs and 14 hits. In four at-bats, he managed only a single.[14]

Life never published the story about Eddie, who wound up winning 21, losing seven and leading the league in shutouts, with five. He hit .368, with 12 doubles, 4 triples, 17 homers, and 74 RBIs. What made these numbers even more amazing is Eddie missed at least 10 potential pitching turns because he didn't join the Gold Sox until they had already played 41 games.

Eddie had another monster year for Amarillo in 1954—a 24-15 won–loss record, .311 batting average, 12 homers, and 68 RBIs.

In 1955, Eddie had a 3-3 mark going into a mid-May game that turned out to be his last in a Gold Sox uniform. In stark contrast to the iron-man performances that had vaulted him into the national limelight, he started and got no one out, allowing five runs on a walk and four hits. "He wants to get out of the league and hadn't been doing his best for us," Amarillo general manager Robert "Buck" Fausett said in announcing his sale to Artesia.

"He'll win the pennant for me," Tom told Fausett.

Eddie was hitting .338, with five homers and 23 RBIs, so there was nothing wrong with his bat.

"Let's don't go into the reasons why Eddie decided this season he wanted to get out of Amarillo and out of the league," Gilstrap wrote. "Let's just remember the many thrills he has given us and wish him well with his new club, for which he is quite likely to perform more miracles like those of 1953."[15]

Eddie did everything for Artesia except win the pennant. The NuMex-ers tied for second.

On the mound, he piled up 211 innings in 38 games, completing 17 of the 25 he started. He posted a 20-7 won–loss record and 3.75 earned run average. At the plate, he batted .355, with 11 home runs, 21 doubles, 6 triples, and 50 RBIs.

"I'd start him, play him in the outfield, and when I needed a reliever, he'd relieve," Tom said. "I sort of felt guilty about the way I used him, but, gosh, when the game was on the line and you had somebody you knew was going to get 'em out, it's hard not to put him in. He just made my ballclub. He did everything except drive the bus."

Eddie regularly borrowed $10 from Tom, reimbursed him on pay day, then got a loan for the same amount again. This continued until the end of the season. Eddie made around $450 a month, more than twice the league average. But he owed Tom $10 and a sizeable amount to the club, leaving him about $15.

"Eddie, what are you going to do?" Tom asked. "The season is over. You owe the club most of what you got coming."

"Well, Skip," he said, "I've got enough money to last me today. I don't worry about tomorrow."

Eddie gave Tommy hitting and pitching tips at Artesia. "He was really, really good at both," Tommy said.

Tommy soon would carry on Eddie's gang-of-one reputation.

* * *

The summer of 1956 was a wonderful time to be a kid.

You could buy a pack of five Topps baseball cards for a nickel. If you were lucky, you might get a Mickey Mantle card, now worth as much as $37,500 in mint condition. Mantle won the coveted Triple Crown in 1956, leading the American League in batting average (.353), home runs (52), and RBIs (130).

Most young boys dreamed of growing up to play pro baseball.

At Williamsport in 1956, *Sports Illustrated* asked nine Little Leaguers about their ambitions. Eight of them said they wanted to continue in baseball. "Just like my father, a baseball player and rancher," Tommy answered. "I'm just like my dad."[16]

Judging from the popularity of toy trains marketed by the Lionel Corporation in the 1950s, there were just as many boys wanting to be train engineers. Lionel sold more engines and rail cars than existed on the real railroads—$25 million worth per year. Joe DiMaggio even hosted a television show titled "The Lionel Club House."

Most of the Roswell players had never been on a train. Boarding the Santa Fe Chief with domed passenger cars at the Roswell train station was almost like stepping onto a spaceship bound for Mars.

Harold Hobson had been on a shuttle train that traveled 180 miles between Carlsbad to the south and Clovis, New Mexico, to the north, but it was nothing like the trains taking the team to Chicago and Altoona, Pennsylvania. He still has the ticket stubs, mementos of the trip and its cost—$48.46 from Clovis to Chicago and $17.16 from Chicago to Altoona. "The train trip was a trip of a lifetime for me," Harold said.

It turned out to be a family affair, as his father, Ed, grandfather, Glen Wheeler, and younger brother, Larry, surprised him when they got on the train. "You've got to go," neighboring farmers urged Ed. "We'll take care of whatever needs to be done."

Ed rushed to Anthony's department store in downtown Roswell to get some clothes for the trip. "He had never done anything like that before," Harold said.

Everything about the trip to Williamsport was a first.

In Chicago, the Roswell players saw their first major-league game— the Detroit Tigers against the Chicago White Sox at Comiskey Park. Tommy caught a ball hit into the stands during batting practice and, instead of keeping it, threw it back on the field like he did at Roswell Rockets games. "That's how disconnected we were from the rest of the world," Harold said.

The Roswell players were not alone.

When they got to Williamsport, other players and their fans asked to see their passports. "They thought we were a bunch of Mexicans from Mexico," Blaine said.

"There was an attitude," Harold said. "We even feel it today with national weather reports. The weather person is always standing in front of New Mexico, covering it up. With a population of a little more than two million, we don't draw enough attention."

Only 800,000 people lived in New Mexico in 1956—30,000 of them in Roswell.

The city is best known for an unidentified flying object (UFO) that supposedly crashed near Roswell in July 1947.

One of the first people on the scene was Tommy Tompson, a Chaves County sheriff and Harold's uncle, who led U.S. military investigators to the site. "He said they wouldn't let him get within 200 feet of it. That's all he knew about it."

Was it a flying saucer with aliens aboard?

Ongoing speculation is fueled by a UFO museum housed in an old movie theater on Main Street in Roswell. "It has brought a lot of people to Roswell," Harold said. "And they're still coming. Unbelievable. I never did believe it. Still don't believe it."

Tommy believes in UFOs. Maybe he knew something because by the end of the week, there were people in Williamsport beginning to think he might be one of the aliens on that Roswell UFO. "They didn't know who I was like I didn't know who they were," he said.

Roswell represented the Southwest region of the United States, an area made up of 408 Little Leagues from Mexico and five states—Arkansas, Louisiana, New Mexico, Oklahoma, and Texas.

Now, Roswell was going up against the big boys, so to speak, the best players from the most populated states in the country—California, Massachusetts, Michigan, New Jersey, New York, and Pennsylvania. Three teams were back from the year before: Auburn, Alabama; Winchester, Massachusetts; and Delaware Township, New Jersey. "We were definitely the outsiders," Harold said. "First of all, we were from Mexico."

They also had to overcome the home state team from a suburb of Philadelphia, Upper Darby, and its fans, who outnumbered Roswell supporters by a thousand to one.

The crowd was loud and boisterous after Upper Darby jumped ahead, 1-0, in the second inning on a home run off Tommy. That was the score until Roswell's Dave Sherrod poked a game-tying homer in the bottom of the fifth. One out later, Tommy rifled a shot over the right-center-field fence. "There were probably 12,000 people rooting for them and seven or eight for us," Tommy said. "Oh, man, that stadium got deafening quiet."

Ferrell followed with another four-base blast to make the final score 3-1. Tommy gave up two hits and no walks, while striking out 13.

Despite another round-tripper by Tommy, Roswell trailed Winchester, 3-2, going into the bottom of the fourth inning of the semifinal game. Four hits and two Winchester errors produced four runs and a 6-3 lead, which was more than enough for Ferrell, who scattered five hits and a walk.

Roswell was one victory away from the magic number 12 needed to be World Series champs. Coincidentally, Tommy's uniform number was 12, and it was his turn to pitch.

The last hurdle was Delaware Township, runner-up the year before and coming off a perfect game in the semifinals by pitcher Fred Shapiro, the first in Little League World Series history. Tommy was unfazed. He figured the Texas teams he beat earlier in the month were better.

Blaine shared Tommy's confidence. "With Tommy out there throwing, I had no doubt that we were going to win."

The players didn't feel the usual pressure to win, and that's because manager Dick St. John placed more emphasis on the fundamentals of hitting and fielding, and, most of all, having fun. "I don't remember anybody telling us that we had to win," Blaine said. "We just went out and played."

St. John operated a coffee shop in a Roswell office building. Sometimes Tommy and the other players popped in for a free milkshake and hamburger. He also passed on to the kids what he learned playing semi-pro baseball in Texas. "He was carefree, but he didn't mind telling you what was on his mind," Blaine said. "He always did it in a good way."

After Blaine belted two homers in one game, St. John told him, "Don't be swinging too hard to try and knock it over the fence again."

In the regional title game, Sherrod asked to be taken out of the lineup after striking out twice. St. John refused and Sherrod homered in his next at-bat to advance the team to the World Series.

It was a different story with Tommy.

"Tommy is a good player, but he won't listen to me," St. John once complained to Tom. "He says, 'I listen to my Daddy.'"

St. John was trying to get Tommy, a right-handed hitter, to pull the ball to left field.

"St. John, what's the count on a home run?" Tom asked. "Don't it count as much to right field as it does to left field? He hits all right. Don't mess with him."

The night before the World Series championship game, Ferrell was selected the "Outstanding Little League Player of 1956" and awarded a full scholarship to Lycoming College in Williamsport.

"It sort of pissed me off," Tom said. "I figured St. John didn't like Tommy too well because Tommy didn't listen to him. So I started to phone St. John and tell him not to pitch Tommy the final game—pitch the number-one player in the United States."

The call wasn't made. So, when Tommy walked to the pitcher's mound to face Delaware Township, Roswell's Main Street was deserted as people gathered around the radio wherever they were—home, work, the barber shop, the pool hall, or, like Tom and Lorene Jordan, in a car on the side of a highway.

Announcing the game was Stan Gallup of KGFL radio in Roswell. He was in Williamsport providing a play-by-play account of the games. At least that's what everyone thought.

He was actually holed up inside the KGFL studio, recreating the games based on cryptic teletype reports directly from Williamsport. Not even his wife or son, Gary, knew the difference. "Mom and I didn't know that he was *not* at the game," Gary said.

It was common practice in the 1950s for budget-minded radio stations to reenact games from their studio with an imaginative announcer and sound engineer.

Stan translated the teletype-speak into action. "S1S" meant strike one swinging, and "B2LO" was ball two, low outside. For hits and outs on batted balls, he rapped a pencil against the microphone to simulate the sound of the bat hitting the ball. The engineer blended in various crowd noises as Stan used a large photograph of Williamsport's Memorial Park to describe what was taking place on the field.

Tom was sitting on the edge of his car seat in the second inning. Delaware Township had runners on second and third base with two outs. "It was pretty damn tense," Tom said. "When I was playing, I never did get excited or uptight."

Stan waited for the news, good or bad. "Jordan winds . . . here's the two-two pitch. It's a swing and a miss for strike three."

The next inning, KGFL listeners heard the crowd cheering a home run by Delaware Township's Henry "Sweet Pea" Singleton that barely cleared the center-field fence. He hit a fastball that moments before Ferrell had told Tommy not to throw. "As he circled the bases he grinned broadly, clapped his hands, and jumped into the air at various times," the *Williamsport Sun-Gazette* reported. "The crowd got a big kick out of it."[17]

Tommy wasn't amused. He didn't allow another hit, striking out nine of the next 12 batters.

Roswell trailed, 1-0, in the bottom of fourth as Tommy strolled to the plate with runners on first and second with two outs.

Delaware Township was leading by two runs in the last inning of its World Series opener when the opposing team's slugger was intentionally walked with one out and the bases loaded to force in a run. The daring strategy preserved a 9-8 decision.

Beyond the right-field fence at Memorial Park was a hill called Lycoming Creek dike. "Everybody talked about how if you were a real baseball player, you could knock the ball over that dike," Blaine Stribling said.

In Roswell's win over Upper Darby, Tommy and Ferrell walloped back-to-back homers over the dike. "They said that if anybody hit a ball over the dike, they could get a ball signed by the commissioner of Little League baseball," Ferrell said. "We were in the dugout arguing over who hit the ball the farthest because we thought they were only going to give one ball away."

The dike was covered with humanity, about two-thirds of the 12,000 people at the game.

Ferrell, a left-handed hitter, waited in the on-deck circle. The Delaware Township pitcher was a lefty, so the percentages favored pitching to Ferrell. "I didn't think they were going to pitch to me," Tommy said. "And they did."

Tommy swung. POW!

"That's the game," Ferrell thought to himself.

The ball soared some 300 feet over the fence in right-center field, landing near the top of the dike. As Tommy rounded the bases, he couldn't believe he had gotten a chance to hit. "I was thinking: 'You haven't been watching these games.'"

It was his third homer in the World Series and eighth in 12 games.

There were two innings to go, but Harold Hobson agreed with Ferrell that the game was over. "For a Little League player, Tommy had a killer instinct. He wasn't going to let anybody get on base, if he could help it."

Tommy walked the first batter in the fifth inning and then mowed down the last six batters on strikeouts to finish with 14 for the game. One of the strikeout victims was Sweet Pea. "I threw all fastballs. He didn't touch them," Tommy said.

In winning all seven tournament games he pitched, Tommy punched out 95 in 43 innings, giving up five runs and 21 hits.

The following day in the *New York Times*, St. John and Tommy are pictured together. A beaming Tommy is holding the World Series trophy as his jubilant manager is lifting both as high as possible.

Sporting News hailed Tommy's performance a "one-boy show," reminiscent of the one-man gang references to Eddie Locke. "Young Tom did a fine job of mixing his pitches, throwing both a high hard one and a curve seldom seen among Little Leaguers."[18]

"NEW MEXICO REIGNS AS KING OF LITTLE LEAGUE," the *Sun-Gazette* declared in a front-page headline.[19]

The newspaper called Tommy's two-hit gem in the title game an early present to his father, whose birthday was 12 days later.

Tom Jordan Jr. hangs on tightly to the Little League World Series championship trophy as Roswell coach Dick St. John celebrated his two-hitter and three-run homer in the title game. The trophy disappeared after the team's first reunion in 1983 and hasn't been seen since despite appeals for its return, no questions asked. *AP photo.*

"Nobody in the whole United States expected them to win, except the boys," Tom said. "Tommy said they were going to win."

Tommy was right. And for one glorious day in 1956, Roswell was known for something other than UFOs.

* * *

The train carrying the new Little League World Series champs stopped a few miles north of Roswell. The players looked out at the vast, barren landscape. "Why are we stopping here?" someone asked.

Years later, Stan Gallup revealed he hopped on the train so when it arrived downtown it would appear he had been with the team all along.

As the train pulled slowly into the station, the players looked in amazement at the crowd squeezed along the tracks and on top of baggage carts and rooftops.

"I didn't know there were that many people in Roswell," Blaine Stribling said.

"We didn't really know what we'd done until we came back to Roswell and 5,000 people were at the train station," Harold Hobson explained. "Then we thought we might've done something."

"You really felt like a hero," Ferrell said.

Crowd estimates ranged from 3,000 to 10,000. Whatever the number, the place was packed. "The crowd was so thick that you couldn't even move," Blaine added.

Tom wasn't around for the celebration. He was with the Carlsbad Potashers in San Angelo, Texas, for a game that night. Lorene Jordan was there. "I'm sorry he missed it," she told a reporter. "It would have been one of the happiest moments of his life."

Lorene said she spoke only briefly with Tommy "now that he is a celebrity."[20]

All 14 players were treated like celebrities.

There was a military band to greet them at the train station. They rode in open-top convertibles through town, waving to cheering fans lining the parade route. They signed autographs and, along with Gallup, did media interviews about their experiences in Williamsport. Ferrell was busy hugging and kissing girlfriends of his older brother.

Three days later, they were feted at a Roswell Rockets game, where the governor of New Mexico made each of the players a colonel on his staff. Joe Bauman, baseball's home run king after slugging a record 72 for the Rockets in 1954, took his cuts against Tommy in a pregame exhibition. He struck out swinging, just as he had promised to do.

Tommy was scheduled to travel to New York City and appear on the nationally televised game show *Two for the Money*, but it never materialized. "I was all ready to go to New York, too," he said.

Tommy was probably the most famous 12-year-old in the United States. He was sitting in a Roswell movie theater when a news highlight film flashed on the screen showing his hitting and pitching heroics in the World Series title game.

Newsreel footage from the Little League World Series the next year featured a team really from Mexico—"Los Pequeños Gigantes," or "The Little Giants," of Monterrey. The biggest of all was Angel Macias, a 5-foot, 88-pound ambidextrous pitcher who tossed a perfect game in the final to inspire a book and 2010 movie aptly named *The Perfect Game*. The Monterrey team was the first from outside the United States to win the World Series and the first to do it in consecutive years, as they won again in 1958.

The fairy tale stories of Monterrey and Roswell captured the imagination of baseball fans and sparked the growth of the Little League World Series into a 10-day television extravaganza that has attracted as many as 8.97 million viewers for a single game. The rise of Little League coincided with the demise of the minors in small towns like Roswell.

"People didn't realize it, but Little League really hurt Minor League Baseball," Tom said. "They had four teams in a league and 15 players on a club. And they had two or three leagues in town. The mother, father, and grandparents of these boys all went to these games instead of the minor leagues."

Attendance at Rockets games in 1956 was 18,367, half the year before. It didn't help that the Rockets wound up ninth in the 10-team Southwestern League. "Couldn't field, couldn't run, couldn't pitch," said Tom, who managed the Rockets most of the season.

Roswell dropped out of the minors in 1957, returned briefly two years later, then was without a team until 2011, when the Roswell Invaders of the independent Pecos League tossed their flying-saucer hats onto the field. In one episode of a 2014 reality television show about the league, a player for one of the teams said he counted every one of the 37 fans in the stands.

The rocky dirt field the Lions Hondo Little Leaguers played on has been replaced by World Champion Memorial Park, a quartet of modern baseball fields complete with a concession stand and lights.

Little League in Roswell is bigger than ever. "The most rewarding thing has been how Little League improved from that time on," Harold said. "People started paying attention to Little League."

The passage of time has made what Lions Hondo accomplished even more special.

"It took a while after it happened for it to really sink in what we had done," Ferrell said. "Nothing like that had ever happened to a New Mexico team."

And it hasn't happened since.

On the 60th anniversary in 2016, approximately 500 people, including current Lions Hondo Little Leaguers and their families, showed up at a Southeast New Mexico Historical Society dinner in Roswell to honor the 1956 champs. Five members of the team were there: Tommy, Ferrell, Blaine, Harold, and shortstop Jimmy Valdez, a Mexican American who received compliments at Williamsport for his excellent English.

Tom missed the team's homecoming at the train station in 1956, but not this celebration. He was almost 97 and oozing with nostalgia. "It was really a pretty thrilling time, my number one thrill in baseball," he reflected.

Harold's uniform, glove, and other memorabilia were on display at the dinner. He couldn't believe the uniform once fit him. "We were just a bunch of little boys playing baseball. The odds of us doing what we did are just astronomical."

Williamsport was the end of the baseball road for Harold. "I was brought up on a farm so when I got out of school, I had to go back to work on the farm."

Tommy, Ferrell, Blaine, and first baseman Dick Storey paced Roswell High School to the state baseball championship in 1960. Ferrell and Dick went on to play at the University of New Mexico.

In 1961, at the age of 17, Tommy signed with the Chicago White Sox for a $10,000 bonus. The White Sox touted his 66-11 record in youth baseball, including a 33-3 mark in American Legion competition.

Tommy was already experiencing soreness in the elbow of his right throwing arm. It became worse his first season at Harlan, Kentucky, in the Class D Appalachian League, where he had a 3-3 won–loss mark and an earned run average of 3.83. In 1962, at Clinton, Iowa, in the Class D Midwest League, he was 3-5, with a 4.45 ERA—similar to the 4-7 record and 3.56 ERA of teammate Denny McLain.

McLain won 31 games for the Detroit Tigers in 1968, and 131 in the majors overall. "It was a real surprise to me," Tommy said. "Denny didn't have much of a breaking ball or anything."

Ironically, Tommy, the kid with the dazzling curveball, never pitched another inning in pro ball. He eventually returned to Roswell and became a truck driver.

Ferrell settled in Texas and spent 38 years in management for Sears & Roebuck Company and Stein Mart.

Blaine wound up working 30 years for the city of Security, Colorado, installing and repairing water and sewer lines.

Harold took over the family farm in Roswell.

Gary Gallup, son of Stan, the sportscaster, capped the 60th anniversary celebration by recreating his father's call of Tommy's game-winning homer in the championship game: "Jordan stands in with two runners on base and two out. He walked in the first and struck out in the third. He's looking for his fifth hit in the World Series and Roswell's first in the game. Here's the pitch . . ."

Gary clicked two pieces of wood together. "It's a long drive to center field . . . way back . . . it's going, going, gone. It's out of here! Roswell takes the lead, 3-1."

"Oh, man, I hit the hell out of that ball," Tommy said. "As soon as I swung, it was long gone."

The World Series trophy also is gone, missing since the team's first reunion in 1983. Public appeals to search attics and basements, as well as a plea to turn it in, no questions asked, failed to produce the memento.

The memories are better than any trophy.

"I told you not to throw that kid a fastball," Ferrell tells Tommy every chance he gets. Tommy claims his dike-clearing homer was longer than the one hammered by Ferrell.

"All my life, I've always been for the little guy," Harold said. "We shut up those boys back east for a little while."

"It's a good thing that Tommy spoke up," Blaine said.

The one time Tommy didn't listen to his dad about baseball turned out to be the best time for Roswell.

6

THE MELLOW IRISHMAN'S
MERRY BAND OF CUBANS

Pat Stasey and the Big Spring Broncs

Big Spring is a city in the middle of nowhere. In Texas, that can be almost anywhere.

It's not the kind of place you'd expect to find a bunch of Cubans, especially from 1947 to 1952, when they were the talk of the town and Minor League Baseball, along with their player-manager-owner, Frank "Pat" Stasey.

The story of how Stasey, an Irishman, teamed with super-scout Joe Cambria, a Sicilian, to bring boatloads of Cuban players to the United States is a testament to the impact baseball had on bringing down the walls of segregation in the southwestern states of Texas, New Mexico, and Oklahoma, where the so-called "Havana horde" mostly toiled.

Cambria and Stasey were the ultimate odd couple.

The pudgy Cambria, dubbed the "Godfather of Cuban Baseball," was a celebrity in Cuba, easily recognizable in a white linen suit, Panama hat, and chomping on one of his own "Papa Joe Cambria" cigars, which he generously gave away.

About the only place the 5-foot-10, 173-pound Stasey stood out was in a Big Spring Broncs team photo because he was usually the only non-Cuban.

Cambria was a fast-talking wheeler-dealer. Stasey was a man of few words.

Al Valdes, a catcher who played three seasons for Stasey at Big Spring, remembered a hitting slump so horrible he wound up sitting and staring zombie-like at his useless bat.

"What's wrong?" Stasey asked.

"The bat's no good," Valdes said.

"He took that bat, went up to the plate, and hit a triple with it," Valdes recalled. "When he came back to the dugout, he just looked at me and said, 'It's not the bat.'"[1]

Cambria had a home in Baltimore, Maryland, but spent most of his time in Havana, where he was co-owner of the hometown Cubans, champion of the Florida International League its first five years of operation (1946–1950).

Stasey went to Cuba every March for tryout camps in Havana, as well as Santiago and Camagüey, the second- and third-largest cities in Cuba. He picked the players he wanted and then arranged to get them to Big Spring, a city of approximately 17,000 people about halfway between Dallas and El Paso.

The one thing Cambria and Stasey had in common is that neither spoke Spanish. Cambria's Spanish was limited to "PEETCH, CATCH, and EL BATTO, accompanied by a whirlwind of gestures."[2]

Stasey had better luck with the Cuban players who translated for him.

Cambria is credited with signing more than 400 Cubans to play pro ball. Stasey had a hand in 187 coming to the United States and playing for him.

Camilo Pascual, a pitcher who won 174 games in 18 big-league seasons, passed through Big Spring. So did another hurler, Mike Fornieles, who won 62 games and saved 55 more in the majors.

The cream of Cambria's crop wound up in the big leagues with the Washington Senators, as he had a working agreement with Clark Griffith, the team's owner and a best friend.

"The Washington training camp is always interesting because you never know what the next tide from Cuba will wash up," *Washington Post* columnist Shirley Povich wrote in 1948.[3]

The Senators and their top farm clubs were awash with so many Cuban players Cambria needed other places to park the talent he was finding on the island.

He hooked up with Stasey in 1947, as interest in baseball was soaring with 10 new minor leagues, one of which was the Longhorn, a Class D circuit that the Stephenville, Texas, native helped organize. He was part owner and manager of the Big Spring entry and looking for the best players he could buy with money out of his own pocket.

The Cubans were bargains, willing to play for about half the salary of American players. They also were exempt from the military draft in the United States, one of the reasons the Senators started recruiting them in the late 1930s. This made them even more attractive to minor-league teams during the Korean War in the early 1950s.

A left-handed-hitting outfielder, Stasey was close to making it to the majors before World War II stopped his climb through the minors at the end of the 1942 season.

Starting at Big Spring in the Class D West Texas–New Mexico (WT-NM) League, he batted .322 and .344 in 1938–1939, then .312 and .277 in 1940–1941 for Moline, Illinois, in the Class B Three-I League. In 1942, he hit .308 for the Minneapolis Millers of the American Association, but instead of going to the big leagues he went into the U.S. Army Air Corps, where he spent the next three years. He turned down a chance to return to the Millers in 1946, so he could work and play ball for the Cosden Petroleum Corporation in Big Spring.

"I think I could have played a few years of big-league ball," Stasey acknowledged. "I had only mediocre speed but was fair defensively, had a big-league arm, and could hit fairly well, especially right-handers. I was a line-drive hitter, and got a lot of doubles and a lot of runs batted in. I usually hit between 15 and 20 home runs a year."[4]

In 1947, the 30-year-old Stasey patrolled right field and laced Longhorn League pitching for a .416 batting average, with 19 homers and 153 runs batted in, to pace Big Spring to the loop's first title. But that wasn't as big of news as the 10 Cubans he used to do it.

All of them were light-skinned and barely distinguishable from the team's six homegrown players. This didn't keep them from becoming targets on the road of what *Big Spring Herald* columnist Tommy Hart termed "open abuse and scathing denunciation."[5]

In a letter to his colleagues in the league's other cities, he urged them to speak out on the subject: "The fact that a man buys a ticket at the gate does not give him the right to hurl foul invective into a man's face and flaunt him at every turn. I think we can do a lot to silence much of that vitriol that spews from the mouths of those so-called citizens."[6]

The taunting may have caused the Broncs to drop out of first place in early June, but they quickly rebounded to top second-place Midland by six and a half games and lead the league in attendance. As one scribe noted, "The boys were given the bird all over the circuit, but just the same, the fans crowded through the gates to see them play."[7]

The Cubans played good baseball, and that was good for business.

"They played hard, and they were hard to beat," said Tom Jordan, a player-manager challenged with stopping the Cubans for two Longhorn League foes, Roswell and Artesia. "They all had good arms. They could all run fast."

Other teams soon jumped on the Cambria bandwagon.

In 1948, the North Texas cities of Sherman and Denison in the Class B Big State League even hired a Cuban manager, Joe Rodriguez, to speak the same language as the 15 Cubans that reported to their team for spring training. They won 102 games—94 regular-season games and eight in the playoffs—to capture both titles.

Meanwhile, Stasey and his merry band of Cubans were the class of the Longhorn League for the second-straight year. An Odessa columnist conceded the pennant to the Broncs mid-season even though they were only one up in the win column over the Odessa Oilers. "If the Broncs ever get a jump on a team, it's like running up a perpendicular hill trying to catch up," he lamented.[8]

The Oilers never caught up, as Big Spring rolled to another pennant, Stasey showing the way with a league-best .389 batting average.

In 1949, Cambria added three more teams to what, in effect, was his own personal farm system, including Abilene, of the Class C WT–NM League. He supplied each club with either a complete or partial roster without signed agreements, and had the final say in moving players throughout his network.

Stasey praised Cuban rookies as more advanced than their U.S. counterparts, pointing out the average one was "fast, has a good arm, and lots of hustle."[9]

Abilene Blue Sox president W. V. Young was still skeptical when he got to Miami, Florida, to pick up a busload of Cubans assigned to him.

"He was doubtful that anybody who couldn't speak more or less perfect English could ever make the Blue Sox ball team," observed a columnist for the *Abilene Reporter-News*.

After the 18-hour ride to Abilene, the Blue Sox boss was singing a different tune. "I'm just flat foolish about these boys," he said. "If they can't play baseball, I'm gonna keep 'em around anyway and form me a glee club. They really can go to town, with melody and harmony."[10]

Big Spring was the New York Yankees of the lower minors in 1949, dominating the Longhorn by finishing 20½ games ahead of runner-up Midland and winning all eight playoff games.

"The people here were just crazy about us," Valdes said a half-century later. "You hit a home run . . . people would put money in the fence. Sometimes there'd be $100 or more stuck in the backstop. Let me tell you, $100 in 1949 looked like $1 million does today."[11]

At the time, an *Odessa American* columnist wrote, "In a Latin lineup that includes such names as Gomez, Mendes, Vasquez, Ramirez, Valdez [sic], and a dozen or so more sounding about the same, the name Stasey stands out like a 'Smith' in the Notre Dame backfield."[12]

Stasey's average of .376 also stood out, giving him back-to-back batting titles.

The success of Stasey's Cubans is even more remarkable given the experiences of Hayden "Stubby" Greer, player-manager at Abilene, then Artesia.

Greer's nickname was inspired by his fireplug shape (5-foot-8 and 160 pounds), but it could easily apply to his short-fused temper.

Stubby was player-manager of Abilene's 1946 championship team, selected in 2001 as one of the 100 best minor-league teams of the previous century. He was not around in 1948, when the Blue Sox finished seventh, prompting the team's ownership to bring him back to lead a roster stocked with Cubans.

The new players sparked the Blue Sox to a second-place tie. Going into 1950, Stubby had high hopes for a pennant and invited 30 Cubans to spring training. By the end of the season, there were only three Cubans playing regularly for the last-place Blue Sox.

Stubby quit in disgust and went to Artesia in the Longhorn League. He took four Cubans with him. In mid-July, Stubby got mad at his Cuban catcher for getting kicked out of a game. They argued and then duked it out in the dugout. Stubby suspended the catcher, upsetting his Cuban mates, who refused to play unless he was reinstated. Stubby canned all of them.

Big Spring was the preferred destination for Cuban players.

Pat Stasey, far right, middle row, was the only non-Cuban on the 1949 Big Spring
team. With Stasey batting a league-leading .376 and Carlos "Potato" Pascual hit-
ting .336, the Broncs captured their third-straight Longhorn League pennant.
Front row, left to right: Cookie Vasquez, Pascual, Felix Gomez, Al Valdes, Bobby
Mires, batboy. Middle row, left to right: Dumbo Rodriguez, Pancho Perez, Bert
Hernandez, Eddy Ramirez, and Stasey. Back row, left to right: Al Aton, business
manager; Julio Ramos; Lazarus Coto; Bert Baez; Paul Molina; Ace Mendez; Bert
Garcia; and Gumbo Helba. *Courtesy of Patricia Stasey Aylor and Maribeth Stasey
Scott.*

When Oscar Rodríguez, manager of the Havana Cubans, informed
two players they were being sent to Abilene, they refused and asked to go
to Big Spring instead.

"That's out of the question," Rodríguez replied. "You've got to go to
Abilene."

"Either we go to Big Spring or we don't go," the holdouts persisted.

"But it will be a promotion," Rodríguez countered. "You'll be playing
Class C ball."

The pair wouldn't budge.

Rodríguez finally relented. "All right, go to Big Spring. Every ball-player we ship out wants to go to Big Spring. I think I'll quit here, pack my bags, and go out there and see what it's like myself."[13]

If he'd gone to Big Spring and spent time around Stasey, he would've seen an easygoing guy that was more a father figure than a manager.

He didn't have a curfew.

"You don't play good, you go back to Cuba," said pitcher Aramis "Tito" Arencibia. "It was very simple."

Stasey often took his wife, Beatrice, and daughters, Patricia and Maribeth, on road trips. Pat sat in the front near the bus driver to help keep him awake on the overnight trips. There was no air conditioning on the old school bus, and it was usually hot and sticky, making it difficult for the players to sleep. So they entertained each other, playing the bongo drums and singing.

Patricia remembered the players doting over her and Maribeth like little sisters many of them had at home in Cuba.

On the field, Stasey kept things simple, using few signals. Pitchers called their own game if they wanted to, and baserunners could steal on their own.

If one of his players got into an argument with an umpire, he casually strolled in from his right-field position to calm down everyone.

"The mild-mannered Stasey is known throughout the Longhorn League as the umpire's friend," one sportswriter reported. "He rarely gives the boys in blue any static. When he protests a decision, he does it without trying to be demonstrative."[14]

The Cubans loved playing for him. "He was a wonderful, wonderful person," Tito said.

"It was never difficult for me to manage those guys," Stasey said. "I gave them all an even break, and they knew it. Most were just extremely grateful for the opportunity to play."[15]

Perhaps the player who most admired Stasey was Carlos Pascual, the "best Cuban player of all," according to a *Washington Post* headline.

"He has the best arm of anybody in Organized Baseball," Senators vice president Calvin Griffith boasted in 1950, shortly after Carlos put on a spectacular Fourth of July show by pitching seven-inning shutouts in both ends of a doubleheader.[16]

"He pitches shutouts, slugs home runs, stars at third base, and is called 'Little Potato,'" another writer added. "He's only 19 years old and is not quite sure whether he is a third baseman, a pitcher, or an outfielder."[17]

Carlos jumped directly from Class D to the majors, a rare feat consistent with his flair for the dramatic.

He couldn't speak English the year before when he traveled by bus from New Orleans to Big Spring.

"He'd keep an eye on his suitcase, and every time they'd take it off the bus to put it on another, he'd follow it," Stasey explained.[18]

Big Spring fans couldn't keep their eyes off Carlos.

At 5-foot-6 and 170-something pounds, he was built like a little potato.

"Everyone called him Potato or Spud," Stasey explained, "and he was the most colorful player in the league. He would pack the park, at home or on the road, with his play, and all of his little mannerisms."[19]

"He would stand up there, rolling the bat from one hand to the other and hitching up his pants," said Jim Waldrip, a pitcher who faced him later in his career. "You'd think you could catch him in between everything, but he was a tough hitter. I didn't want any part of him."

Waldrip wasn't alone. Pitchers didn't dare throw at him or appear to be doing so.

"He could probably whip anyone in the park," Waldrip said.

No one wanted to find out.

He was one hot Potato in 1949, burning up the league with a .336 average, 25 home runs, and 125 runs batted in. He had a bazooka for an arm, his throws from third to first base so powerful that both of his feet left the ground.

"He was a third baseman with one of the greatest arms I've ever seen," Stasey said. "He could throw the ball on a line for 150 feet, and it would never get more than five feet off the ground."[20]

Stasey decided to let him pitch in 1950. He gunned down hitters just like he did pitchers. In the twin shutouts that made national headlines, he pitched a stretch of 10⅔ innings of hitless ball, while allowing 5 hits and striking out 10. Overall, he fanned 103 batters in 85 innings to compile a 7-2 record.

Potato ended up hitting .345, with 16 homers and 100 RBIs, almost identical to Stasey's numbers: .346, 8, and 101, respectively. But a bad start had Potato thinking about quitting baseball altogether.

Stasey properly concluded that Potato's struggles at the plate were caused by the pressure of filling in at so many other positions—shortstop, second base, and center field. He put his star at third base to stay except for occasional pitching assignments.

The Senators envisioned Potato as a pitcher. That's how he was used when he was promoted late in the season.

Potato made his big-league debut on September 24, 1950, against the Philadelphia Athletics at Griffith Stadium in Washington, DC.

The season was over for the Broncs. They finished a disappointing third despite the heroics of Potato.

The eyes of Big Spring were now fixed solely on Potato. He was the pride of the West Texas town, the envy of every player who ever put on the uniform of a Class D team, the squatty little guy that tugged at the heart strings of couch potatoes everywhere.

The game meant nothing in the American League standings. The Senators were in fifth place, the Athletics buried in last. The crowd of 2,731 wasn't much bigger than some at Big Spring.

Potato pitched like the 10-year veteran some folks in the Longhorn League believed him to be. In just 94 minutes, he shredded the Athletics, 3-1, with a sneaky fastball that held them to an unearned run, five hits, two walks, and a hit batter.

Four days later, at Boston's Fenway Park, Potato faced a more daunting task—a potent Red Sox lineup featuring Ted Williams, Dom DiMaggio, Bobby Doerr, Vern Stephens, and Walt Dropo, American League Rookie of the Year, with 34 homers and 144 runs batted in. He scattered seven hits, blanking Williams, Stephens, and Dropo, but still lost, 4-3.

"He's crude, but he has a chance to stick," Senators manager Stanley "Bucky" Harris said heading into the 1951 season. [21]

Bucky wasn't so sure when a lovesick Potato reported to training camp nine days late, showing more interest in returning to Havana and pitching woo to his sweetheart. "Pascual he homeseek," a fellow Cuban pitcher related, wiping imaginary tears from his eyes. [22]

Teammates claimed that while Bucky's back was turned, Potato picked up a bucket of water and poured it over his face to make it look like he was crying.

In his first (and only) spring outing, Potato was "virtually pitching and ducking in the same motion" as the Athletics pounded him for eight hits in three innings. [23]

"Why don't you go home?" Bucky suggested.

Potato said he would play in only two places—Havana or Big Spring. Bucky didn't care where he went so long as it wasn't back on the mound for the Senators. "I don't want to be troubled by any homesick Cubans," he muttered. [24]

Potato played most of the next three years in Havana; injured his throwing arm; got married, with Stasey attending the wedding; then re-connected with his favorite boss at Hobbs, New Mexico, in 1955.

Taking Potato's place in Big Spring was his younger brother, Camilo. He quickly became known as "Little Potato," although he was four inches taller.

Camilo was exclusively a pitcher—one that relied heavily on a devastating curveball that made him the strikeout king of the American League three straight years (1961–1963) while amassing a career total of 2,167—66th all-time entering the 2018 season, one behind Clayton Kershaw of the Los Angeles Dodgers.

The Longhorn League was reclassified from D to C in 1951, and the player limit per team upped by one to 16—five veterans, eight limited service, and three rookies.

The Korean War was draining baseball of young prospects.

"The good-looking 19-year-old rookie, once the goal of every club owner, has now been devalued," Povich opined in the *Washington Post* in early 1951. "He's under the gun of the Selective Service." [25]

Stasey's Cubans were not only draft proof, but also they qualified as lower-cost rookies and limited-service players with more than 45 days' experience but less than three years. This meant Stasey was one of the few owners in the league turning a profit.

One owner proposed a cap of five Cubans on a team.

"We favor a small number of Cubans on Longhorn League teams, if they are going to be used at all," a Sweetwater, Texas, columnist wrote. "Call it discrimination if you like." [26]

The general manager of the Vernon, Texas, team complained that Big Spring's Cubans were perennial limited-service men: "They play under their own name one year, under their mothers the next, and their cousins the next." [27]

Hart defended the Cubans in his *Big Spring Herald* column: "The Cuban lads who come here are, for the most part, without much baseball background. They succeed because it provides a chance to escape a humdrum existence. They regard it as their life's work. If you're going to discriminate against the Cubans for that, then you might as well outlaw the game and let the people seek other means of entertainment."[28]

Big Spring's top pitching prospects in 1951 were Camilo, barely 17; Mike Fornieles, 19; and Raúl Sánchez, 20.

Camilo had a 2-1 record and 5.14 ERA, walking 12 and giving up 10 runs (8 earned) and 18 hits in 14 innings pitched. He spent the rest of the season with teams in Oklahoma and New York.

Fornieles won 17 games, and his 2.85 ERA was the lowest in the league.

Sánchez completed all nine games he started, winning six. He went on to pitch in the majors for the Senators and Cincinnati Reds.

Stasey captured his third batting title in four years with a .387 average, thumping 14 homers and driving in 118 runs, but his Broncs were denied another pennant, placing second. They were runners-up again in 1952, Stasey hitting .344, with 13 homers and 120 runs batted in.

The ace of the pitching staff for first-place Odessa in 1952 was Cuban southpaw Evelio Ortega, a 23-game winner. Another Cuban and a former Broncs infielder, Julio De la Torre, starred for archrival Midland. Throughout the lower minors, Cubans were the ticket to winning both on the field and at the box office. They were the lifeline of surviving teams as the number of minor leagues plunged from an all-time high of 59 in 1949 to 23 a decade later.

Stasey worked a miracle in Big Spring, his teams winning three championships, placing second twice and third once. Counting playoffs, the Broncs won 189 more games than they lost.

But he could see television antennas popping up on roofs throughout town and hear the whirring sounds of new air conditioners. As the club's business manager, he knew ticket and concession sales were falling like a tumbleweed downhill. After the 1952 season, he sold the Broncs for $12,000 and purchased the Roswell Rockets. "Roswell has a better park and a larger drawing area," he explained.[29]

He took four Cuban players with him, one of whom was Ossie Álvarez, a future big-league infielder, and added several more after financial problems forced Big Spring's new owners to shut down operations at the end of July. The Broncs returned to the league in 1954.

Stasey tried blending the Cubans with the Rockets' holdovers he inherited. The strategy didn't work, as Roswell finished fifth, with a 60-70 record, and attracted only 35,459 fans, sixth in the league and less than any of his Big Spring teams.

The Rockets managed only 47 home runs, six less than Joe Bauman personally accounted for at Artesia. Bauman was looking for a place to pump more four-baggers and some gas at a Texaco station he wanted to own and operate. Stasey offered him an opportunity to do both in Roswell.

Youth, speed, and pitching made up Stasey's winning formula at Big Spring. In signing Bauman and another proven oldster, Stubby Greer, 34, he was departing from that. As the team's new co-owner, Greer would help run things off the diamond and turn in his usual all-star performance on it.

At age 37, Stasey was reduced to a part-time role in 1953. He appeared in 80 of the Rockets' 130 games, batting .341.

The lone Cuban in the Rockets' day-to-day lineup in 1954 was the fancy-fielding Alvarez. Pitching was by committee, a dizzying array of Cubans rotating around an 18-game winner with the all-American name of Tom Sawyer.

Bauman had opposing pitchers fearing for their lives in 1954, smacking 72 home runs to set an all-time single-season record for pro baseball. He was able to hit 19 more homers than his previous high because he batted fourth in the lineup, between Stubby and Pat.

"Stubby never hit many home runs, but he was a hell of a good hitter," Bauman said.

Greer hit 13 homers, and his .398 average was second in the league, behind Bauman's .400. Pat batted .295, with 8 homers.

"Pat was really a better hitter than his statistics that year," Bauman said. "He hit to the opposite field all the time, and he just slammed it."

For all of mighty Joe's clouts, the Rockets ended up second in the standings and fourth in attendance. Stasey sold his share of the team to Greer so he could build a new club from scratch in Hobbs, about 115 miles from Roswell, near the New Mexico–Texas state line. He wanted to take one more crack at a championship and do it Big Spring–style, relying primarily on Cubans.

Álvarez and three other Cubans from Roswell followed Stasey to Hobbs, with Potato Pascual joining them for the latter part of the season. Another late addition was Alejandro "Alex" Crespo, a 40-year-old out-

Pat Stasey, right, was a regular customer at Joe Bauman's Texaco station in Roswell during the 1954 season, when he was player, manager, and co-owner of the Roswell Rockets. Stasey usually batted behind Joe in the lineup. Pitchers still walked Joe a whopping 150 times. *Courtesy of Patricia Stasey Aylor and Maribeth Stasey Scott.*

fielder who starred for the New York Cubans of the Negro Leagues in 1940 and later in Mexico and Cuba.

"We've been trying to land him for 10 years," Washington's Calvin Griffith said in 1955, after Crespo arrived at spring training camp in Orlando, Florida, and had manager Charley Dressen doing somersaults over line drives he was lashing to all fields.[30]

"I pitched him outside and tight, high and low, fastball and curve, but it didn't stop him," veteran Senators pitcher Francis "Spec" Shea said after throwing batting practice to the 6-foot-1, 206-pound Crespo.

Dressen was incredulous: "I don't care if he's 58, if he keeps hitting like he's been hitting down here, I can use him pinch-hitting."

Crespo opened the season at Charlotte, North Carolina, in the Class A South Atlantic League before winding up in Hobbs and hitting .324, with 16 homers in 87 games. He was one of the few bright spots for Stasey, who ended his playing career and then had to endure his worst season as a manager—a 62-77 won–loss mark and sixth-place finish.

Crespo remained in Cuba and retired in 1956, but Stasey cheered himself knowing he'd have Potato the entire season, as well as a working agreement with the Senators that ensured talented youngsters needed to be a contender in the new Class B Southwestern League. The 10-team circuit was made up of cities previously in the Longhorn and WT–NM loops.

Stasey's biggest plum was Dan Dobbek, a strapping 21-year-old out-fielder who would go on to play in the majors for the Senators and Minnesota Twins. He batted .340, with 23 homers and 144 runs batted in, while Potato was almost as dangerous, hitting .323, with 34 round-trippers and 120 RBIs.

Potato was voted the most popular player by Hobbs fans, followed closely by Dobbek. The Sports cruised to the pennant with 90 victories. "That '56 club was really great," Stasey said. "It was very well-balanced, with good speed and great defense. Everyone pulled together, and everyone thought we would win."[31]

Unfortunately, winning didn't keep Stasey from losing $100 to $300 every home game and wondering if he could finish the season.

"I don't know what to do," he admitted in early August to columnist Art Gatts of the *Hobbs News-Sun*.

I thought all Hobbs wanted was a winning ballclub. That, we have. We've been in first place from May 19th on. We have a hustling, entertaining ballclub. Other cities draw twice as many fans when we play in them than they do for any other team. Yet, we can't draw 1,000 fans a night. I'm on the last rope.[32]

Attendance for the year was 44,206—fifth in the league and less than half of the 102,000 Stasey said was needed to keep the team financially stable.

"Pat used to coach third base," Dobbek said. "He'd spend more time counting people in the ballpark. He kept track of just about everything."

That's how he knew it was time to sell the team and get out of Minor League Baseball. The Senators wanted him to be their assistant farm director, but he turned down that position and another one as a full-time scout. He moved his family to San Angelo, Texas, and got into the financial planning and insurance business.

Stasey got along with Cuban players when others gave up on them. He gave them both a chance to succeed in the United States and a ticket to freedom for themselves and their families. At the same time, he helped the lower minors outlast the Korean War and hang on as long as possible during the tough economic times that followed.

When Pat left baseball in 1957, Hobbs was one of eight teams left in the Southwestern League. By August, that number was down to four. The loop disappeared entirely in 1958, replaced by the Class D Sophomore League, which lasted through the 1961 season. Pro baseball was history in Hobbs, Roswell, and the sleepy Texas town of Big Spring, which Stasey and his Cubans once had in the national limelight.

In 1998, Stasey was inducted into the Texas Baseball Hall of Fame for his contributions to the game.

"You really can say that I lived the American dream," Stasey said.[33]

He wasn't done.

When the San Angelo Colts, a member of the Longhorn League from 1948 through 1955, were resurrected in 2000, as a member of United League Baseball, he became a limited partner and advisor to the team's owners. He served two years as the Colts' bench coach, receiving a championship ring after they won the United League title in 2002.

He died in 2005, at the age of 88, inspiring a *San Angelo Standard-Times* headline that read, "STASEY DEVOTED LIFE TO BASE-BALL."[34]

"He helped a lot of people find a better way of life," Patricia said of her father.

The stories of two Cuban pitchers, Aramis "Tito" Arencibia and Esteban "Steve" Nunez, are proof of that.

* * *

Tito and Steve couldn't speak English when they first stepped on U.S. soil.

They found out the best way to learn the language was to make friends with a local girl.

"You want to learn English, you have to go out with a girl," a teammate advised the 19-year-old Tito. "She will talk with you continuously and you'll get adjusted to it."

Someone arranged a date for him.

"Go with her," he was told. "Don't worry about it. She gives you a kiss, you kiss her."

They went to a rodeo. "When I walked in, I saw all these strange people," Tito recalled.

He found another girl more to his liking—a high school student named Wanda Woods. She was four years younger than Tito. They began meeting almost every weekday afternoon at a TG&Y variety store in Big Spring.

"I kept asking her for a date, and she said, 'No, you need to learn English.'"

"Somebody will teach me," Tito said wishfully.

Eventually, Wanda agreed to go out with Tito. They went to a place called Lover's Lane and shared a watermelon.

"I dated her, and my English picked up right away," he said. "I was amazed."

Steve met Frances Valdez, a waitress at her parents' Valdez Café in Roswell. She spoke some Spanish and told him what to order.

"Hamburger is one word I could say all the time," Steve said.

Frances expanded his vocabulary to include "fried chicken" and "pork chops," then decided to throw in a few other words. "I'm going to teach you how to speak English," she announced.

Future conversations were in English, not Spanish.

Tito arrived in Big Spring on July 4, 1951. As he stepped from the airplane into the scorching sun, he discovered what Texas has in common with hell. "The heat was unbelievable," he said. "I wanted to get back on the plane and go home."

The urge to return to Cuba got stronger the more he sat in the dugout and bullpen.

Nine days passed before he pitched a scoreless inning in relief to win his first pro game. He continued to wait for a chance to start a game.

Stasey was waiting, too. He wanted the 6-foot, 141-pound Tito to add some weight so he wouldn't shrivel up and die in the Texas furnace.

"He didn't think I could last five innings," Tito said.

Finally, Tito went to Humberto "Bert" Baez, a bilingual jack-of-all-trades—pitcher, infielder, outfielder, coach, and interpreter.

"If he won't let me pitch, I'd like to go home," he told Baez, who translated the message for Stasey.

"Tell him he's going to pitch tomorrow," Stasey said.

Every spring from 1947 through 1952, Pat Stasey, front row, fifth from left, returned from Cuba with players that made the Big Spring Broncs winners on the field and at the box office. One of Stasey's recruits was Tito Arencibia, a big smile on his face as he exits the plane, third from the top. Tito arrived in 1951, married a local girl, and was still living in the Big Spring area in 2018. "People think I was born here," Tito said. "They say they saw me in a high school uniform." *Courtesy of Patricia Stasey Aylor and Maribeth Stasey Scott.*

"I'll shut them out," Tito predicted upon receiving the news.

Those were bold words, as the opponent was the first-place San Angelo Colts, with a hard-hitting lineup featuring Bob "Round-Trip" Crues, coholder of baseball's single-season home run record.

"They throw me to the tigers," Tito said. "I think Pat did it on purpose."

Tito responded with a four-hit shutout, floating knuckleballs that confounded the Colts. He beat the eventual league champs again a month later, limiting them to a single run and six hits. He won seven of nine decisions and posted a 3.09 earned run average—third best in the league.

Tito spent the winter at his home in Pinar del Río, Cuba, exchanging letters with Wanda. The wife of Broncs' co-owner Al Aton became a pen pal. "I had two people writing me, and my English got better," Tito said.

On the mound he used pinpoint control to compile a 16-7 record and 3.58 earned run average. He walked only 62 batters in 201 innings. The hellish Texas heat didn't faze him, as he completed 18 of the games he started.

In Cuba, Tito got star treatment, Havana's 18 newspapers touting his achievements with glowing stories and box scores that detailed games he pitched.

When Stasey visited Cuba in early 1953, he stayed two nights at Tito's home and attended a festive banquet honoring his ace. They went to see one of Tito's best friends pitch.

"I recommended Pete Ramos," Tito said. "He was like my own brother."

Pedro Ramos pitched 15 years in the majors, winning 10 or more games seven straight seasons, mostly for last-place teams. The Senators signed Ramos, but he didn't accompany Tito to Roswell, where Stasey was starting over.

The summer of 1953 was a long one for both of them. Stasey suffered through his first losing season, and Tito battled loneliness and a windswept ballpark in Roswell to post a 12-11 record.

Stasey tried to help by letting Tito stay in Big Spring when the Rockets were playing in nearby cities. The wind in Roswell was another matter.

"Roswell was the worst place to pitch," he said. "The wind was blowing out all the time, and it carried the ball with it."

Tito and Wanda got married in 1954, and had their first child, a girl named Elizabeth. He returned to Big Spring to notch a 14-11 mark, then, soon after starting an offseason job with Cosden, the local oil company, he was drafted by the U.S. Army.

"Everybody told me when I got drafted, go to Cuba," Tito said. "You don't have to go. You're not an American citizen."

But he was married to one, making him eligible for the draft.

He joined the army and became a U.S. citizen, and by the time he got out of the military in 1956, he had a sore arm from pitching in cold weather for a team in the Chicago area. His pro baseball career was over, and he returned to Big Spring to stay.

Steve Nunez arrived in Roswell seven weeks into the 1954 season, going from the Sweetwater Spudders at the bottom of the Longhorn League standings to the Rockets at the top.

Stasey scouted Steve in Cuba so he was confident the 20-year-old right-hander could help compensate for the loss of Tito.

Steve won his first five decisions with the Rockets and had 13 victories entering the final week of the season. He had a blazing fastball and decent curveball. He needed a pitch like the screwball to get over the hump and perhaps realize his dream of reaching the majors.

The screwball is a reverse curveball. The pitcher snaps his wrist and forearm inward at the last second, forcing the ball to break in the opposite direction from a curveball.

"A screwball is like a curveball to a left-hander," Steve explained. "I said to myself, 'I'm going to learn how to throw that pitch, so I can be a good right-handed pitcher to left-handed batters."

Fernando Valenzuela, a 20-year-old Mexican pitcher for the Los Angeles Dodgers in 1981, used a screwball to trigger a national frenzy called Fernandomania, which Dodgers announcer Vin Scully said "bordered on a religious experience" for Mexican fans as they "grabbed onto him with both hands to ride to the moon."[35]

The first and only pitcher to capture Rookie of the Year and Cy Young Award honors in the same season, Fernando went on to become a cultural icon while winning 173 games in the majors.

Steve was looking for a pitch that would raise him above the crowd of other pitchers. "I was trying to be different than everybody," he said.

The screwball is as difficult to throw as it is to hit. The threat of a career-ending injury to the shoulder and elbow hovers over a screwball pitcher like a dark cloud.

"The successful screwball pitcher must overcome an awkward sensation that feels like tightening a pickle jar while simultaneously thrusting the wrist forward with extreme velocity," Bruce Schoenfeld wrote in a *New York Times* story about the disappearance of the pitch from modern-day baseball.[36]

Pitchers were self-taught in the 1950s. Minor-league teams didn't have pitching coaches, and veteran hurlers were reluctant to pass on tips to youngsters for fear they'd take their jobs. Steve was on his own.

He practiced throwing the screwball, not knowing he was doing it the wrong way. He twisted his entire arm instead of just the wrist and hand.

The Spudders were perfect for testing a new pitch in game conditions, as they won only 29 games the entire season. In previous encounters, he beat them easily with his usual stuff. Besides, it was "Joe Bauman Night" at Roswell's Fair Park, and attention would be on the Rockets slugger and his quest to become baseball's new home run king.

Just before throwing a screwball to begin the second inning, Steve asked himself, "Okay, you think you're ready?"

Recalling that moment 61 years later, he grinned and said, "I guess I wasn't ready."

Steve fired a screwball as hard as he could. The ball sailed into the grandstand, and he fell to the ground. He got up, gently pulled on his right arm at the wrist, and heard a rattling sound. He hollered to Alvarez at shortstop, who rushed to his side.

"I think I broke my arm," he said in Spanish.

Steve tugged on his wrist so Ozzie could hear the rattle.

Stasey trotted to the mound, took one look at Steve's arm, and agreed that it was broken. "He had never heard of a pitcher breaking his arm throwing a baseball," Steve said.

Steve wanted to be different, but not that way.

The medical diagnosis was a "torsion fracture between the shoulder and elbow."[37]

Steve's arm was pieced back together with a plate and two screws, and placed in a cast. It didn't heal properly so it was broken again and put back in a cast for a month. "When I started pitching again, I was throwing better, faster than before I broke it. Actually, my arm got stronger."

He pitched four more years, the apex in 1956, when he notched a 11-6 mark and 3.71 ERA at Fort Walton Beach, Florida, in the Class D Alabama–Florida League. He averaged almost a strikeout per inning—134 in 136.

Steve messed around with a screwball only once in a game, and it screwed up his five-year career.

"They knew about my broken arm, and I think they held that against me," he told Toby Smith, author of the book *Bush League Boys*. "I am not bitter anymore. Frances wouldn't let me be that way."[38]

Steve married Frances in 1957 and settled in Roswell. "Everything she said was in English and, then, she'd translate into Spanish and what it meant."

By the time he became a U.S. citizen in 1963, he was singing the national anthem and reciting the Pledge of Allegiance and the Preamble to the U.S. Constitution. He could still do it more than a half century later.

Steve and Frances put all five of their children through college. "Out of the whole bunch, I got three teachers, a lawyer, and a handyman," Steve said. "None of them speak Spanish. Everything we said at the dinner table was in English."

After a long battle with cancer, Frances died in 2007, a week after she and Steve celebrated their 50th wedding anniversary. Steve passed away in 2017, the screwball incident still fresh in his mind.

He didn't see Bauman blast his 64th homer later in the game because he was at the hospital. He was still there the following Sunday when Joe jolted a trio to hike his total to 72.

"He never hit a homer off me," Steve said proudly.

Tito was one of the Big Spring pitchers who reportedly pitched around Joe the last week of the 1954 season.

"I pitched to him," Tito insisted. "The second baseman asked me to give him an easy ball to hit and I said, 'No, he have to hit what I throw.' He hit one foul ball that they never could find."

The Big Spring ballpark still stands. Tito showed it off to a visitor in 2015. "I love this park. The guy who used to be my catcher. He died, and they spread his ashes on the field."

Almost 60 years had passed since he left the army and went to work for Cosden in Big Spring. He worked four hours at night for another company and, in his spare time, sold Studio Girl Perfume. "I had three jobs, and Wanda had two shifts at the hospital."

They had a growing family to support. A second daughter, Viena, was born in 1957, and a son, Bill, in 1958.

Tito also had five older brothers and two sisters he wanted to get out of Cuba after Fidel Castro assumed power in 1959.

One brother, Carlos, escaped in 1961, with his 14-year-old son, Carlos Jr. They were among six Cubans rescued by the U.S. Coast Guard after their sailboat sank in the Gulf of Mexico near Brownsville, Texas. Carlos landed a job in a handbag factory in Miami, Florida.

Another brother, Erasmas Raul, came to the United States via Spain. At one time, Raul was a lieutenant in the Cuban army and head of the palace guard in Havana.

A sister, Celida, was unable to leave Cuba until the early 1970s. "She was the last to get out because her husband belonged to the union and it was controlled by the Communist Party," Tito said. "So they wouldn't let them go."

Tito paused to reflect on his proudest achievement. "I brought 37 members of my family from Cuba. I think that's a record."

As Tommy Hart of the *Big Spring Herald* observed, Tito is "repaying, in part, a nation that has been so good to him."[39]

It all started with Stasey bringing Cubans to play baseball in Big Spring. It not only helped Minor League Baseball hang on a little longer, but also transformed and even saved the lives of hundreds of Cuban players and their families. That's a legacy to be remembered and celebrated.

* * *

Across the road from the baseball field, there's a farmhouse. Kevin Costner is nowhere to be found. Instead of tall stalks of corn beyond the right-field fence, there's 1,204-foot Chalk Mountain, white from the chalky rock that inspired its name. The surrounding area is teeming with rattlesnakes, copperheads, and creatures ranging from wild hogs to bobcats to coyotes.

Welcome to Stasey Field, established in 1992, three years after the movie *Field of Dreams* was released. It may not be the original, but it's a real one based on the hopes and aspirations of Pat and his younger brother, Billie Joe, who were born on the land in Erath County, Texas, about 17 miles east of Stephenville.

Billie Joe told folks that Pat had the same inborn fondness for baseball that he had for land. "He loved baseball, but the land held his heart,"

Patricia Stasey Aylor noted in *Stealing Home*, a book about the family's history. "Pat loved the land, but baseball held his heart."[40]

Billie Joe liked to quote architect Daniel Burnham, the father of the skyscraper: "Make no little plans; they have no magic to stir men's blood and probably themselves will not be realized. Make big plans; aim high in hope and work."[41]

Billie Joe achieved his goal of owning 1,100 acres and 100 mama cows. In so doing, he preserved a ranch that has been in the family for 100 years and is now the site of Stasey family reunions the second weekend in June.

For these events, red, white, and blue bunting adorns the backstop and chain-link outfield fence. Three flags wave in center field—the U.S. and Texas state banners and one honoring Confederate ancestors who came to Texas after the Civil War. Wood replicas of jerseys worn by Pat and Billie Joe decorate the right-field fence.

There are two tin-roofed dugouts and a press box with a scoreboard where numbers are hung from two nails on a wooden board.

"I remember driving up to the field and being in awe of the field and thinking how cool it was to cut a ball diamond out of a cow pasture for this event," said Jeff Smith, public address announcer for athletic events at Texas Christian University who has been the voice of reunion softball games since 2002. "I've called at least 25 home runs and set off the cannon shots after each one."[42]

The national anthem is sung before the game between Pat's Slammers and B. J.'s Bombers, followed by "Take Me Out to the Ball Game" during the fifth-inning stretch. There are no strikeouts. Kids' runs count, but their outs don't.

"We developed a code where we could contact one another after death," Billie Joe said in 2012. "He got in touch with me and said, 'They still have baseball up here. They have diamonds and everything just like we read about in the Bible.'"[43]

Several years after Pat's death, a piece of paper was found stuck in the crack of a drawer in his old desk. It was a quote by an American statesman, Dean Alfange, titled "My Creed" and first published in *Reader's Digest* in 1952.

> I do not choose to be a common man—
> it is my right to be uncommon if I can.
> I seek opportunity—not security . . . .

> I prefer the challenge of life to the guaranteed existence,
> the thrill of fulfilment to the State calm of Utopia. [44]

Pat and many of his Cuban players followed this creed. They chose opportunity over security, challenges instead of guarantees, freedom above all else.

The climax of every Stasey reunion is a Texas-sized fireworks show. The field goes dark except for the flagpoles, illuminated by spotlights, and a string of lights reading "Stasey" and the phrase "WHATEVER IT TAKES" in capital letters.

And then the sky lights up with fireworks as dramatic as any Fourth of July celebration. Music plays over the loudspeakers, culminating with country music singer Lee Greenwood proclaiming, "I'm proud to be an American where at least I know I'm free."

The words soar with the fireworks and spark images of Pat and his Cuban players walking onto the field as the final blast turns the sky into a sea of swirling color. It's dazzling stuff, the kind that makes great movies.

7

THE BOBO AND JOJO SHOW

Bobo Newsom and Joe Engel

By the time Louis Norman "Bobo" Newsom got to Chattanooga in 1949, he boasted of 305 victories under his sizable belt, 205 of them in the majors, the most of any active pitcher. He had already played for 18 teams, nine in the big leagues. He could sing "I've Been Everywhere" long before it became a country music classic.

Newsom called himself and everyone else Bobo or Bo for short. When you've traveled so many places, it's hard to know who's who.

He insisted that he was born in 1909, not 1907, as listed in most baseball books. "The Newsom family Bible will prove that."[1]

Early in his career when he answered to his boyhood nickname, Buck, one writer said he looked like a cross between actor Gary Cooper and a well-scrubbed pirate. By 1949, however, Bobo could pass as a double for Joe Engel, portly owner of the Chattanooga Lookouts, a Class AA minor-league team that played in the Southern Association and had a working agreement with the Washington Senators.

Bobo still bragged about fogging hitters with his fastball, but he caused more fog with a tantalizing blooper pitch that appeared to come out of heaven to make the hitter look like hell. The ball climbed as high as 15 feet and then dropped across the plate, batters flailing at it and missing badly.

From 1938 to 1940, when he was at the top of his game, posting 20 or more victories three-straight years, he both comforted and confused his managers by telling them variations of, "Don't worry, be happy, Bobo will win 20 games for you."

Bobo was bodacious, brash, blustery, and bombastic. Nobody talked a better game. That's how he became the only non-Hall of Famer to make it into Ogden Nash's classic ode to baseball immortals, *Lineup for Yesterday*:

N is for Newsom,
Bobo's favorite kin.
You ask how he's here,
He talked himself in. [2]

No one was listening to Bobo in 1949, the year *Sport* magazine published Nash's poem, not even Clark Griffith, the Washington Senators owner who, according to *Washington Post* columnist Shirley Povich, was an "incurable Buck Newsom fan." [3]

Four times Griffith acquired Bobo, each time dealing him away. In 1949, Bobo wanted Griffith to sign him again, so he could claim five terms in the U.S. capital, one more than President Franklin D. Roosevelt.

Three years earlier, in 1946, after posting a 14-13 record, Bobo predicted, "Two fifty by fifty." This was his five-year plan to have 250 big-league victories by the end of 1950. [4]

He made it to 205 in 1947, by winning 11 games—four for the seventh-place Senators and seven for the pennant-winning Yankees, who also won the World Series.

Bobo moved across town in 1948, to the New York Giants. "Relax, chum," he wired Giants manager Mel Ott. "Old Bobo will straighten everything out." [5]

Old Bobo was winless in four decisions when Ott cut him loose. He remained in New York City, working out with the Giants and Yankees when they were in town. When he didn't get any nibbles, he went home to Hartsville, South Carolina, to pitch for a local semipro team. In a key playoff game, Bobo was hammered and humiliated in front of some 5,000 fans.

Bobo's future was bleak until he got a letter in early 1949, from Griffith, inviting him to Orlando, Florida, for a visit during spring training. The Senators had already snubbed Bobo for a coaching job and rejected his request to work out with them. If he couldn't sweet-talk his way onto the field, he'd sit in the grandstand of Tinker Field, the Senators' ballpark. That's where he was the afternoon Engel was watching the Senators with some friends and mentioned the Lookouts were desperate for pitchers.

"Why don't you talk to Bobo Newsom?" one of them said.

Engel walked over to where Bobo was sitting in the stands and asked about the condition of his right throwing arm. "My arm is never out of shape," Bobo crowed, offering to put on a Lookouts uniform and mow down the Senators in an exhibition the next day.[6]

Engel liked the idea.

The Lookouts didn't have a uniform large enough for Bobo's 6-foot-3, 230-something-pound frame so he wore a Senators uniform. "This is not one of Engel's gags, as far as can be learned," *Chattanooga Times* sports editor Wirt Gammon assured readers.[7]

Engel was referred to as the P. T. Barnum of the Bushes. In 1931, he sent a 17-year-old girl pitcher to the mound in an exhibition game to face legendary New York Yankees sluggers Babe Ruth and Lou Gehrig. "She couldn't pitch hay to a cow," Engel admitted, "but both of 'em let her strike 'em out."[8]

No stunt was too preposterous for Engel.

He staged elephant hunts, jackrabbit races, and circus parades; placed 50 cages of singing canaries in the stands because the "team wasn't making enough noise to keep the customers awake"; and traded a smart aleck shortstop for a 25-pound turkey that he roasted and served to local sportswriters—his own way of giving them the bird.[9]

Bobo's appearance for the Lookouts had all the makings of a gag. Engel entered the ballpark in a motor cavalcade escorted by police with sirens blaring. He stepped out of his car at home plate onto a carpet rolled out by his chauffeur.

Bobo was scheduled to pitch three innings. It didn't look like he'd make it past the first as the Senators roughed him up for three runs on four hits. His old pals didn't get another hit, swinging in vain at blooper pitches that had them baffled and Bobo beaming. He had so much fun he stayed on an extra inning.

Engel immediately offered Bobo a Lookouts contract and said he'd pitch Opening Day. But Bobo continued to shop around for a spot on a big-league roster. "In his mind he still is a major leaguer," Gammon wrote. "In his arm, he is almost one."[10]

Eighteen days passed before Bobo accepted Engel's offer. "I was able to land Bobo, who should be a winning pitcher in the Southern, because of his love for me," Joe jested. [11]

Bobo once was the highest-paid pitcher in baseball, making approximately $45,000 after posting a 21-5 record and winning two games in the 1940 World Series for the Detroit Tigers. Engel never revealed what he gave Bobo, but it was estimated to be twice the big-league minimum of $5,000, with Washington's Griffith covering half.

Upon Bobo's arrival in Chattanooga, Engel had him try on the biggest Lookouts uniform available. It was too small. "Bobo's too big for his britches," one photo caption read. [12]

Bobo offered another explanation as to why the uniform didn't fit. "It hurts here," he said to a baseball writer, drawing his hand across his chest. "This is where it should say W-A-S-H-I-N-G-T-O-N instead of Chattanooga." [13]

Bobo played in the Southern Association on his way up to the big leagues, and now, on his way down, the league was considered by some a "way station to baseball oblivion." [14]

The stage was set for "The Bobo and Jojo Show"—the two greatest showmen in baseball combining their talents and egos to spread joy and laughter throughout the land.

"It seems to be one of those coy tricks of fate that Bobo Newsom should wind up with Joe Engel at Chattanooga," observed Whitney Martin, a wire service correspondent. "Together, the two should make a rainbow look like a fog over a prairie. Instead of the Chattanooga Lookouts, it should be Chattanooga, look out!" [15]

The Lookouts were his 19th team since he turned pro in 1928, his 23rd move in 21 years. He had piled up a slew of nicknames along the way: Baseball's Traveling Man; Baseball's No. 1 Rover Boy; the Original Rambling Rose of Baseball; the Wandering Minstrel of Baseball; Marco Polo of the Majors; Nomad of the Diamond; Road Map; and Bobo the Hobo.

He was the perfect guy for Engel, a "superb showman with a natural flair for the spectacular." [16]

Prior to buying the Lookouts in 1929, Engel pitched and then scouted for the Senators, his prized discoveries being two future Hall of Famers— Joe Cronin and Stanley "Bucky" Harris. During several offseasons, he

Bobo Newsom joined the minor-league Chattanooga Lookouts in 1949, so he could entice one of his nine former employers in the majors to give him another chance. The Lookouts were Bobo's 19th pro team in 21 years, earning him a spot in baseball's "Haul of Fame" and nicknames ranging from "Baseball's Traveling Man" to "Bobo the Hobo." *Courtesy of the Chattanooga Public Library and University of Tennessee at Chattanooga.*

costarred with two Washington clowns, Nick Altrock and Al Schacht, in a vaudeville act titled, "Punch Drunk with Joe Engel."

"I always try to look on the light side of things, and I live every day just as if it were New Year's Eve," Engel said. [17]

During the Great Depression in 1936, Engel gave away a fully furnished house and garage complete with a Lincoln Zephyr. A crowd of 24,639 packed 12,000-seat Engel Stadium, spilling over into the outfield. A grocery clerk making $12 a week won the drawing.

Opening Days produced the best (and worst) stunts. For one, a stuffed ostrich laid an egg at second base, followed by a stuffed duck, which left one twice as big. Another time, eight brass bands and a circus marched into the ballpark with city officials riding camels and elephants at the front of the parade.

For the Lookouts' home opener in 1949, Bobo hid away in Jojo's private box on the roof of Engel Stadium. He was still waiting for his special-order, size 52 uniform to arrive. Jojo also wanted to hold him out two days and attract more fans to an Easter Sunday doubleheader.

A crowd of 8,071 turned out to see Bobo in his new uniform. The pants were too large, so he put on an old pair and pitched despite a swollen right ankle he sprained shagging fly balls during practice the previous day. His ankle was iced down between each of the four innings he pitched, but he couldn't cool off the other team, allowing six hits, including two homers and five runs, to lose, 7-1.

Asked why he pitched on a bum ankle against the team doctor's advice, Bobo said, "They've advertised that Ol' Bobo is going to pitch, and it wouldn't be right for me to let the fans down." [18]

Lookout fans had to wait two weeks to see Bobo again. Even then they struggled to find him in the heavy fog that shrouded the field and forced the game to be called off in the bottom of the sixth inning. Bobo often gloated about fogging hitters with his fastball, so it was only fitting that his first victory for the Lookouts was in the first game ever to be fogged out in Chattanooga.

"The misty stuff was rolling off of the roof of the right wing of the grandstand, as if Joe Engel were pouring it into the park with a fog machine," the *Chattanooga Times* reported. [19]

It was so foggy that Bobo called center fielder Earl "Junior" Wooten to the pitcher's mound for a meeting, possibly to confirm he was on the field. Bobo couldn't see the 5-foot-11, 160-pound Junior, who he once described as a "skinny little nut-brown half pint."[20]

Bobo and Junior were both from small South Carolina towns and good friends off the field. They needled one another every chance they got.

"When does the blimp go up?" Junior asked. "I want to get a ticket."

"If they charged by weight, you couldn't even get on board," Bobo countered.[21]

Bobo owned an old Cadillac that Junior loved to drive. After home night games, they cruised around downtown Chattanooga, Junior at the wheel, wearing a chauffeur-like cap, and Bobo sitting in the back seat, where he could easily access cold beer in a built-in refrigerator.

Bobo didn't need Mother Nature after his fog-aided win. He won four of his next five decisions to take a 5-2 record into June. Win or lose, he was the consummate "apostle of color."[22]

After watching Bobo beat the New Orleans Pelicans for his second victory, the *Times'* Gammon praised him as an "artist on the mound, with his wide variety of stuff, soft and hard."[23]

In another win over the Pelicans in New Orleans, Bobo repeatedly questioned the judgment of the home plate umpire. When he walked to the plate to bat, "he tipped his hat and bowed several times as half the crowd booed and half cheered."[24]

In Memphis, he argued with the umps, clowned with the fans, and beat the Chicks with his arm and bat, belting a home run and double.

Bobo was cruising to his sixth victory in Little Rock when the Travelers knocked him out of the game and into the locker room showers. He was dressed in street clothes and sitting in the dugout in the bottom of the ninth when Lookouts manager George Myatt got ejected for protesting a balk call. Upon hearing unkind remarks from Bobo, the umpire wheeled around and shouted, "You, too, Newsom, you (censored)."[25]

Bobo stormed onto the field, in civvies, to go chin-to-chin with his antagonist. It took five players to hold him back. Bobo was fined $50 and suspended five days. He looked on the bright side: "I need five days' rest."[26]

Newsom returned to action with an iron-man performance against the Birmingham Barons at Birmingham's Rickwood Field. He started both games of a doubleheader, something he'd done several times in his career. Bobo lost the seven-inning opener, 3-2, on a walk-off home run by the opposing pitcher. The second game was tied at four-all in the top of the seventh when he hurt himself running out a double.

Bobo thrived on physical abuse. Ignoring a doctor's orders to stay off a broken toe for at least 10 days, he pitched and won two complete games during that time, including a nifty three-hitter. With eight wins, he was tied for the league lead.

Bobo lost three-straight games as the Lookouts managed a grand total of three runs. They scored only five times in his next two starts, but it was enough for Bobo to win both. He blew a five-run lead in a loss to Memphis to go into the Southern Association All-Star Game with a 10-7 record.

Bobo was the only Lookout selected to play in the All-Star Game. This convinced the *Times'* Gammon that Bobo deserved another chance in the majors. "The fellows like him, he's been helpful to all, and has been bearing down with all he has. A comedown to the minors is a humbling thing, but it has done many a man good who has tried the harder to go back."[27]

Bobo's accomplishments were even more impressive considering his injuries and the ineptness of the Lookouts, who were last in hitting and fielding, and next to last (seventh) in the standings with a 35-53 record.

On May 26, Engel announced, "I'm leaving town. So are a lot of other fellows."[28]

On June 9, he changed managers, replacing Myatt with Fred Walters.

"Not one player on his team has lived up to expectations fully," Gammon wrote, later acknowledging that Bobo was an exception.[29]

Engel signed Bobo and other big-league veterans, hoping they would win a pennant to mark the team's 20th anniversary under his leadership. Instead, Engel had to settle for a special day in his honor. A crowd of 4,638 turned out on Sunday, July 3, for Joe Engel Day. They clapped, yelled, and sang when the band played "For He's a Jolly Good Fellow."

The fans almost rendered Engel speechless with a new Oldsmobile station wagon filled with gifts ranging from a fishing rod to clothing to cases of food. "I just don't know what to say, for once in my life," Joe confessed.[30]

The Lookouts lost both games of the doubleheader, a *Chattanooga Times* headline summing it up best: "FANS HONOR ENGEL WITH AUTO; TEAM HUMILIATES HIM."[31]

No one would've blamed Engel for swapping the station wagon for a home run hitter, but at his wife's request, he exchanged it for a sedan. Engel kept the handkerchiefs he received. He was going to need them to wipe away the tears the rest of the season.

* * *

The second act of "The Bobo and Jojo Show" began with the Southern Association All-Star Game in Nashville, Tennessee, on July 12, 1949. The event matched the first-place Nashville Vols against the best players from the other seven teams in the league. The All-Stars were leading, 18-6, when Bobo took the mound in the bottom of the ninth inning.

The first batter walked, and the next singled. Coming up were Babe Barna and Carl Sawatski, the league's top two home run hitters, and Bob Borkowski, the eventual league batting champ.

Memphis Commercial-Appeal columnist Walter Stewart elevated his prose to match Bobo's blooper pitch:

> He threw Mr. Barna an eephus (gopher or bloop) pitch, and Mr. Barna, cutting with all the intensity of 235 pounds of vibrant muscle, raised an infield fly little taller than the Newsom delivery. Mr. Sawatski swung from his grandfather's heels and missed the ball so severely that it was almost necessary to call time while the Nashville catcher untied the knot which had formed in his gizzard.

Sawatski called for another blooper, and Bobo obliged. "Mr. Sawatski bashed at it with the elfin grace of a mule falling down three flights of stairs. The ball's upper epidermis was hardly ruffled when Mr. Newsom picked it up and lobbed to first base."[32]

Borkowski popped out on a blooper pitch to end the inning.

In a game featuring 24 runs (nine in a single inning), 34 hits (including four homers), 5 hits by one player (three of them doubles), and 4 other records, Bobo stole the show with his blooper pitch. "Ol' Bobo left them laughing," Stewart concluded, "but pretty unhappy."[33]

Bobo wasn't happy either. "There's no future for me in the minors," he said after the game. "I think I've done everything asked of me so far in Chattanooga, but unless I can go back up I am through."[34]

The last straw was when the Senators spurned Bobo for Allen Gettel, a Chicago White Sox pitcher with two wins for the season. Bobo read about the $10,000 deal in the paper the morning after the All-Star Game.

He called Engel to question how hard he was trying to help him get back to the majors. "Engel said he contacted all the big clubs and that they didn't want me," Bobo lamented.

Bobo couldn't believe that, so Engel told him to find out for himself. The first team he contacted expressed interest. "I called Engel back and accused him of not making the try," said Bobo. "He hung up on me. Hung up on me in my face."[35]

Engel explained later that he wasn't contractually obligated to let Bobo go to the majors. "It's just a gentleman's agreement," said Engel. "The question is whether I'm a gentleman."[36]

Bobo still showed up at Chattanooga's train station the evening of July 13, to say goodbye to his Lookouts teammates before they departed for their next series in Little Rock. Several of the players tried to get Bobo to board the train. The train left without him. "We thought the Chattanooga club would walk out on Bobo first," one wag wisecracked.[37]

"Of all the screwy things to pull," Engel said. "I thought I was nutty. That Newsom's nuttier than me."[38]

Engel suspended Bobo without pay for the season. "This is a case of ole Bobo facing ole Jo-Jo, and this time Jo-Jo has the winning hand."[39]

The entire thing smacked of another Engel publicity stunt or a ploy by Bobo for more money, with one exception—Griffith. He was a father figure to Bobo, who named his only son Allan Griffith. Bobo was stunned when Griffith vowed, "He'll never wear a Washington uniform again."[40]

For all their stubborn pride, Bobo and Jojo were showmen to the core and knew the show must go on. "I'm sorry it all happened," Bobo said. "Engel's a wonderful fellow and more power to him."[41]

Engel reduced Bobo's suspension to 10 days, ending just in time for him to pitch against the league-leading Nashville Vols at Engel Stadium. Bobo held the mighty Vols to seven hits to win, 4-2.

Four days later, he tossed another seven-hitter to beat the Atlanta Crackers by the same score. He struck out 17 batters in the two games combined, walking only one. "I had to con him a bit," Engel claimed later.

He told Bobo there were eight big-league scouts in the stands, but they were doubtful he could go the distance. "Gimme that ball and I'll show 'em," Bobo said.[42]

Bobo made it three-straight by edging Mobile, 5-4, then he gave up nine runs, six earned, to New Orleans in an 18-7 loss.

Most managers found Bobo a headache bigger than his ego, but Walters and his predecessor, Myatt, were among his biggest fans. "He has a great competitive heart," Walters said. "He'd pitch every day if I asked him to."[43]

Going into a doubleheader against Little Rock on August 9, the Lookouts pitching staff was in tatters from injuries and overwork. Bobo typically rested three days between starts. Since he was scheduled to pitch one of the games against the Travelers, Walters asked if he'd try the ironman role again. Bobo agreed.

He had to overcome five errors to win the seven-inning opener, 10-6. After showering and putting on a fresh uniform, he returned to the mound to pitch nine more innings and win again, 9-6.

Altogether, Bobo pitched 16 innings spanning four hours in muggy, 90-degree weather to improve his record to 15-8. "It was an unheard-of feat for a man of more than 40 years of age," Russ Walker wrote in the *Chattanooga Times*.

"Get yourself the best suit of clothes in town and charge it to me," Engel announced to Bobo over the public address system at Engel Stadium immediately after the second game.[44]

Bobo declined the offer. "I pitched and won that doubleheader for the fans of Chattanooga and the ballclub, not for ol' Jojo."[45]

Amazingly, Bobo pitched $10\frac{2}{3}$ innings in his next start against the Memphis Chicks. The game was tied, 2-2, in the top of the 11th when the Chicks scored four runs after usually sure-handed shortstop Willy Miranda bobbled a potential inning-ending grounder. A disgusted Bobo stormed toward the home plate umpire, tore off his cap, bowed, and said thanks before flinging his glove into the dugout. He was ejected, fined $25, and suspended for three days—his third suspension of the season and second for run-ins with umpires.

Bobo's mouth was as tireless as his arm. Whether on the bench or the field, he was constantly harassing opposing players or disputing ball and strike calls. "It's more a filibuster than a ballgame," one writer observed. "He throws and dares the ump to call it a ball. . . . He fumes, he fusses. He frets. Fans love it."[46]

Prior to a game in Chattanooga, Bobo was hitting fly balls to the outfield while jawing with Little Rock catcher Marland "Duke" Doolittle. "I could hit you any time you stepped on the mound, even when you were young," Duke shouted.

They faced one another later in the season in Little Rock, and Bobo buried a fastball in the middle of Duke's back. When it was Bobo's turn to bat, he looked at Duke crouched behind the plate and said, "See, ol' Bobo can hit you, too."

He was center stage at Engel Stadium in late August for Bobo Newsom Day. The plan initially was for Bobo to play the iron-man role. But he had pitched eight-plus innings two days earlier and Walters decided to use him only in the second game of the doubleheader against Birmingham.

A crowd of 5,215 showed up to honor Bobo and hear him introduced in the pregame ceremony as 39-year-old Louis Norman Newsom. He took over the microphone and thanked Engel, "who gave me a little rest a few weeks ago."[47]

He thanked his teammates and Chattanooga fans, saying he would always remember them "whether I'm back next year or not."[48]

Bobo had a two-hitter and a 2-1 lead entering the seventh and last inning. He walked a batter that he thought should've been called out on strikes. Visibly upset, he allowed a homer and three singles before the inning ended with the Barons ahead, 4-2. As he walked off the field, he had a few choice words for the plate umpire, who, in turn, made Bobo's day even more special by kicking him out of the game.

Bobo was all about Bobo—most of the time. He had a ready explanation for that. "We once had a band in Hartsville, South Carolina, my hometown. We found we had only 13 pieces, so we got a boy just to hold a horn, so it wouldn't be bad luck. But the boy never made a dollar. Why? He never did toot his own horn."[49]

Junior Wooten never tooted his horn, so Bobo did it for him. He went directly to Gammon's office at the *Times* to propose the last day of the season be made Junior Wooten Day. "He deserves it more than I did," Bobo said.[50]

Two days later, Engel announced the popular Junior would have his own day. "It's been worth the price of admission just to watch him play center field," one fan said.[51]

The day before Wooten Day, at 3:15 in the morning, Bobo stopped to pick up a hitchhiker. As he leaned over to open the car door, he was attacked by two other boys in a surprise ambush. One of them demanded his money and car before they were frightened away by an approaching truck and car. "There was nothing to it," Bobo said. "I didn't lose a thing."[52]

Junior was honored before the doubleheader against Nashville, and the Little Lookouts, champions of a local boy's league, were recognized between games. The crowd was still buzzing over Bobo's hitchhiker escapade, which made the front page of the *Chattanooga News-Free Press*. Engel used this as a teaching moment for the Little Lookouts: "There is just one piece of advice I want to give you boys. Never pick up a hitchhiker at three o'clock in the morning."[53]

Bobo took the mound in the second game like nothing had happened.

The Vols' Carl Sawatski was itching for another shot at Bobo's blooper pitch. He had a league-leading 45 homers and was eager to add more. Sawatski poked a single in his first at-bat and, then, grounded out on the next one. Third time up, he caught a blooper pitch with his bare left hand, flipped the ball in the air, and slammed it into deep right field, turned, and headed for the dugout as the plate umpire called him out. He went to bat a fourth time, expecting more bloopers. Instead, Bobo fired three straight fastballs, striking him out.

Bobo beat the first-place Vols, 3-1, to finish the season with a 17-12 record. "With any luck, he'd have won 25," Engel said.[54]

He had a league-high 141 strikeouts; pitched 237 innings, third most in the league; and was primarily responsible for the Lookouts setting an all-time Southern Association attendance record for a last-place team—155,468.

Chattanooga fans showered Junior with a truckload of gifts that wound up being going-away presents. On the day he was feted, Junior was sold to the Kansas City Blues, a Yankees farm club.

Bobo was still waiting for a big-league team to call.

* * *

In early 1950, millions of Americans were doing the boogie-woogie to the foot-tapping beat of Red Foley singing "Chattanoogie Shoeshine Boy," also known as "Chattanooga Shoeshine Boy."

The song was number one on the music charts when Bobo got a contract from Engel for $100 a month. "Who does he think I am," bellowed Bobo, "the Chattanoogie shoeshine boy?"

"Sure, I offered him just $100," Jojo snickered. "Why not? He would turn down the first contract anyway."[55]

Bobo and Jojo began their mating dance in early February with a series of staged photos spread across eight columns of a page in the *Chattanooga Times*. One of the four shots had Engel pushing a contract and pen toward Bobo, who was fending them off with a hand while looking away.

The fake holdout was the opening bell for the third act of "The Bobo and Jojo Show."

"When I sign him," Engel said, "I'm going to have my picture taken with my pockets sticking out empty and Bobo walking off with my wife, or maybe Bo and me hugging each other."

"Plain to see, the thing to look for here is fun, not trouble," Gammon wrote. "The two are like kids with an electric train."[56]

Joe Engel, left, and Bobo Newsom hammed it up for a series of publicity photos showing them haggling over Bobo's contract for the 1950 season. Here, Bobo refused to sign, saying, "Not for me, Jojo." Engel once offered Bobo $100 a month. "Why not?" he asked. "He would turn down the first contract anyway." *Courtesy of the Chattanooga Public Library and University of Tennessee at Chattanooga.*

Bobo spent most of the spring working out with the Senators in Orlando, making sure visiting managers could see that he was a slimmed-down 220 pounds.

Bucky Harris was in the first year of his third stint as manager of the Senators, a last-place team that had lost 104 games the year before. Harris had so many troubles he saw no reason to add another one in Newsom.

Bobo pestered Griffith, who nagged Harris until he agreed to let him pitch for the Lookouts against the Senators in an exhibition game near the end of spring training. This was Bobo's chance to prove he should be pitching for the Senators instead of against them. He was bombed, allowing five runs on five hits in three innings. He also walked four, leading to speculation that "he was pitching with one eye on the batter and one eye watching Clark Griffith's reactions."[57]

Bobo finally signed a Lookouts contract. "Why that penny-pinching Engel," he said, "he couldn't do without me."[58]

Bobo's signing called for another publicity photo, one that captured their friendship and common goal to entertain. The result was a shot of Bobo and Jojo in bed (500 pounds of weight combined), Jojo pretending to wake up a slumbering Bobo. "KITCHY-KITCHY-KOO," the caption heading read.

"Engel and Newsom make an ideal pair," *News-Free Press* sports editor E. T. Bales wrote in the accompanying story. "Bobo's flare for publicity fits perfectly into Engel's scheme of things, and in addition to all this, both are good actors." [59]

The photo of Bobo and Jojo side by side in bed prompted columnist Fred Russell of the *Nashville Banner* to suggest that Bobo preferred the small bed over the narrow confines of Sulphur Dell, content to "rest on his laurels" from the 1949 Southern Association All-Star Game, when Nashville sluggers swung wildly at the bloopers he threw the one inning he pitched. [60]

The Lookouts opened the 1950 season against the Vols, beginning with a three-game series in Nashville, followed by games in Chattanooga. Opening Day was custom-made for Bobo because the crowd was usually big and boisterous, just like him. But he wanted no part of Sulphur Dell, opting instead to pitch the Lookouts' first game in Chattanooga.

Bobo called Sulphur Dell a "drained-out bathtub."

Most pitchers shared his disdain for the Dell, a sulfur spring and a picnic spot in pioneer days. The right-field fence, topped by a 30-foot screen, was only 262 feet from home plate. "When a guy walks into this telephone booth of a park," Bobo complained, "it's so small he starts to look for a nickel to put in a pay telephone."[61]

He was one strike away from pitching a scoreless 10th inning in relief when a left-handed batter lofted a pitch he was fooled on over the right-field screen for a game-winning homer. "Not until yesterday did I know the great Newsom could be struck speechless by anything," Russell wrote. "He grabbed his jacket and continued to the clubhouse without opening his mouth."[62]

Bobo rebounded four days later at Engel Field. He arranged for an electric cooling box to be installed in each clubhouse and stocked them with a new soft drink he was promoting. Free drinks for every player and as much as they wanted to drink, compliments of Bobo. On the field, he pitched six innings to beat the Vols despite a blister between his index finger and thumb on his throwing hand.

Bobo relished being the center of attention, but going into New Orleans for a series against the Pelicans, an 18-year-old pitcher named Paul Pettit was the talk of the town.

Bobo was well-versed on the record $100,000 bonus Pettit received to sign with the Pittsburgh Pirates two months earlier. That was as much money as Joe DiMaggio was making. Pettit was untried, unproven, still to throw his first pitch in a professional game that counted in the standings.

When the Pelicans announced Pettit would make his pro debut in the opener of a Sunday doubleheader, Bobo insisted on pitching against him. A crowd of 10,832 jammed Pelican Stadium, flowing onto the outer edges of the field.

"Most of this crowd has turned out to see me," Bobo teased Pettit before the game. "You know it was in my contract that I'd pitch any time we met the Pels and you pitched. I do my best before a crowd. And I feel at ease pitching against $100,000 stuff."[63]

"I vaguely knew that he had pitched in the big leagues," Pettit recalled. "As I got to be a little more of a student of the game, I realized how much he had done."

One thing he knew for sure was the fans were there to see him, not Bobo. "It was really amazing because we only drew about two or three thousand every night. It was a big moment in my life—something I'll never forget."

Bob Ross hasn't forgotten the Newsom–Pettit showdown either.

Ross had a ringside seat—the Lookouts bench. He was a 21-year-old, left-handed pitcher in the Dodgers organization who the Lookouts had drafted the previous winter hoping he could recover from a sore arm.

He grew up in Fullerton, California, about 30 miles from Lomita, where Pettit pitched six no-hitters and averaged 14 strikeouts a game during his four years at Narbonne High School. Pettit was 15 when they faced one another in a semipro game. "I don't know how the game came out, but if you ever saw a baseball prospect, it was Paul Pettit."

In later years, they lived about 10 minutes from one another and became good friends. "Paul and I talk about it a lot," Ross said of his pro debut.

"Paul is the youngest guy in the league; Bobo is the oldest," Ross continued. "Big matchup. Full ballpark. People standing and sitting in the outfield. They put up ropes to keep them back near the fence so they wouldn't get in the field of play. All you had to do was hit the ball in that crowd; you got a double—a ground-rule double."

The Lookouts jumped on Pettit in the first inning for two runs, but his teammates answered with three off Bobo in the bottom half. Bobo opened the second with an infield single. Pettit walked the next two batters, then gave up a grand-slam homer. The Lookouts didn't score another run until the eighth, but Bobo had what he needed to withstand a three-run rally in the ninth to win, 7-6.

Bobo scattered seven hits in nine innings, striking out seven and walking three. Pettit lasted 7⅔ innings, allowing seven hits and fanning nine. His downfall was 11 walks.

"I was trying to impress everybody that I was a big bonus player and all that stuff, and I went out there and just threw everything as hard as I could throw it," Pettit said. "I was always wild but never that wild. I was just so pumped up. The one thing I remember is I threw 152 pitches that game."

In Bobo's next start, he lost a heartbreaker, 2-1, and then was shelled for five runs in the first inning of another game, a 12-1 blowout that provoked an irate fan to sound off in the *Times*: "If Blow Blow is so darn good, he should be ashamed to allow a hit in this league much less get knocked out in the first."[64]

The one team that made the Lookouts look good was the Little Rock Travelers, losers of 17 straight after Bobo beat them, 7-3, in the first game of a Sunday doubleheader.

The previous day, Engel had attended the Kentucky Derby at Churchill Downs in Louisville, Kentucky, to cheer Hallieboy, a horse named after his wife, Hallie, and bred on their farm before it was sold to a friend. Hallieboy was a 100-to-1 long shot—a "busher among the plutocrats."[65]

The colt collapsed upon arriving at the Downs, exhausted after traveling 1,000 miles in a tiny van from Providence, Rhode Island. "At least, they say he collapsed," cautioned the *Banner*'s Russell. "I have a feeling he was merely practicing sliding into home plate as taught by Joe Engel."[66]

Hallieboy finished 10th in a field of 13—"better than Joe Engel's baseball clubs have for the past two years, for he was four places better than last."[67]

"Didn't expect you back so soon," someone joked upon Engel's appearance at Engel Stadium shortly after the Derby. "Thought you'd stay up there until Hallieboy got in."

"Hallieboy got more publicity than any horse ever entered in the Derby," Engel raved. "Dream horse they called him."[68]

Nothing could dampen Engel's enthusiasm except the Lookouts' nightmarish play. The Lookouts were in seventh place, now looking over their shoulders at the Travelers, who were rebounding from a league record 21-game losing streak.

Since beating the Travelers in early May, Bobo had only one win—a five-hitter to beat Memphis, 4-3. He pitched well in a 4-1 loss to Memphis, then, unthinkable for Bobo, asked to leave a game against Little Rock after five innings, complaining of fatigue.

A Ladies Night crowd of 5,247, including 600 employees of a refrigerator company, turned out to see Bobo face the Atlanta Crackers, the team that had KO'd him in the first inning. Bobo got past the opening frame this time, but not before he surrendered an inside-the-park, grand-slam homer to Ebba St. Claire, a catcher not known for his power or speed.

Bobo left the game in the fourth with no outs and the bases loaded, showered and dressed, and went to the roof of Engel Stadium, where Joe was sitting just outside the press box. As he listened to Bobo bemoan St. Claire's home run, Joe accused Bobo of being in such bad shape that he could beat him in a fight. "If you whip me, it would be the first one you've won in a long time," he goaded.[69]

Those were fighting words. They jumped to their feet to punch it out. "No one actually knows what prevented the two from swapping blows unless it was the ability of each to realize how futile such an act would be if held in privacy," Bales commented in the *News-Free Press*.

The Crackers belted the Lookouts, 12-5. During a postgame ceremony to give away a refrigerator, Engel was jeered. "I know you want to boo me, so give me a good blast. I'm sorry for this lousy game."[70]

Most pitchers run every day to stay in condition. "I ain't no runner; I'm a pitcher," Bobo argued.

Rules and roommates were for other players, not Bobo.

He had a hotel room to himself on the road. Regardless of what time he went to bed after a night of carousing, he'd be up and in the lobby at about six in the morning. "Doesn't that guy ever sleep?" clerks asked.[71]

Bobo coped with the extreme summer heat and humidity of Southern Association cities by consuming copious amounts of beer. "In the Southern, the story was that when you went home, your mother wouldn't recognize you because you lost so much weight," the 160-pound Bob Ross chuckled. "It took me about three or four days to get it back. He'd drink the beer and get the weight back."

Bobo's throwing arm was as resilient as the Michelin Man's. "He had a rubber arm," Paul Pettit said. "He threw kind of sidearm—three-quarters sidearm—and he just had a real natural motion. He looked like he could throw all day."

As Bobo got older, he relied less on the speed of his fastball and more on trickery and the turmoil he created. Ross estimates the velocity of Bobo's fastball was between 85 and 90 miles an hour. "That isn't very much these days; for a guy his age, that was remarkable," he added. "He had tremendous control. He could hit that low, outside corner with his sinking fastball. He threw a slider, or what is called today a cutter. He'd start the ball over the plate and break it out away from the plate four to five inches. He could make 'em reach for that ball a lot."

Bobo often used a windmill windup, lifting his arms up over his head and back down. "He'd do it once, twice, maybe three times," Ross said. "Or maybe he'd shorten it up a little bit. The effect would be sort of a quick pitch to the hitter. He was nobody's fool on the mound."

Engel was no one's fool either. He knew his rooftop tirade would fire up Bobo.

He allowed only 14 runs in his next 6 starts, winning 4 of them to even his record at 8-8. One of the wins was a five-hitter to beat New Orleans, 3-2.

Pettit was nursing a sore left arm injured three weeks earlier so he sat out the Chattanooga series. "I started throwing too soon after I hurt my elbow, and, then, I hurt my shoulder and my shoulder never did get well. I was throwing with both of 'em hurtin.' That was miserable."

Bobo was back on track, but it was Ross, with a 5-3 won–loss mark, who the Senators called up to the majors in mid-June. "I had no business being in the big leagues," he said. "I was 21 years old—just a kid."

Bobo wished Ross well. Al Sima, another Lookouts lefty who was older and more experienced, wasn't so gracious. "Al was pretty pissed," Ross said. "He made no bones about it."

A month later, Ross and Sima traded places. "The thing that struck me about the whole situation was that Bobo was the best pitcher on our team," Ross said. "He should've gone to the big leagues. He never said a word about it."

Bobo didn't bellyache about the Lookouts' feeble hitting either. "You give up three runs, you're beat," Ross said.

Bobo lost four straight, three by the score of 3-2. He was one strike away from blanking Nashville in his first start at dreaded Sulphur Dell when Sawatski drilled a line drive that barely cleared the right-field screen for a game-tying, two-run homer.

It took Bobo two months to win his 10th game. "In justice to Bobo, it should be pointed out that his pitching record (10-15) is a libel," the *Times'* Gammon wrote in early August. [72]

The Lookouts finished last in runs scored (about 3½ per game), home runs (36), and batting average (.249). They had two six-game and three nine-game losing streaks. "It was really hard to win with that team," said Ross, who at 10-10 was the only pitcher to win as many as he lost.

Bobo pitched 235 innings, second in the league; completed 16 of the 34 games he started; and posted a 13-17 won–loss mark. "You can't believe everything you read," he said, claiming he was 15-13. [73]

"Bobo never let facts get in the way of a good story," Ross said.

He did, however, let something get in the way of a highly anticipated rematch with Pettit in the season finale at Engel Stadium.

In a guest column for the *Times*, Bobo criticized teams giving large bonuses to youngsters like Pettit because "it only takes a couple of seconds to make a pitch, but it takes years to make a pitcher, and for a young ballplayer base on balls, home runs, and a few losses can kill his confidence and embarrass him more than anything else."[74]

Without mentioning his name, Bobo had predicted what would happen to Pettit. He won two games in 1950 and only one in two brief flings with the Pirates.

The day before he was scheduled to face Pettit, Bobo left Chattanooga to tend to some business matters he wouldn't discuss. A few days later, he was doing plenty of talking in a three-week trial as a radio broadcaster for the St. Louis Browns. Bobo called Engel and asked to be released from his contract.

"Why, no, I can get good money for you," Engel joshed.

"What? After all the hard work I did for you?" Bobo protested. "Look, you're just small-time down there. I'm either going into the movies, broadcast Major League Baseball, or pitch for some major-league club. I ain't decided which."[75]

* * *

"The Bobo and Jojo Show" was over. Or was it?

Bobo got good reviews in the broadcast booth, but the starting salary of $125 a week was far below what he expected. "When ol' Bobo can't get more than that out of his mouth, he'll go back to his arm," he announced. "It made me a lot more than that, and it ain't got me in trouble yet."[76]

In his annual "State of Bobo" interview with Shirley Povich of the *Washington Post*, Bobo asked, "Man, don't they want to win a pennant?"

Povich went on to report, "If worst comes to worst, Bobo would sign with Chattanooga again."[77]

This was quickly refuted by the Lookouts.

Bobo was saying all the right things about Jojo. He called him "one of the finest men in baseball" and offered to "give over my spot to some kid who is trying to make the grade" so Engel could build a younger team.[78]

Harris was still manager of the Senators. When someone reminded him Newsom was available, he snorted, "Let him remain available."[79]

Harris didn't want Bobo near the pitcher's mound during spring training in 1951, after one of his warm-up tosses in batting practice busted one of the fingers on the throwing hand of Mickey Grasso, the Senators' starting catcher. "Here I go right off and louse up their best catcher with a little old curveball," Bobo said dejectedly.[80]

Engel was under orders from Griffith to play "youngsters who have a chance of becoming major leaguers" rather than "lose again and again with oldsters who are not going anywhere."[81]

In a column datelined April 1, 1951, Povich announced Bobo was going to pitch for the Birmingham Barons because he liked Birmingham people. "You know, funny thing, they like me," Bobo said.[82]

It was no April Fool's Day joke, although it looked like one a week later when the Boston Red Sox belted Bobo for eight hits and nine runs in one inning of an exhibition game. Barons fans took solace in a comment made by Engel: "He reported to us last year weighing 220, but he didn't really start pitching good ball until he got up around 235. That's when his arm got in shape. The rest of his anatomy doesn't matter."[83]

The Barons were Bobo's 20th team. He lost three straight before winning his first game a month into the season. "Ask the scouts who is the best pitcher in the league," *Birmingham News* sports editor Zipp Newman wrote in late June, "and the chorus will be Bobo Newsom. The record shows six and six, but the Barons know it should read 10 and two."[84]

Bobo won seven of his next eight decisions, and 10,796 fans showed up at Rickwood Field on August 11, for a Blooper Ball Birthday Party celebrating his 40-something birthday. He gave up two runs in the first inning, then retired the next 25 Little Rock batters. "Maybe the fans gave Ol' Bobo a lot of nice things tonight, but the Barons didn't," one fan groused after the 2-1 loss. "They gave him one skinny run—and that wasn't enough."[85]

Little Rock staved off the second-place Barons down the stretch to win the pennant. But not even a black cat could save the Travelers in the Southern Association playoff finals.

Of the almost 1,000 games Bobo pitched in 25 years, none was wackier or more symbolic of his colorful personality than the second game of the Barons' best-of-seven series against the Travelers in Little Rock.

As Bobo stepped out of the dugout, a doctor and rabid Little Rock fan jumped out of the stands and stuck a black kitten in his face as a news photographer snapped a picture. The whammy didn't work in the first inning, but in the second the Travelers scored six times to knock Bobo out of the game.

Three women waited by the dugout to shower a disgusted Bobo with scraps of paper he considered unlucky. The doctor rushed toward Bobo, waving the kitten. Bobo retaliated by firing his glove at the cat man. He missed, setting off a frenetic search in the stands to recover it. A Barons fan found the glove and sat on it until it was safe to give back to Bobo. "That cat didn't hex me," Bobo said after the Barons rallied for a 9-8 victory. "But that guy with the cat better not ever let Bobo get his hands on him."[86]

In the fourth game of the series, Newsom tossed a six-hitter to win, 6-1, and give the Barons a playoff sweep. He ended up with 18 wins, two in the playoffs. For the regular season, his 16 victories tied for the league lead. He was tops in innings pitched (237), second in complete games (17), tied for third in strikeouts (132) and shutouts (3), and fourth in earned run average (3.04).

The Barons went on to beat the Houston Buffs, the Texas League champions, for the Dixie Series title. In contrast, the youth movement in Washington resulted in a seventh-place finish for the Senators and eighth, or dead last, for the Lookouts.

"You've been marvelous," Bobo told Birmingham fans just before the Barons released him. "We all love you."[87]

* * *

The question in the spring of 1952 was whether anyone wanted Bobo. No Southern Association team was interested in him. That was fine by Bobo. "I'm tired of the minors," he complained.[88]

The Senators let Bobo pitch batting practice at their spring training facility in Orlando, but Harris was still manager and resisted any temptation to sign him.

Bobo had hitters leaving the batting cage "muttering to themselves and wondering why, on a club that needs pitching, somebody didn't flourish a contract under Newsom's nose."[89]

Harris finally relented, saying, "He'll be a relief pitcher with us."[90]

"This makes my fifth term in Washington so I'm one up on Roosevelt," Bobo said proudly.[91]

He lasted 68 days, pitching only 12⅔ innings in relief and posting a 1-1 mark. "This is hard to take," he said, of the inactivity.[92]

At a time when Bobo needed to know someone cared, an old friend from Philadelphia offered him a job. Philadelphia A's owner Connie Mack once ordered a coach to stay close during a meeting with Bobo so he wouldn't hire him again. Bobo played 2½ years for Mack in the mid-1940s, an eternity for the restless hurler. To the 89-year-old Mack, Bobo was "just a boy at heart." His team was perfect for the storybook ending to Bobo's nomadic baseball career. [93]

The A's had Harry Byrd, a talented pitcher from Darlington, literally down the road in South Carolina from Hartsville, Bobo's hometown. He couldn't throw strikes consistently. "You're bendin' back so far in your motion, Bo, you lose control." [94]

Byrd corrected the flaw and won 15 games to become Rookie of the Year in the American League.

Bobo played the role of senior statesman as much as relief pitcher for the A's in 1952–1953, compiling a 5-4 won–loss record. He pitched 87 innings, the equivalent of a few weeks work in Chattanooga. He didn't start in 1953 until the last day of August, against the Tigers at Detroit's Briggs Stadium.

The heat and humidity were too stifling for a fat, old man to last long. But, lo and behold, there was Bobo huffing and puffing into the fifth inning with a nine-run lead. Errors by his teammates that inning cut the margin to six.

"It was brutally hot out there, uncomfortably sticky even sitting in the dugout," said A's manager Jimmy Dykes. "Along about the seventh inning I thought I'd better inquire about Bobo's condition. I asked him how he felt. 'If you mean am I as fresh now as when I started, I ain't,' he told me. 'But I'm feelin' fine. I'm getting them out, and that's enough for me.'"

Bobo could smell victory—his 200th in the American League, 211th in the majors, and 350th as a pro. He strutted and postured, making a behind-the-back catch of a throw from his catcher and getting Fred Hutchinson, the Tigers' player-manager, to foul out on a blooper pitch. He finished the game, allowing 4 runs, 1 earned, and 11 hits. "My arm doesn't hurt a bit," Bobo boasted after throwing 135 pitches. "I'm ready to pitch again tomorrow." [95]

Wherever Bobo played, he led the league in laughs and sometimes wins, losses, and getting kicked out of games. He said what many people thought and did what they could only imagine. As a showman, he was at his best when teamed with Engel. Together, they blurred the lines between work and play, fantasy and reality, a three-ring circus and baseball.

"Ring Lardner, with all his genius, couldn't have invented Joe Engel," one editorial writer mused after Engel's death in 1969. [96]

Syndicated columnist Bob Considine was fascinated with Bobo and followed his adventures closely. "He has never done anything that dissuaded me from believing that the Almighty, in some antic moment, created him from an old Ring Lardner baseball story. He's Jack Keefe, who knew a guy named Al."[97]

Ring never wrote about Newsom, but in 1957 his son, John, did the quintessential story about Bobo for *True* magazine titled, "The One and Only Bobo."

Baseball has forgotten Bobo and Jojo, although Engel's beloved stadium has made a comeback of sorts.

The Lookouts played their final game at Engel Stadium in 1999, moving to a modern ballpark downtown. In 2004, ownership was transferred to the University of Tennessee at Chattanooga, and in 2009, it was added to the National Register of Historic Places. In 2012, Engel Stadium was

Bobo Newsom, center, liked to boast that he served five terms in Washington, D.C., putting him one up on President Franklin Delano Roosevelt. Bobo was in his fourth term when he and New York Yankees pitcher Allie Reynolds greeted President Harry S. Truman, FDR's successor, prior to the 1947 season opener. *National Park Service, Abbie Rowe, Courtesy of Harry S. Truman Library.*

used as a movie set for the motion picture *42*, the story of Jackie Robinson breaking Organized Baseball's color barrier.

"When Newsom dies," Bucky Harris once said, "they ought to cut off his right arm and place it in the Hall of Fame at Cooperstown."[98]

Bobo's amazing right arm is buried in a family plot at Magnolia Cemetery in Hartsville. A simple marker features a glove, bat, and ball. His birth year is listed as 1907, not 1909, as it was supposedly recorded in the Newsom family Bible.

Bobo died of a liver ailment on December 7, 1962, the same day as J. G. Taylor Spink, the publisher of *Sporting News*. In a 1945 editorial, Spink correctly observed that Newsom represented an era: "He is a member of a picturesque, if picaresque, tribe which is becoming only a faint memory and soon to be reduced to nothing more than a hazy legend . . . of color on the diamond."[99]

Only in Hartsville is that legend preserved.

On Fifth Street downtown, there's a mural featuring a large black-and-white photo of Bobo shaking hands with President Harry S. Truman, who had just thrown out the ceremonial first pitch to open the Senators' 1947 season. After the picture was taken, reporters wanted Bobo to tell them what President Truman said. He quoted himself instead: "I told the president that he had a mighty good blooper pitch."[100]

The same photo is part of an exhibit at the Hartsville Museum across the street in an old post office building. There are pictures, baseballs, bats, trophies, and Newsom baseball cards in a showcase. The centerpiece is a baseball-shaped time line covering the highlights of Bobo's baseball journey, which spanned four decades.

On the south edge of town, there's a 10-mile stretch of South Carolina State Highway 151 that's named Bobo Newsom Highway and runs past his boyhood home. The ultimate tribute to a swaggering, slick-talking nonconformist like Bobo Newsom is not a cookie-cutter bronze Hall of Fame plaque, but a highway that carries his name and symbolizes his legacy as baseball's rambling man.

8

"A BOY NAMED KINGSTON"

Al Pinkston

The players in the gray traveling uniforms worn by the Philadelphia Athletics the year before were strangers to the sportswriters at Connie Mack Field in West Palm Beach, Florida.

"Do you know any of these guys by sight?" one asked. "They all look to me like guys from Kansas City."[1]

That made sense because the Athletics had just moved to Kansas City, and it was the first week of 1955 spring training camp for the Kansas City Athletics under a new manager, Lou Boudreau. He was sitting on a bench alongside one of the dugouts, chatting with Red Smith, a renowned sports columnist.

"See that big fellow over there? A boy named Kingston. Moves pretty well, swings that bat pretty well, reminds you a little of Luke Easter."[2]

That was tall praise, as Easter was a fence-busting sensation for the Cleveland Indians in the early 1950s.

The problem is that the name wasn't Kingston, as Smith dutifully reported. It was Pinkston. And his first name was Al, a detail left out of the story carried by newspapers throughout the United States. Boudreau's comment about a "boy named Kingston" defines the career of Al Pinkston, the greatest hitter no one ever heard of.

Pinkston spent his entire career in either the Negro Leagues or the minors. He won a record-tying six minor-league batting titles and was runner-up four times. His career batting average of .352 ranks eighth all-time in the minors.

Altogether, Pinkston played 15 years in Organized Baseball—8 in the United States and Canada, and 7 in Mexico. He was widely known as "Pinky," and in Mexico he also was called "El Gigante" (The Giant) and "El Monstruo" (The Monster). He was inducted into the Mexican Baseball Hall of Fame in 1974.

Standing 6-foot-5 and weighing anywhere from 230 to 250 pounds, Pinkston could've easily passed for a visitor from another planet.

"He had an unusual body," said Clyde Kluttz, who managed Pinkston at Savannah, Georgia, in 1954, when he won the South Atlantic (Sally) League batting championship with a .360 average. "His legs looked 10 feet long."

By comparison, he had a small, stubby upper torso—a mass of muscles atop two stilts.

Pinkston was the biggest guy in the A's camp and the center of attention from the first day of spring training, when he blasted a monstrous shot over the center-field fence during batting practice. At one point, Pinkston pounded nine balls over the right-field fence, 330 feet away from home plate.

"Boudreau was pitching batting practice," Pinkston said. "He asked me to put on an exhibition for the players."

The A's new owner, Arnold Johnson, witnessed the show. So did a *Sporting News* correspondent, who wanted to know the name of the unusual-looking slugger.

"Why, that's Pinky," A's coach Oscar Melillo said.

The writer found out Pinky "likes to wear sporty clothes but says his biggest difficulty here is getting clothes to fit his massive frame."[3]

Little was known about Pinkston because he wasn't on the A's 40-man roster. He belonged to the Columbus Jets, the A's farm team in the Class AAA International League. He was invited to work out with the A's after impressing Boudreau at a rookie camp in Sanford, Florida, prior to spring training.

Pinkston already had won two batting titles. In addition to leading the Class A Sally League in 1954, he was a Triple Crown winner in 1952, with a .360 average, 30 home runs, and 121 runs batted in for St. Hyacinthe, Quebec, in the Class C Provincial League.

Al Pinkston was a familiar face in the baseball guides published annually by *Sporting News*. This photo of Pinkston first appeared in the 1955 guide after he won the 1954 Sally League batting title. The same shot was featured in the 1960, 1961, 1962, and 1963 guides, as Pinkston was top batsmen in the Mexican League four-straight years. *Author's collection.*

He broke into Organized Baseball in 1951, by hitting .301 for another Provincial League team in Farnham, Quebec.

After his banner year at St. Hyacinthe, he was signed by the A's and sent to Ottawa in the International League. He flopped there, batting .198 in 45 games, and was demoted to Williamsport, Pennsylvania, in the Class A Eastern League, where he rebounded to hit .331.

John Sosh managed Pinkston at St. Hyacinthe. "He hit some vicious line drives. And he hit towering home runs," Sosh related. "I'll tell you who he reminded me of—Ted Kluszewski. That was the type of player Al was in the minor leagues. He looked something like Klu."

Kluszewski was nicknamed "Big Klu" because of his size and 279 big-league homers. The peak of his career was the previous year, 1954, when he paced the National League with 49 home runs and 141 RBIs.

In the A's spring opener against the Pittsburgh Pirates, Pinkston had Branch Rickey Jr., the son of the Pirates' president and general manager, raving about him. "I watched that boy quite a bit, and he fascinates me. He has that long, loping stride that usually denotes a runner. His other actions are good, too, and he takes a good cut at the ball."[4]

In his first at-bat, Pinkston lined a double off the right-field fence and, to Rickey's delight, stormed into second. "There's a guy who can really fly once he gets underway," Rickey said. "I'd like to see him in a race against some of these fellows who take short strides and create the illusion of flying. He'd run away from them."[5]

"Pinkston's drive was easily the hardest-hit ball of the day," commented Joe McGuff of the *Kansas City Star*. "He probably is still too inexperienced to make the A's squad, but there are a good many baseball men, including Rickey, who believe that Pinkston could eventually become a star."[6]

Pinkston recalled Ted Williams, the last player in Organized Baseball to top .400, watching him hit in batting practice and telling Boudreau, "Nothing you can do for him. Just let him swing cause he's got the best coordination I've ever seen."

The 1954 Athletics finished last in the American League, 60 games behind the first-place Indians. They had the worst won–loss record in the majors—51-103. "The A's have no more than five major-league players on the roster," manager Eddie Joost grumbled after he was fired.

"We had what I'd call raw material," Boudreau said. "Arnold Johnson had just purchased the club from Connie Mack. It was an old club—

veteran players. Mr. Johnson wanted to build in Kansas City. Early that spring, we went to Sanford and brought in about 100 players. We were looking for a nucleus of young blood."

Any hopes of Pinkston making the team were dashed during the exhibition season, as he batted only .226 and failed to homer or drive in a single run. He was sent to Columbus.

"He needed experience—game experience going against major-league pitching," Boudreau said.

> In intrasquad games, he hit the ball well. When we got to the exhibition games, the pitchers were a little ahead of him. I wanted to keep him as long as I could to build up his confidence, then I was going to send him out—let him get started about a month or so in the minor leagues and bring him back up.

Pinkston got off to a fast start in Columbus with an 8-game hitting streak. Through 24 games, he was batting .321, with 4 homers and 13 RBIs. "They didn't have no other choice but to bring me back," he said. "But, then, I got hurt."

He broke his left arm sliding back to first base on an attempted pickoff play and was sidelined for six weeks. "Came back and tried to play; I couldn't," he said. "My batting average started to fall."

Pinkston ended up hitting .300, but that wasn't good enough. "In this game, you've got to be in A-1 condition," he reflected. "I wasn't myself."

The spring of 1955 was the closest Pinkston came to playing in the majors.

He appeared in only 12 games for Columbus in 1956, batting .182, mostly as a pinch-hitter, before he was sent to Columbia, South Carolina, in the Sally League. "I had no business down in A ball," Pinkston insisted. "I got down there and didn't care. I was a bad influence on the younger guys. I didn't hustle."

The sulking Pinkston finished the season in Jacksonville, Florida, with four homers and a batting average of .293—the first and only year he missed the .300 mark.

The A's virtually gave up on Pinkston, assigning him to Abilene, Texas, of the Class B Big State League.

"He never did develop in the minor leagues," Boudreau said. "He didn't get started the way I thought he would. His hitting didn't come around."

"I'm sure I'd made some owners in the major leagues real happy over my performance," Pinkston said. "But when you don't get that real good chance, there's nothing you can do."

He didn't make it to Abilene, hooking up instead with the Amarillo Gold Sox of the Class A Western League. The manager of the Gold Sox in 1957 was Eddie Bockman, a former big-leaguer and shrewd judge of talent who went on to scout for 45 years.

"Skip, don't worry about me hitting against lefties," the left-handed Pinkston told Bockman soon after joining the club. "Don't pinch-hit for me or move me in the lineup. I can hit 'em."

"And he did," Bockman added. "I left him alone and let him swing."

Pinkston made a believer out of Bockman in the Gold Sox' season opener at their new ballpark, Potter County Stadium. The Gold Sox trailed the Pueblo Dodgers, 6-0, going into the bottom of the ninth. Pinkston began the inning by popping out.

"We started chipping away," Bockman said, "and I'm thinking to myself, 'God, there's some way I've got to get Pinkston to hit again.'"

The score was 6-5 when Pinkston returned to the plate with two runners on base. The first pitch was a fastball up around his cap. He clobbered it over the center-field fence for a three-run homer to win the game, 8-6.

"He hit the ball downtown," Bockman said, using a baseball term for long home runs. "People started sticking money through the fence."

Pinkston held up both hands stuffed with cash and hollered at Bockman, "Hey, Skip, look-ee here. This is more than I make in an entire month."

"He was a line-drive hitter," said Clay Dalrymple, a catcher for the Gold Sox who played 12 years in the majors. "If the ball elevated at all, then he had a chance to get it over the fence. But he could really pop the line drives to all fields—right-center on over to left field. It was just amazing."

"I tried to hit line drives—hit behind the runners and get them from first to third," Pinkston said.

He credited John Sosh with teaching him at St. Hyacinthe how to be a line-drive hitter.

"You don't need to stride as long as your legs are," Sosh told him. "Just spin your toes and heels. Nobody will get you out."

If the ball was anywhere close to the plate, Pinkston swung at it. "I used to go after the 'cap-ville special' and 'shoe-toe special.' I didn't believe in balls and strikes. You didn't need an umpire for me. You can't wait .300; you have to swing .300."

A perfect swing is needed to hit .400, the Holy Grail of hitting. Pinkston was batting over .400 until late July, when he went into a slump on a road trip. He was found talking to his bat in the locker room. "Look here, bat, we've got to pick up some points during this homestand. I'd say about 70 points would be enough, and now is the time to start trying to sew up the batting title."

"Did you say seven points, Pinky, or 70?" a teammate asked.

"I said 70, not seven," Pinkston said with a big laugh. "Don't you think I can make it?"[7]

Pinkston slashed three hits that night, but the best his bat could do was .372, two points behind the league leader. He still managed to drive in a circuit-high 133 runs and poke 23 homers.

Amarillo newspapers listed Pinkston's age at 30 to begin the 1957 season. The 20-year-old Dalrymple suspected he was older, perhaps in his late 30s or early 40s.

Gold Sox pitcher Hugh Blanton didn't think he was that old. "He not only looked younger, he acted younger," Blanton said.

Road trips were particularly grueling, as the Gold Sox traveled by bus to the league's far-flung cities. Albuquerque was the closest, at 288 miles, and Des Moines the farthest, at 801. Others ranged from 300 to 500 miles away from Amarillo.

"Poor Al's knees," Dalrymple said. "I'll always remember him saying, 'Oh-h, my knees,' and massaging them on the bus."

The Gold Sox bus driver was named Chung. He doubled as the team's trainer.

When Dalrymple's foot swelled up after fouling a pitch off his instep, he was instructed to stick the foot in the toilet and keep flushing until it got better. "Chung's whirlpool," the players called it.

Pinkston figured rubbing his aching knees was better. "I always took care of myself. I didn't drink or smoke, got my sleep, and ate the right foods. I knew that to compete with these young kids I had to stay in condition."

In Pinkston's second year at Amarillo in 1958, his average fell to .337, but he tied for most hits (204) and paced the league in four other catego-

Al Pinkston batted .372 for the Amarillo Gold Sox in 1957, two points behind the league leader, but his 133 runs batted in were tops in the Western League. He played two seasons for Amarillo, his last stop in the United States before going to Mexico, where he terrorized pitchers seven more years. *Author's collection.*

ries—doubles (44), total bases (330), slugging percentage (.545), and runs batted in (126). He also rapped 24 homers.

"As long as he could go to that plate with that bat, he was going to have a job somewhere," Bockman said.

In February 1959, the Gold Sox sold Pinkston to the Portland Beavers of the Pacific Coast League. The Beavers were his best chance to get another crack at the majors, but before he could put on a Portland uniform, they peddled him to the Mexico City Reds in the Class AA Mexican League. He didn't want to go. "That league is for the old boys," he said, without realizing he was one of them.

The Mexican League turned out to be the perfect place for Pinkston to spend the twilight of his career. He went from the obscurity of the United States to fame in Mexico.

Mexican fans marveled at Pinkston's powerful arms and huge hands, and how savagely he ripped the ball. They were reminded of the great Josh Gibson and other Negro League stars who once played in the Mexican League. Pinkston didn't bash homers like Gibson, but he hit for a higher average than everyone else.

He won back-to-back batting titles for the Reds in 1959 and 1960, and the second year drove in 144 runs to shatter one of Gibson's hallowed records.

The Reds enraged their followers after the 1960 season by sending Pinkston to Veracruz for a run-of-the-mill Mexican player. "They wanted all Mexicans," he said.

He hit .374 for Veracruz in 1961 and .381 in 1962, to give him an unprecedented four consecutive Mexican League batting crowns and earn an invitation to the Cleveland Indians' spring training camp in 1963. He never went because of a broken elbow suffered in a winter league game.

A broken hand kept Pinkston from making it five straight in 1963. He was injured with one week left to play in the season, and all he could do was watch as Monterrey's Vinicio Garcia passed him, .3684 to .3680. Then he sat out the last two games. "You had to be better than the Mexicans," he said.

One reason was he made a lot more money—$2,000 a month plus living expenses during the season.

"Most of the guys [Americans] who had the potential to be real good, they didn't want them," he said of Mexican League teams. "Too much money. They wanted to take care of their own ballplayers."

Going into the 1964 season, Pinkston announced, "I'm too old for this job."

He revealed that he was born on October 22 in 1917, not 1926, making him 46 instead of 37.

Several Mexican sportswriters couldn't believe he was nine years older.

"I have proof—a birth certificate," he insisted.

"They didn't want to believe me," Pinkston chuckled. "They started calling me 'Viejo'—Old Man."

Viejo batted .364 in 1964, to finish second again. In 1965, his average dropped to .345, still best on the Veracruz team but seventh in the league.

It was time to retire, as he was worn down by the bus travel and playing too many games in poorly lit ballparks. "I just got tired of killing my body," he said.

Veracruz tried to change his mind by promising he could play only at home. Pinkston knew that wasn't practical because he was the team's biggest drawing card on the road.

"I could've played more," he admitted. "That last day I went 5-for-5—two doubles, two singles, and a home run. It was a long one. About 400 and something feet."

Pinkston quit a month shy of his 48th birthday with a lifetime batting average of .372, the highest in Mexican League history. His string of four-straight batting titles is still tops, and he continues to own the RBI record he wrested from Gibson. All of this was done after Pinkston turned 40.

"I wasn't surprised at anything he did with the bat," Bockman said.

Pinkston was 37 in 1955, when Lou Boudreau got a glimpse of his star potential at the A's spring training camp.

"I thought Al Pinkston was going to become a very outstanding major-league ballplayer," Boudreau said. "He was quick, he was studious about the game, and he had good power. I felt he could improve in the outfield, but I wasn't looking for that at the time. I was looking for some hitting. I thought Pinkston was the answer."

He sent Pinkston back to the minors to gain the confidence needed to be a star in the majors. "I knew that if I kept him with me that he would be on the bench. I figured that by playing every day he would improve so I could bring him back by May 1."

That didn't happen, and Pinkston drifted through the minors until he got to Mexico and became a superstar.

"I couldn't understand why some big-league team didn't pick him up, and then I realized he was just happy to be playing in the Mexican League," Boudreau said. "He had the confidence down there. He knew he could hit in that league and be a star. When you have the confidence that you can do something, you usually do it."

Boudreau only wished Pinkston would've had the same confidence in Kansas City. Maybe he could've hit in the majors like he did in Mexico.

* * *

The manager of the Savannah Athletics in 1954 was Clyde Kluttz. He was 36 years old. His star player, Pinkston, was 26. Or so Kluttz thought.

Upon learning later that he and Pinkston were the same age, Kluttz was incredulous. "I played against Luke Easter, and it was obvious that he was older than he said he was. But I lived with these guys every day in the clubhouse, hotels, and buses. There's no way possible he could've been 36 years of age. It's unbelievable."

"Well, you know how it is," Pinkston snickered.

At about the time Pinkston divulged his long-kept secret, Easter admitted to trimming a decade off his age. "My baseball age is 42," Easter announced in 1963, at Rochester, New York, where he was playing for the Red Wings. "But I'm 52 years old today."[8]

It was common for Negro League players to lower their age and enhance their chances of making it to the bigs.

"Everybody was doing that," said Hector Lopez, a Panamanian who played with and against Pinkston in the Provincial League before starring for the Athletics and New York Yankees. "You could tell Pinky was an older guy. But I didn't know that he was that old."

Most players shaved two or three years off their age, so Pinkston was pushing the boundaries of believability by lopping off nine.

"He just went through a stage where he forgot to have birthdays," deadpanned Bockman.

"If he's in the big leagues and he's 36 years old and doing the job, nobody says a word," Kluttz said. "But when he's in the minor leagues . . . well, there was all the motive in the world for him to lie about his age."

Pinkston arrived in Savannah as one of the most promising "young" players in the A's organization. His Savannah debut against the Yankees in an exhibition game at Savannah's Grayson Stadium was the stuff of legends.

Despite breaking his bat, he muscled a home run over the right-field fence off Ed Lopat, the southpaw ace of the Yankees pitching staff. That was Pinkston's lone spring highlight, as he got off to a horrible start with only 24 hits in his first 100 at-bats for a .240 average.

"The guy was giving 100 percent all the time, but he just couldn't hit," Kluttz said.

He passed up a chance to trade Pinkston to Augusta, another Sally League team that was shopping for a black player. "Augusta didn't have anybody that could replace Pinky on my club."

The usually amiable and low-key Pinkston accused the North Carolina–born Kluttz of giving him a hard time because he was black.

"I really went at him nose-to-nose," Kluttz recalled. "I told him, 'You're just as white as I am and I'm just as black as you. Don't you ever bring that up to me again. I have only one thing in mind with this ballclub and that's to develop ballplayers and win whenever I possibly can. You or nobody else is going to stop me.'"

Kluttzs' wife asked him afterward, "What if he'd started after you?"

"Well," he replied, "I'd had to dig a hole in the ground."

The incident bonded the two men.

"His attitude changed drastically after that," Kluttz said.

"Clyde Kluttz was a good man and a good manager," Pinkston said.

Kluttz took solace in the home run Pinkston hit off the Yankees' Lopat during spring training. "That's what made me believe that somewhere along the line he had to snap out of it."

At Augusta in late May, Kluttz pulled Pinkston aside to tell him he could steal the catcher's signs from his position in the third-base coaching box. "Pinky, what I have to say I don't want anyone else on our club to know about. Any time that I call your name, Pinky, it's a curveball. When I don't say anything, you know it's a fastball."

Midway through the game, Kluttz yelled, "Come on, Pinky!"

"It was a curveball," Pinkston said. "Swoosh. I hit the ball out of there. Into the seats. That got me going."

Pinkston went on a .534 tear (31-for-50) prior to the Sally League All-Star Game in early July to raise his batting average to a team-high .327. He said,

> I hit in cycles. I'd get four, five hits in one game. Next game I might not get a hit. I was never in a slump. I never used that word. Gee, I'd knock an outfielder down catching the ball. That's not a slump. That's bad luck. You've got to have luck in this game. I hit a ball once that hit an infielder on the chin, bounced to another infielder, who threw me out. That's bad luck!

He wasn't selected to play in the All-Star Game, leading one observer to predict, "Years from now when someone looks at the box score of the All-Star Game he'll wonder why Pinkston wasn't playing."[9]

Pinkston continued his torrid hitting during the next two months, going on a record-breaking 37-game hitting streak. In one stretch, he had hits in 55 of 56 games.

"When he got hot, I quit calling pitches," Kluttz said. "He'd gained his confidence, and he didn't need my help."

Pinkston finished the season with a league-leading .360 average, 27 home runs, and 102 RBIs—numbers that compared favorably to those compiled by Hank Aaron and Frank Robinson, two future Hall of Famers. Aaron had posted a .362 average, 22 home runs, and 125 RBIs the previous year at Jacksonville. Playing at Columbia in 1954, Robinson had a .336 average, 25 home runs, and 110 RBIs.

"I've seen guys like Stan Musial and other great hitters in the minor leagues," Kluttz said. "But during that short period, he was probably as good a hitter as you'll ever want to see. He didn't think any pitcher could get him out."

Joe Stanka of Macon, one of the league's top pitchers in 1954, with a 16-5 won–loss record, joked, "I held him to 5-for-10."

Pinkston's performance was even more amazing given how racially divided the Deep South was at the time. "It was a difficult time for black athletes," Kluttz said. "It was especially difficult in Savannah."

The color barrier in the 50-year-old Sally League had been broken the year before by outfielder Fleming "Junior" Reedy and infielder Elbert Isreal in Savannah, and Aaron, Felix Mantilla, and Horace Garner in Jacksonville. Savannah had two blacks in 1954—Isreal and Pinkston.

"They couldn't do the same things as the other players," Kluttz said, continuing,

> When we stopped to eat along the highway, we had to take food back to the bus for Al and Elbert to eat.
>
> There were some people in Savannah trying to get Al and Elbert off the club, and suddenly they were coming out to see them play. At the end of Al's 37-game hitting streak, they gave him a standing ovation. He just made those people love him.

Pinkston was cause for excitement in a beleaguered A's organization that was talent poor, cash starved, and about to relocate from Philadelphia to Kansas City under new ownership.

The A's were hoping Pinkston could follow in the footsteps of Aaron, who jumped from the Sally League to the majors and launched his sensational career with 13 homers and a .280 average for the Milwaukee Braves.

A big-league catcher for nine years, Kluttz didn't get caught up in the hoopla.

"I didn't feel he'd help the A's that much," he said bluntly. "He could've hit big-league pitching. He had trouble with certain pitches, but there's no question he had the power and strength. At that time a big bat wasn't enough."

Kluttz elaborated, "Al was a bad outfielder. He was so tall and clumsy. It took a tremendous amount of work to make him respectable. His arm was all right. He was a hard runner, but he had those long legs and had trouble getting down on ground balls. Just couldn't do it. And I must've hit him 5,000 of them."

Teammates attested to Pinkston's awkwardness in the outfield and running the bases.

At Farnham in 1951, Pinkston collided with Joe Taylor in the outfield and broke Joe's jaw.

The same year, Hector Lopez, playing shortstop for St. Hyacinthe, was spiked by Pinkston trying to break up a double play at second base. "I had to have 17 stitches," Lopez recalled. "He played hard and rough. He played to win. You see Pinkston coming, you'd better get out of the way in a hurry."

The first black to don a Philadelphia A's uniform, pitcher Bob Trice played with Pinkston for almost three years. A peaceful guy off the field, Al could be barbaric on it. "Pinkston was a big fellow, and he didn't have the finesse," Trice said. "He would rather run over you than slide around."

At Savannah, Pinkston almost caused a riot when he barreled standing up into Macon's Chico Fernandez, knocking the skinny second baseman to the ground in an attempt to jolt the ball loose. The entire Macon team charged Pinkston, with several players landing punches before he was rescued by teammates and Savannah police.

"What happened is he would run over smaller ballplayers, and 90 percent of the time, he wound up getting hurt himself," Trice said. "It was a clumsiness and the inability to grasp the finer techniques of the game."

This could explain the injuries that plagued Pinkston throughout his career.

Several major-league teams were interested in Pinkston after he dominated the Sally League, one reportedly offering the A's $100,000, a hefty sum in the 1950s.

Kluttz recommended that the A's trade or sell Pinkston. "It was evident to me that he was never going to be a top-notch big-league ballplayer. If they could get some money or another player for him, that was the time to do it. My report was on record."

The A's hung onto Pinkston for two more years. "We can't afford to get rid of players who hit .360," Kluttz was told.

"I understand the reason they gave me," Kluttz said. "They made a mistake."

The A's admitted as much later.

"They realized that the batting average he carried with me in Savannah was misleading and that he wasn't major-league caliber," Kluttz said.

That candid assessment by Kluttz shouldn't diminish what Pinkston did at Savannah and Amarillo or in the Mexican League.

"The year he put in for me, he was from July on as good looking a hitter as I ever wanted to see," Kluttz said.

Only the legendary Smead Jolley can match Pinkston's half-dozen minor-league batting titles. He stands alone atop the Mexican League in lifetime batting average and holds a slew of other records.

Even though he didn't play his first game in Organized Baseball until he was 33, he amassed 2,368 hits, of which 250 were home runs. After turning 40, he had a remarkable .367 batting average and a slugging percentage of .567.

Pinkston is enshrined in the Mexican Baseball Hall of Fame, along with such Negro League greats as Gibson, Roy Campanella, and Monte Irvin. Yet, he remains unknown in the United States except by those who saw him play.

"I'll never forget him," said Eddie Bockman, his manager at Amarillo. "I'll never forget him."

* * *

Clyde Kluttz was in Baton Rouge, Louisiana, to scout a promising catcher on the Southern University baseball team. The size and unusual shape of the black first baseman looked familiar.

"What's the boy's name at first base?" he asked the team's coach.

"Al Pinkston," the coach replied.

It was "Big Al's Son"—the nickname for Al Pinkston Jr. He was built just like his daddy.

In 1974, Big Al and Junior, then 28, traveled to the Mexican Baseball Hall of Fame in Monterrey.

As they walked into the museum for the induction ceremony, Junior started singing "Walking Cane," a song about strolling down memory lane.

Big Al looked at Junior and said, "I didn't know you could sing."

Junior didn't know much about his father either.

Big Al was gone most of the year playing baseball. When he was home, he worked on the riverfront as a longshoreman.

"All of the accolades that he accomplished in his life, we didn't know anything about," Junior said. "When he came home, he never talked about baseball."

Alfred Charles Pinkston Sr. was talking baseball in 1975, as he relaxed in the living room of his small wood-frame house in the Lower Ninth Ward of New Orleans, one block from the industrial canal connecting the Mississippi River to Lake Pontchartrain.

Big Al was sort of a mystery in the United States, as he didn't get much publicity. Everything he did in Mexico stayed there because the newspaper and magazine stories about him were in Spanish.

Big Al grew up in Newbern, Alabama, a predominantly black community about 30 miles south of Tuscaloosa.

He was the fifth of nine children (five boys and four girls) born to Ed and Viola Pinkston, a true power couple at 6-foot-9 and 6-foot-2, respectively.

The Pinkston brothers flexed their muscles in baseball as the Downtown Boys, regularly beating the Country Boys, the other all-black team in town. "We'd run them to death," Big Al said.

The Downtown Boys disbanded when the Pinkstons joined the Newbern Gray Sox, a sandlot team. "All of my brothers played. I was the pitcher. I pitched from 15 up until I was about 20. When I was 17, I hurt my arm."

Researchers claim he played first base briefly for the St. Louis Stars of the Negro National League in 1936, at the age of 18. Big Al never mentioned it. "I was 23 when I entered the Army in 1941; 28 when I got out in 1946."

While stationed at the U.S. Army's Air Corps base in New Orleans, he married a local girl, Velma Lewis. The first of their two children, Nancy, was born in 1943, and Junior in 1946.

Big Al played for various teams in Louisiana until he belted two homers against a club led by Wesley Barrow, a highly respected manager in the Negro Southern Association. "Where's that young man you call Al Pinkston?" Barrow asked after the game.

Pinkston was told the Cleveland Buckeyes of the Negro American League needed a power-hitting catcher and to report immediately to their spring training camp in Florida. "They took a look at me and said, 'You're too large to catch.'"

He switched to first base and played for three teams in 1948—the Buckeyes, the Chicago American Giants, and the New Orleans Creoles.

Big Al was the Creoles' big stick in 1949 and 1950, with a combined 70 home runs and batting averages of .385 and .380, respectively. But the team's big draw was second baseman Toni Stone, described by one newspaper as a "husky woman who handles the duties around the keystone sack like a man."[10]

Toni was the only woman in professional baseball and the team's big newsmaker on barnstorming tours throughout the Midwest and Canada. When Joe Louis, former world heavyweight boxing champ, showed up for a Creoles game in Council Bluffs, Iowa, the local newspaper ran a photo of him and Toni together with the caption, "Slugger Meets Slugger."[11]

In 1951, Big Al headed for the Provincial League in Canada with dozens of black players. "The majority of them were old guys," he said. "The Canadian teams wanted to build up their clubs immediately and figured they weren't going to get any whites to come in there."

He went to Farnham, a mostly black team assembled by Sam Bankhead, a longtime Negro League star and the first black to manage in Organized Baseball.

One of the outfielders was hard-hitting Joe Taylor. Josh Gibson Jr., the son and namesake of the Negro League great, was an infielder. Eudie Napier, the elder Gibson's backup with the Homestead Grays, was the catcher.

Farnham pitcher Bob Trice recalled Bankhead telling him, "Why lie about your age? If you can play ball, you can. If you can't, it doesn't make any difference if you're 10 years old."

Big Al was 33 at the time. "I didn't tell anybody my age. I thought if I can get around it, don't tell. It's something I knew would come out sooner or later."

Bankhead put Big Al in right field to hide his defensive deficiencies as much as possible. "They said I looked awkward out there. I caught everything I could get. I made my plays. I threw people out."

The Farnham team folded in 1952, sending Big Al to St. Hyacinthe, where he won his first batting championship. "Some people are afraid when they don't hit. I hit so much I was afraid that year. I was looking for the knockdown pitch. They threw at me every now and then. But they found out it didn't do any good. It made me bear down more."

Big Al got better with age, although no one knew just how true that was at the time. "I won the batting championship at Savannah in 1954, but it wasn't my greatest season. My best was at Amarillo in 1957. I hit .400 almost all year until I dropped down to .372."

He put it all together at age 41, when he got to the Mexican League. "I began to watch the pitchers more. When they wound up, my eyes followed the ball. After they turned it loose, they didn't have any more to do with it. I'm the boss then. It's got to come by me."

He laughed at the thought of the balls that didn't make it past him. "Tell me who I didn't hit? I hit .372 the whole seven years there. I broke lots of records of a lot of great players. Josh Gibson is one of the greatest hitters that ever lived. I broke his record for runs batted in."

He rattled off some of the others. "Most total bases in a season (366), most hits in a season (225), most consecutive batting titles (4)."

When Big Al got back to New Orleans at the end of the 1965 season, his last in baseball, he was greeted by Hurricane Betsy, the most destructive storm in New Orleans history until Hurricane Katrina came along 40 years later. "Betsy wiped out everything we had," he said. "It was like I'd just been born into the world. All I had was my shoes on. Everything was destroyed. We came back into this house, threw everything away, and started again."

He repaired his house, then he helped others do the same. He worked on a full-time basis as a longshoreman and got involved in a small neighborhood church, doing whatever needed to be done to keep it going.

In 1975, he was building a house in Newbern. "I'm going to live there when I retire——about four years if I live."

On their way to the Mexican Hall of Fame the year before, Big Al had told Junior about a knot he had in his stomach that wouldn't go away. He thought it was an ulcer. Velma believed it was an old baseball injury. It turned out to be cancer.

He died on March 18, 1981, at the age of 64. "They said it was a heart attack, but he had cancer," Junior said.

Sporting News reported Big Al's death a month later. The five-line story only mentioned his Mexican League accomplishments.

In 2005, Hurricane Katrina washed away the house Big Al rebuilt after Betsy. Velma was still living in it. "A big barge from the canal hit the house, and it just floated down the street," Junior explained.

When Junior and his wife, Barbara, went to the Lower Ninth Ward several months later, they found an open field where the house used to be. There were some bricks from the foundation scattered around. Junior picked one up.

"I'm going to take this brick," he said to Barbara. "This is the only memory of the house I grew up in."

His father's Hall of Fame plaque and the photographs, newspaper, and magazine articles chronicling his illustrious career were gone. "There's nothing that reflects that Mr. Pinkston was ever here," Barbara said.

In 2007, actor Brad Pitt established a project to rebuild 150 homes in the Lower Ninth Ward. The Pinkston house was one of them.

In 2009, Junior received a telephone call from a writer who had photographs of his father and tape recordings of him talking about his life and baseball.

Junior could finally walk down memory lane with his father.

9

PLAYING DRUNK

Joe Taylor

A short walk from the National Baseball Hall of Fame in Cooperstown, New York, is the Doubleday Café, a popular restaurant pub that offers souvenir t-shirts reading, "A drinking town with a baseball problem."

Joe Taylor was a baseball player with a drinking problem. If he had spent less time drunk, he might have a plaque at Cooperstown alongside Harmon Killebrew, Frank Robinson, and other power-hitting greats of the 1950s and 1960s.

George Bamberger was a teammate of Taylor's in both the minor and major leagues.

"If Joe would've come along today, he'd wind up a superstar," he said. "Joe had what we call 'power plus.' In other words, real great power. You rarely found anybody with excellent power. Maybe Harmon Killebrew. Joe had Killebrew power."

In the minors, that power was unleashed—264 home runs in 13 booze-stained seasons, half of them in the Pacific Coast League (PCL) cities of Portland, Seattle, Vancouver, and San Diego. As a pinch-hitter and part-time outfielder, he belted only nine shots in five jigger-sized trials in the majors with the Philadelphia A's, Cincinnati Reds, St. Louis Cardinals, and Baltimore Orioles.

"Joe Taylor could have been one of the great home run hitters in all of baseball had he stayed clean," said Eddie Basinski, a teammate in Portland and Seattle. "Everybody that played against him knows that to be true."

Maury Wills, a base-stealing star for the Los Angeles Dodgers in the 1960s, played with Taylor in 1957, at Seattle. "He wasn't the all-around player that Frank Robinson was, or Willie Mays, but he could hit," said Wills. "He could really hit. Everything else he was short on would've been overlooked. He could've accomplished as much as Frank Robinson."

"Great hitter," recalled Al Moran, a teammate at Vancouver in 1962, noting, "Low-ball hitter, highball drinker."

Bob Trice broke into Organized Baseball with Taylor in 1951, at Farnham, Quebec, Canada, in the Class C Provincial League. They remained in the same league in 1952, playing for St. Hyacinthe, Quebec, and moving up the Athletics organization through Ottawa in the Class AAA International League. In September 1953, Trice became the first black to play for the Athletics and Taylor the third when he joined the team in August 1954. "He was one of the few fellows that could hit while drunk or sober. He hit the best of 'em ossified."

"Joe had all the makings," Bamberger said, continuing,

> What he needed was one opportunity where he was thrown into the lineup in the big leagues and told, "You are my left fielder, right fielder, center fielder, whatever it may be, and you will play, let's say, two or three months straight—every day." Joe would've turned out to be an outstanding ballplayer.

Taylor's managers in the majors weren't too sure about the condition he was in even if he made it to the ballpark on time. With Baltimore in 1959, he overslept and was late for a doubleheader in Chicago against the White Sox. "Taylor will make his next appearance for Vancouver," announced Orioles manager Paul Richards.[1]

Taylor didn't appear in another big-league game.

In 1954, Joe was considered a cinch for a starting job with the Athletics after tearing up the International League with a .323 batting average and 23 homers for Ottawa. Two weeks after the Canadian city honored him with a "Joe Taylor Night," he was arrested for drunken driving and sentenced to seven days in jail.

Trice was Joe's unofficial chaperone, trying to keep him sober and making sure money was sent home to his wife and two sons in Pittsburgh as soon as he got paid. Trice went to pay a $100 fine and get Joe out of jail. "He tells me he needs the rest. So, he spent a couple of days in jail to get some rest," Trice said.

The next month, in Philadelphia, Joe was again charged with drunken driving after a car accident at three o'clock in the morning near the A's ballpark, Connie Mack Stadium. He was driving a car owned by Trice's wife, Henrietta.

In 1955, the A's had a new home in Kansas City and a new manager, Lou Boudreau, who began spring training by announcing "rules with a strict taboo on liquor of any kind" and a "midnight curfew."[2]

In an exhibition game against the Brooklyn Dodgers at Vero Beach, Florida, Joe hit a towering double and a homer that traveled almost 400 feet off Brooklyn ace Don Newcombe. "Man, you got it made," Dodgers catcher Roy Campanella said to Joe after his home run blast.

"I thought I had it made, too," Joe said.

Back at the A's training camp in West Palm Beach, Joe showed up in the clubhouse well ahead of the other players so he had ample time to sit in the whirlpool. "I had a bad leg, but I hadn't said anything to anybody."

"You're drunk!" Boudreau said upon seeing Joe.

"How can I be drunk and playing ball like I'm playing?"

Joe told Boudreau about his leg, but Boudreau wasn't buying it. "He figured because I came in early that I'd been out drinking."

Boudreau concluded that while Joe was a big-league hitter, he also was "his own worst enemy." He sent him back to the minors.[3]

Drinking was only one of the problems Joe had with the A's. "I can't go into all the other things, but it was more than drinking," Trice said. "Any ballplayer in the country other than Hank Aaron, Willie Mays, Mickey Mantle, would've paid to hit the ball the way Joe hit the ball."

Taylor went from Kansas City to Columbus, Ohio, in the International League, and then to the Portland Beavers in the PCL.

The Beavers had several former big-leaguers. They included Basinski, a onetime Dodger; first baseman Ed Mickelson of the St. Louis Browns; and second baseman Artie Wilson, an ex-New York Giant. Artie was assigned to room with Joe on the road.

Joe landed in Portland at six o'clock on a Sunday morning after an overnight flight from Columbus. The Beavers had a doubleheader against the Oakland Oaks that afternoon, but he was told to go to his hotel and get some rest. Joe played anyway.

He led off the second inning by belting the first pitch over the center-field wall.

With a runner on base in the fourth inning, he swatted the ball over the left-field wall for a two-run homer. In the sixth inning, Joe drilled another shot to deep center. "The ball would've gone out if the center fielder hadn't jumped so high to catch it," Mickelson said.

The 6-foot-1, 185-pound Taylor strolled to the plate in the eighth inning with the crowd yelling, "Hit another!" On the first pitch, he bashed another homer into the center-field seats.

In four at-bats, Joe blasted three home runs and came within inches of a fourth. *Oregonian* sports editor L. H. Gregory called it the "most sensational debut any player ever made" in the 52-year history of Portland's Vaughn Street Park.[4]

"They were three of the longest home runs ever hit in that park," Basinski said. "All of a sudden, this guy is going to be the black Babe Ruth."

Taylor joined the Beavers in mid-May. By July, he was hitting at a .345 clip. "You shouldn't be down here," Artie Wilson told him. "You ought to be in the majors."

Several times after a road game Artie ushered Joe directly back to the hotel. "Next day he couldn't hit the side of a building. So I told him, 'Don't come in tonight.'"

Joe stayed out until five o'clock in the morning and slept until Artie woke him up to go to the ballpark. "He'd get out there and hit and catch everything," Artie said.

If Joe staggered under a fly ball, Beavers fans would holler encouragement: "Stay with it, Joe, stay with it!"

"In the field, his reflexes were slower," Trice said. "But once he walked up to that plate, it seemed like he was a machine."

The machine sputtered in July, Joe's average dropping 45 points to .300.

"Whenever he was singing or whistling coming up into the dugout, our manager would run and take his name off the starting lineup," Mickelson explained.

Portland manager Clay Hopper decided Taylor was unable to play the first game of a doubleheader. Basinski slashed a line drive into left field and toward the bullpen where Joe and several pitchers were sitting. Everyone got out of the way except Joe.

"He jumped up out of a fog and fielded the ball and threw it back into play," Mickelson said.

Basinski coasted into second base thinking he had a run-scoring double. Umpire Vinnie Smith, an ex-player, walked up and said, "Ed, I hate to tell you but you're out. Taylor was sleeping on the bench down there in the bullpen, and the ball came rolling by him and he picked it up and tossed it to the outfielder."

Mickelson watched from the Beavers dugout. "I could hear Basinski calling him names and Hopper was running down the left-field line as hard as he could with the reddest face I ever saw."

Also looking on was a crowd of almost 5,000 that had turned out to honor Frank Austin, the team's black shortstop, for playing in 600 consecutive games. They could easily hear Hopper, a Mississippian, use the "N" word and drop the "F" bomb to vent his anger. "He called him all kinds of names," Basinski said.

Gregory, of the *Oregonian*, called Taylor's one-handed stab a "boner," as well as an "old-fashioned, country-fair type of pure bonehead play" and a "freak of baseball stupidity."[5]

Joe played in the second game of the doubleheader, going hitless in four at-bats and committing an error in right field. He quietly disappeared from the lineup, not playing another inning for the Beavers. Ten days later, he was shunted to the Toronto Maple Leafs in the International League. At the time, Joe was batting .295, with 10 homers, 18 doubles, 4 triples, and 55 runs batted in.

Responding to fans curious to know what happened, Gregory wrote, "The crux of it was that Taylor got to misbehaving and paying no attention to training rules, not for the first time in his baseball career. About everything was tried, including one fine—not a very heavy one—but nothing worked."[6]

At Toronto, Joe slammed four home runs the first week and 10 in 33 games. "Nothing happened [off the field] and how that man hit for us," said Luke Sewell, the Toronto manager.

Sewell thought so highly of Joe that when he became manager of the Seattle Rainiers in 1956, he convinced the Rainiers to buy him from the Athletics. "I have never seen a better power hitter," he said.[7]

Taylor's power came in surges, like the one that produced 15 home runs in the first half of the 1956 season. He ended up with 24.

The Rainiers had a new manager in 1957, Francis "Lefty" O'Doul, a Coast League institution after 22 years at the helm of four PCL teams. The 1957 season would be his last managing, as he opened a bar and restaurant in San Francisco so he could spend more time golfing and drinking Bloody Marys. In fact, there's a Bloody Mary mix named after Lefty.

Maury Wills was a shortstop for the Rainiers. Said Wills,

> We weren't too sure of Lefty half the time. Sometimes he would come in just before the game started and give the coach the lineup, leave, and come back in the fourth inning. He wanted to know who's playing, where, what's the score. If we were winning, Lefty would come out and take over. If we were losing, he might not suit up at all.

The night before the Rainiers opened the season at home with a double-header, there was a banquet at a downtown Seattle hotel to introduce the players. Joe showed up drunk. Lefty calmly sent him home to sleep it off. The next day, Joe socked three homers and batted in nine runs. "It was amazing to all of us that he could hit the ball as well as he did being in the condition that we felt he was in," Wills said.

Through 64 games, Joe was leading the league with 14 home runs. Seven of those came during an 11-game stretch.

"Taylor's home runs have two distinguishing characteristics," Len Anderson wrote in the *Sporting News*. "Almost all of them are of awesome proportions, and they come in clusters."[8]

"When Taylor is 'right,' he is definitely a major-league hitter," Lefty said. "He has great reflexes, terrific wrist action, and tremendously quick hands. He has as much power as almost any hitter in the game and an easy, nearly perfect swing."[9]

Joe had a .305 average, 22 homers, and 72 RBIs in early August, when Cincinnati brought him up to the majors in exchange for Bob Thurman, another outfielder.

"Cincinnati was his last shot, so he was really going to bear down," Thurman said.

Joe was 31 and running out of chances. He didn't stop drinking, but he cut back. "I was trying to prove something to friends of mine at home— that I could hit the ball without drinking."

Reds manager George "Birdie" Tebbetts had a degree in philosophy from Providence College, but he was using psychology when he immedi-

Joe Taylor is congratulated by manager Lefty O'Doul after hitting a home run at
Seattle in 1957. When Joe belted a homer and three doubles in another game,
Lefty quipped, "That's what happens when a guy sobers up." Joe rapped 22 hom-
ers in 115 games for Lefty, earning a second chance in the majors. *Dave Eskenazi
Collection.*

ately placed Joe in left field and moved Frank Robinson, a budding young superstar, from left to first base. Joe had five multihit games in his first 10 starts.

"He tried to lay off the bottle, but he wasn't the same ballplayer," said Thurman, who rejoined Cincinnati in late August.

Joe's batting average dropped steadily from .333 in mid-August, to a season-ending .262. He hit four home runs.

"I asked him why he had to drink," Thurman explained. "He said that in order for him to have the nerve to stay in there and swing the bat, he had to have a drink—to build up his confidence at the plate."

Thurman empathized with Joe. "Fear plays a big part in a hitter's life. Not just the fear of being hit with the ball, but also the fear of being made to look bad at the plate. Pride. Joe just couldn't stay in there on a curve. He'd wave at them when he was sober. Now, when he'd had a drink, why, he didn't budge."

In December 1957, Joe was sent to the St. Louis Cardinals in a five-player deal, along with Curt Flood, a 19-year-old outfielder. Cardinals manager Fred Hutchinson had tried to get Joe from Seattle for pinch-hitting, but the Reds had a working agreement with the Rainiers and grabbed him instead.

Taylor and Flood opened the 1958 season at Omaha, the Cardinals' farm club in the American Association. By June, they were wearing St. Louis uniforms and rooming together on the road. By the end of July, Flood was a leading candidate for National League Rookie of the Year, and Taylor was playing for the Baltimore Orioles after they claimed him for the waiver price of $20,000.

Joe had a .304 batting average, with 7 hits in 23 at-bats. He was batting .333 as a pinch-hitter—4-for-12, with 2 doubles and a home run. The homer came in his last at-bat for the Cardinals in a game against the Reds in Cincinnati. That was exactly one week before the Orioles deal.

"Radio, radio, radio," Joe said. "Sitting in a bar drinking. In St. Louis, good friend of mine owns a bar. And I heard it on the radio. Even my buddy says, 'What?'"

The next day, the Cardinals had a twilight doubleheader at Busch Stadium against Tebbetts's Reds. He took batting practice and returned to the clubhouse before Hutchinson confirmed that the radio report was true. Joe was going to the Orioles.

Hutchinson was in his third and last year as the Cards' manager and Vaughan "Bing" Devine in his first as general manager. Hutch had bristled over previous front-office decisions made without his knowledge. "Bing Devine sold me and never told Fred," Joe said. "Fred cried like a baby when I got sold."

Joe felt like crying, too. "At that time, I was playing good ball. I was the best pinch-hitter they had. That's what I don't understand."

While Joe didn't go on the wagon in Cincinnati and St. Louis, he stayed out of management's doghouse and the newspaper headlines. It was a different story in Baltimore. "When I went to Baltimore, the first thing the man said was, 'I bought you to send to the minor leagues.'"

The "man" Joe was referring to was Paul Richards, manager of the Orioles.

"You're going to send me out of the major leagues the way I'm hitting?" Joe protested. "I'm not going."

Richards kept Joe around for pinch-hitting and spot duty in the outfield. He batted .273, with two home runs. One was an inside-the-park homer at New York's Yankee Stadium off of Whitey Ford, the Yankees pitching ace.

"He hit a line drive off the left-field fence that got in a trough at the bottom of the fence and just rolled around it," said Charlie Beamon, a teammate with the Orioles and later in Seattle.

> The outfielders couldn't catch up with the ball, and Joe was flying. Anyway, when he got to home he just did make it into the dugout before he regurgitated. It was alcohol and stuff, but, I mean, Joe was really trying to do the right thing when he was at Baltimore. He was as good a hitter as anybody I saw in the majors. He was hitting the Yankees just as hard as Mantle was hitting Baltimore.

Joe started in just half of the 36 games he played for the Orioles in 1958. Two days after the season ended, he was arrested at a tavern in Baltimore for disorderly conduct.

"You're the ballplayer, aren't you?" the judge inquired at his hearing. "The Oriole man?"

Joe nodded.

"You hit several home runs since you've been here, and I'm certainly sorry to see you in trouble," the judge said after setting bail at $100.[10]

There was no bailing out Joe with Richards. He quickly shipped him to the Orioles' Vancouver farm club in the PCL.

Throwing knuckleballs in batting practice and getting arrested for disorderly conduct was ample cause for Richards to permanently exile Joe to Vancouver.

Perhaps the greatest testament to Taylor's hitting ability is that he made it back to Baltimore in 1959.

In 60 games for Vancouver, Joe batted in 48 runs, while stroking 13 homers. The Orioles were last in hitting and runs scored when he rejoined them in mid-June. He lasted slightly more than a month, hitting a measly .156, with one home run in 14 games.

The backbreaker was when Joe overslept and reported late for a doubleheader in Chicago. Richards was so irate he had police remove him from the dugout. In Vancouver, manager Charlie Metro was so elated he would've provided a police escort for his return.

Georg N. Meyers, sports editor of the *Seattle Times*, good-naturedly accused Metro of sending Joe to Baltimore without an alarm clock. "It was only a matter of time before Joe would oversleep and incur the wrath of Paul Richards," Meyers wrote. "Now Joe will keep Coast League pitchers awake."[11]

Soon after returning to Vancouver, Joe overslept and was tardy for another game. He was fined and put right back in the lineup.

"I loved the guy," Metro said. "He played his heart out, to the best of his ability. He could hit. He could have been fabulous. But I just don't know if anybody in the big leagues would have put up with him long."[12]

Metro stuck with Joe, and he delivered 23 homers, 77 RBIs, and a .292 batting average.

"Charlie Metro was one tough cookie," said Dick Fitzgerald, a pitcher for the Mounties.

But Metro seemed to have a soft spot for Taylor.

When he arrived at the ballpark for a home game against the Sacramento Solons, he could hardly walk. The team's trainer helped him shower and put on his uniform.

"He sat in the dugout during the game because he couldn't play," Fitzgerald said. "He nagged Charlie the whole game: 'Put me in, I'll break this game open.'"

Joe pinch-hit in the bottom of the ninth inning with a runner on base and the Mounties trailing, 3-1. "I had my doubts, but he kept at me until I let him go up to the plate," Metro wrote in his autobiography, *Safe by a Mile.*

Fitzgerald had just pitched two scoreless innings and was pulling for Joe to snap out of his stupor long enough to hit a game-tying homer. "If Joe hits one out, I might get a win in relief," he said.

The usually free-swinging Taylor didn't move his bat as three-straight strikes whizzed past. On the way to the locker room after the game, he chastised Metro, saying, "Charlie, you shouldn't have sent me out there. You knew how drunk I was."[13]

"Some managers would let him go ahead and drink," Thurman said. "They'd tell him, 'Be ready to play the game. I don't care how much you drink as long as you play.' That made him feel better. He didn't go overboard with his drinking."

In 1960, Taylor moved to Seattle from Vancouver, along with general manager Cedric Tallis. "I want this man on my ballclub, as long as he can afford to pay his fines," he said, tongue only partly in cheek.[14]

Joe almost didn't have enough money to pay the fines.

In mid-May, he crashed a car that was believed to be stolen. The incident was the off-the-field equivalent of the bonehead play that got him run out of Portland five years earlier.

Taylor went to a tavern after a night game in Seattle. He left in the wee hours of the morning, got into a car that looked like his, stuck the key in the ignition switch, and took off for a friend's house. Later, he was driving home in the rain when he rear-ended a vehicle driven by a nurse on her way to work. Police confirmed Joe's car looked like the one he had wrecked, and the ignition key fit both cars. They found the crashed car against a utility pole a few blocks away.

"It was the strangest story," said Johnny O'Brien, the Rainiers' third baseman and team captain. "He thinks he's in his own car and he isn't."

The actual owner of the car had reported it stolen and was at his house talking to the police when Joe drove by. He was eventually arrested and jailed. "He probably thought he was in the batting cage when he woke up," joked O'Brien.

Joe was convicted of drunken and negligent driving, fined $250, and had his driver's license suspended for 30 days. The Rainiers added a fine of their own.

In the fourth inning of a game on July 5, he was hit by a pitch and, running to first base, stumbled over the bag and almost fell down.

"Spectators detected nothing awry when Taylor failed to show in left field the next inning," Meyers reported in the *Times*. "He had been hit by a pitched ball. The supposition was that Joe had suffered a minor injury."[15]

Manager Dick Sisler thought otherwise and had the team doctor check to see if Joe was intoxicated. They decided he was and removed him from the game.

"They said I was drunk," Taylor said. "I didn't feel I was drunk. But if they felt I couldn't do the job, that's up to them."[16]

Tallis suspended him indefinitely for drunkenness and insubordination.

Joe blamed the suspension on his reputation, saying, "I've had this bad reputation for eight years. Any little thing I do, they jump on it."

"Nobody ever has called Taylor a 'bad man,'" Meyers wrote, "and that is the reason he has had more than one second chance in baseball."[17]

Taylor got those second chances because of his power hitting. In the game before he was suspended, Joe homered, doubled twice, and tripled to score three runs and drive in four. He had a team-high 16 homers, 17 doubles, 4 triples, 46 RBIs, and a batting average of .296.

"Joe was basically the muscle of the team," O'Brien said. "And when he was going good, everything was going good."

O'Brien represented the players at a meeting with Tallis, Sisler, an assistant to Rainiers owner Emil Sick, and Edo Vanni, a longtime Rainiers player and coach.

"Joe's gone," Tallis announced, "he's out of here."

"What the hell are you talking about?" Vanni protested.

He reminded everyone that they were sometimes guilty of drinking too much. "And now you want to throw Joe off the team. We need Joe."

The Rainiers were in fourth place, only six games behind league-leading Spokane.

"Joe was our cleanup hitter," said center fielder Buddy Gilbert. "We needed his bat if we were going to get in the first division."

The final decision was left up to the players, and they wanted Joe back in the lineup.

To make sure that happened, Joe had to breathe on team trainer Freddie Frederico prior to every game. If no alcohol was detected, he could play.

Joe was sober as a judge his first game back. And he looked like one, too, striking out twice. He continued to pass the sniff tests and whiff at the plate.

"He just looked awful," Gilbert said. "I used to tell people I could get him out underhanded."

After managing only five singles in 35 at-bats, he finally homered—a prodigious poke that carried 500 feet over the high wall in straightaway center at Seattle's Sick's Stadium, the first hit in the history of the 22-year-old park.

Edo Vanni came up with the idea of giving Joe a shot or two of vodka, like a dose of medicine, immediately after he passed his daily sobriety test.

Joe belted four homers in five games and finished the season with a career-best 30, tops on the team. He batted a solid .291 and paced the Rainiers with 94 RBIs.

"He needed a lubricant, let's call it that," O'Brien added. "The problem he had was that, on occasion, he took too much lubricant."

Thurman put it more bluntly: "He had no control over his drinking problem. This is what really got him because you never knew when he'd show up for a ballgame. If he ever showed up, and was able to play, nine times out of 10 he was going to help you win a ballgame."

The classic example of this was a game between Vancouver and Seattle in 1962. Joe was now playing for the Mounties, managed by Jack McKeon. The '62 season was Taylor's last in the PCL. It was McKeon's first at the Triple-A level. He went on to manage 16 years in the majors.

The Mounties acquired Taylor from the Hawaii Islanders a week into the season. McKeon didn't know much about Taylor, so George Bamberger, a veteran Mounties pitcher, gave him the low-down.

"He's a good guy," Bamberger said. "He won't bother anybody. He'll have a few drinks, just leave him alone."

That's what McKeon did.

"Just go out and do your job," he told Taylor. "If you want to go out and get bombed, just don't take any of the younger guys with you."

McKeon stayed cool even when Joe sauntered in late for the game against the Rainiers in Seattle. "He got dressed in a hurry and headed to the bullpen so nobody could talk to him," McKeon chuckled.

One of the pitchers in the Mounties bullpen was Jim Rantz, head of the Minnesota Twins' farm system from 1986 to 2012. "Joe had a head start on happy hour," Rantz recalled. "When he had a few, he was very talkative."

The bullpens at Sick's Stadium were a short walk from the dugouts down the foul lines.

In about the third inning, Rantz rushed in from the bullpen to tell McKeon, "Skip, you've got to bring Taylor up to the dugout. He'll have us all bombed. He's loaded."

Taylor was still in the bullpen in the sixth inning when Rantz paid McKeon another visit. "Joe Taylor says, 'Put 'em in and he'll break up this no-hitter.'"

Pitching for Seattle was Dave Morehead, a 19-year-old signed to an $85,000 bonus contract by the Boston Red Sox. Morehead had a no-hitter and a 1-0 lead going into the top of the ninth inning.

"Send Taylor down here," McKeon hollered to Rantz in the bullpen.

The manager could hardly believe his eyes. "He's staggering up to home plate. The first pitch he sees, he banks off the left-field wall for a single. Breaks up the no-hitter."

The next batter, Ron Henry, homered, and the Mounties won the game, 2-1.

On at least one occasion in 1962, Taylor never made it to the ballpark.

The Mounties had just played the Padres in San Diego and were scheduled to fly from Los Angeles to Honolulu for a series against the Islanders. Taylor missed both the team bus to LA and the flight to Hawaii.

Joe was last seen at the San Diego hotel where the Mounties stayed, but the team's business manager admitted, "We can't find anyone who has seen him or heard from him since."[18]

"We went to Hawaii," Rantz said. "He went to Mexico."

Wherever Joe was, he needed money, and McKeon had the players' paychecks with him. "He's calling me in Hawaii to send him his check. I said: 'I'm sending you nothin'. Meet us in Salt Lake.'"

A week later, Taylor was in Salt Lake City to pick up his check and sit in the bullpen, where he spent most of his last month as a Mountie.

Joe's 13 home runs and 37 RBIs were exactly half of what they were the year before. His batting average of .246 was a career-low in the minors. "He was at the end of the line," McKeon said.

Taylor's last stop was the Mexican League in 1963, beginning in Puebla and ending in Mexico City. He bashed 19 homers—parting shots of an amazing slugger fading away in an alcoholic haze.

"That Joe Taylor was something," Thurman said. "He had a tremendous drinking problem. But he didn't know it. He said he could handle it. He always thought that. That was the difference between him and the others that drank."

* * *

Beer is as much a part of baseball as popcorn, peanuts, and Cracker Jacks.

Sick's Stadium in Seattle was named after Emil Sick, the owner of the Rainiers and the brewery that produced Rainier beer.

Today, the St. Louis Cardinals, Colorado Rockies, and Milwaukee Brewers play their home games at ballparks named after beer sponsors—Busch Stadium in St. Louis, Coors Field in Denver, and Miller Park in Milwaukee.

The most enduring image of Brooklyn's Ebbets Field is the Schaefer beer sign atop the scoreboard in right field, which read, "A *real* hit! Schaefer—*real* beer!"

In the 1950s, the Yankees had Ballantine beer and its advertising slogan "Baseball and Ballantine." Bronx Bomber home runs were hailed as "Ballantine Blasts" by Mel Allen, the team's radio and television voice.

Announcers were pitch men for beers sponsoring their team's broadcasts.

Curt Gowdy of the Boston Red Sox plugged Narragansett beer with the catchphrase "Hi, neighbor, have a Gansett."

Ernie Harwell of the Detroit Tigers used tense situations in a game to tell fans to "hang on to your Stroh's."

Harry Caray was the ultimate beer salesman, promoting Budweiser and Griesedieck beers for the Cardinals, Falstaff for the Chicago White Sox, and Budweiser for the Chicago Cubs.

In Taylor's hometown of Pittsburgh, Bob Prince promoted Iron City beer by urging Pirates fans to "pump an Iron." They could sing along with this advertising jingle for the beer: "Well, you can't pump an Iron in Cincinnati, Candlestick Park and Wrigley, or Shea, you can't pump an Iron too far away from Pittsburgh, PA."

Joe was 10 years old in 1936, when his father, George, and mother, Mary, moved from Chapman, Alabama, to Pittsburgh in the midst of a devastating flood that left 110,000 people homeless. George went from driving a team of mules in Alabama to working in a steel mill. Mary was a maid.

Following in the footsteps of his father and 22 uncles, Joe played baseball. "All I knew was baseball, baseball, baseball," he said.

Joe was 14 in 1940, when some friends double-dared him to pump his first Iron. "My mother beat the hell out of me. That's why I can remember the first beer I drank in my life."

He dropped out of high school in 12th grade. "I had no education—just a dummy. But I loved baseball. I knew baseball."

Joe was 18 on D-Day, June 6, 1944, when his U.S. Army battalion invaded Le Havre, France, as part of the Normandy landings that liberated Western Europe.

Upon returning home after World War II, Joe played softball and then baseball at Kennard Field, a Pittsburgh playground. That's when he learned a couple of beers "make the ball look real good."

Earl Johnson, a sportswriter for a weekly newspaper, the *Pittsburgh Courier*, started chronicling his long-ball-hitting exploits. "He kept pushing me, kept pushing me."

Joe was 23 in 1949, when he joined the Chicago American Giants in the Negro Leagues, playing alongside Ted "Double Duty" Radcliffe. Double Duty often pitched the second game of a doubleheader after catching the first.

In 1950, he moved to the Winnipeg Buffaloes of the independent ManDak League in Manitoba, Canada, and North Dakota.

In 1951, he joined manager Sam Bankhead at Farnham in the Provincial League. Bankhead lived in Pittsburgh and was a drinking buddy. "Joe, you can run and throw," he said. "Go to the outfield."

"I can't do it, man. I don't know how to play the outfield."

Taylor reluctantly agreed to play center field. He was hitting .360, with 10 homers, when he broke his jaw in an outfield collision with Al Pinkston. "Sure, I could run. But I was a catcher—a good one," he maintained. "My buddy put me in the outfield, and I couldn't do it."

Taylor and Pinkston played side by side in the outfield at St. Hyacinthe in 1952. Joe posted a .308 batting average, with a Provincial League–leading 35 doubles, 25 homers, and 112 RBIs.

Joe Taylor, left, and Al Pinkston were teammates at Farnham, Quebec, in 1951, when they collided in the outfield, Joe sustaining a broken jaw that sidelined him the rest of the season. They were at spring training together with the Kansas City Athletics in 1955, before winding up at Columbus, Ohio, in the International League. *Author's collection.*

"Joe wasn't a bad outfielder," said St. Hyacinthe manager John Sosh. "He was a 3-to-1 better outfielder than Pinkston."

Joe was 28 in 1954, and hitting .325, with 16 homers and 24 doubles, for Ottawa when Branch Rickey, vice president and general manager of the Pittsburgh Pirates, filed the following report:

A tall, rough, sea-going Negro who allegedly plays a great game when sober. He has a reputation for being a complete rounder—a fence screeching tomcat with not enough females in sight. 'Tis said he even plays a good game with a snoot full. This fellow can run and he can throw, and he can hit the ball "a fur piece." I don't know how old he is. So far as I can find out, no one does. My guess is somewhere between

20 and 40. Age doesn't matter because he is fast, agile, and obviously full of confidence. . . . Taylor bears such a vile reputation that I guess I couldn't have the remotest interest in him, but he impressed me very much as a player. [19]

In November 1975, Joe was almost 50. He was a janitor for the Pittsburgh Housing Authority (PHA) and living with a woman named Madaline and her son, Loren, in a two-bedroom apartment in Terrace Village, part of the PHA.

Joe had just finished pumping a can of Iron and walked to the kitchen to reload. He returned to his seat in the living room, a cold Iron in one hand and a burning Salem cigarette in the other.

"I guess I didn't help my reputation any. I'd say, 'Throw it to my whiskey! Throw it to my whiskey! Throw it to my whiskey!' I said it everywhere. Fastball. POW! Running around the bases, I'd yell, 'You threw it at my whiskey.' Maybe it hurt me because, like a fool, I never tried to stop it. I let it go."

That's the closest Joe came to expressing any regrets.

Joe sipped the beer to demonstrate how he tricked pitchers into thinking he was drunk. "I'd take one little taste—one little taste. I'd say, 'Whew, man, I was drunk last night.'"

"He'd kid with everybody on the field," Thurman said. "The players would say, 'Ah-h-h, Joe's got his head bad. Watch out.' He'd tear the ball up."

"I was actually sober as a judge," Joe insisted. "But everybody thought I was drunk. I'd take that one drink and get beside you—WHOOSH!"

The drinks helped Joe relax and, as he once told Thurman, cope with the fear of failure. "Gave me a whole lot of courage. Couple of beers and I'm not scared of you," Joe said.

Joe jumped to his feet to show where his whiskey was located.

Knee-high, baby. If you throw it knee-high, you're hurting. Outside, inside—doesn't make no difference. I was a first-pitch hitter. They knew it. But they think I'm drunk. Wow, here comes a fast ball. POW! They always wondered, until Gaylord caught me, why I hit so many home runs on the first pitch.

Gaylord Perry won 314 games in the majors to earn a Hall of Fame plaque that one opposing manager said should be permanently attached to a tube of K-Y Jelly. He was widely suspected of doctoring the ball with K-Y and throwing a spitball.

In 1961, the 22-year-old Perry won 16 games for the Tacoma Giants of the PCL. Taylor, then 35, poked 26 homers for the San Diego Padres.

One afternoon, he rushed into a restaurant and up to the bar: "Give me a drink! Give me a drink!"

Joe grabbed the shot glass of whiskey, sipped half of it, and said, "I gotta go play ball."

Joe didn't see Gaylord behind him having lunch.

"A lot of the players said he was a heavy drinker, but they had nothing to back it up," Gaylord said. "They'd kid about it. That was part of the game everybody talked about—not in a bad way. It was in a comical way. We looked for it every time we played them. The first thing you did was go out on the field and find out."

One of Gaylord's teammates in Tacoma was James "Dusty" Rhodes, hero of the 1954 World Series for the New York Giants. Dusty was a so-called gin-head. He offered Gaylord some sage advice: "Look, when Joe acts like he's had a lot to drink, that's when he's going to hit the ball the best."

Gaylord often hung around the batting cage with other players so he could hear their bantering. Joe walked up to Gaylord before one game and said, "Man, you know I had a rough night last night."

Gaylord could smell the whiskey on Joe's breath.

"I'm drunk. I'm sick."

Gaylord thought to himself, "Why would a guy want to do something like that to himself?"

And then he remembered the warning from Dusty: "Don't believe him!"

"Throw it to my whiskey," Joe joshed.

"Oh, no," Gaylord said. "You ain't getting no fastball tonight, you son of a bitch."

The incident at the restaurant confirmed what Gaylord suspected. "He'd get the young guys to throw him that good fastball in there the first time because they'd think, 'Well, he can't see the ball.' But, believe me, he could see the ball. It didn't take me too long to catch on to him."

"Gaylord knew that I was bullshitting," Joe said. "I didn't play drunk. I took one drink to make him think I was drunk."

"Joe used certain psychology to get the pitcher like I used to try and get the hitter when I was going through all the motions," Perry said.

> Whether you did or not, a lot of times it worked. I heard our infielders talk. Maybe they relaxed a little bit more when he was up there. They said, "He can't hit the ball anyway. He can't see it." All of a sudden, the ball would go by them, and if they'd really been ready, they'd got it. He put on a pretty good show.

"I never had a drinking problem," Joe said. "Don't get me wrong, I drank. But it wasn't a problem. I swear it wasn't."

Joe was asked what he'd have done differently.

"The only thing I'd do over again is play it again—play it! Because it's been beautiful. The excitement . . . the anticipation . . . the drama when you hit a home run to win a ballgame. As old as I am, you see what I'm doing?"

Joe pounded his right fist into a dusty baseball glove.

"Here's my catcher's mitt."

He was holding a first baseman's mitt.

"But that's my catcher's mitt. That was my whole life—catching. I had a good throwing arm. I'm not going to make any comeback, but I'm going to play again."

The glove hadn't been used in 10 years.

"I've got my gloves, see. I'm getting them out and put that Neatsfoot oil on them and get them soft and go out there with the kids. I want to show them something—what I've learned. Going out with the kids. Going out with the kids."

* * *

Joe turned 50 on March 2, 1976.

Four days later, he was chatting with his mother, Mary, in her well-preserved two-story brick home in Pittsburgh's dilapidated Hill District.

"People don't pay much attention to drinking until you get in the public's eye," Joe said. "And then they watch you."

"I had a newspaper article once," Mary said. "Can't find it. But some reporter said, 'Babe Ruth spilled more whiskey than Joe Taylor could drink.'"

Babe Ruth and Mickey Mantle are the most famous of baseball's heavy drinkers. Right up there with the Yankee greats is Grover Cleveland Alexander, the alcoholic pitcher who won 373 games and was portrayed in the movie *The Winning Team* by Ronald Reagan, the 40th president of the United States.

The Negro Leagues had their share of boozers.

Josh Gibson was Babe's equal both with the bat and the bottle. A favorite drinking companion was Sam Bankhead, a teammate, friend, and, after Gibson's death, a surrogate father to his son, Josh Jr.

Sam was managing a team in Caracas, Venezuela, when he received a telegram on January 21, 1947, informing him Josh was dead. "He went out that night, got drunk, came in, and tore up everything in the room," said Bill Cash, the team's starting catcher.[20]

In a 1952 *Pittsburgh Courier* poll, Sam was named to the all-time Negro Leagues all-star team as a utility player.

In 1942, five years before Jackie Robinson broke the color barrier in the majors, *Courier* sports editor Wendell Smith urged the woeful Pittsburgh Pirates to give tryouts to Bankhead, Gibson, and two other members of the all-black Pittsburgh Crawfords, as they "would add what the Bucs lack now."

Smith praised Bankhead as the "ballplayers' ballplayer" because he could play both the infield and outfield. "He can hit, run, and throw. He is dynamite in the clutch and a great competitor."[21]

The Pirates agreed to a tryout but at a "future date."[22]

That date never arrived.

A Bankhead played for the Brooklyn Dodgers in 1947, but it was Sam's youngest brother, Dan, the first black to pitch in the majors

"The Dodgers came to town, Dan pitched, and Sam wouldn't go see him play—his own brother," confided Frank "Fuzzy" Walton, a former Negro Leaguer. "Why? He was jealous. Sam Bankhead won't let anyone be better than he was as a player. That's a shame."

Sam was Joe's first manager in Organized Baseball and the one responsible for making him an outfielder. He lived in Pittsburgh so Joe arranged a meeting.

"Sam just left his house to go to Herron Street," Joe said. "If we don't find him quick, he'll be drunk."

A brick street with old train tracks running down the middle, Herron, in the mid-1970s, was a mishmash of bars, barbecue joints, and ramshackle buildings awaiting the wrecking ball.

Joe walked into a noisy, crowded tavern and up to a table where Fuzzy Walton was sitting with three other people. Fuzzy was 17 in 1930, when he first played in the Negro Leagues for the Baltimore Black Sox.

"We're trying to find Sam," Joe said. "You know where he is?"

Fuzzy didn't know but got up to join the search. He returned shortly with a key to an abandoned building nearby.

"This is condemned," Fuzzy said as he entered the building, a Concerned Citizens sign hanging over the entrance.

Joe appeared minutes later with a tipsy Sam.

"This is our hangout," Joe said. "We come here to drink and talk."

It was the ultimate man cave. There was a shoeshine stand. Next to it was a vintage refrigerator with an empty Iron City can on top.

One wall was decorated with lettered cards spelling, "STEELERS GO GO," and crepe paper streamers in the Pittsburgh Steelers' black and gold colors.

Another wall was covered with photos of the 1975 Steelers, Super Bowl champions, and two local heroes: the Steelers' All-Pro defensive tackle, "Mean" Joe Greene, and Manny Sanguillen, a three-time all-star catcher for the Pirates in the 1970s.

Joe steadied a wobbly Sam as they climbed up on the shoeshine stand.

"When Joe come up on my ballclub," Sam began, "I said I had nothing to worry about. But he got hurt. We were right in contention for the championship. When Joe got hurt, I had nobody else to play."

"We only had 14 men," Joe said. "When I got hurt, it killed the club."

"He was a good outfielder," Sam said. "He could do it. He could run."

"Sam says I was a helluva outfielder," Joe said. "I'm trying to tell you I was poor in the outfield."

"As a catcher, Joe was one of the best," Fuzzy said.

"I don't think he was the best catcher," Sam argued.

"I want you to say what you know," Joe said. "That's what we're here for."

"What I know is this is my man," Sam said as he slipped his right arm around Joe's shoulders. "I could never put you over Josh Gibson."

"Who could you put over Josh Gibson?" Joe asked.

The conversation switched to Joe's reputation as a fifth-a-day man.

Sitting on a shoeshine stand in an abandoned building in Pittsburgh's Hill District in March 1976, Joe Taylor, left, and Sam Bankhead debated whether Joe was a better outfielder than catcher. Joe was a catcher before Bankhead, his manager at Farnham in 1951, moved him to the outfield. They remained good friends and drinking buddies long after leaving baseball. *Photo by Mark Von Wehrden.*

"A fifth-a-day man?" Fuzzy said. "I drink a fifth a day now—working every day."

"I don't have that much money," Sam sighed.

"Don't condemn a man because he drinks," Fuzzy said.

"I wish I had me a drink," Sam quipped.

"All ballplayers drink," Fuzzy said. "They are worse than us now. They are using dope."

Fuzzy pointed to Sam and then Joe. "What about the punishment we had coming up? Any little technical thing they could find on us."

"Yeah, yeah!" Sam cheered.

Fuzzy was referring to how black players were treated differently than whites.

"We could't afford to go out and have over three drinks," he said. "If we took over three drinks, they condemned us: 'There he is—a drunk.'"

"But here's a ballplayer," Fuzzy pointed to himself, "who won't condemn Joe. I won't condemn you, Joe."

"You want my opinion why Joe didn't stay in the majors longer?" Sam asked. "He didn't take care of himself."

"That's what he wants—your honest opinion," Joe said.

"He was too old," Sam added.

Joe was 28 when he broke into the majors with the A's.

"He was a great hitter," Sam said. "How do you think he made the major leagues? Not on his fielding ability or his life living. Maybe he didn't suit the personalities that were there—the people that he was playing for."

Of the 1,615 games Joe played in Organized Baseball, he caught in only one of them—the next to last game of the 1956 season with the Seattle Rainiers. Most of his teammates had no idea he was a catcher in the Negro Leagues.

"At that time we didn't have many good catchers," Joe explained.

> As a good catcher who could hit, I had a better chance than in the outfield. I couldn't throw that good to be in the outfield. Guys would run on me. But as a catcher I could throw the ball. I had a quick throw, but not a long and a hard throw like an outfielder should have. That's why I say I had a better chance as a catcher.

"I think he had a good enough arm to be a top-notch catcher," Sam said.

"He never got to see me catch," Joe lamented.

Sam quickly changed the subject. "Who can hit?"

"Me!" Joe shouted with glee.

"Heh-heh-heh. He ain't lying."

* * *

Joe Taylor is one of those players who got others wondering "What if?"

What if he was younger when he broke into the majors?

What if he had controlled the booze rather than the other way around?

What if his big-league managers had played him every day?

As far as Dick Fitzgerald is concerned, Taylor "should've been in the Hall of Fame. He was apart from everyone else as far as pure power. Of all the players I played with, he had the greatest talent of any of them."

That's saying something, because one of Fitzgerald's teammates at Vancouver in 1959 was Brooks Robinson, a human vacuum cleaner who went on to become a Hall of Fame third baseman for the Baltimore Orioles. Said Fitzgerald, "I used to go home and tell my friends about this guy named Joe Taylor and they'd go, 'Who?' They didn't know much about him."

Even the staunchest baseball fans know little about Joe. He died in obscurity, just like his pal, Sam Bankhead.

On July 24, 1976 (almost five months after the Herron Avenue meeting), Sam was shot in the head and killed during a locker room argument with Nelson Cooper, a lifelong friend and fellow dishwasher at the William Penn Hotel in downtown Pittsburgh. Cooper testified in court that Sam was "very drunk" and "threw him to the floor" before he reached for a handgun in his locker. The gun accidentally fired as they fought over it.[23]

Pittsburgh fans had to be reminded by *Pittsburgh Post-Gazette* sports columnist Al Abrams, that the slain man once was a shortstop for the Homestead Grays and a "top player making the Negro all-star teams of his era seven times."[24]

Joe was 67 when he died on March 18, 1993. The *Post-Gazette* carried a brief obituary that read in part, "Mr. Taylor played pro baseball for the Cincinnati Reds, the St. Louis Cardinals, and the Baltimore Orioles in the late Fifties and early Sixties."[25]

There was no mention of the Philadelphia A's, Joe's first team in the majors, nor any of his achievements in the minors. For all of his baseball accomplishments, Joe is remembered mostly for what he didn't accomplish.

"If Joe had just taken better care of himself, I wonder what would've happened?" Fitzgerald mused. "He was the best player ever who didn't make it in the majors."

10

A WHIFF OF THE BIG TIME

Joe Brovia

The roommates were an odd couple.

At 6-foot-3 and 200 pounds, Joe Brovia was so menacing with a bat in his hands that pitchers feared he might club them over the head if he didn't get a hit. He was sometimes called the "Davenport Destroyer" after his hometown in California, because of his ability to wallop a baseball hard and far.

The 5-foot-7, 150-pound Marino Pieretti was a pitcher nicknamed "Chick" and "Half Pint." What he lacked in size, he made up for with a pesky persistence.

"Joe hated pitchers with a vengeance," Marino said. "No matter who they were, they were terrible. All pitchers were bad except when I was his roommate. The sportswriters would say, 'Joe, you don't like pitchers. What about your roommate?' Joe would say: 'He's on my side; I like him.'"

Marino and Joe were roomies the six years they played together with the Portland Beavers and Sacramento Solons (1949–1954) in the Pacific Coast League (PCL).

"The only thing I didn't like about Joe was he'd wake me up in the night to discuss a new way to hit a ball," Marino said.

One night after going hitless in Seattle, Joe returned to his hotel room, where Marino already was sleeping, getting extra rest for the game he was pitching the next day.

Marino was awakened by Joe lying in bed moaning about going hit-less and what he was doing wrong. At about one o'clock in the morning, Joe turned on the light and jumped out of bed.

"I think I got it!" he exclaimed. "I think I was dropping my back shoulder. Take a look at my swing."

Marino couldn't believe his eyes.

Joe was swinging a clothes hanger in the middle of the room "with no clothes on and his balls dangling back and forth."

A sleepy Marino advised, "You're not dropping your back shoulder. Your problem is your nuts are too heavy."

Joe almost fell down laughing, and in the next game Marino said, "He hit three line drives and told everybody that I corrected his swing by swinging straight out."

Brovia was one of the PCL's all-time great hitters and a real-life version of the fictional character Ring Lardner described shaving with a straight razor in the middle of the night in his classic sports story *My Roomy*: "Instead o' doin' it in the bathroom he'd lather his face and then come out and stand in front o' the lookin'-glass on the dresser. Of course he'd have all the lights turned on, and that was bad enough when a feller wanted to sleep; but the worst of that was he'd stop shavin' every little while and turn round and stare at the guy who was makin' a failure o' tryin' to sleep. Then he'd wave his razor round in the air and laugh, and begin shavin' agin."[1]

Joe once had a nightmare that startled his roommate so much he blabbed it to a wire service reporter, who spread the story nationally. "Hell's bells, another strikeout!" he shouted in his sleep. "The ball was two feet high and four feet outside, but I had to swing at it like any busher. Brovia, I'm a bum."[2]

He was 18 years old in 1940, when he broke into pro ball with a bang by hitting a league-leading .383 and driving in 103 runs in 104 games for the El Paso Texans of the Class C Arizona–Texas loop.

El Paso manager Cy "Spec" Williamson advised El Paso fans to "get a good look at him now" because it will cost them "more to see him play in a few years—he's sure to go to the majors."[3]

Brovia finally made it to the majors in 1955, with the Cincinnati Reds, but at the age of 33, it was a case of too little, too late. He lasted 39 days, appearing in 21 games as a pinch-hitter and getting only 2 hits in 18 at-bats for a puny .111 average. He struck out six times.

George "Birdie" Tebbetts was the Reds' manager at the time. "Of all the ballplayers I've ever known I've rooted more for him and felt more badly about the fact that he was getting a shot so late in life," said Tebbetts. "I even tried to find a soft spot for him to hit. I couldn't find it."

Joe spent the rest of his career in the minors, playing mostly in the PCL cities of San Francisco, Portland, Sacramento, and Oakland. In 12 seasons, he ravaged the league's pitchers, hitting .304 and belting 174 home runs.

"It's just a shame that his career had to be wasted in the Coast League," Pieretti said. "If he were born in this time with the designated hitter rule, he'd probably be a great star."

Marino was born in Italy and migrated to the United States just like Joe's father, Pietro, and mother, Maria. When the two friends were on opposing teams, Marino was the "mortal enemy" and incurred Joe's wrath by throwing off-speed or so-called "junk" pitches. "Being a power hitter, he'd try to pull the ball. He'd ground out or something and scream, 'You ain't got enough to hit, you little Dago.'"

"Brovia was as good a fastball hitter as I've ever seen in my life," said Chuck Stevens, a former big-leaguer who played nine years in the PCL. "I'm talking about Joe DiMaggio, Ted Williams—guys like that. It was like putting a pork chop on the table for a dog when you threw him a fastball. He'd begin to lick his chops. The harder you threw, the better he liked it."

At San Francisco's Seals Stadium, home of the PCL Seals and the Giants in 1958–1959, after they relocated from New York, there was a white star next to a 404-foot sign on the 30-foot-high center-field fence. The star marked the spot of a rocket shot by Brovia in 1947, which was still rising as it cleared the fence. The ball traveled an estimated 560 feet from home plate. Even Willie Mays, the Giants' superstar center fielder, was amazed, saying, "Hey, that's a $5 ride in a taxicab."[4]

Nowadays, it's about $45—slightly less than the fare from AT&T Park's Willie Mays Plaza to San Francisco International Airport.

Brovia joined the San Francisco Seals in 1941, and immediately captured the attention of Bob Stevens, a young sportswriter for the *San Francisco Chronicle*.

"Joe came up to the plate, then backed away and went into the traditional act of knocking dirt out of his spikes with his bat," Stevens wrote a decade later.

He made only one mistake, besides trying to do it with the barrel end of the Louisville. He got his legs crossed, slammed the bat into his right ankle, knocked both feet off the ground, and fell into a heap at the side of the Padre catcher. Nonplussed, Brovia painfully regained his feet and proceeded to nearly tear the pitcher apart with a line drive through the box. [5]

The things Brovia did and said were beyond the imagination of most writers.

"The best way to fly is to go by air," he mused in 1950, as he piled up 39 homers for the Portland Beavers. [6]

After he was suspended in 1954, for abusive language and spitting in the face of an umpire, he explained, "I was frothing. Some of the froth must've landed on the umpire." [7]

Brovia was convinced the official scorer for Portland Beavers games was cheating him so he wouldn't have a higher batting average and get a raise the next year. He was griping about it in the clubhouse when Bob Blackburn, the Beavers' play-by-play announcer, appeared.

"Bob, come over here," Joe said. "Yesterday I got 3-for-4. Look at this paper: 1-for-4."

Blackburn glanced at the box score and said, "Well, Joe, that's a typographical error."

"Error, shit!" Joe protested. "Those were line-drive hits."

A riled-up Brovia was always good for a laugh.

Dwight "Red" Adams pitched for Portland three of the four seasons Brovia played there (1949–1952).

"We'd just wait for him to come back to the dugout when he'd make an out because we knew he was going to do something funny," Adams said. "One game he hit a couple of line shots right at somebody. That just killed him when he hit a ball hard and didn't get a base hit. He came back to the dugout, and he was beside himself. He looked up at the sky and, like he was talking to the Lord, said, 'Are you living up there?'"

At Portland's Vaughn Street Park, there was a battered old door from the clubhouse runway into the Beavers dugout. Two panels were missing, one of them with a message in white chalk reading, "Brovia kicked out this panel August 16, '49 after lining out." [8]

The panel was high on the plywood door. When Joe kicked a hole through it, his foot got stuck. He was trapped.

Teammates at Sacramento in 1953–1954, Joe Brovia, left, was as high-strung as Bob Dillinger was low key. Playing his first game in Portland as a Sacramento Solon, he was ejected for trying to go into the stands after an abusive fan. "What happened?" Bob asked Joe back in the dugout. "The guy threw beer on me," Joe growled. "You should've drank it!" Bob quipped. *San Diego History Center.*

"We're out in the field and we've got no right fielder," Beavers short-stop Eddie Basinski recalled. "So everybody is saying, 'Hold it! Where the hell is Brovia?'"

He was found hung up on the door, screaming for help.

A year later, one door panel was still intact, with a handwritten reminder: "Reserved for Brovia."[9]

By then Joe had moved on to bigger, more dramatic things.

In a game against Sacramento at Vaughn Street Park, Joe was camped under a fly ball near the screen fence in left field when suddenly, he staggered and fell to his knees without the ball. L. H. Gregory, sports editor of the *Oregonian*, reported Brovia was hit in the head by the ball and "got one foot caught in [the] bottom part of the screen and almost dragged the contraption down in struggling to pull free to pursue the ball."[10]

The noggin-bashing triggered a 9-for-15 hitting spree that included a homer, 3 doubles, and 6 runs batted in. Gregory suggested in his column that fans might want to donate "toward an iron hat for Joe."[11]

The next time Gregory walked into the Portland clubhouse, Brovia screamed, "Hey, you son of a bitch, get out of here or I'll kill you."

Beavers third baseman Leo Thomas could see the fear in Gregory's eyes. "It's a wonder Gregory didn't die of a heart attack," Thomas said, "It scared the hell out of him."

The madder Brovia got, the better he hit.

He batted in 114 runs for the Beavers in 1950, but Gregory claimed he wasn't a "top clutch man," reasoning, "If Joe's homers came in game-winning spots, he wouldn't stay here long."[12]

"I'll show you up good for that," a deeply offended Brovia told Gregory at the start of the 1951 season.

Gregory changed his tune, writing two weeks later: "Joe Brovia's big bat is really slamming runs home in the clutch this spring."[13]

Brovia ended the year with 133 runs batted in and 32 round-trippers, while improving his batting average 23 points, from .280 to .303.

Joe was no Phi Beta Kappa. Nor was he a country bumpkin or buffoon. Early on, sportswriters depicted him as a colorful character, and while he protested every now and then, he enjoyed the attention and usually laughed along with others.

"He was just a big overgrown kid," Thomas said. "Everybody liked him. Even the opposition liked him. But they feared him at the plate."

Most of Brovia's wrath was reserved for pitchers.

"I never met a pitcher I ever liked," he said. "Off the field, yeah. But on the field, no. They were all son of a bitches to me."

He harassed pitchers constantly. "Throw the ball, you cunny-thumb sucker," Joe hollered, trying to provoke a fastball that he could jack out of the park.

Joe detested left-handers, especially Glenn Elliott, a pitcher who wore glasses and relied on a baffling assortment of pitches that were slow, slower, and slowest.

"Glenn Elliott probably couldn't throw hard enough to bust a pane of glass," Pieretti said. "He used to get Joe out something pathetic."

Coast League teams played seven games against one another during a weeklong series. If Joe faced Elliott on a Tuesday night, they'd meet again Saturday night. "You syphilitic son of a bitch, I'll get you Saturday," he might scream after going hitless against Elliott.

"If we're leaving town, he'd say, 'I'll get you next trip,'" Pieretti said.

In a game near the end of the season, everyone on the team except Joe had a hit off Elliott.

"Last time up he hit a rope—probably the first rope he hit off Elliott," Pieretti recalled. "Right at the first baseman. He came back to the bench and was flipping the bat up and down, screaming and yelling, calling him a four-eyed everything you could imagine."

He stopped, realizing the season was over. There was no game Saturday or next trip. Finally, he shouted, "Okay, I'll get you in the Winter League."

Ironically, after the 1952 season, Portland traded Joe and Marino to Sacramento in exchange for Elliott and another hurler.

In Sacramento, Joe was reunited with "Chesty" Chet Johnson, a left-handed pitcher who was a teammate at El Paso in 1940, briefly with the Seals in 1941, and at Tacoma in 1942. Chet had a cameo appearance with the St. Louis Browns in 1946, returning to the Seals in 1950, to win 22 games.

"He was one of the finest left-handed hitters I ever saw," Chet said. "It didn't matter who was pitching, what they were throwing, he just wanted to hit."

Chet gave Joe fits the first time he faced him. "I knew he didn't like pitchers," Chet said, "but we roomed together, and I figured I was pretty close to him."

He teased Joe with slow pitches, admitting, "I couldn't throw a fastball by him."

Joe swung as hard as he could and hit a pop fly for an easy out. Before he reached the bench, the next hitter did the same thing. They entered the dugout at about the same time.

According to Chet,

> All of a sudden I heard this screaming and swearing, calling me everything in the book. I couldn't believe Joe would do this to me. I thought it was the other guy. So when he came up the next time, I decked him.
>
> He yelled, "What did you throw at me for?"
>
> I said, "I don't want you yelling and cussing at me."
>
> He said, "That wasn't me! That was Brovia!"

Joe had popped out again and was screaming about it in the dugout. "I'm gonna get you, you screwy left-hander!" he screamed.

Chet laughed as he reflected on the eye-opening scene.

"Here was Joe—my friend, my buddy who I'd taken care of when he was sick—just cussing me up one side and down the other. I'd always thought friendship was more important than hitting, but it wasn't. We got along fine—until I had to play against him. He hated me. He could've killed me."

* * *

The road was slick as ice from the dust spewed into the air by the nearby cement plant. Suddenly, a big, black limousine slid off the pavement, hitting a eucalyptus tree.

A teenage boy walking along the road rushed to the limo. The chauffeur got out first, followed by his famous passenger: Herbert Hoover, president of the United States from 1929 to 1933, during the Great Depression.

No one was hurt, and the limo was undamaged, except for a flat tire. The boy fixed the tire and the former president showed his gratitude by giving him 50 cents.

This was Joe Brovia's greatest claim to fame before it was discovered he could throw a baseball hard and hit one even harder.

Joseph John Brovia and his twin sister, Virginia, were born February 18, 1922, in Davenport, a sleepy California town of about 200 people, nine miles north of Santa Cruz on the scenic Pacific Coast Highway.

The year before, 1921, Pietro and Maria Brovia moved to Davenport from Torino, Italy.

Pietro owned a share in an artichoke and Brussels sprouts farm until a depressed local economy forced it to shut down in 1934. He took a job with the town's biggest employer, the Santa Cruz-Portland Cement Company, and moved his family into one of the company-owned houses.

"They cut my dad back to two days a week, $3 a day," Joe said. "He had to grow sprouts on the side to raise us kids. He was fortunate to have a job. You had about 5,000 people waiting at the gates to get a job."

To help his father, Joe worked in the fields from sunup to sundown for $1.25 a day, baled hay at a dairy farm for 10 cents an hour, and sold some of the smelt he caught fishing for one and two cents a pound. On spring and summer nights, he listened to radio broadcasts of Seals games.

"I practically felt like I knew the players because I listened every night," Joe said. "Dom DiMaggio was my idol. I said to myself, 'I want to play ball.'"

Brovia was 15 in 1937, when Dom became the last of the three DiMaggio brothers to play for the Seals. Vince DiMaggio led the way in 1932, followed by Joe and Dom. By the end of Dom's third and last season with the Seals in 1939, Brovia was a standout pitcher at Santa Cruz High School, attracting the attention of big-league scouts.

He was 16 in October 1938, when he attended a Cincinnati Reds tryout camp. The Reds considered him a "good prospect" and placed him on a "honor roll," saying they might call him back when he was older. [14]

As soon as Joe turned 18, he quit high school to sign with the Seals. "My folks didn't have any money. They couldn't afford to pay my sister's way to high school. I was the only one that went. I thought I might as well go out on my own and give baseball a try."

Brovia was listed as a pitcher when he arrived at the Seals' spring training camp in Boyes Hot Springs, 46 miles north of San Francisco.

"Joe is the first Italian reporting to the Seals this year who positively is not related to the DiMaggios," *Sporting News* informed readers. [15]

Seals manager Lefty O'Doul wasn't sure they weren't kinfolk after watching Joe rifle six shots in his first six exhibition game at-bats. One of the blasts was a triple against the wind, and another was a home run. "Kid, take that toe plate off," Lefty ordered. "You're going to be one of my outfielders."

By the end of spring training, Lefty was calling Brovia the best natural hitter he'd laid eyes on since Ted Williams. He also said Brovia was a second Smead Jolley. That was cause for the Seals to send him to El Paso so he could learn that a glove is intended for more than taking phantom swings in the outfield.

Midway through the 1940 season, Seals president Charles "Uncle Charlie" Graham traveled to Texas to see if Joe was as good as his press clippings. Uncle Charlie wound up adding to the hype with a lavish description of a "terrific triple" that "smacked against the fence 410 feet away" from home plate and a line-drive smash that tore through the second baseman's glove, "cracked his shoulder and knocked him down."[16]

A few months later, Brovia played in a Catholic Youth Organization benefit game at Seals Stadium against a major-league all-star team headed by Joe and Dom DiMaggio. The previous year, he watched the annual contest from the grandstand. Now he would be in right field for the minor-league stars, facing Joe and his hero, Dom. It was a chance to show he belonged on the same field.

Joe homered, and Dom slapped two hits and made a sparkling shoe-string catch. Meanwhile, Brovia ripped three singles, scored a run, and drove in another. "A junior Smead Jolley," observed Walter Judge of the *San Francisco Examiner*, noting "right field proved a trifle too big for him. But keep your eye on Joe. He can swing that bat."[17]

Judge had just rendered a verdict on Brovia that would stand the test of time: good hit, no field.

In Joe's first start for the Seals in 1941, he whacked three hits off the best pitcher in the PCL, Lancelot "Yank" Terry of the San Diego Padres. He also made three errors in left field.

"The balls were all hit hard—line drives," Brovia said. "One hit me in the chest. Another hit me in the knee. I went back on another one, stumbled, and it went over my head. I just had a miserable night, that's all."

Joe made five miscues the entire season, but the three-error game overshadowed a .318 batting average and labeled him. "Once they put the old tag on you—whoosh. That's it."

Joe spent most of the 1942 season at Tacoma in the Class B Western International League, posting a .290 average. With the Seals, he had only 6 hits in 36 at-bats for a .167 average.

"In those days, nobody helped you," Brovia said. "The players were out for blood. They wanted to play. They weren't about to let you take their job."

Things got tougher because of World War II.

Joe had a chance to join the U.S. Army's special services unit and play in Hawaii and other Pacific islands along with hundreds of other ballplayers, notably the DiMaggio brothers. Instead, he waited to be drafted in 1943 and was sent to France and the front lines of the war against Nazi Germany. "If we're in a war, why should I play baseball and the rest of 'em have to fight? I didn't figure that was right," he said.

Joe spent 20 months in combat. When the fighting ended in 1945, he joined U.S. occupational troops in Germany and played baseball. Every afternoon during practice, a pretty blonde named Gretchen rode her bicycle in front of Joe in right field, evoking cuss words that didn't faze her because she couldn't understand English.

"I'm going to stop that son of a bitch one of these days," he boasted to a teammate.

They started dating and got married in 1947. "She saw me playing baseball and fell in love with my hitting," Joe told friends.

Meanwhile, Joe returned to the Seals in the middle of the 1946 season. Images of him in the outfield were still fresh in Lefty O'Doul's mind. "He thought I was a big, slow, lumbering outfielder so why work with me," Joe said.

Lefty used him as a pinch-hitter nine times and then shipped him to the Salt Lake City Bees in the Class C Pioneer League.

The Salt Lake City ballpark, Derks Field, was destroyed by fire immediately after the fiery Brovia left town or else he would've been accused of arson. As it was, he burned up the league when he wasn't searing the ears of box-seat patrons with battlefield-caliber profanity.

"Every time he'd whiff or fail to hit, he'd come back and whack the wall in the dugout, mouthing unsavory oaths in anger," reported Harry Borba in the *San Francisco Examiner*. "The fans used to flee back three or four rows in fear. Every knuckle on Big Joe's big right paw is mashed and scarred. So are the ears of the Salt Lake fans."[18]

Brovia excelled in extremes.

He survived a hitless streak that extended 38 at-bats and then pounded hits in a league-record 29 straight games. In one game, he belted three triples, and in another, he got picked off second base twice. In fact, he was caught napping off a base four times in three games.

Joe batted .373 in 53 games, including the playoffs.

Up to this point in his career, he had a mere 10 homers. By comparison, he had 30 triples, and that had nothing to do with his speed.

"All his long hits went into center field and were caught," said Mickey Rocco, a left-hander who slugged 52 homers in his two years with the Seals. "If he pulled those same pitches into right field, they'd be home runs instead of outs."

At Seals Stadium, it was 400 feet from home plate to Joe's power alleys in center and right-center, and usually he was hitting against a stiff wind.

Joe had to learn to pull the ball down the 365-foot right-field line.

"Lefty was always trying to get Joe to pull the ball," Rocco said. "He tried different things to eliminate the hitch in his swing and nothing seemed to work."

Joe stood in front of a mirror at night, practicing his swing with a coat hanger as Lefty's words repeatedly went through his mind: "You're hitching!"

"When the pitcher threw the ball, Joe hitched his bat," Rocco explained. "It's sort of cocking your wrist is what it is. The bat would come up and go down real fast, and by that time the ball was by him. That little hitch made him swing late."

Joe couldn't ditch the hitch. "He could hit over .300 in the majors," Lefty told reporters. "He's mean when he swings that bat. I mean MEAN."[19]

The meanest bash of all was the one that almost scalped Bob Feller, the great Cleveland Indians pitcher. A perennial 20-game winner and strikeout king, and one of the highest-paid players in baseball, Feller faced Brovia in a March 1948 exhibition game at Seals Stadium.

Joe ripped a pitch that "almost knocked a few hundred thousand dollars' worth of pitching flesh out of commission," the *Examiner* reported. "The line drive barely missed the priceless Feller head by inches, maybe only by an inch."[20]

Joe could've been a bigger menace to Coast League pitchers if he'd been in the lineup every day. He played in only 114 of the Seals' 187 games in 1947, batting .309, with 10 homers and 63 runs batted in. He was on a rampage in 1948, when he was cut down by an appendicitis attack and sidelined almost five weeks. He ended up making the PCL all-star team with a .322 average, 9 homers, and 89 RBIs.

Veteran center fielder Bernard "Frenchy" Uhalt finally gave Joe the help he needed on defense.

"I had a sure pair of hands," Joe said. "When I got to a ball, I never dropped it. Uhalt saw me standing straight up."

"Joe," Frenchy said, "you've got to get up on your toes so you can go either way on the ball."

"I started concentrating on it, and, dammit, my fielding got better," Joe said. "In 1948, I was one of the most improved ballplayers in the PCL. I was slow, but I got a better jump on the ball. I made some good plays."

Of course, there were the bad plays—the Smead Jolley moments.

Sometimes fog crawled into Seals Stadium just as a fly ball was hit. One night, Joe was poised to catch a ball hit to right field when suddenly it disappeared into the fog and he couldn't see it.

"The ball ended up hitting him in the chest, but he could have just as well been hit on the top of the head," Rocco said. "Things like that always seemed to happen to Joe."

The wind and fog at Seals Stadium prompted Seals owner Paul Fagan to install a 12-foot-high, 101-foot-long shatterproof glass backstop in a semicircle behind home plate to protect fans in the choicest seats from the evening chill. If the glass fogged up, groundskeepers rushed to mop off the moisture.

A banker and shipping tycoon, Fagan knew far more about growing pineapples on his Hawaii plantation than popups or putouts. He bought a one-third share of the Seals in 1945, and assumed full control at the end of the 1950 season.

Fagan wanted Seals Stadium to be a showpiece and his players to be well-groomed models of decorum both on and off the field. He hired a "fog man" to chase fogs that settled around Seals Stadium, banned peanuts at the ballpark, and made women's restrooms as plush as those at his resort hotel on Waikiki Beach in Hawaii. Electric razors were placed in the clubhouse for daily shaves, and a barber chair was installed for semi-monthly haircuts. The players also were given combs and brushes sterilized daily and a clean handkerchief to carry in their hip pocket and use to wipe runny noses.

"What the hell does that man want to make me—a movie star?" Brovia complained. "Baseball is a rough game. It's not a pretty boy's game."

He rolled the bill of his cap, tilted it to the right, and pulled it down over his eyes to block any glare from the lights at night. Instead of tucking the bottom of his pants six inches below the knee, as required by the rules, he let them droop down around his ankles. Joe continued cussing and chewing tobacco, and spitting whenever and wherever he pleased. He refused to use a hanky.

Fagan was accustomed to having his way. "If a player is a troublemaker, out he goes," he said. "No matter how skillful he is. We want athletes worthy of wearing the Seals uniform representing San Francisco. That's an honor."[21]

A showdown was inevitable. It happened in early 1949, when Joe asked for $100 more than the $1,000 a month raise the Seals offered. He was coming off his best year in the PCL, plus he and his wife, Gretchen, were expecting their first child in June.

The Seals balked.

Joe went to see Lefty at the Seals' spring training camp at Boyes Hot Springs. "You have to see Charlie," Lefty said.

Uncle Charlie was dead, so in this case, Charlie was his son, Charles J. Graham, the Seals' general manager. "I went to see him in San Francisco, and he wouldn't have anything to do with me," Joe said.

He drove back to Boyes Hot Springs. "They gave me the run-around," he fumed.

Finally, Lefty informed Joe that a deal was in the works with another Coast League club and to go home and wait until it was done.

That's how Joe landed in Portland and Lefty in the middle of the biggest firestorm in his 17 years of managing the Seals.

O'Doul was a San Francisco landmark as popular as Coit Tower, Fisherman's Wharf, and the Golden Gate Bridge. His bar and restaurant downtown was a tourist attraction. He was Mr. San Francisco and scoffed at leaving to manage in the big leagues. "I already am in the major leagues," he said after leading the Seals to the 1946 PCL pennant. "This is major class. This is a major city, the Pacific Coast League is a major league."[22]

At $40,000-plus a year, Lefty was the best-paid manager in baseball. Life was rolling along like a smooth cable car ride until Brovia got railroaded out of town.

The Seals virtually gave Joe away for $4,000. They received no players.

"Whenever a .322 hitter doesn't fit into your plans, it's time to change your plans," argued Curley Grieve of the *Examiner*. "You don't pick .322 hitters out of trees, and seldom get them in trades, especially the kind that hit a long ball. There's a star on the fence at Seals Stadium where Brovia cleared it at the 404-foot mark."[23]

Lefty phoned Grieve to clear up what the columnist termed "the mysterious, inexplicable (to the fans) dismissal" of the Seals' most popular player.

"First, it was not a case of money," Lefty said. "Second, don't blame anyone else but me. I'm the guy who made the decision. Brovia just didn't fit into my plans."

Lefty found himself "cornered by public opinion" and in the awkward position of knocking a player that he liked personally and respected as a hitter. "What's so great about a .322 hitter?" he asked Grieve. "There are other things a ballplayer has to do besides hit."[24]

The Seals' first regular-season game was less than four weeks away. They would host Portland and a revenge-minded Brovia. "I was never mad at O'Doul," he said. "I was mad at the front office—Fagan and Graham. I made up my mind I was going to kill them after what they did to me."

For a while it looked like Seals fans would do Joe's dirty work for him.

"Great cascades of letters poured into the stadium office, and the telephone trunks were loaded to the bursting point with irate customers protesting the cruel, inhuman, barbaric, cannibalistic, deplorable, and slightly phooey firing of old Joseph, today a martyred man," Stevens wrote in the *Chronicle*.

"What have we done?" Charlie Graham Jr. wondered. "You'd have thought we not only fired poor old Joe, but kicked his mother in the teeth and poured ground glass into the baby-to-be's Pablum."[25]

Fagan was mum. "Maybe he was taking one of his pals on a tour around the new women's dressing rooms and lounge," quipped a disgusted fan.[26]

Lefty mused, "All you had to do was bring up his war record, sing the 'Star-Spangled Banner,' and take a picture of me stuffing the flag down his throat, and you'd have completed the job."[27]

Lefty's humor usually defused tense situations, but this time it was at the expense of another local hero and provided fans a script that could be used against him.

Every Brovia at-bat "will prove a climax of some sort or other with the air both acrid and pungent," predicted Jack McDonald, sports editor of the *San Francisco Call-Bulletin*.[28]

"You can't hit left-handers," O'Doul told Brovia when he was with the Seals.

"Bullshit," Joe said. "I can hit left-handers."

Lefty planned on starting southpaws in at least four of the six games in the weeklong series.

A crowd of 8,451 showed up to see the first act of what the *Call-Bulletin* billed as "Hero Brovia" versus "Villain O'Doul (Hiss!)."[29]

The deck was stacked against Lefty. Most of Joe's boyhood friends and neighbors from Davenport and some 300 fans from Santa Cruz, where he moved after the war, were in the stands, poised to cheer their hero and jeer the villain.

They rattled Lefty with a thunderous ovation for Joe when the lineups were announced. And, then, they rocked the house in the first inning after he slashed a run-scoring single to right-field. A "Joe Brovia Fan Club" banner was raised, and anti-O'Doul placards popped up everywhere.

The sign that really got under Lefty's skin proclaimed, "Marble Head O'Doul."

Joe had his fans jumping again in the third inning with another single off Seals left-hander Cliff Melton. He added a third hit to wind up 3-for-5.

The Seals won the game, but the boos and cries of "Marble Head" were still ringing in Lefty's ears.

"The verbal stoning cut deeper than any physical beating," said *Examiner* columnist Prescott Sullivan. "It was a hideous night for Lefty."[30]

He joked about it, saying, "The Brovia people put on a good show. Trouble was there wasn't enough of them. I expected a larger turnout."[31]

Brovia was 4-for-7 against lefties and 7-for-16 overall in the series—a robust .438 batting average. He might've made it worse for Lefty, but he sat out two games after crashing into the left-field fence and cracking a vertebrae in his lower back. "There must be a jinx around my neck," he grumbled.[32]

It was a long, miserable week for Lefty, a preview of the trouble ahead. The Seals floundered, losing 103 games to finish seventh in 1949. The next two years under Lefty they placed fifth and eighth, respectively—the PCL cellar, with no wine for drowning his sorrow when Fagan fired him at the end of the 1951 season. Charlie Jr. sold his one-third interest in the team to Fagan in late 1950 and bought a piece of the Sacramento Solons.

"It was sad that a man like O'Doul had to pay the price," Joe said. "But the Seals just quit drawing. The fans of San Francisco lost interest. I hurt 'em badly. They just couldn't get me out."

Lefty became manager of the San Diego Padres in 1952, but he was still being blamed for the Brovia deal, which continued to haunt the Seals.

Tired of taking the rap for firing Brovia, Lefty finally revealed that Fagan was the culprit and he and Charlie Graham were ordered to cover for him. He accused Fagan of having more crazy ideas than a dog has fleas, then apologized for libeling dogs.

Brovia would ultimately be reunited with both Charlie Jr. and Lefty, but first he had something to prove in Portland.

The Beavers acquired Brovia to take aim at the right-field fence in their Vaughn Street Park. It was 305 feet down the line and 360 to right-center, mere putts for mighty Joe.

Beyond the fence was the roof of a foundry with three fire barrels lined in a row. Portland manager Bill Sweeney had visions of Joe blasting the ball past the third and last barrel for what one Beaver slugger coined a "three-barr'l homer."[33]

"I bought you to hit 25 to 30 home runs a year," Sweeney told Joe.

This meant he needed to master pulling the ball to right field, something he was unable to do for Lefty.

"I tried, but I couldn't do it in '49 because I had back problems," Joe said. "I recovered but not fully."

He missed 70 of the Beavers' 187 games, and while he batted .303, he produced only 11 homers. They were numbers as disappointing to Sweeney as the team's 102 losses, one less than the Seals.

"Joe, you're not going to hit 11 home runs for me again," Sweeney warned. "You hit 25 to 30 or I'm dumping you."

A sore back limited him to pinch-hitting the last month of the 1949 season. "That's when I started dropping down my arms," Joe said. "It hurt to bat my normal way."

The payback was immediate. "Boom! I hit the ball over the right-field fence for a home run."

He tinkered with his batting stance. "I had a little crouch and held the bat straight up, right against my belt buckle."

Mickey Rocco joined the Beavers in 1950 and picked up where he left off with Joe in San Francisco, helping him work out the bugs in his swing. Joe hit until his hands bled.

"He's standing there like a wooden Indian," Rocco explained.

> His bat being low and his hands low with it, he moved forward into the ball as the pitcher threw it. The bat stayed back so that automatically cocked it for him. He'd hit right from there. Without any hitch. He did himself what O'Doul was trying to do all these years. It was just a beautiful thing to see Joe able to pull because he had all this power that for years he hadn't been able to utilize.

"Took me 10 years to get the whole thing together," Joe sighed.

Rocco poked 26 homers for the Beavers in 1950, while Brovia piled up 39, a number of them "three-barr'l" blasts that scattered workers watching the game on the roof of the adjoining foundry. The right-field fence was made of tin. It was actually the side of the foundry that went higher and was painted red. When a ball hit this area, it made the distinctive sound of a home run—boom-boom!

"I used to have the hitch, but now it's boom-boom!" Joe said in describing his transformation into a pull hitter. "People couldn't understand how I could hit the ball. I just come up and go forward. The ball is on its way and I'm coming forward. It was unorthodox for me, but it was the only way I could hit."

Brovia thought he'd get a shot in the big leagues after his breakout performance in 1950.

"Geez, don't hesitate on that guy," Rocco urged scouts. "He can always do the job with the bat. Even if he plays part time, he can help you."

The Boston Braves expressed interest, but the price was too high— "half the Braves ballclub and $75,000," a Boston scout confided to Joe.

Brovia continued to boom homers for the Beavers, 32 in 1951, and 21 in 1952.

One shot landed on the foundry roof behind the right-field wall at Vaughn Street Park. "How can a man hit one that far?" the opposing catcher wondered.

Joe Brovia became a dangerous home run hitter when he developed this batting stance, which made it look like he was "trying to hide his bat from the pigeons," according to Johnny Mize, a four-time National League home run champ. The joke was on pitchers, because the stance eliminated a hitch in Brovia's swing and enabled the left-hander to pull the ball, turning long fly outs to center into homers over the right-field fence. *Doug McWilliams Collection.*

He found out when he picked up the bat and saw a hole that Joe had tried to cover with resin and tobacco juice.

"The year I hit 39 home runs, I probably pulled 20 balls foul over the right-field fence," Joe said. "I was swinging a 42-ounce bat and still getting around early on the ball. That's why I went to a lead bat."

He drilled a hole in his bat and stuck lead in it. "It didn't make me hit more home runs; it made the ball go further."

He did this for the first month of the 1951 season, before he was caught and ordered to get the lead out of his bat.

Joe was stuck with lead feet that allowed defenses to overshift to the right side of the diamond and turn sure hits into outs. "The right-fielder would play up against the fence, and the second baseman would play halfway out into right," Joe said. "I hit shots over the second baseman's head and they'd still throw me out."

He hammered one of the longest drives of the 1952 season at Sacramento's Edmonds Field, the ball hitting the flagpole in center field and ricocheting back onto the field, still in play. Joe was thrown out at third, but he was unapologetic. "I hit the ball good, and it took a perfect relay to get me."[34]

Joe thrived under the easygoing Bill Sweeney, but playing for crusty Clay Hopper in 1952, he was unhappy, and it showed in the key statistics. His batting average dropped from .303 to .290, RBIs from 133 to 85, and home runs from 32 to 21.

Late in the 1952 season, the *Oregonian's* Gregory reviewed a new baseball novel titled *The Natural*, by Bernard Malamud. He localized the story, commenting that if "Joe Brovia himself could hit as Roy Hobbs does with his special bat, our Portland Bevos would be pennant winners by about 20 games."[35]

The columnist wasn't so kind after the fourth-place Beavers traded Brovia and Pieretti to the cellar-dwelling Solons for two pitchers: Orval Grove and Glenn Elliott, Joe's number-one tormentor.

"Compared to Portland, this Sacramento is big-league," Joe said, claiming he had never gotten a pay raise despite hitting 103 homers in four years.[36]

On the first day of spring training camp, he found two ham sandwiches and a pint of milk in his locker. "This club is big-league," he repeated, noting the Beavers required players to pay 40 cents apiece for sandwiches and 15 cents for a carton of milk.[37]

Gregory was indignant, writing that Joe was "always in a sour state of mind at something or someone" and that O'Doul was right all along: "'He doesn't fit into our plans.'"[38]

No one realized it at the time, but soon Brovia would fit perfectly into O'Doul's plans. It would come after Lefty found redemption in San Diego and Joe returned to California and played two years in Sacramento, about 150 miles from his home in Santa Cruz.

The Sacramento ballpark was a graveyard for home run hitters. From home plate to the fence, it was 330 feet down the foul lines, 377 feet via the power alleys in left-center and right-center, and 436 feet to center. "It wasn't a left-handed hitter's ballpark," Joe said. "Wind was always blowing in from right field. I got smart and started going to left field more."

He had fewer homers, 20 in 1953, followed by 13 in 1954, but he batted .314 and .303 and knocked in 97 and 91 runs, respectively.

Joe gave up on making it to the majors long before Lefty guided the Padres to the 1954 PCL pennant, then quit to manage the Oakland Oaks. "I get a chance to pour it on the Seals from another angle," Lefty explained. "I'll be closer than I was in San Diego, and it will burn more when I pour it on."[39]

There was no better way to get revenge on the Seals than to hook up with another guy who had his heart broken in San Francisco.

"The Lefter," San Francisco humorist Herb Caen wrote, "was strictly San Francisco, with everything that implies in the way of dash and color."[40]

Brovia was just as colorful in his own way. "Color is interpreted by some as comprising dash, vigor, comedy," *Oakland Tribune* columnist Alan Ward wrote. "Others see it as stark drama. Still others know color as an explosive quality, exciting because it doesn't happen often, but when it does—whoosh."[41]

At least once during a game, Joe was likely to rock the crowd with a whoosh of his bat. His bash, mixed with Lefty's dash, would smash the Seals for running them out of town.

Lefty took credit for bringing Joe to Oakland.

"This is my deal," Lefty quickly pointed out. "The first thing I asked of Brick Laws (Oaks' owner) when I became manager was to get me Brovia. He's the best hitter in the Coast League and he ought to hit a million home runs into those short right-field stands at Emeryville."[42]

Oaks Park in Emeryville was considered the Fenway Park of the Coast League, the right-field bleachers 305 feet down the foul line. The distances gradually got deeper but were still within easy reach of Joe's line-drive shots.

Joe hit .405 in the first 12 games, clouting 5 homers and driving in 18 runs. At the end of June, he was batting a robust .332, with 15 homers and 58 runs batted in.

He was asleep in his Seattle hotel room when Lefty called at 8:30 in the morning.

"Joe, pack your stuff," Lefty said. "We've sold you to Cincinnati."

Lefty wasn't kidding, and Joe wasn't dreaming. He had waited 16 years for this chance, but he had mixed emotions. He was 33, an age most players are leaving the majors, not going up for the first time. "I'm a little bit old," Joe said. "I want to play up there, but I don't want to pinch-hit."

Lefty had won two National League batting titles, the first at age 32 and the second at 35. "There's no reason why Joe won't hit .300 or more," he told reporters. "I had my best years after I was 30, and there's no reason why Joe can't too."[43]

Joe pondered the moment he thought would never come. "Maybe it's only for a cup of coffee, but at least when my kids ask me if I was ever in the big leagues, I'll be able to answer, 'Sure.'"[44]

Joe hurried off to Cincinnati. He was so excited he left his favorite bats behind in Seattle.

* * *

It was the first of July, and Cincinnati was in fourth place and struggling to remain a contender in the National League pennant race. They needed a fence-busting pinch-hitter to spark the team the last half of the season.

"We were looking for a pinch-hitter and only a pinch-hitter," said Reds general manager Gabe Paul.

Lefty recommended Brovia, telling Paul, "When you put a bat in his hands, he should be able to hit major-league pitching. Don't put him in the outfield."

On his way to Cincinnati, Brovia stopped briefly in Oakland to gather his personal belongings and meet with Laws. "I want to play regularly up there," he reminded the Oaks owner. "I don't want to pinch-hit."

Laws urged him to talk with Paul as soon as he got to Cincinnati. "I have an unorthodox batting stance," Joe said, pleading his case to Paul. "I have to be in the lineup every day."

"You're just going to pinch-hit for us and play in spots," Paul replied.

There was no room for Joe in the Reds outfield. Wally Post and Gus Bell were fixtures in right and center field, and on their way to 40- and 27-homer seasons, respectively. Left field was by committee, infielders Ray Jablonski and Chuck Harmon taking turns with outfielders Stan Palys, Sam Mele, and Bob Thurman.

Tebbetts spent 53 years in the majors as a player, manager, and scout. "Birdie was the finest manager I ever played for," said Bell, Joe's roommate in Cincinnati who batted .281 with 206 homers in his 15 years in the majors. "He was just a highly intelligent man. He was real fair with everybody. He knew how to talk with people. He got the best out of them."

Birdie was scouting for the Yankees in 1975, when he was asked to revisit Brovia's "cup of coffee" with the Reds in 1955.

Tebbetts began,

> We had Brovia because he was strong, and we had a ballpark to fit him. His power was to center and right-center. Our park was built for that kind of hitter.
>
> Thousands of guys came up like he did, but they weren't Brovias. He was a household word in the Coast League. They made so much of him. Don't believe the man ever received so much attention.

Brovia was a feel-good story the national media couldn't resist.

Sporting News devoted almost a full page to his rise to the top. *Sports Illustrated* featured a photo of Joe writing a letter about his big-league debut to his wife, who was with their two daughters, Jeany and Irene, in Germany visiting her parents.

"The first time he came to the plate everybody in Cincinnati knew who he was," Birdie recalled.

> When a guy comes up, he should be unknown. When he steps up to the plate for the first time, the fans should be asking each other, "Who's this John Smith?" That's the way it should be.
>
> Brovia, before he ever got to Cincinnati, was a celebrity. There's no greater pressure on an athlete, especially a baseball player, when

people come from miles around to see him prove he's as great as everyone says. He didn't even have a hit and he had this heat on him. I don't think anybody with Joe's background, at his age, could've survived the pressure.

The first pitcher Brovia faced in the majors was Warren Spahn, a left-hander who won 363 games on his way to the Hall of Fame. Joe struck out.

"Don't feel bad, Joe," Birdie said as he returned to the dugout. "He's done that to a lot of 'em. He's one of the best."

"I can hit that guy," Joe groused. "I can hit that guy. He's like everybody else. He throws a curveball and a fastball."

The next day, Joe batted against a pitcher he knew well from the Coast League—Warren Hacker of the Chicago Cubs. "Hacker was one man I could hit. I used to kill him. But I got just one crack at him. I topped the ball and hit into a force play."

Prior to starring for the Milwaukee Braves and compiling a 203-144 record in the big leagues, Lew Burdette pitched for the Seals in the PCL. He grounded into a run-scoring force play against Burdette, leaving him hitless in five at-bats.

"Joe got the opportunity to go up to the plate and hit," Birdie said. "I'm sorry it was against Spahn and Burdette. That's the way the game is. He came to that kind of a club. He had to hit against that kind of opposition, which is the toughest job in the world."

He went into the All-Star break with one hit in seven at-bats. During the three-day recess, the Reds let Joe play left field in an exhibition game against the Detroit Tigers at Crosley Field.

There was a terrace in left field that began 20 feet from the concrete wall and sloped upward at a 15-degree angle. "Everybody had a pretty tough time playing it," Bell said.

Joe looked like Smead Jolley on one line-drive hit to left. "I went up for the ball and got it, but, son of a bitch, I almost fell down."

He slammed a double and home run that he hoped would earn him a spot in the lineup.

"Joe begged me to play him more. 'Birdie,' he said, 'I've always been a regular. I've never pinch-hit.'"

Joe watched from the bench as Jablonski and Harmon, both infielders, trotted out to left field. He stormed into the Reds clubhouse and ripped off his shirt. "They play #*#*#* infielders in the outfield. I've played outfield all my life in the Pacific Coast League. I'm not that gawddamn bad! Play my ass or get rid of my ass."

"Joe, you are our number-two pinch-hitter," Birdie said calmly. "You pinch-hit with two outs. Thurman pinch-hits with one out."

"I knew the situation," Joe acknowledged. "Thurman could run faster than me. He could keep out of the double play."

Lou Smith, a columnist for the *Cincinnati Enquirer*, was less flattering: "Brovia, the big guy with the Abe Lincoln profile, runs like Charlie Laughton, the rotund actor."[45]

Joe continued to pinch-hit. He faced such premier pitchers as Robin Roberts, a future Hall of Famer; Jim Hearn; Curt Simmons; Murry Dickson; Clem Labine; Hoyt Wilhelm; and Don Newcombe, a 20-game winner in 1955.

Joe whiffed three-straight times, the last against the Giants' Wilhelm, the knuckleball artist enshrined at the Hall of Fame. "He came up four strikeouts ago," a Cincinnati sportswriter quipped to another scribe, who wrote, "A minute later the number was five."[46]

As Joe flailed away, the *Enquirer's* Smith peppered him with potshots.

"The lead-footed former Coast-Leaguer," he wrote, "has been of little or no help to the club," noting he "looks like a spear carrier when he takes his stance at the plate."[47]

A few days later, he quoted Johnny Mize, a four-time National League home run champ, as saying, "Looks like that big guy, Brovia, is trying to hide his bat from the pigeons."[48]

When Joe fouled out against Roberts after sitting idle for seven games, Smith suggested he came out of "cold storage."[49]

Joe got one more chance.

"Grab a bat, Joe, you're hitting!" Birdie said.

"I went up there and struck out," Joe said. "The fans booed me out of the ballpark."

The Reds sold him back to Oakland.

"I was just crushed when I had to tell him he had to go back to the minor leagues," Birdie said. "I can't think of anything that was tougher, mostly because I was pulling for him so much."

Joe spent 39 days in the majors. "A Whiff of the Big Time," the *New York Daily News* called the whirlwind fling.[50]

He appeared in 21 of the Reds' 40 games during that period. He singled twice, walked once, hit a sacrifice fly, and made 16 outs. He whiffed in his first big-league at-bat, as well as his last—six times altogether.

"Joe Brovia probably had more pressure on him than anybody who ever came to the big leagues," Gus Bell said. "After being in the minors and thinking all those years about what you have to do to make it to the major leagues, he says, 'Well, I must've done something right—they're calling me up. Now I've got to watch what I'm doing up here. If I do one thing wrong, I'll be gone.' Evidently, it pretty much happened that way."

Joe never cussed out a pitcher in the big leagues. "I wasn't in there enough," he said. "If I'd gone up there four times a game, I'd been on their ass. I'd told them: 'You son of a bitch, I'll get you next time.'"

There was no next time, and that's what galled Brovia. Back in Oakland, he complained that 18 at-bats was not a fair chance.

"I just happened to be the manager of a club when this guy came up with a flashlight," Birdie said wistfully. "I wish he'd made it."

News of Joe's demise in Cincinnati ruined the day for Stevens, the *Chronicle* sportswriter who had witnessed his first at-bat with the Seals, when he fell down knocking dirt from his cleats.

"It was like throwing back a damaged old toy in your closet of dreams," he wrote upon learning of Joe's return to Oakland. "Glad to have it back, but, alas, will it ever work again?"

Stevens's answer to the question was right on target: "The long trip back will be the hardest, unhappiest, most disillusioning thing that has ever happened to Ol' Joe, a lovable guy with the pride of a king."[51]

He walloped one ball into the bleachers his first game back with the Oaks and finished the season with 19 homers, 73 RBIs, and a .325 batting average. But he wasn't the same brash and brazen Brovia.

"I didn't care anymore," he said. "I figured I was at the end of the line. I went up there and I failed. To come back and face the Coast League fans, I just felt very embarrassed. I hated to go out in right field. I hated to come out of the dugout. I'd hit and hide. I couldn't wait for the ballgame to be over with."

In 1956, Lefty moved with the Oakland franchise to Vancouver, British Columbia, and the Oaks became the Mounties. The Vancouver ballpark was bigger, and Lefty wanted faster outfielders. "I saw the writing on the wall," Joe said. "I went on to Buffalo."

In 46 games at Buffalo, he hit .230, with only six homers. He finished the season strong at San Jose, a Class C league team, hitting .361, with 22 homers. It didn't matter much to Joe. "I was so torn up inside that I went from the majors to Class C in one year. I'd lost all incentive."

He began 1957 at Veracruz, Mexico, in the Class AA Mexican League, and was hitting .313 when a severe case of food poisoning ended his season and colorful career.

It so happened that Brovia's last Coast League game came in 1955, and it also was the finale for Portland's ancient Vaughn Street Park, where he had hit so many three-barr'l homers. Usually, Joe batted fourth in the lineup, but Lefty wanted to do something special for him. "Joe has 19 home runs and is after 20 for the season, so I'm letting him lead off so he'll have an extra at-bat," he explained.[52]

It was a gesture that showed Lefty's respect and affection for a Coast League great who no longer fit into anyone's plans.

* * *

Joe squeaked when he walked and squawked about doctors and politicians when he talked. The two were related.

Upon leaving baseball, Joe became a truck driver for a bakery in Santa Cruz. He quit that job when he was diagnosed with lung cancer that turned out to be walking pneumonia.

Joe resumed driving a truck, this time for a beer distributor. One day in 1970, he reached down to rotate a case of king-sized Coors and felt a snap in his back, which had already been operated on because of a ruptured disc. He continued working until his legs weakened and he started tripping over curbs. He had lost almost all feeling in the lower part of his left leg when he began wearing a squeaky drop-foot brace to help lift his heel and keep from falling.

The squawking was from the medical tests and insurance hassles he went through during a five-year period, only to be told nothing could be done to eliminate the back pain.

Joe was 53 and unable to work. He was living off his disability paycheck and income earned by his second wife, Cathy, who worked at a savings and loan company near their modest one-bedroom home in Santa Cruz.

Cathy listened as Joe vented his anger. "Since he's got hurt, he's let everybody have it," she said.

He ripped politicians, saying, "Those bastards are all left-handed pitchers throwing bullshit. They are for the birds. They ain't for you and they ain't for me."

The pain that plagued Joe in 1975 got worse. "I couldn't get any pain pills," he declared. "I drank like hell to try and kill the pain."

A fourth surgery in 1980 finally detected pelvic damage and scar tissue pressing on the nerves in his back. Arthritis had ravaged his hip joints, leaving his left leg eight inches shorter than the right. Joe couldn't move either one.

He had two hip implant operations to extend the leg and stretch the muscles. A physical therapist came to the house and tried to help him with the exercises he was supposed to do for 45 minutes, three times a day. He bitched about doing them.

Joe got an earful from Cathy, just like he gave the pitchers who threw him slow-breaking curveballs. "You played baseball," she reminded him. "You should know how to exercise."

He began cooperating with the therapist and working out on his own. Soon he was walking three miles each night.

By May 1984, he was a poster boy for the Cabrillo College Stroke Center in Santa Cruz. The center teaches people with physical disabilities how to rebuild their lives through arm and leg exercises, and doing things on their own. He even joked to a local reporter about his long battle to get back on his feet. "If I wrote a book, it would be called, 'Twelve doctors and 11 years later.' I owe that place an arm and a leg."[53]

Joe lived another 10 years. He was 72 when he died of cancer on August 15, 1994—three days after major-league players launched a 232-day strike, the longest and most damaging in baseball's history.

"The only strike Brovia knew was a missed swing," observed Dave Newhouse, a syndicated columnist for the *Oakland Tribune*."[54]

In 1984, Brovia was a guest on a radio show hosted by Newhouse. Listeners were invited to call and talk with him

"Joe Brovia, you're my hero!" one caller proclaimed.

"You were my hero, too," Newhouse said.

This was 10 years before the strike, almost 30 years after Joe had made it to the majors.

"You're a hero to a lot of people, and you'll always be one to me," Newhouse said in signing off.[55]

Joe found out that a whiff of the big time could last a lifetime.

11

UNWANTED

Bob Dillinger

The focal point of the cartoon entitled *The St. Louis Kid* is a big black sedan, a tommy gun hanging out the passenger side window, blazing off into the darkness. Streaming over the top of the car is a caption reading like the newspaper headlines that once followed an infamous bank robber: "DILLINGER HAS STRUCK AGAIN. . . ."

Artist Willard Mullin got the inspiration for this 1947 *Sporting News* cartoon from two Dillingers—John, a gangster and public enemy number one in 1934, at the height of his notoriety, and Bob, a speedy basestealer for the St. Louis Browns who Mullin dubbed "catchers' public humiliator number one."

"There was a lot of larceny in J. Dillinger," wrote *Sporting News* publisher J. G. Taylor Spink. "There is larceny in B. Dillinger, too, but it is all in his feet."[1]

Bob put the Dillinger name back in the headlines. Instead of the front page, they were in the sports section, heralding his latest exploits: "BAD-MAN DILLINGER GETS AWAY AGAIN."[2]

In six big-league seasons, Dillinger consistently ranked among the game's best basestealers and hitters.

But in the spring of 1952, after hitting .301 for the Chicago White Sox the year before, he was banished to the minors—the Sacramento Solons of the Pacific Coast League (PCL).

The other 15 big-league clubs could've bought Dillinger for $10,000, the price paid by Sacramento. All of them snubbed a hitter with a lifetime batting average of .306—eighth best among players active at the time and higher than such superstars as Hank Aaron (.305), Pete Rose (.303), Willie Mays (.302), Mickey Mantle (.298), and Barry Bonds (.298).

The exile of Bob Dillinger to the minors for the rest of his career was as big a mystery as John Dillinger's famous escape from an Indiana jail with a wooden replica of a gun. He went from being the most wanted player in the American League to the most unwanted in the majors.

It is a case study in what happened if a player got on the bad side of team management in the days when there was no proactive union to take up his cause or free agency to find a better situation. "I was not a well-liked fellow," Dillinger said. "I guess I never gave management the respect they thought they had coming."

Dillinger didn't get the respect he had coming either.

He led the American League in stolen bases three consecutive seasons—34 in 1947, 28 in 1948, and 20 in 1949. Three times he batted more than .300—.321 in 1948, .324 in 1949, and .301 in 1950. He hit a combined .292 for the White Sox and Pittsburgh Pirates in 1951. His lowest batting average was .280 in 1946, his rookie year, when he was used sparingly.

He was named to the American League all-star team in 1949, but ignored in 1948, despite a league-leading 207 hits.

At Sacramento in 1953, he was left off the PCL all-star team despite winning the batting title with a .366 average—a mark that lasted 26 years. In the winter draft that year, every team in the majors had a chance to grab him for $15,000. None did.

"For sheer God-given ability, he was the best that I saw," said Chuck Stevens, a teammate with the Browns and a lifelong friend. "If he'd had Pete Rose's appetite for hustle, it's beyond my imagination to visualize what he could have accomplished."

Two years earlier, Bob was the "baseball equivalent of the Hope diamond" and sought after "just as furiously as the FBI chased the other Dillinger in days gone by," according to a story titled "EVERYBODY AFTER DILLINGER EXCEPT FBI."[3]

The Browns placed a $300,000 price tag on his head. Five American League clubs were in hot pursuit: the White Sox, Cleveland Indians, Boston Red Sox, New York Yankees, and Philadelphia Athletics.

On July 16, 1948, at Yankee Stadium, Dillinger was at the plate ready to bat against Yankees ace Allie Reynolds. Stevens, batting second in the lineup, called time out and got Bob back to the on-deck circle. "Are you aware that they have pulled the Williams shift on you?" he asked, referring to the extreme shift used against Ted Williams, a left-hander.

The right-handed-hitting Dillinger primarily pulled the ball to left field. So, the Yankees bunched everyone except the first baseman and right fielder on the left side of the diamond. He lined three singles and a bases-loaded triple into right field that game and added three more hits the following day against another Yankees star, junkballer Ed Lopat.

"This is the kind of ability he had," Stevens said.

> If I look back now at all the fine-looking hitters that I played with or against, he would be in the top five. He was just absolutely classic. Any time that he walked to the plate he was in control. He could move the ball around. And the amazing part of this is that you take those Coke-bottled glasses off of him, he couldn't see across the room.

The bidding for Dillinger got as high as $250,000 before the Browns decided to keep him.

In his four years with the Browns (1946–1949), they finished next to last or last three times. Each winter, they cashed in on their best players. "The theme song when you were on the Browns was to get your salary up to a certain level and they'd sell you," explained Stevens, who played parts of three seasons for the team.

Through most of the 1949 season, Dillinger was neck and neck with George Kell and Williams in the race for the American League batting title. Hobbled by injuries near the end, he finished third.

Dillinger was the only Brown selected to play for the American League team in the 1949 All-Star Game. He entered in the sixth inning as a pinch-runner and sprinted home from first on a double by Joe DiMaggio. In the seventh, he lashed a run-scoring single and again scored from first on a double. "Dillinger stole the show in his rinky-dink uniform," raved Walter Winchell, a syndicated radio commentator and newspaper columnist.

The Browns lost 101 games in 1949. Attendance dropped to 270,936—roughly 3,500 fans per game. After the season, the Browns put any player age 28 and older up for sale or trade. Dillinger was 31 and making approximately $20,000, one of the highest salaries in baseball.

"Specs no bar," read the caption on this 1946 *Los Angeles Times* photo showing **Bob Dillinger** in a St. Louis Browns uniform. Dillinger's Coke-bottled glasses didn't stop him from hitting .306 in six big-league seasons, but they caused him problems at third base, where he was tagged a "flagger" for waving at hot smashes. *Los Angeles Times Photographic Archive, Library Special Collections, Charles E. Young Research Library, UCLA.*

The Browns hauled in $100,000 plus four players for Dillinger and outfielder Paul Lehner from the usually frugal Connie Mack, owner and manager of the A's.

Mack was 87 years old and beginning his 50th year at the helm. The deal was viewed as a "final cast with the dice" for baseball's "Grand Old Man."[4]

For Dillinger, it was a chance to play for a winning team—his first in the majors. The A's placed fifth, with an 81-73 record, in 1949.

"I'm tickled to death to come to Philadelphia," Dillinger said. "Connie Mack always has been my idol, and I think he's a great man to play under. He won't be sorry he got me."[5]

Mack had just bet the farm on a guy widely panned for not hustling, missing ground balls, and drinking too many highballs. Dillinger developed a throwing phobia in the latter stages of his major-league career, confessing, "I became a little bit of a bad third baseman."

But Ferris Fain, the A's All-Star first baseman, attributed most of Dillinger's defensive problems to the thick glasses he wore to correct poor eyesight.

"It was not a deserved reputation, but he was supposed to be a little bit lackadaisical at third base," Fain said. "Balls that were hit real hard, he'd say howdy-do and give it the 'whoo-ee' and let them go by. That was the reputation he had."

Fain and Dillinger served together in the U.S. Army Air Force during World War II, playing on teams in California and Hawaii. They were drinking buddies.

"I was pretty much responsible for Bob coming to the Athletics," Fain said. "They came to me and said, 'We've got a chance to get Bob Dillinger. You and he were friends in the service. Do you think you can handle Bob Dillinger? Can you see that Bob is on the straight and narrow?'"

"Hell, yes, he's no problem," Fain assured the A's.

He was the right guy to tame Dillinger's tosses because he knew his friend tightened up when he had to make a throw. "Just turn the ball loose over there," he told Bob. "Bounce it and I'll catch the damn ball for you. You don't have to worry about me not catching the ball because you're not going to throw it over my head."

Dillinger started the season with a 12-game hitting streak. He ranked among the league leaders in hits, batting a team-high .309 in late July, but the A's were buried in last place.

The acquisition of Bob Dillinger by the Philadelphia A's in 1950 was called a "final cast with the dice" for 87-year-old Connie Mack, the A's owner and manager. The A's lost 102 games to finish last, and Dillinger was the fall guy, despite a .309 batting average. *Courtesy of Eleanor Dillinger.*

"The Old Man had a meeting," Fain said. "He never knew anybody's name. It was either 'Young Man' or 'That Fellow' or 'Our Third Baseman' or whatever."

Except for Fain, Mack lambasted everybody for not hustling. He singled out Bob by name, stating, "And, you Mr. Dillinger, you aren't worth the money that we gave for you!"

He was the highest-paid player on the club, making $25,000 annually.

Fain was incredulous as he recalled the incident. "Bob was leading the ballclub in hitting. He was actually getting in front of balls and knocking them down . . . putting his body in the way. He was bustin' his ass. And I'm a son of a bitch if it wasn't just two or three days later, he was on his way to Pittsburgh."

The Pirates acquired Dillinger for $50,000, enabling Mack to get back half of his investment. "Dillinger was the biggest disappointment I ever had," Mack groaned.[6]

Mack sent assistant manager Jimmy Dykes into the clubhouse to tell Dillinger he was going to Pittsburgh. "He had a can of beer in his hand and threw it clear across the room," Dykes said. "Best throw he made all year."[7]

Dillinger went to Fain's house afterward.

"We were having a few suds," Fain said. "After a while he got a little cryin' jag on: 'I don't know who the hell is going to catch my balls for me now.' He was a sensitive son of a gun. A lot of that bullshit that they laid on him was totally unwarranted."

For the A's to sell Dillinger to the Pirates, a National League team, the other American League clubs had to waive their rights to buy him for $10,000. One writer said it looked "suspiciously like the boys were trying to get Connie off the hook, financially."[8]

A wire service survey found "every club in the American League figured it had a third baseman at least as good."[9]

There was no place to go and nothing Dillinger could say to get his reputation back.

"I'd like to make one thing clear," he told *Pittsburgh Press* columnist Les Biederman on joining the Pirates. "I never had any trouble with anyone on the Athletics. With all these stories following me, maybe it would have been better if I had."[10]

"The word was out," Chuck Stevens said. "He could've hit .380 and I don't think it would've made any difference."

The Pirates were in the cellar just like the A's. One big difference was the Pirates attracted almost 1.2 million fans in 1950, four times more than the A's or Browns. Most of them showed up to see Ralph Kiner, the king of swing, with seven straight National League home run titles from 1946 to 1952.

A crowd of 34,016 turned out to see Dillinger's debut, 9,000 more than usually attended a Friday night game at Pittsburgh's Forbes Field. Dillinger singled twice, Kiner homered, the Pirates lost, and everyone was happy, as a *Pittsburgh Press* headline suggested: "DILLINGER DEAL ALREADY PAYING OFF."[11]

Dillinger hit a combined .301 for the A's and Pirates in 1950. That wasn't good enough for his detractors.

In the ninth inning of a game against the Brooklyn Dodgers near the end of the season, Dillinger failed to slide on a close play at home plate and was tagged out, denying the Pirates the tying run. Pirates manager Bill Meyer scolded him for loafing, saying, "We won't tolerate that kind of playing, last place or not."[12]

For the Pirates' new boss, Branch Rickey, the play epitomized the team's losing record (57-96) and spirit. It was a "shocking episode," he told the media after being named executive vice president and general manager. "It was one of the worst sights I ever looked at from a major-league team. The men who play for me must have a great desire to win."[13]

Rickey had a reputation of his own. He was renowned for paying players as little as possible, prompting sports columnist Jimmy Powers to call him "El Cheapo."

Dillinger was the lone unsigned Pirate going into a face-to-face meeting with Rickey, who boasted he never had a holdout in 31 years running the St. Louis Cardinals and Dodgers.

Dillinger described his discussion with Rickey at a lavish hotel in Beverly Hills, California.

> Gets me up in his room and he says, "You know, Mr. Dillinger, you are the most highly overpaid ballplayer I've met in my life."
>
> I looked at Mr. Rickey and said, "What do you want me to do? Play for nothing."
>
> And he says, "Well, what have you ever done?"

I said, "Look at my record. What 150 other ballplayers have done what I have done? I'm not overpaid. I'm making a little more than the peons that you won't give any money to."

Rickey cut me 25 percent.

A publicity photo showed Rickey handing Bob a pen to sign the contract and keep his cherished record intact. It was vintage Rickey. He had already asked waivers on Dillinger, once again making him available to any team that wanted him.

Dillinger sealed his fate with the Pirates when he didn't show up for a Sunday game. Rickey refused to set foot in a ballpark on Sundays for religious reasons. "He went nuts. I said if it was good for him to stay away on the Sabbath, it should be even better for his players."[14]

The White Sox grabbed Dillinger for $10,000. "The last fellow around here by that name got shot," one Chicago pundit wisecracked.[15]

He was referring, of course, to J. Dillinger, who was gunned down at a Chicago movie theater by G-men's bullets.

The big-league career of B. Dillinger also ended in the Windy City. Instead of bullets, he was done in by a series of run-ins with Paul Richards, a manager as sharp as his middle name, Rapier, a double-edge sword used for quick thrusts and slashing. "He was smart," Dillinger conceded. "Too smart in a way. I didn't particularly like him, and he didn't like me."

Richards was a so-called hustle specialist, who in his first year as manager transformed the White Sox, a sixth-place team in 1950, into the Go-Go Sox and a pennant contender. Richards was asked if he could "convert the one-time 'Boy Bandit.'" He replied, "I'm going to let him work out his own salvation."[16]

The Dillinger name was again making crime news in Chicago, as thieves stripped his car shortly after he arrived in town. Police found the abandoned vehicle on jack stands at the side of a road. All five tires and wheels were missing, plus eight bats with Dillinger's signature. Eighteen bats were left next to the car.

Dillinger didn't need them at first, as he sat on the bench for two weeks after going 3-for-6 in his only start. When he finally cracked the lineup, he went on a .359 tear in June, including an 18-game hitting streak.

The White Sox were in first place at the All-Star break in July, then lost 15 of their next 20 games to slip to fourth. They stayed there as

Dillinger mostly watched from the dugout, starting only 14 games the last two months.

"I was a little bit of an agitator," Dillinger said. "Not nasty. I never told them that they were bush-bush. But they got the general idea."

Richards prided himself as a teacher and innovator. One day in practice he had the batting cage moved to within 30 feet of the pitcher's mound—half the normal distance.

"Get in there Dillinger!" Richards ordered.

"I ain't goin' in there," Dillinger balked.

"What's with you?"

"I ain't going to screw up my timing to hit from there."

At spring training in Pasadena, California, in 1952, Richards unveiled a plan to improve Dillinger's throwing accuracy from third base. "It got to where I'd field the ball and think, 'Where am I going to throw it now?'" Dillinger said. "I was scared to throw the ball."

For six days, he practiced throwing to first base, starting with 50 balls and increasing by five each day up to 75 at the end.

"He didn't throw less than the prescribed number, but what was more important, he didn't throw any more either," Edward Burns wrote in the *Chicago Tribune*.[17]

As far as Richards was concerned, Dillinger had just counted himself off the team and out of the majors. "The White Sox boss evidently came to the conclusion that Dillinger didn't want to hustle, didn't like baseball, and didn't care whether he played or not," Burns reported.[18]

In his last big-league at-bat, Dillinger faced Satchel Paige, the legendary pitcher. Ironically, he got an infield single. "It was a leg job. Ball bounced over his head, shortstop fielded and threw it, but I beat it out."

Dillinger always could run. In the end, he was run right out of the big leagues.

* * *

"Bob was just an unfortunate, misrepresented son of a buck," Fain said. "They had him pegged totally wrong."

Fain didn't realize it, but he was echoing the title of a *Baseball Digest* story about Dillinger published in September 1951: "They Got Me Wrong!"[19]

The Chicago media attributed Dillinger's fast start with the White Sox to a "new spirit" Richards had instilled in him with a long, blistering lecture on hustling.

"BALONEY! JUST PURE UNSLICED BALONEY!" Dillinger told Milt Richman, an award-winning sportswriter for United Press International. "They don't know what they're talking about because I've had the same spirit all the time."[20]

He debunked other charges that questioned everything but his ability to hit and run.

People were getting things wrong about Robert Bernard Dillinger from the day he was born in Glendale, California—September 17, 1918.

He was mistakenly identified as a girl on his birth certificate. His family name was listed as Pittman, but that wasn't an error. He changed it to Dillinger after his parents, Grace and Roy Pittman, divorced and Grace married Charles Dillinger, a commercial artist.

In 1936, the name Dillinger was a natural for a swift, shifty All-Southern California fullback who had scampered around and away from would-be tacklers to earn the moniker "Badboy" and propel Glendale to the Southern California high school football championship game at the Rose Bowl in Pasadena.

Dillinger was so talented on the baseball diamond that his high school coach arranged a tryout his senior year with the Los Angeles Angels of the PCL. Angels' manager Truck Hannah sized up the bespectacled 5-foot-11, 159-pounder and pronounced, "You better forget all about baseball, kid. You'll never make a ballplayer—not with them eyeglasses."[21]

Dillinger didn't need glasses to escape tacklers on the football field, so the University of Idaho gave him a two-year football scholarship, envisioning him leading the team in touchdowns, not broken collarbones. The first of two occurred in a scrimmage against the varsity. The following year, he cracked the same bone in a game. That was it for football. He returned home and started playing semipro baseball in the Los Angeles area.

A tryout with the St. Louis Cardinals ended the same way as the one with the Angels. "You can't make it as an infielder wearing glasses," he was told.[22]

The only major-league infielder to wear glasses up to that point was George "Specs" Toporcer, a utility man for the Cardinals from 1921 to 1928.

A junior-college teacher tipped off Browns scout Jack Fournier on a "young kid with glasses who could pound the ball at the plate, run like a deer, and field ground balls with as much skill as any youngster in California."[23]

Dillinger was as good as the glowing report. He was signed immediately and sent to Lincoln, Nebraska, the Browns' farm club in the Class D Western League. "Fournier was the only scout who had the guts to sign me," Dillinger said.[24]

Lincoln fans went silly over Dilly, his nickname locally, as he batted .314 and burned up the base paths with 32 doubles, 21 triples, and a league-high 67 steals. His sprinter's speed was showcased in a 100-yard race against Jesse Owens, the world's fastest human, after winning four gold medals at the 1936 Olympic Games. Owens spotted Dillinger five yards and then nipped him by a foot.

Nobody could catch Dillinger in 1940, at Youngstown, Ohio, as he swiped 67 bases for the second-straight year. "You've got to do something that will bring attention to you," he said. "I could run and steal bases so that's what I tried to do everywhere I played in the minor leagues."

Dillinger was a model of consistency moving up the minor-league ladder. He hit .312 at Youngstown in Class C; .291 in 1941, at San Antonio, Texas, in Class A, despite being sidelined for three weeks because of pneumonia; and .305 in 1942, at Toledo, Ohio, in Class AA. He was considered a fielding wizard, playing second base and third at Toledo.

The only time Dillinger's glasses caused a problem was at Lincoln, when he offered them to future big-league umpire Lynton "Dusty" Boggess after two questionable strike calls. Boggess calmly put on the glasses, readjusted his mask, and ordered, "Play ball!"

Upon hearing the sound of the next pitch hitting the catcher's glove, Boggess bellowed, "Stree-rike three!"

"Where was that last pitch?" Dillinger asked.

"I don't know," Boggess said. "I couldn't see with your glasses and you couldn't see without them, so it's strike three and you're out."[25]

Going into the 1943 season, World War II was raging. More than 200 major leaguers were wearing military uniforms as teams scurried to find replacements. A prospect's draft status was as important as his statistics.

Dillinger appeared to be a shoo-in as the Browns' next third baseman. He could hit, run, and field, plus he was classified 4-F because of his bad eyesight. He tried to enlist in four different branches of the military, and each time he was rejected. In early April, Dillinger had another physical examination. This time he was ruled fit to serve in the special services unit of the Army Air Force and assigned to the baseball team at its McClellan Field base near Sacramento.

Military teams provided much-needed entertainment and relief from the stress of war. The teams were uplifting for troop morale, and by the end of the war some of them were as good as the patchwork clubs in the majors.

Dillinger fit right in with the mixture of major- and minor-league stars that put the McClellan Commanders in the big leagues of military baseball.

Fain, previously a member of the San Francisco Seals in the PCL, played first base. At shortstop was Dario Lodigiani, formerly of the White Sox. Two of the outfielders were Mike McCormick, ex-Cincinnati Red, and Walt Judnich, a .313 hitter with the Browns in 1942. Catcher Charlie Silvera and pitcher Rinaldo "Rugger" Ardizoia were talented Yankees farmhands.

"Right off the reel Bob was a tremendous addition," Fain said. "We could see that here is one helluva ballplayer. He could run like crazy. It was amazing what he could do with the bat with those Coke-bottled glasses that he wore."

In 1944, Dillinger and several of his McClellan mates joined the Seventh Army Air Force Fliers, stationed at Hickam Field in Hawaii. That's where he was when Walt Dobbins, sports columnist for the *Lincoln Journal Star*, received a letter from a navy officer named Zeke wondering whether the Dillinger playing third base for the Fliers was the same one that had patrolled second for the Lincoln Links five years earlier. "He wears glasses and walks like he had a board for a spine, but he is fast on his feet and fields anything that comes his way," Zeke wrote.

He listed Fain and Dillinger's other teammates, including second baseman Joe "Flash" Gordon of the Yankees, the American League's Most Valuable Player in 1942, and shortstop Jerry Priddy, an ex-Yankee. The center fielder was Joe DiMaggio. "The only player leading Dillinger in hitting is DiMaggio, and he hasn't played as long as Bob," Zeke added. [26]

Dillinger upstaged DiMaggio in 1944, as documented by a *Sporting News* headline reading, "BETTER THAN DIMAG." [27]

The Army Air Force Fliers participated in the Central Pacific Area (CPA) Service League and the Hawaii League for both civilian and military teams. Dillinger's .400 batting average and 24 stolen bases paced the Hawaii League, while his .367 mark was third best in the CPA.

Stomach ulcers limited DiMaggio's playing time and kept him out of the Service World Series between the army and navy. He also was going through the breakup of his marriage to actress Dorothy Arnold. "We had a guy named Will Leonard," Dillinger said. "DiMaggio would have Leonard write letters to her because DiMaggio did not quite have the gift."

Playing for the Bellows Fliers in 1945, he hit .489, to lead the Honolulu League. Later in the year, he was on one of three Army Air Force teams that toured the Pacific islands of Saipan, Tinian, and Guam. "My last game in the service in Guam, I played center field because DiMaggio had gone home. That was the first time I played in the outfield."

In Hawaii, Dillinger went from being virtually unknown in the minors to the most talked-about player in the Pacific. That was saying something because there was DiMaggio, Pee Wee Reese, Phil Rizzuto, Enos Slaughter, and plenty of other major-league stars.

As sportswriter John Lardner pointed out in a nationally syndicated column, Hawaiians took greater interest in Dillinger and Fain "because they figure they got to know these coming stars before the major-league fans had a chance to."[28]

Dillinger excelled on the mightiest of military teams. The Army Air Force Fliers won 28-straight games during one stretch and McClellan 30 out of 35. He was Player of the Pacific, a rookie gift-wrapped by Uncle Sam.

Browns manager Luke Sewell didn't know what to think or say about his good fortune. He complimented Dillinger during spring training but then criticized players coming out of the military for not taking baseball seriously enough. "The army and navy were too busy winning a war to get the service ballplayers into condition. And the ballgames were just— well, they were just recreation."[29]

It was a curious statement. Sewell's greatest success as a manager was in 1944, when the big leagues were at their weakest. He stocked the Browns roster with 18 4-F players, the most in the majors, to win the American League pennant. "Their strength," author William B. Mead wrote in *Even the Browns*, "was in superior weakness."[30]

One of the holdovers from the 1944 team was Mark Christman, a 32-year-old third baseman and brother of Paul Christman, a two-time All-American quarterback at the University of Missouri. Dillinger was 27, the same age as Chuck Stevens, a rookie first baseman with the Browns. "Luke Sewell had no faith in young ballplayers," Stevens said.

Sewell accomplished in three days what no one in the military could do in three years—stop Dillinger. When he went hitless the first two games of the 1946 season, Sewell benched him. He didn't start again for a month. By mid-August, he had only 27 starts in 110 games.

"Mark Christman was the third baseman who got him in the World Series," Dillinger said of Sewell. "So he's going to stick with his ballplayer. I understood that. But I understood also that I want to play. And I knew I was a better hitter."

Sewell put him back in the starting lineup two weeks before he was forced to resign. In that period, Dillinger had eight multihit games to hike his batting average 40 points, to .292. He wound up starting 51 games and hitting .280—22 points higher than Christman. His eight stolen bases led the team.

Christman was sold just before the 1947 season began under new manager Herold "Muddy" Ruel. Soon there was a newspaper headline reading, "THIS DILLINGER IS A 'PISTOL.'"[31]

He was hitting .415 after 16 games, running wild on the bases, and making plays at third base that had some folks suspicious of an imposter wearing his uniform. "The Bob Dillinger of 1947 just isn't the same man," Dent McSkimming wrote in a *St. Louis Post-Dispatch* story entitled "It's Browns, Not Me That Changed."

"I'm wearing the same glasses I used the latter half of last season," Dillinger said. "My bat is the same. I'm not doing anything at the plate I didn't try last season."[32]

Dillinger was hitting .316 and leading the league in hits and stolen bases in mid-July. His 23 steals in less than half the season matched the total of the entire team in 1946. He ended up with 34, tops in the majors, and a team-high .294 batting average.

The Browns were as bad as Dillinger was good. They lost 95 times to finish last again.

In the November 1949 issue of *Sport* magazine, writer J. Roy Stockton began a story asking Dillinger how it felt to be "a winner in the ranks of a loser, a sort of lonely little orchid in an onion patch?"

"It's tough," Dillinger said. "When you're with a loser, in a long losing streak, there's nothing to lift you out of a slump. You get to worrying, and that makes it all the harder to shake it off."[33]

The A's and the Pirates also were in the cellar when he played for them. This prompted a Pittsburgh sportswriter to muse that "'Cellar'-brated Bob Dillinger" couldn't get out of last place. "Each change of uniform—Browns, Athletics, and Pirates—has left him in the same spot."[34]

In early 1948, Bob's teammates dubbed him "The Team" after the revamped Browns were described as a "bunch of nobodies surrounding Bob Dillinger, who is the whole team."[35]

"Team, hell!" Dillinger scoffed. "I'm just one of the leftovers."[36]

"He had the misfortune of being on a lousy ballclub," Stevens said. "Had he been on a good, productive, winning ballclub, he would've really broken some records in basestealing."

Dillinger stole a league-high 20 bases in 1949, but he was faulted for not stealing more. "If you can lead the league with 20—unless you're going to get the sign and help the team score a run—why get more than 20? In a way, that's all I was interested in—leading the league in what I could lead it in," he said.

Dillinger checked the box scores daily to make sure he had at least one more stolen base than his closest competitor. This baffled most folks.

"He has the ability if he'll only use it," said Zack Taylor, the Browns' boss in 1948–1949. "But the boy has a peculiar disposition."[37]

One of Dillinger's nicknames was Goofy.

"He was on occasion kind of Goofy," Ferris Fain said. "I heard him say, 'No, I ain't going to hit any more than this because they'll expect it. Piss on 'em.' That's why he didn't steal any more bases. He just wasn't going to be bothered because they didn't seem to appreciate it."

Dillinger used a big, thick-handled bat. "The thicker the better because if you hit the ball on the fist or under the trademark, it will go far enough to get over the infielder's head."

In 3,202 big-league plate appearances, he hit only 10 homers but struck out a mere 203 times—five less than the Yankees' Aaron Judge as a rookie in 2017.

"Put the bat on the ball" was his hitting philosophy, and if the bat needed a little doctoring to do that, no problem. He might cork a bat to make it lighter or flatten the barrel to ensure contact with the ball.

"He was as big a cheater that ever pulled on a baseball uniform," Fain said. "He was constantly screwing around with that bat."

"Oh, I did everything," he admitted.

Dillinger was a craftsman at flattening his bat.

"There's an area on the bat maybe a half-inch wide where you are going to hit the ball solidly," Fain said. "He'd file the area and then use a bone to rub it down and make the bat harder. Instead of an absolutely flat half-inch spot, it was more like a gawd-damn paddle."

Fain tried using one of the bats. "I couldn't make it work," he said. "But he made that thing work like a charm."

One of Dillinger's bats was tossed out of a game because it wasn't round enough.

"This isn't cricket, y'know," the umpire said.[38]

"They give you a round ball and a round bat and they tell you to hit it square," Stevens said.

> Dillinger just wanted to even the odds a little bit. He corked his bat because it was a no-no. Now, had a decision come down from the commissioner's office saying that everybody had to cork their bat, Dillinger wouldn't have corked his. He did everything that he wasn't supposed to do for just the hell of it.

"Everybody liked him because of his nonchalance and a kind of a dry wit," Fain said.

Dillinger said things that confounded management.

"If I knew any other way of making this much money," he told Browns co-owner Charley DeWitt, "I sure wouldn't put on this monkey suit every day."[39]

In 1949, Dillinger committed 25 errors, six more than any other American League third baseman. He was called a "flagger" because sometimes he looked like a matador waving his red cape at a charging bull.

The Browns and the Cardinals shared Sportsman's Park. The constant use and summer heat made the infield hard as a rock.

"The way the infield was, he had to do like he was a matador," said Roy Sievers, a rookie outfielder for the Browns in 1949. "A lot of times he'd give it that kind of fadeaway catch at the ball. Sometimes he'd miss it."

Pitcher Charles "Red" Embree joined the Browns in 1949, and in his first start, the leadoff batter hit a three-hopper to third base that he thought was an easy out. "The batter gets a stand-up double, and I'm staring at Dillinger there at third, wondering how in the world he missed that ball," Embree recalled. "He sees me and yells back, 'Welcome to the Browns!'"[40]

Fain and Dillinger bunked together in the army. He remembered Bob taking off his glasses at night and hanging them on the end of his bunk bed. Every now and then someone in the barracks would hide them. "He was absolutely blind when that happened," Fain said.

He pondered this when Dillinger joined the A's in 1950. "He wasn't starting after the ball as quickly as he should, and people thought he was lazy. He was zeroed in at 60 feet, six inches with those glasses."

That's the distance from the pitcher's mound to home plate. It's 90 feet from the plate to third base and another 10 to 15 feet to where Dillinger was usually positioned. Said Fain, "I'm not an eye doctor, but I honestly believe he didn't see the ball until it was almost to him."

Dillinger tried contact lenses, but at the time they were as big as a thumb. He continued wearing glasses and tending the hot corner. "None of them were smart enough or wanted to put me in the outfield where I couldn't hurt them," Dillinger said of his big-league managers.

Unwanted in the majors, Dillinger was banished to Sacramento in the spring of 1952. There he proved he wasn't washed up. And for one season at least, he found redemption by surpassing everyone's expectations.

* * *

Sacramento player-manager Joe Gordon sidled up to Dillinger prior to an exhibition game between the Solons and White Sox. "They're going to get rid of you," Gordon said. "Would you like to play for me in Sacramento?"

A week later Dillinger was wearing a Sacramento uniform.

Sacramento was a homecoming of sorts for Dillinger.

He had played on the baseball team at nearby McClellan Field during World War II. Two of his teammates were Gordon and Solons outfielder Mike McCormick. They also played together in Hawaii against another Solon, catcher Vinnie Smith.

"They were named the Solons, but I called them the Saloons," Dillinger said. "That's the only reason I played for them—drinkers."

Sacramento manager Joe Gordon, far right, wanted Bob Dillinger, center, when no one else did. Dillinger joined Gordon and outfielder Mike McCormick, both teammates in the military, at Sacramento in 1952. Gordon solved Dillinger's defensive woes at third base by moving him to the outfield. The next year, he hit a league-leading .366. *San Diego History Center.*

Every team had its drinkers, and no one cared much as long as they did their job on the field and stayed out of trouble off it. "I'll take all of the drinking guys in the world because I know that they might be hurtin' and dyin' a little bit, but they're going to play," Fain said. "The milkshake drinker, he's going to trip over a foul line and be on the disabled list for three weeks."

Dillinger's salary in Sacramento the first year was $15,000—the same as what he got from the White Sox. "If you couldn't play major-league ball, you might as well play in the Coast League."

He enjoyed playing in Sacramento for his pal, Gordon. He liked being out of the spotlight. Gordon had hit 43 homers the year before and was the main attraction. Veteran outfielder Joe Marty and shortstop Richie Myers were local boys and fan favorites.

"After a ballgame, I'd go to the bars and there would be nobody on the street," Dillinger said. "They couldn't say, 'Hey, I saw Dillinger out there gassed again.'"

Dillinger was happy in Sacramento and let it be known he had "no ambition whatever to return to the majors."[41]

Roger Osenbaugh was fresh out of Stanford University—a self-described "college hot dog." At 22, he and Myers were the youngest on a mostly veteran, 30-something team. "Your name as a rookie like me was always Bush," said Osenbaugh. "They never called you by your name. It was, 'Hey, Bush.'"

The 5-foot-6, 150-pound Myers had already spent parts of three seasons with the Solons, never hitting above .222.

"He was a little small, but he had talent," Dillinger said. "He could play shortstop. Had a gun for an arm. Hitting was a little difficult. I didn't go out of my way to help everybody or to tell them how to play the game of baseball. It's tough enough trying to play it yourself. But I liked him. He was a nice fellow."

Soon after joining the Solons, Dillinger offered to help Myers, saying, "I think I can make you a better hitter if you want to try it."

Myers was shocked. "I was a little afraid of him," he admitted. "I knew his record up in the major leagues. I knew he was an excellent hitter. I knew he had trouble throwing in the infield and getting along with Richards. He liked me, and I liked him. And we got along great."

The 1952 Solons were terrible. They were last in fielding and hitting, averaging slightly more than three runs a game, and at the bottom of the standings, losing 114 games.

Myers raised his batting average to .250. Dillinger led the team in hits (168) and stolen bases (12), but his average was a disappointing .287.

Late in the season, Gordon moved Dillinger to left field. "I don't know why it wasn't done before," Dillinger said, "because I could've probably played and hit .300 in the big leagues and I wouldn't have hurt them as bad in the outfield as I would at third base."

The Solons were impressed enough to put him in center field in 1953. "Players of the opposition agree that Dillinger fits into center as if to the manor born," wrote Bill Conlin of the *Sacramento Union*. "He gets a quick jump on the ball and has the speed to go after and round up the long ones."

Dillinger was amused. "Maybe you're right about me being a natural center fielder," he told Conlin. "Say if I am, then I sure fooled 'em for six years in the majors, didn't I? I wonder what those smart masterminds up there have to say now!"[42]

Dillinger went on a rampage in 1953, reminiscent of his namesake, the hitting streaks more resembling shooting sprees.

One 17-game streak featured two five-hit rampages within a day of one another. During a 22-game skein, he was 40-for-82—a whopping .488 average. Through August 19, Dillinger was hitting .343, and runner-up Artie Wilson of Seattle .329. He kicked it up a notch, sewing up the batting title with a torrid .667 stretch—22 hits in 33 at-bats—to finish at .366, well ahead of Wilson, at .332.

"Mandrake the Magician is what we called him," said Eddie Bockman, referring to a comic-strip superhero popular in the 1950s. Bockman took over at third base when Dillinger moved to the outfield. "Best two-strike hitter I ever saw," raved Bockman. "With two strikes, you didn't have him. He had you."

Dillinger feasted on curveballs. "I like garbage," he said. "A good fastball I could hit it, but I didn't like it. I waited longer than a lot of other people did. So the fastball would almost be by me before I would get with it. If it was junk, I could wait, wait, and wait. I loved to wait."

"He was very still—held the bat straight up and hardly moved it until the pitch," Myers said, describing Dillinger at bat. "I don't know how he waited so long. You'd swear that he could never hit the ball. He wouldn't be ready. But he was. Even when he wasn't getting base hits, he was hitting line drives."

He embarrassed some of the best lefties of his era, hitting .419 against Hall of Famer Hal Newhouser and .340 off of Mel Parnell, a 25-game winner for the Red Sox in 1949. "No left-hander gave me any trouble," Dillinger boasted.

In 1953, Myers used batting tips from Dillinger to improve his average 18 points, to .268. He was hitting .303 in 1954, when he was shelved by a knee injury halfway through the season. "I cut my strike outs way down and became a much better two-strike hitter."

Winning the PCL batting title in 1953 wasn't enough to earn Dillinger a spot on the PCL all-star team or another shot in the majors. "I thought I might go back as an outfielder," he said. "By the same token, I was 35. They had too big of a pool of other younger players to come up."

Dillinger's batting average dropped to .301 in 1954, and the Solons wanted to slash his salary the following season. He had already agreed to a $5,000 pay cut after his first year in Sacramento.

In 1955, the team had new ownership. Cutting costs to save a dying franchise was a top priority. Bob was offered $5,000, a third of what he made when he joined the Solons. "I just got pee-o'd and said, 'I ain't goin' to play no more.' So, I held out for two weeks and, finally, I got six."

Solons manager Tony Freitas was a local legend. He won 342 games in the minors, the most ever by a left-hander. Most of those victories came in Sacramento, where he won 20 or more games six-straight times. He almost single-handedly produced the city's only PCL pennant in 1942.

Freitas took over halfway through the 1954 season, leading the Solons to a 73-94 record and a seventh-place finish. He strictly enforced a curfew, in contrast to Gordon and his successor, Gene Desautels, who didn't bother with one. Freitas didn't drink anything stronger than soft drinks.

"It is a known fact that Freitas has not liked Dillinger since he arrived for spring training," Tom Kane reported in the *Sacramento Bee*.[43]

"I played for a little while and said, 'To hell with it,'" Dillinger said. "When they started not playing me, I came home."

The Solons enticed him back with a box of his favorite cigars. By late May, attendance was down almost 50,000. Loyal fans were deserting the Solons, according to Kane, because of the front office's failure to replace older players and Freitas's indecision and inability to handle any of them. "Tony has his favorites, and they are carrying him and the club down to disaster," he wrote.[44]

Two days after the story was published, the Solons dropped the hammer on Dillinger, infielder-outfielder Nanny Fernandez, and third baseman Leo Thomas, all big-league veterans. At 36, Dillinger and Fernandez were the oldest position players on the team.

Dillinger called Freitas the "worst I ever played for in 16 years in the game."[45]

Conlin likened Dillinger's tirade to "taking a dive off the high board without looking to see if the pool was filled. Only a rockhead would make this move."[46]

In what turned out to be the last game of his career, Dillinger rapped three hits against the Oakland Oaks to finish with a .281 batting average, best among the team's outfielders. "When I think about it, they might of played me to see if Oakland wanted me," he said.

Dillinger batted .317 in his three-plus seasons in Sacramento. In 513 games, he accumulated 613 hits—508 singles, 87 doubles, 18 triples, and no homers. In 2,090 plate appearances, he struck out only 85 times—one in approximately every 25 at-bats.

Freitas was fired at the end of the season as the Solons finished in the PCL basement for the third time in four years.

Solons pitcher Bud Watkins expressed a view shared by many of his teammates. "Bob just absolutely talked himself right out of a job. He ripped one of the grandest guys you'd ever meet in your life. He was no manager, granted, no manager. But I'll tell you what, he was a fine human being, and he did not deserve that."

Some Sacramento players questioned Dillinger's desire.

"Easy come, easy go," Bockman said. "That was the way he played the game. The only time he really focused was when he had a bat in his hands."

Osenbaugh and Myers had a different take.

"He did everything so effortlessly that it made it look like he was not hustling," Osenbaugh said. "He was faster than greased lightning, and he moved with fluidity and ease. I never ever recall Dillinger not hustling."

"Once you got to know him, you understood him," Myers said. "He wanted to win as bad as anybody."

A frustrated Dillinger once asked a reporter, "What do they want me to do, stand on my head out there? I give the best I have every time out, and if it looks like I'm not hustling, I can't help that."[47]

As L. H. Gregory of the *Oregonian* once observed, "Dillinger unluckily isn't the least bit dramatic. If he had only a little bit of that dramatic 'touch,' he'd be a baseball idol, fans would flock to see him, and his pay would always be in the very top bracket."[48]

"They just assumed that it was a born deficit in his makeup and they weren't going to do anything about it," Stevens said. "Nobody ever bothered to pat his ass and tell him that he was the greatest guy since the electric light bulb, go get 'em. It would have been interesting if somebody had done that."

After leaving Sacramento, Dillinger became a grip man, setting up cameras in a Hollywood television studio. He ended up working 22 years for the city of Los Angeles as a construction inspector.

Robert L. Burnes, a columnist for the *St. Louis Globe-Democrat*, followed Dillinger from the beginning of his big-league career with the Browns. He summed up the ending as "typical in character" because he "left in the bitterness which marked a good part of his career and unfortunately hurt it."

Now that his baseball career was over, Burnes wondered if Dillinger had any regrets. He concluded, "Apparently not."[49]

* * *

Dillinger was the ultimate loner.

Midway through the 1953 season, Osenbaugh was in the Solons clubhouse, dressed in street clothes, and saying goodbye to a teammate. He had just received orders to report for active duty at the U.S. Marine Corps base in Quantico, Virginia.

Dillinger rushed up to the other player.

"Where is he?"

"Who?"

"The guy that's going into the marines."

"He's right here."

Dillinger turned and looked at Osenbaugh and said, "Good luck, Meat!"

Those three words—"Good luck, Meat!"—are the only three words Dillinger said to Osenbaugh in the two seasons they were teammates.

There's more to the story, and it's the most revealing part.

In the early 1960s, Osenbaugh was retired from baseball and working in the insurance business. He lived in Arcadia, California, about 30 miles from Dillinger's home in the San Fernando Valley.

"I get a phone call one Sunday afternoon," Osenbaugh recalled. "The voice on the line says, 'Hi, this is Bob Dillinger.'

"Now, 'Hi, this is Bob Dillinger.' What is that? Five words. That's more than he said to me all the time I played with him, which was, 'Good luck, Meat!'"

Most people saw only the crusty, gruff exterior of Dillinger's loner side. He didn't say much, on or off the field, and what he said came out in what sportswriter Milt Richman described as a "flat-toned, semi-snarl" that gave "strangers the mistaken impression he is constantly irritable."[50]

"A newspaper guy would ask him a question, he didn't take any prisoners," Stevens said. "He didn't know that it might call for a moment of finesse."

Dillinger was difficult to know. "It's that gruffness," Stevens explained.

> I've been around him with hundreds of people, and he scared most of them with that attitude. I don't think anybody took enough time to find out what kind of guy he was. Through osmosis, I found it out. We ate, slept, played ball, and drank together. So, I got to know him as well as anybody.

Dillinger's bluntness overshadowed a quiet, unassuming personality and wry sense of humor.

"These golden years aren't what they're cracked up to be," he grumbled to a writer one morning in May 2000. They met outside a restaurant in Santa Clarita, California, and then spent the rest of the day at his home nearby.

Dillinger was driving a 1986 Chevrolet pickup truck, conspicuous because it was lowered and sported racing stripes on the side. "This sucker has been lowered. I go down the street, you know, and these gangbangers see this truck with a disabled license on it and give me the finger."

Dillinger was 81. The thick crop of blond hair that earned him the nickname "Blond Bandit" was now silver. Two hip replacements had him moving slowly, and he was facing cataract surgery. "I'm going to go to 85 and then I'll hang it up. I think the guy will be out of jail then, too. You know, Dr. Death!"

Dr. Death was the nickname for Dr. Jack Kevorkian, a pathologist who was in prison at the time for helping terminally ill patients commit suicide. Near the end of the daylong interview, Dillinger announced, "This is the last one of these that I do. The next time I see you, bring one of those pills that Dr. Death carries around."

Bob and Eleanor Dillinger were high school sweethearts. They married in 1940, when Bob entered pro baseball, and had their only child, Judith Ann, in December 1943, just before he joined the army.

"He's different," Eleanor said of her husband. "He tells you what he thinks. He doesn't K.A. anybody."

"I felt you could pat me on the back and get more out of me than you could by telling me, 'You're H.S.!' Tell me, I'm H.S., I'll be H.S. Tell me I'm a good ballplayer, I'll be a good ballplayer. That, to me, is a good manager."

H.S. stood for "horseshit" and K.A. for "kiss ass."

"I knew all the radicals and reprobates," Bob said. "Priddy and I were pretty good friends. He tried to bomb that boat, you know."

Gerald Priddy, a teammate with the Browns and Army Air Force Fliers, was convicted of extorting $250,000 from a cruise ship company by threatening to blow up one of its vessels off the coast of Baja California.

"Hank Thompson liked me real well. He said I was the only guy who treated him good when he came to the Browns. He killed a guy in Houston."

Thompson, a black third baseman, played briefly for the Browns in 1947. The following year, he shot and killed a man in self-defense during a barroom brawl. After leaving baseball, Thompson served three years in prison for armed robbery.

"And then Blackie Schwamb . . . he and another guy killed a doctor. When I was at Sacramento, he would write me for baseballs and I'd send them."

Schwamb, who pitched briefly for the Browns in 1948, spent 12 years behind bars at San Quentin.

"Like I say, boy, I was more at home with the Mafia than I was those frickin' blue-nosed baseball owners."

Left off of Dillinger's list of "radicals" was Fain, who was imprisoned in the late 1980s for growing and selling marijuana.

When they were teammates in Philadelphia, Dillinger received a package of huge lobster tails every month. "I know damn well that the guy who sent him these lobsters wasn't one of the church deacons," Fain said. "We'd barbecue them and drink up a half-dozen cases of beer."

Bob mixed self-depreciating quips into many of his comments.

During the 1947 season, one national magazine published a story titled, "Dillinger, the Silent."[51]

"'Silent' could have been from my mouth being full of chew," wise-cracked Dillinger.

At one point in 1948, he had a 28-game hitting streak. "I'm half as good as Joe DiMaggio. In my next life, I'm going to hit 56 and tie him."

Whatever the subject, Dillinger didn't pull any punches. "I was a lousy drinker—a nasty talker. Not abusive but, in other words, 'Oh, shove it up your ass.' It's lucky I didn't get belted a few times. But wearing glasses, they don't dare hit you I assume. I quit about five years ago."

Dillinger once answered a telephone call from a sportswriter by saying, "Ya want Dillinger the bank robber or Dillinger the ballplayer? Either way, ya probably got the wrong guy."[52]

Dillinger had a few regrets. "I'm sorry I didn't do better with Connie Mack and the Athletics," he once said.

He felt badly about the way his career ended. "I ripped him [Tony Freitas] and I shouldn't of."

Dillinger's lifetime Browns average of .309 ranks fifth on the team's all-time list. He was the last Brown to collect 200 hits, score 100 runs, and steal 30 bases in a single season, and the last Brown to get a hit in an All-Star Game. "The two things that pleased me more in playing baseball were going to the '49 All-Star Game, scoring twice and getting a base hit, and then coming out to the Coast League—the year after they ran me out of the big leagues—and leading the league in hitting. That made me quite happy."

One of the few baseball mementoes displayed at Dillinger's home was a framed letter from a fan in Florida who had just met Bob at a Philadelphia Athletics Historical Society event in the Philadelphia area. "Unlike so many players, you have a real personality and sense of humor," the letter read. "I wish you could've been with the A's much longer and maybe they would have had more success and not had to leave town. Well, Connie Mack traded Nelson Fox, too, so what can we expect?"

Fox, a second baseman, was traded to the White Sox after the 1949 season. He went on to become a 15-time All-Star; win the American League's Most Valuable Player Award in 1959; and be selected to the Hall of Fame, along with George Kell, a 10-time All-Star third baseman the A's sent to the Tigers in 1946.

As Dillinger watched a visitor read the letter, he appeared to have tears in his eyes.

In late 2000, Dillinger visited Fain at his home in Georgetown, California. They had not seen one another since they were teammates in 1950.

Fain was in a wheelchair. "The body is gone, but I still got a brain or two functioning halfway properly," he said.

Wally Westlake, a big leaguer for 10 years, described Fain, a lifelong friend, as a "red-ass—prime time" who "wouldn't back down from a chainsaw."

Fain challenged Dillinger to a foot race. "You don't argue with Ferris, so I just said, 'Yeah, you could beat me.'"

They smoked a turkey and swapped stories about the good old days when they washed down barbecued lobster tails with rivers of beer.

"He hadn't changed one bit," Fain said. "He was still as nonchalant, didn't much give a shit, knew he could do this, and cared less about anything else."

They laughed like kids.

They finished eating and said goodbye to one another for the last time.

"Bob was the best damn friend I ever had," Fain said. "I enjoyed watching his graceful ability on the field. The guy was just a tremendous player, and he never got credit for it."

Fain died in 2001, and Dillinger in 2009, at the age of 91.

As the years passed the Browns became lovable, and longtime sportswriters like Joe Falls of the *Detroit News-Free Press* waxed romantic, remembering the brown piping on their rinky-dink uniforms and Bob Dillinger because "he made you think of John Dillinger, the bank robber," the way he stole bases. [53]

At long last, Bob was getting some respect. In turn, he began letting others see behind the crustiness that kept most people at bay.

After the interview in 2000, Dillinger sent several personal notes to the writer he playfully accused of being Dr. Death.

"Just got back from walking on water," he joked. "Me and the Lord. You know what I mean."

"Myers was a nice young ballplayer," he wrote in another. "Too bad he could not get several years in the majors. He could play short."

Richie Myers finally made it to the majors in 1956, with the Chicago Cubs, appearing in four games and batting once.

Most revealing of all was this quip, handwritten on replica "American Base Ball Club of Philadelphia" stationery: "Poor Mr. Mack got a lemon in John Dillinger. Oh, well, there were a few others." (Even Bob Dillinger, the ballplayer, confused himself with John Dillinger, the bank robber.)

12

MADE FOR HOLLYWOOD

Carlos Bernier

Fans either loved or hated Carlos Bernier, depending on whether he played for or against their team.

He was the darling of Hollywood Stars fans during the heart of the 1950s—as big a celebrity locally as the movie stars who owned stock in the team and filled the box seats at home games.

One of them was George Raft, an actor best known for his roles in gangster films. "He wanted to take me to the studio and put me in the movie business," Carlos recalled. "I say, 'Now, George, I like you and you like me, but I want to play baseball.'"

Carlos could play, too.

He made his Hollywood debut in 1952, by hitting .301 and leading the Pacific Coast League (PCL) with 105 runs scored and 65 stolen bases.

"Calling all Coast League catchers," one Los Angeles sportswriter wrote. "Be on the lookout for Carlos Bernier, alias 'The Bandit.' He's out to steal you blind!"[1]

Carlos dazzled crowds much like another Puerto Rican, Roberto Clemente.

"Everybody was impressed with his speed," said Wes Parker, a six-time Gold Glove Award winner at first base for the Los Angeles Dodgers and a teammate of Maury Wills, who swiped a record 104 bases in 1962. "You see the basics when you're a kid—the strongest, the fastest, the showiest."

Parker was 12 years old in 1952, when Carlos had Tinseltown in a tizzy, running the bases for the pennant-winning Stars like the nicknames he accumulated—The Bandit, Carlos the Comet, Jet, and Human Outboard Motor.

"Oh, he was showy," Parker said. "When he was running the bases, he was always running around and diving—kind of like a Maury Wills."

Chuck Stevens was one of many former big-leaguers on the Stars roster. "Carlos was a big draw in Hollywood," said Stevens. "It was a show town, and obviously they liked his routine."

Bobby Bragan managed the 5-foot-8, 180-pound Bernier in Hollywood for two years (1954–1955) before taking charge of the Pittsburgh Pirates in 1956, the first of three big-league teams he guided. "He was strong—built like a boxer. Strong from the base up. He was fast . . . got a quick jump on the ball."

Bragan was one of Carlos's biggest boosters. "He could do as much or more than many big-league outfielders. He had the speed. He could steal bases with anybody in the big leagues. He could hit, he could run, he could do it all. He had flair like Willie Mays. He was exciting to watch—the opposition always knew Bernier was playing today."

So did the umpires.

"I remember vividly that Carlos was never out at first," Stevens said.

> That's real good when it's a tap-tap play. But it's not good when you're obviously out. The umpires have the last say, and if you aggravate them, they can come back to haunt you. We had a good ballclub, and we knew we'd be in the thick of a pennant race come September. We didn't want Carlos aggravating umpires—raising hell on plays where he was obviously out.

Cesare "Cece" Carlucci was an umpire in the PCL for 12 years and witnessed most of Carlos's adventures, good and bad. Carlos played 11 seasons in the PCL—five at Hollywood, two at Salt Lake City, and four at Hawaii.

"He was nothing but trouble for the umps," Carlucci said. "You never could call a strike on him or call him out. If you called him out, it was a beef. Called a strike on him, it was a beef. If you knocked him out on a third strike, geez, he'd go crazy. Remember he slapped Chris Valenti."

Valenti was the home plate umpire in a game played on August 11, 1954.

Umpire Cece Carlucci used his body as a buffer between Carlos Bernier, far left, and several members of the San Diego Padres, including Milt Smith, far right, and Luke Easter, who is visible to Carlucci's right. Ten days later, Carlos slapped an umpire and was suspended for the rest of the 1954 season. *San Diego History Center.*

"He called me out on three high pitches," Carlos said. "Same spot—right here on neck."

He pointed to his throat.

Carlos turned to argue and bumped Valenti.

"That's all for you, Carlos!" he hollered.

"I go like this to argue with him, and I hit him in the face."

Carlos gestured with his right hand to show what happened.

"It was an accident."

Bragan called it a slap—"kind of like you'd tap a girl on the cheek."

Tap or slap, it didn't matter.

"Hitting an umpire was like shooting the president," said Irv Kaze, publicity director for the Stars. "He could've been nailed for life, hitting an official."

PCL president Clarence "Pants" Rowland was sitting in a box seat near home plate and would decide Carlos's fate.

A distraught Carlos, tears streaming down his face, apologized to Valenti after the game. "I'm sorry what happen," he said. "I don't try to hit you."

Carlos was suspended for the rest of the 1954 season—34 games. He was batting .313 and leading the league with 38 stolen bases at the time. The Stars were in first place, two and one-half games ahead of the San Diego Padres. They wound up tied, the Padres winning a one-game playoff for the title.

"Losing Carlos cost us the pennant," Bragan added.

It probably cost Carlos another shot in the majors.

He hit only .213 in 105 games for the Pittsburgh Pirates in 1953, but he led the team in stolen bases, with 15. Carlos spent the next four years in Hollywood, racking up 127 more steals.

The Stars and the PCL were run out of Hollywood in 1958, by the arrival of the Dodgers and Major League Baseball. They moved to Salt Lake City and became the Bees. Local sportswriters quickly dubbed Bernier "Colorful Carlos."

"Colorful Carlos" lived up to his new nickname, hitting .332, with 34 steals and a league-leading 11 triples and 121 runs scored.

In 1959, his batting average dropped to .281, and the number of stolen bases to 21.

"He was just a step slower," reported *Salt Lake Tribune* columnist John Mooney. "He was taking the called third strike and arguing. The fans who applauded his colorful disputes in 1958, became disgusted with Carlos's attempts to 'cover up' his shortcomings by arguing."[2]

He split the 1960 season between Columbus, Ohio, and Indianapolis in the American Association. The Hawaii Islanders rescued him from Indianapolis in May 1961.

The Islanders were new to the Coast League and asked Carlucci, the veteran umpire, to recommend players who could help them on the field and at the gate. "Carlos Bernier!" he blurted out. "Helluva ballplayer. But he's trouble."

The Islanders signed him anyway.

He proceeded to win the PCL batting title with a career-high .351 mark, which landed him on the Triple-A all-star team and earned PCL Player of the Year honors from Topps, the baseball card company.

Carlos was 34, but the National League's addition of the New York Mets and Houston Colt 45s in 1962 gave him hope of another shot at the majors. "The Mets wanted to buy my contract for $25,000," Carlos said.

That was half the amount the Islanders wanted. Carlos played three more seasons in Hawaii, totaling 90 homers, 68 doubles, and 17 triples, compared to 61 stolen bases.

He retired after playing part of the 1965 season at Reynosa in the Mexican League. His numbers in the minors offer a glimpse of the star potential unfulfilled in the majors—.297 batting average, 2,374 hits, 1,594 runs scored, 312 doubles, 129 triples, 212 homers, and 594 stolen bases.

"Carlos Bernier today could steal a hundred bases a year," said Orlando Cepeda, a Puerto Rican first baseman who joined the San Francisco Giants in 1958, and went on to slug 379 homers in a Hall of Fame career. "In those days it was so hard for a Latino and black player to make the big leagues. I was very fortunate because when I came to the Giants, they had to give me the opportunity."

"In a way, Bernier was ahead of his time," said Art Spander, longtime San Francisco sports columnist.

Spander grew up in Los Angeles, rooting for the Los Angeles Angels, the Stars' bitter crosstown rivals. "He was a showboat. That was looked down upon greatly by some people, me included, at the end of the twentieth century. People didn't do that. They hit a home run, they ran around the bases. They didn't posture; they didn't pose. He did."

In the end, Carlos's fiery temper and the fighting were his undoing.

"No, no, he wasn't blackballed—nothing like that," Bragan insisted. "I know there wasn't any organized conspiracy to keep Carlos out of the big leagues, but it's very possible that the slapping incident influenced the decisions of others. After all, it got him a bad reputation."

"I like to fight all the time," Carlos admitted. "Close plays I'd be out, and I'd argue. The umpire would say, 'No.' I'd say, 'Yes.' Who is the loser? Carlos Bernier. I don't think I win one argument yet."

Carlos's return to Hollywood in 1955 was greeted by a *Los Angeles Times* story that began as follows: "Coast League umpires beware—Carlos Bernier is coming back!"[3]

The men in blue were seeing red. They believed Carlos got off with a tap on the wrist for a slap in the face.

"The umpires weren't going to take any crap from him at all," Carlucci said. "When he got out of line a little bit, we knocked his butt out of there."

Carlos was on his best behavior—too good for Bragan.

"He's afraid to fight," the Stars manager said soon after his return. "He's trying so hard to be good that he's playing under a sort of suppression. He needs an outlet for emotion. He needs to blow off steam. But I can't tell him that at the risk of having him run out of baseball."[4]

Bragan eventually told Carlos, "Don't be afraid. You have to fight a little bit."

"I know I can't play baseball if I have my heart blocked," Carlos said. "I have to once in a while say something. That's what I did."

He learned to argue with his hands behind his back. And he tried to be nice to the umpires.

"When he came back, hell, he dusted the plate off for us and picked up things," Carlucci said. "It was unbelievable. But it was just an act. He still had the same attitude. You couldn't call anything on him. He was always going to say something."

One time in Portland, Carlos turned around to gripe about a strike call by Carlucci. "Don't f*#* with me," the umpire warned. "Just play ball."

Carlos was still upset when the game ended and waited for Carlucci outside the umpires' dressing room, blocking the door. "Look, the game is over," Carlucci said. "Tomorrow is another game. Just get out of my way."

Carlos wouldn't budge. "He started pushing me around, and I hit him once with my mask," Carlucci said.

It took two policemen and Carlos's own teammates to restore order.

"He only got a fine," Carlucci said. "He should've been suspended again."

As much as the umps and Carlos disagreed, they agreed that he argued too much.

"I got thrown out 25 to 30 times every season," Carlos estimated. "The thing that cost me another chance in the big leagues is I argue all the time with the umpires."

Carlucci agreed with his longtime nemesis. "If he would've just played ball and let the umpires do their jobs, he could've put up 10 years in the bigs."

* * *

The town of Juana Dias is on the southern coast of Puerto Rico, about one and one-half hours by car from San Juan and light years from Hollywood.

Carlos Eugene Bernier Rodriguez was born in Juana Dias January 28, 1927. At the time, most of the town's 8,000 residents worked in the sugar cane fields and lived in mud houses.

One of seven children, Carlos was nine years old when his father, a carpenter, was killed in a fall from a house he was building. Two months later, a younger sister died of yellow fever.

Carlos quit school in the eighth grade to support his mother, Rosario, by cutting sugar cane and shining shoes on the side. Next, he became a plumber's assistant, and, then, just before turning 16, he upped his age to 18 so he could join the army. He didn't tell anyone until he called his mother seven months later.

"Ma, I went to the army by myself and never asked you," he said. "You better take me out. This is not for me. I'm too young."

Carlos returned to Juana Dias and started playing ball locally. He caught the eye of a neighbor—Ceferino "Cefo" Conde, a Puerto Rican League pitching great.

Cefo was like a father to Carlos and took him to Mayaguez to play. He went hitless in his first 23 at-bats. The team's owner wanted to unload him but was talked out of it by manager Joe Buzas, an ex-New York Yankee who went on to a distinguished career as a minor-league club owner.

The next day, Carlos lashed a triple and two singles. He was off and running on a Puerto Rican League Hall of Fame career that would span three decades, from 1946 to 1966, and feature a record 285 stolen bases, including 5 basestealing titles and the single-season mark of 41, which lasted 31 years.

In 1948, Buzas arranged for Carlos to play pro ball in the United States at Port Chester, New York, a Class B league team.

Carlos bought a Spanish–English dictionary and at night looked up words he heard during the day. He had plenty of time to study because in a game during the Fourth of July weekend, a pitched ball struck him on the left side of the face, just below the temple.

"I spent two months in the hospital with a fracture of my head," Carlos said. "Before I got hit on the head I was one of the coolest men you'd ever see in your life. I argue with nobody; I fight with nobody. But when I got hit in the head, that changed everything."

In an interview after the slapping incident, Carlos blamed the beaning for "nasal hemorrhages" he suffered in Pittsburgh and "recurring nervousness and illnesses" that "caused him to lose his temper at the least provocation."[5]

In 102 games at Port Chester, Carlos stole 24 bases, fifth best in the Colonial League, and batted .248, with 3 homers. He lost his cool only once when, according to one news account, "he became so enraged" over being called out on a double play "that he went after the umpire with homicide in mind."[6]

At Bristol, Connecticut, in 1949, Carlos gave up switch-hitting to bat solely from the right side of the plate. The payoff was a .336 batting average, 15 home runs, and a Colonial League–high 89 stolen bases. He had a midsummer trial with Indianapolis of the American Association. Manager Al Lopez looked him over in batting practice and pregame warmups and decided "he was not suited to Triple-A baseball, nor to a future major-league career."[7]

He started the 1950 season at St. Jean, Quebec, Canada, in the Class C Provincial League, batting .335, scoring 69 runs in 64 games, and swiping 41 bases. He returned to Bristol to hit .287 and pile up an amazing 53 steals in 52 games. Combined, he belted 24 round-trippers.

"Carlos Bernier is a hard-running, aggressive ballplayer on the diamond, but off the field is one of the nicest young men you'd want to meet," one newspaper reported.[8]

The 1951 season paired Carlos with Ben Chapman, manager of the Tampa Smokers in the Class B Florida International League. Chapman is best known as the Philadelphia Phillies pilot who heaped racial insults on Jackie Robinson his first year in the majors.

Except for his caramel-colored skin, Carlos had a lot in common with Chapman. They had terrible tempers and constantly feuded with umpires, Chapman striking one in the face and drawing a year-long ban from baseball. As a player, Chapman earned the nickname "Alabama Flash" by topping the American League in stolen bases four times.

Chapman sharpened Carlos's base-running skills. He stole home six times. Overall, he had 51 steals, 21 triples, and 124 runs scored, all league bests, and sparked Tampa to the pennant—his fourth championship in as many years.

The Hollywood Stars were a farm club of the Pittsburgh Pirates, headed by Branch Rickey, the mastermind behind the powerhouses built by the St. Louis Cardinals in the 1930s and Brooklyn Dodgers in the 1940s. Rickey loved speed and prodded the Stars to select Carlos in the minor-league draft.

Carlos had never played above Class B, and in the PCL, one notch below the majors, he would be facing wily veterans with a lot more stuff than the youngsters he batted .271 against at Tampa.

The Stars were loaded with former big-leaguers accustomed to winning. They won the PCL title under manager Fred Haney in 1949, placed third in 1950, and came in second in 1951.

Haney shared Rickey's passion for speed. He pilfered 63 and 71 for the Stars in 1933–1934, respectively, giving him four stolen-base crowns in the eight seasons he played in the PCL.

"The three parts of swiping a base are jump, speed, and slide," Haney said. "Carlos is outstanding in all three, but it's his jump that really turns the trick."[9]

The Stars' skipper rated Carlos as the fastest player in baseball.

"Fred Haney told me when I join Hollywood ballclub: I want you to hit .250 and have a lot of stolen bases. You run on your own."

In the early 1950s, the Stars were the closest thing to "Showtime" in Los Angeles sports. The Lakers and Dodgers had yet to arrive in LA, and the Rams of the National Football League, the city's only claim to big-league status, played second fiddle to the USC Trojans and UCLA Bruins, local college football powerhouses. The Angels were the other baseball team in town, but in contrast to the Stars, they were as stodgy as their Chicago-based boss, chewing-gum magnate Philip K. Wrigley.

The Stars were owned and operated by Bob Cobb and his actress-wife, Gail Patrick. They bought the team in 1938, with the help of a few Hollywood friends who regularly hung their hats at Cobb's Brown Derby restaurants and savored the Cobb salad he invented—Gene Autry, Gary Cooper, Bing Crosby, Cecil B. DeMille, George Raft, Robert Taylor, and William Powell.

The following year, the Stars moved into a new ballpark, 12,000-seat Gilmore Field. The wooden grandstands hugged the playing field, placing fans and players so close they could sometimes read one another's minds.

"When Rita Hayworth walked in, everybody stopped and watched her move around," said Rinaldo "Rugger" Ardizoia, a Hollywood pitcher.

Singer-actor Jimmy Durante sat directly behind Stevens, the Stars' first sacker. Stevens warned the entertainer that the wild throws of third baseman Jim Baxes made his seat the most dangerous in the ballpark. That evening an errant Baxes toss sailed into the stands, sending cups of beer and a mustard-covered hot dog flying over Durante and drenching his clothes. He arranged for a new seat after the game.

Raft was another regular.

"He was always dapper—just like you'd see him in the movies," Irv Kaze said.

The gangsters Raft portrayed in the movies had their own rules. Whatever it took to get the job done, they did. Carlos took the same approach on the basepaths.

"He was dangerous—a dirty player the way he'd steal bases," said Eddie Basinski, a shortstop for the Portland Beavers. "He'd spike you or knock you down if it looked like the throw was going to beat him."

Opponents had their own dirty tactics to use against Carlos.

Angels second baseman Gene Mauch admitted tossing a handful of dirt in Carlos's face as he slid into second. On one play he leaped high for a throw and came down on top of him. "Just kind of walked all over him," Mauch related. [10]

Carlos had 27 steals before he was caught for the first time 68 games into the 1952 season. He pestered pitchers into committing balks, making wild throws trying to pick him off base, and generally getting under their skin. Regardless of the situation, he was running.

"He stole a lot when it didn't mean anything," said Tom Saffell, another Stars speedster. "Fred would turn him loose. He'd let him run when he wanted to. I thought a lot of times he ran when he shouldn't have been running, like with a big lead or way behind."

Haney defended Carlos publicly, saying, "I let Bernier steal whenever he wants to, particularly at home. The fans come out to see him run. Why should I disappoint 'em, since it doesn't hurt me."

Haney told opposing managers Carlos wasn't trying to show them up when he tried to steal third with two outs and the Stars way ahead. "He's giving fans a thrill. It's showmanship!"[11]

Others saw it differently.

"He was your typical hot dog," said George Freese, a teammate with the Stars in 1955, and later a rival with the Angels and Portland Beavers.

Carlos shrugged off the label. "Some say Carlos Bernier is a big show off—a hot dog. Most fans think Carlos Bernier is a good ballplayer."

One night in Salt Lake City a young man ran up to Carlos in center field and threw two hot dogs at him. "That's what you are—a hot dog with mustard," the fan screamed.

Carlos chased the fan back to the bleachers, getting in a couple of whacks to the back before the guy jumped into the stands. "I want to jump into the bleachers, too, but the players in the bullpen no let me go up there."

"Carlitos," as Clemente called him, "was a bullet running." He won Coast League Rookie of the Year honors, surprising everyone by hitting .301, with 9 homers and 79 RBIs. His 65 stolen bases almost doubled the runner-up, at 33. The Stars rolled to 109 victories and the PCL flag.

Whenever Haney wanted to fire up his players in Hollywood, he threatened to send them to Pittsburgh, the Siberia of the majors. Now, he was headed there as manager. He took Carlos with him.

The '52 Pirates won only 42 games to finish 22½ games behind the seventh-place team in the standings and 54½ games out of first. "We lost 13 of our first 15 games, and then we had a real bad slump," explained Pirates catcher Joe Garagiola.

The big question about Carlos during spring training was whether he could reach first base. He answered critics two weeks into the season with eight hits in three games, including four triples and two doubles. The capper was a 4-for-5 outburst against the Reds on May 2, featuring a record-tying 3-straight triples, 3 runs scored, 3 RBIs, and a stolen base. The spree jacked up his batting average to .429.

The Pirates began platooning Carlos, and by the end of May, his average was down to .258. In the outfield, he already had three errors. He was even getting thrown out on the bases. Five of his first seven steal attempts were foiled, and he was picked off first base once.

As frustration mounted, his average continued to tumble, and he was thrown out stealing a league-high 14 times. "I was happy before when I was playing every day," he said. "But when I'm sitting on the bench watching the other guys playing, I don't feel like Carlos Bernier."

He blamed Rickey for the decision to platoon him. "Haney wanted to play me every day. In Hollywood, Haney do everything he want. In the big leagues, he take orders from the big man."

Most of the shots called by Rickey in 1953 backfired. The Pirates wound up in the National League basement again with a 50-104 record, 55 games behind first-place Brooklyn.

Carlos summed up his relationship with Rickey: "We not get along too well. I don't think he like me. I don't like him either."

He went to spring training with the Pirates in 1954, but Carlos was soon on his way to Hollywood. "I no want come back here," he confided to a Pittsburgh writer. "I like play every game, and that not happen with me for Pirates." [12]

When Carlos rejoined the Stars in 1954, there was a highly popular show beginning its second year at Gilmore Field titled "Barbing the Ump" and starring the team's colorful player-manager, "Bombastic" Bobby Bragan.

If Carlos was a showman–hot dog, Bragan was a showboat and the whole enchilada with outrageous behavior intended to show up umpires and gain an edge for his players. The act worked for Bragan in 1953, as the Stars won their second-straight title, despite ranking fifth in batting and tying for fourth in fielding.

Bragan had the turnstiles turning and the pundits pontificating on whether his antics were making a mockery of the game. "Fans either hate him or love him; there is no middle ground with this guy," the *Sporting News* reported. [13]

Bragan was so upset with the umpiring in one game that he used eight pinch-hitters in the same batting spot. "I used all the players I had in the dugout."

The night after losing a 21-inning game that Bragan thought should've been stopped because of curfew, he sent a coach to meet the umpires at home plate with watches lining his arms from wrists to elbows and an alarm clock hung around his neck. "He was ejected before he got to home plate," Bragan said, laughing.

Bragan was catching for the Stars when he turned in his finest performance—a striptease following a disputed call on a bunt play. "I tried to find creative ways to let them know when they were wrong."

Tom Saffell played and coached three years for Bragan. "Bobby was a very, very intelligent baseball man. He always had the game worked out three innings ahead of everybody else. But he had that thing about the umpires. He never saw an umpire he liked. Every chance he got to show them up, he did it."

Bragan was just as explosive as Bernier. Together, they harangued umpires and infuriated foes in devilish ways, raising hell wherever they went.

Carlos had a bull's-eye on his forehead going into a weeklong, seven-game series in early June against the Angels, the Stars' backyard enemy. The Angels–Stars rivalry was one of the most intense in baseball.

"I would stack it up to the Dodgers–Giants, Yankees–Red Sox, and Cubs–Cardinals," said Kaze, the Stars' publicist. "The rivalry was just as heated and emotional as any of those at their best."

"The Angel ballclub think it better than us and we think we better than them," Carlos explained. "That's why all the time we have fight and argument."

The fiery Mauch joined the Angels in 1954, and for the next three years, he and Carlos played the chief villain roles as well as any movie actor.

"The Hollywood fans hated the Angels, and the Angel fans hated the Stars," Bernier said. "The fans of the Angels hated Carlos Bernier and all of the Stars. Same way with the Hollywood fans. They hated Gene Mauch and the Angels. Everybody hated each other."

The opener of the June series at the Angels' ballpark, Wrigley Field, was fairly typical of what LA newspapers referred to as a civil war.

"There were gory brawls in the stands," the *Los Angeles Mirror* reported. "Tempers flared on the field, an umpire reversed a decision, a player was thumbed out, there were 22 hits and 22 strike outs, some terrific plays and some boners."[14]

The expelled player was Carlos. He blew up and made an obscene gesture at an umpire after being called safe but then out on a play at second base.

Mauch was chased in the second game for arguing a called third strike, and Carlos stomped on the foot of Angels first baseman R. T. "Dixie" Upright, sparking angry words that almost led to blows being exchanged.

Bragan and Stars pitcher Bob Hall were ejected from the third game, Hall pointing to all three umpires and then giving them the choke sign by clutching his throat.

The seventh and last game of the series featured a free-for-all touched off by Carlos after LA shortstop Bud Hardin tagged him hard sliding into second base. When Carlos lashed out with his spikes scrambling to his feet, Hardin cut loose with a haymaker that missed.

"I jump up to throw a punch at him," Carlos said. "Gene Mauch came in behind me and I turn around and punch him. What happened is everybody fight and I sit on the bench. I don't know how I got on the bench. I think the umpire take and sit me on the bench. I tried to get up, but the policemen wouldn't let me."

Mauch hit Carlos alongside the head before park police halted the fight.

Bernier and Hardin got the heave-ho, Carlos holding his nose and spitting as a fan waved a handkerchief at him as he returned to the Hollywood dugout. He lingered there, heckling the umpires. The Angels' Upright took one of the insults personally and dared him to come back onto the field. Finally, Bragan stepped in and ordered Carlos into the clubhouse.

The *Los Angeles Times* called it a "mob fight." Carlos was suspended five games "for insulting the fans and for action that could have caused a riot."[15]

The *Los Angeles Mirror* cited an off-the-record prediction made three weeks earlier by a Coast League umpire: "Carlos Bernier is begging for trouble, and he's going to get it. He's going to get socked before the season is over."[16]

Bragan wasn't concerned, telling *Mirror* columnist Sid Ziff, "I don't uphold all that beefing when you don't have anything to beef about. But I don't want to discourage it. I like a fighting, base-running ballclub."[17]

Not even Bragan expected what happened next.

"BERNIER STRIKES UMP BEFORE THOUSANDS," announced a headline in the *Mirror*.[18]

It was the unidentified umpire's warning come true.

"I'm my own enemy," Carlos said. "Because when I lose my temper, that's it. Off the field, I friendly with everybody. The only hot blood is on the field."

Shortly after Bernier was slapped with a season-ending suspension, Bragan received a three-game ban for cursing and threatening an umpire. He denied the charges but admitted to commenting on the ump's "white hair and false teeth."[19]

Times columnist Al Wolf tagged Bragan the "Dr. Jekyll and Mr. Hyde" of baseball—"clever, affable, and accommodating off the field but frequently rash, defiant, and insulting thereon."

Bragan's actions had gone from "hilarious" to "just plain ornery," Wolf maintained. "And the evidence indicates all too plainly the adverse influence Bragan has asserted on some of his men." As an example, he cited how Bernier's "excellent" behavior under Haney in 1952 "steadily worsened" with Bragan at the helm.[20]

Carlos had nothing but praise for Bragan. "Bobby Bragan was one of the greatest managers I ever played under in my life. He say, 'You have to play the way you play all your life. It doesn't matter. I'm going to be behind you. That's what I like from you.'"

The following spring, they posed for a *Times* photo showing Bragan holding a halo over Carlos's head.

"I'm good boy now," Carlos said. "I know my mistake cost Stars the pennant. No more trouble, and we win this year. I play for family and teammates now and play hard."[21]

The Stars' Kaze wanted fans to know that Carlos was a "happy-go-lucky kind of guy" off the field. He arranged a pre-Mother's Day story in the *Times* about Carlos and his cigar-smoking mother: "I have to watch her, or mamma will raid my supply. So I see to it she has her own. I buy her boxes for holidays, birthdays, any occasion."[22]

Mama Bernier almost had to verify that her son was indeed the Stars' new third baseman and not a stand-in actor. The guy looked like Carlos but sure didn't act like him.

He went an entire month before debating an ump's call. By the end of the second month, the kinder, gentler Carlos was cause for alarm.

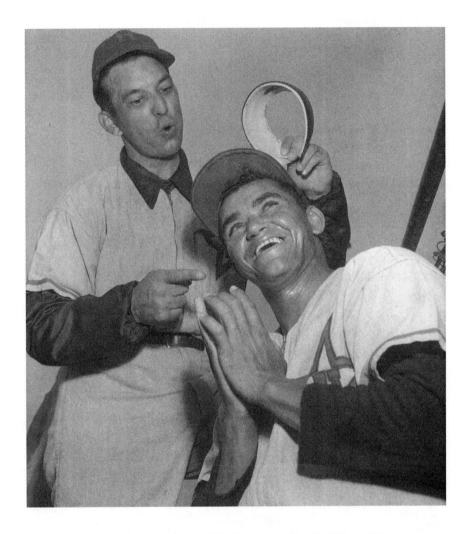

There was no making an angel out of Carlos Bernier, but Hollywood Stars manager Bobby Bragan had fun trying at spring training in 1955. Early in the season, Carlos played without his usual fire, prompting Bragan to tell him, "Don't be afraid. You have to fight a little bit." *Los Angeles Times Photographic Archive, Library Special Collections, Charles E. Young Research Library, UCLA.*

"The fire has gone out of the Puerto Rican," Sid Ziff declared in the *Mirror*. "His color is gone. He has become just another player and not even a very effective one."[23]

The Stars were in last place, and through 43 games, Carlos was hitting only .276, with 7 stolen bases. "I argue a little bit, but I'm afraid they throw me out of the game and the president of the league would say, 'He no learn his lesson yet' and suspend me again. That's why I try to cool off a little bit."

Carlos was ejected once during the entire season. He even teamed with Bragan to prevent a brawl and kept his cool after Angels pitcher Don Elston hit him in the head, shattering the plastic helmet he was wearing. Five days earlier, Elston had popped him on the shoulder.

The Stars rebounded to finish in a third-place tie with the Angels, but Carlos struggled to the end, batting .279 and swiping 29 bases, both Hollywood lows up to that point.

"Unzestful," is how Kaze characterized Bernier's postslap play. "I don't know that he ever was the same again. I just think that it took something out of him."

Bragan moved up to the majors in 1956, to manage the hapless Pirates, leaving Carlos behind in Hollywood to carry on with the show.

Carlos could still captivate and arouse a crowd, but he was no longer the toast of LA. That distinction belonged to the Angels' Stout Steve Bilko, a beer-drinking Sergeant of Swat built like a 1953 Hudson sedan. Bilko bashed 148 homers in three seasons in LA, including 55 in 1956.

Some Stars fans were weary of Bernier's behavior, the LA media suggesting at the end of both the 1955 and 1956 seasons that he had worn out his welcome and wouldn't be back. That proved wrong, but Carlos's bad-boy reputation overshadowed his performance on the field. He was thrown out of only 2 games in 1956, and led the league in triples (15) and stolen bases (48), while batting .283, but he spent most of the year in the doghouse of Stars manager Clay Hopper.

The white-haired Hopper was responsible for developing such promising youngsters as second baseman Bill Mazeroski, a future Hall of Famer, and pitchers Bob Purkey and Luis Arroyo, who went on to star in the big leagues. Hopper had no patience for a moody veteran who didn't fit into the parent club's plans. "I'm going to give it to him good," he promised near the end of the season.[24]

Carlos was suspended for three games. "He gave me a lot of lip," the fed-up Hopper explained after a heated argument under the Gilmore Field stands during a game.[25]

Carlos outlasted Hopper to play the Stars' final season in Hollywood and seal his legacy as the most electrifying player in the team's history. No one could match Carlos as a lightning rod for trouble and controversy. "He raised the emotions for fans," Kaze said.

One woman was so enamored with Carlos that she sent him a bag to save as a souvenir one of his golf-ball-sized wads of tobacco he chewed, to become known as "the jaw with the biggest chaw in the Pacific Coast League."[26]

A broken thumb caused Carlos to miss one-third of the 1957 season and steal a mere 12 bases. But when the curtain came down on the Stars' 20-year rivalry with the Angels, he was back at center stage, kicking and screaming when an umpire reversed a call and then making the last out.

Carlos Bernier, the showman, and Hollywood, the show town, were made for one another.

It took the Dodgers to usher Carlos out of Hollywood and Sandy Koufax, Don Drysdale, and Maury Wills to push him back in the memory banks of LA baseball fans.

"Those were the best days of my life, playing for Hollywood," Carlos said.

They were also some of the best days for baseball in LA.

* * *

In the early 1960s, Hawaii was a refuge for former big-leaguers with a troubled past.

The first signed by the Islanders was Ralph "Blackie" Schwamb, a former St. Louis Browns pitcher trying to make a comeback after serving time in prison for killing a man in a robbery attempt. Blackie lasted a month into the 1961 season before he was released with a 1-2 won–loss mark and 5.14 earned run average.

A few days after Blackie left, Carlos arrived from Indianapolis.

In 1962, the Islanders took a chance on Joe Taylor, hoping the aging slugger would improve with age like the whiskey Old Taylor. A week into the season, Joe had a lone hit—a home run—to show for 10 at-bats and was sent to the Vancouver Mounties.

The most famous refugee was Robert "Bo" Belinsky, a petulant play-boy pitcher with more girlfriends than the 11 major-league victories he

Infielders were fair game when Carlos Bernier was running the bases. Here, he upended Los Angeles Angels shortstop Jack Caro in a failed attempt to break up a double play. Looking on is George "Sparky" Anderson, a 23-year-old second baseman for the Angels in 1957. He went on to become a Hall of Fame manager. *Los Angeles Times Photographic Archive, Library Special Collections, Charles E. Young Research Library, UCLA.*

had in late May 1963, when he was demoted by the Los Angeles Angels. The Islanders were a farm club of the Angels, one of two expansion teams added by the American League in 1961.

"Most baseball players are like robots," Bo said. "The management winds them up and then turns them loose. I guess I am just a nonconformist."[27]

Bo was engaged to actress Mamie Van Doren at the time. "I like the way he walks, the way he talks, the way he pitches," Mamie purred.[28]

The Angels also liked the way Bo pitched as a rookie in 1962, winning 10 games, including a no-hitter. Bo proposed to Mamie on April Fool's Day 1963 and proceeded to lose seven of eight decisions.

It took Bo two months to report to the Islanders, but when he finally did, he wowed men and women fans alike, compiling a 4-1 won–loss record and 2.50 earned run average to get another shot with the Angels.

The troublemaker label dogged Carlos from Hollywood to Hawaii. It probably cost him a spot on the PCL all-star team after he won the batting title in 1961, with a .351 mark, 41 points higher than his closest rival. The league's managers snubbed him, while Topps tabbed him PCL Player of the Year and baseball writers throughout the country named him to the All-Triple A team.

Irv Noren joined the Islanders as player-manager in 1962. He played 11 years in the majors, mostly for the Washington Senators and New York Yankees.

"His reputation when I arrived was that he'd fight at a drop of the hat," Noren said. "Heard he was trouble . . . hard to handle. This turned out to be untrue. I had no problems with him. He'd do anything to beat you on the field. Off the field, he was a quiet guy who didn't break any curfews or cause any trouble."

Carlos looked more like a tourist around town, sightseeing with his wife, Delia, and two boys, Néstor Rubén and Horacio Enrique. He usually wore a colorful sports shirt and wide-brimmed straw hat, and chewed a cigar with the paper band still on it.

Carlos reinvented himself as a power hitter in Hawaii. He began wearing glasses and adjusted his swing to take advantage of Honolulu Stadium's short right-field fence, which one scribe called the "laughing stock of the league."[29]

"The right-field fence was close—305 feet," Carlos said. "'I no stupid!' That's what I told everybody who ask why I hit to right field."

Of the 90 home runs he poked in four seasons with the Islanders, 74 were at Honolulu Stadium, the most by any player. Every time Carlos parked one at home, he and his family were treated to a free dinner at a local restaurant. He was the most popular player in the 27-year history of the Islanders.

Noren found out for himself in 1963, when the parent Angels insisted he bench Carlos and play Dick Simpson, a 19-year-old hotshot who had slammed 42 homers in a Class C league the year before.

"The big bosses, they say I'm too old," Carlos said during spring training. "I don't think I'm too old. I feel like a 19-year-old. I think I am better than anyone here."[30]

Carlos slammed 20 homers in 1962, but his batting average dropped to .313, prompting the Islanders to try peddling him to a team in Japan.

"I worked for the Angels, and if they wanted me to play Simpson, I had to play Simpson," Noren said. "I played Simpson in center field, not Bernier. Used Carlos as a pinch-hitter."

"You take your order and play him," Carlos told Noren. "You're going to have to explain to fans why you don't play me."

Simpson went hitless in his first four games as Islanders fans jeered.

"I took a lot of abuse from the fans," Noren said. "There was a radio program where people called in. They jammed the lines asking why I didn't play Bernier."

Carlos was soon back in the starting lineup, hitting at a .300 clip and socking 26 homers. Simpson wound up batting .232, with seven homers.

Noren was still reeling from the Simpson controversy when he learned Belinsky was headed his way.

"Waikiki needs Belinsky like another tidal wave," quipped Red McQueen of the *Honolulu Advertiser*. "If Noren thinks he's had trouble handling the tempestuous Bernier, wait 'til he gets Belinsky."

Carlos was around to say hello and goodbye to Belinsky, and, in 1964, he put an exclamation point on his adventures in paradise with a .294 batting average and five two-homer games, giving him a career single-season high of 27.

The Washington Senators replaced the Angels as Hawaii's sugar daddy in 1965. Jack Quinn, the Islanders' new 27-year-old general manager, reasoned the team "could have finished 45 games out of first place just as well without Bernier as we did with him."[31]

Quinn unceremoniously dumped Carlos and his team-high $15,000 salary in Reynosa, Mexico, and a lower-level league. It was a shabby way to treat a player known as the "people's choice" and the last link to the team's beginnings.[32]

Carlos delivered Hollywood-style action and drama not even the flamboyant Belinsky could match in his three Hawaii gigs. Bo pitched for the Islanders in 1968 and 1969, even throwing a no-hitter. But compared to Don Carlos, Bo was a one-night stand.

* * *

Carlos was standing in front of a television, a bat in one hand and a half-smoked cigar in the other. He watched intently as New York Yankees catcher Thurman Munson and then manager Billy Martin futilely argued an umpire's call. It was as if Carlos was watching a playback of himself.

"Billy Martin argue too much," he said.

It was the summer of 1976, and Carlos was showing a visitor around his three-bedroom house on a tree-lined street in Paterson, New Jersey.

The night before Carlos worked the graveyard shift at U.S. Bronze, an aluminum powder manufacturer. He got home at eight o'clock in the morning and fell asleep on a couch in the den.

Carlos sat on the same couch, smoking a cigar as he talked about growing up in Juana Dias. "It's a friendly town. Wonderful people," he said.

> The only problem with Juana Dias is the people drink too much. Everybody drink—rum . . . beer. Especially when he's going to the ballgame.
>
> I no finish the eighth grade. I quit school to go to work and support my little sister and my mother. My older brother was sick and couldn't do nothing.

From his first pro team in Port Chester to his last in Reynosa, Carlos recalled his career in vivid detail.

"I don't want to go to Mexico," he said of his sale to Reynosa prior to the 1965 season. "But the president of the minor leagues say if I don't report to Mexico, he's going to suspend me. My wife say, 'Go there and try. If you don't like it, quit and come home.' So I did."

In 87 games, he batted .281, with 12 homers and 5 stolen bases.

Carlos pulled out a scrapbook that he hadn't looked at since leaving baseball.

A crumpled photo from Hollywood got his attention. "See how skinny I was. I weigh 165 to 170 pounds. I now weigh 165 pounds, and I drink a lot of beer."

Each picture turned back the clock, resurrecting a faded memory.

"This is in Hawaii. Look how fat I'm here. I used to eat too much."

He came to a photo of him jawing with an umpire. "You see how I argue? With my hands in my pocket. Look at how he look at me."

He held up a picture of kids grouped around him in Hawaii. "This is me signing autographs. I'm the only one to sign autographs for the kids all the time. I love kids."

Carlos waved another photo. "This is home run I hit in Hawaii. That's when I won Player of the Year. They gave me a trophy that I have in the basement."

Carlos went to the basement. Trophies lined the walls: 1961 Honolulu Quarterback Club, Hawaii Athlete of the Year; Topps Minor League Player of the Year, Hawaii 1961; Tacoma Giants Booster Club, 1961.

I appreciate this more than any other one I have here," he said, picking up the Tacoma award. "It was given to me for outstanding sportsman-ship."

In a game against the Giants at Tacoma, Washington, in 1961, Carlos was caught in a rundown between home plate and third base. Tacoma catcher John Orsino tagged him hard on the back. "I turned around and punched him back. We started a free-for-all," Carlos said.

In subsequent games, Tacoma fans booed and insulted Carlos louder than ever. They waved a banner: "Bernier, you're a bum."

The ringleader was the president of the Giants booster club, who sat in a box seat behind first base. In one game, Carlos hit a ground ball to the shortstop and decided to have some fun. "I run with all my speed. I was out. I continued running and jumped. I kissed him right here."

Carlos pointed to his cheek and laughed. "After that, the old man really loved me."

Tacoma fans honored him with a special day and the sportsmanship award.

He added,

> The fans like the aggressive ballplayer. He like to see the action. That's the same way when you go to the movie. You see dull picture, you go asleep. When you go to the ballpark and you see two or three ballplayers hustle all the time, the fans like that. They like to see ballplayers fight and everything.

Carlos returned to the den and switched on the television to watch the Yankees, his favorite team.

> Every time I watch ballgame on television and I see those averages, I say to my wife, "Look at that—.190." When I play baseball, you have to spend seven, eight years in minors before you went to the big leagues. And some guys never have the chance to go to the big

leagues. Now anybody can go to the big leagues. In a way, I was born 30 years too soon.

For almost two decades, he played baseball 11 months a year, averaging more than 200 games. "I miss it," he said. "I still love baseball. I play baseball all my life and I cry—just like that. Really, I can't take it. I cry all the time."

The comment didn't seem all that significant at the time.

The next year, Carlos quit his job at U.S. Bronze after 10 years and moved to Juana Dias. Delia remained in Paterson.

"She didn't want to go and live in Juana Dias," explained their son, Nėstor. "She just didn't like Juana Dias."

In December 1988, when Nėstor visited his father in Juana Dias, he was living in a house on the same street as his mother and two sisters. He was a coach for the Juana Dias Poets, an amateur baseball team. He was struggling financially despite working for a local oil refinery and managing a downtown parking lot.

"I took care of all the bills, but I think that Dad was just depressed," Nėstor said.

Carlos often became melancholy in recalling certain moments of his career. "Nėstor, I knew it was time to quit the day I dropped that fly ball."

He was a reserve outfielder for Arecibo in 1965–1966, his final season in Puerto Rico. According to author Thomas E. Van Hyning, fans at Hiram Bithorn Stadium in San Juan called Carlos an old woman—"Vieja! Vieja!"—when he made a play in the outfield or stepped to the plate. [33]

"I know that he missed baseball incredibly," Nėstor said. "Even to the point that I think he would avoid it sometimes."

Carlos was asked by the Hawaii Islanders to participate in their 25th anniversary celebration, but he declined.

Nėstor has mentally replayed many times this conversation he had with his father just before Christmas 1988.

"You know, Dad, I envy you in a good sense," he said.

"Why is that?" Carlos wondered.

"You've had the opportunity to play baseball in the major leagues and to play with some of the greatest players, even in the minor leagues. I wish I could've done that."

Nèstor was 32 and on his way to earning a doctorate in pharmacology and toxicology, and working as a research scientist and then educator focused on helping other Latinos and African Americans do what he did.

"No, actually, I should envy you," Carlos said, "because you were able to go to school and I wasn't. I don't know what I would've done if I didn't play baseball."

On April 6, two days after the Pirates' season opener in 1989, Carlos hung himself with a rope in the shower of his Juana Dias home. Outside of Puerto Rico, where it was major news, Carlos's death largely went unnoticed.

It might've ended differently for Carlos if he'd known what *Honolulu Advertiser* columnist Ferd Borsch wrote after learning of his death.

> Carlos might be gone, but what he did on the playing field will last a long time—both in the record books and in the memories of the fans who watched him play.
>
> The stadium became a stage, with Carlos playing the lead role. What he did on that stage is the stuff of legends.
>
> I never saw Carlos turn down a youngster. After all, he was really a kid at heart.
>
> Once he had his uniform on, Carlos never walked. He always ran or trotted. That is how he played the game and that is how he lived.
>
> Carlos Bernier was one of a kind.[34]

* * *

Why?

"No one seems to know why he did it," said Marcos Perez, sports editor of the *San Juan Star*. "It came as a surprise to those who knew him."[35]

Carlos didn't leave a note, but police were certain it was suicide.

Delia Bernier wasn't so sure. She confided to Nèstor: "If you told me your father died trying to save someone else or because he got involved in a scuffle helping someone, I would understand that. Not committing suicide. That wasn't your father."

Baseball allowed Carlos to blow off steam on the field and still be easygoing off it. "I have hot blood," he said of his time in Hawaii. "Made me play with more energy."

The madder he got, the better be played. This probably explains how he made so many sportswriters eat their words after they declared him washed up.

Borsch recalled a 1964 spring exhibition game in Palm Springs, California, between the Islanders and Angels. Many of the spectators had followed the Angels and the Stars in the Coast League.

"You mean he's the same Carlos who played for the Stars way back when?" one of them said in amazement as his name was announced over the public address system.

"How old is he?" another fan asked. "Forty? Forty-five?"[36]

Carlos adopted Nèstor in 1956, a month after marrying Delia. Horacio was born in 1960. He had two children by a previous marriage—Carlos Jr. and Ivonne.

Nèstor was old enough to remember all the free dinners his father's home runs produced in Hawaii but too young to know how big a star he was in Hollywood.

Nèstor learned more in 2004, when he attended the induction of his father into the PCL Hall of Fame at a meeting of the PCL Historical Society in Carson, California.

Parker, the ex-Dodger, was there. "All of us wanted to be just like your father," he said to Nèstor. "He played baseball the way it should be played."

He met Carlucci, the umpire who once got into a wrestling match with Carlos after a game in Portland. "I didn't mind having it out with your dad," Carlucci said. "It was part of the age."

What really upset Carlucci was messing up the suit he was wearing to see his girlfriend and future wife. "You know how dirty I was after rolling on the ground with your father?" he asked.

Nèstor apologized.

"I know that my father was competitive to a fault. And I know that smacking an umpire is disrespectful. But I know that he was under severe pressure of the times."

In *Necessities, Racial Barriers in American Sports*, published in 1989, Phillip M. Hoose writes, "To white fans, the Latin baseball player is a cheerful, peppery character from south of the border, a stablemate of Cisco and Pancho, Cheech and Chong, Ricky Ricardo, Jòse Jimenez, Trini Lopez, and Walt Disney's motor-mouthed, cigar-chomping parrot Josè Carioca."[37]

The Latino stereotype was reinforced in Pittsburgh by *Press* columnist Les Biederman, who phonetically spelled Carlos's broken English.

"Hollywood, I like," Carlos was quoted as saying on one occasion. "Fans they like me. I like fans. I go movie studio. I meet many stars. Kirk Doglas, Robair Taylor, Yvonne de Carlo, oh, oh, and Marilyn Monroe, oh, oh, oh!"[38]

Biederman related another comment by Carlos: "I like major leagues—so far. Efryboty guud to me but some humpires, I no understand. In minors, you can say to humpire, 'You miss play,' and then he say, 'You make errors sometime, too.' But here in majors you no say nossing."[39]

Carlos was ejected from just one game in the majors, but sportswriters covering the Pirates still voted him the most temperamental player on the team.

"We're actually talking about Dr. Jekyll and Mr. Hyde," Nèstor said.

> On the field, he was a fierce competitor, even when he managed the Juana Dias Poets. He was a guy who would go an inch off an umpire's face or roll a player on a dispute. But off the field, you'd never meet a kinder man. He loved children. He was compassionate. I want people to know that.

There are two more things Nèstor wants people to know about his father.

First, the accomplishments that got his father elected to the Puerto Rico Baseball Hall of Fame in 1992 came against such big-leaguers as Clemente, Willie Mays, Henry Aaron, Orlando Cepeda, and Sandy Koufax, all Hall of Famers. Second, Carlos made his debut with the Pirates on April 22, 1953, and should be recognized by the Pirates and Major League Baseball (MLB) as the first to break the color barrier in Pittsburgh. Currently, Curt Roberts, an African American second baseman, has that distinction, even though he didn't join the Pirates until 1954.

Carlos's skin was not as dark as that of Clemente or Vic Power, contemporary Puerto Rican stars in the 1950s, so most of the white media did not view him as black. Such black-owned publications as the *Pittsburgh Courier*, a weekly newspaper, and *Jet*, a national weekly magazine, included Carlos in their coverage of black players. In fact, *Jet* referred to him as a "Negro Coast Star" after he slapped umpire Valenti in 1954.[40]

"He was still called the 'N' word more times than you can imagine," Néstor said. "He and my mother were kept from staying at hotels in Kentucky while traveling as newlyweds. Why was he treated like a black man if everyone thought he was white?"

The debate led to a 2013 story by Joe Guzzardi in the *Pittsburgh Post-Gazette*.

"Many argue that Bernier should be classified as Puerto Rican," Guzzardi wrote. "But, first, Puerto Ricans are American citizens. And, in the 1950s, baseball owners considered players as black or white—Caribbeans, whether Puerto Rican, Cuban, Venezuelan, or Dominican—weren't categorized separately."

Guzzardi concluded Carlos was "unquestionably black."[41]

That hasn't changed the position of the Pirates or MLB that Roberts, not Bernier, was the first black to play for the team.

"Listen, the case of my father is greatly predicated on his alleged controversial approach to the game," Néstor said. "He was not liked by many people in baseball."

Even in death, Carlos Bernier is causing controversy. That's only fitting. The show must go on.

When George Raft told Carlos he ought to get into the movies, the actor didn't fully realize his friend already was in show business. Bernier's performances were unscripted but just as entertaining as any of the screen stars memorialized on the Hollywood Walk of Fame.

He played with his heart, not his head. If he sometimes got too hot under the collar, it was because of the passion burning inside. He was a bolt of lightning streaking around the bases. He was fury unleashed, starting a brawl, chasing a taunting fan off the playing field, going nose-to-nose with an umpire, all the things that made him one of baseball's most colorful and controversial players.

Carlos Bernier was a showman, not a showoff. He was a baseball star made for Hollywood.

13

A TALE OF TWO LEGENDS

Ron Necciai and Steve Dalkowski

The legendary Branch Rickey once was asked to name an all-star team from players who competed for his teams in St. Louis, Brooklyn, and Pittsburgh. He listed Cardinals greats Stan Musial, Rogers Hornsby, Frank Frisch, and Dizzy Dean, and Jackie Robinson of the Dodgers. And then he said, "The greatest all-round pitcher I ever saw never was a major-league regular. He had the best fastball; he had all the learning aptitudes. He was great." There was silence when he mentioned Ron Necciai.[1]

Cal Ripken Sr. was a coach for the Baltimore Orioles and father of the Hall of Fame shortstop by the same name. He was asked about Steve Dalkowski, a flame-throwing left-hander he caught in the minors but who never made it to the majors. "He threw harder than anyone," Ripken said. "I saw Nolan Ryan from the coaching box, and I know you might think I'm stretching the point, but Ryan didn't compare with Steve. I believe if Steve had pitched in the big leagues, he was capable of striking out 21 batters a game."[2]

When Dalkowski was released by the California Angels at the age of 26, the *Sporting News* called him a "baseball legend in his own time." The story ends by listing his lifetime record with 11 teams in nine leagues from Class D to Triple A: "46 wins, 80 defeats, a 5.67 earned run average—and an incredible 1,396 strikeouts and 1,354 walks in 995 innings."[3]

Necciai was 19 in 1952, when he achieved legendary status pitching for the Bristol Twins of the Class D Appalachian League. He tossed a no-hitter that was different than any no-hitter anyone had ever thrown—before or since. "Rocket Ron," as he came to be known, struck out 27 batters in a nine-inning game.

The catcher in Rocket Ron's game for the ages was Harry Dunlop. He was player-manager for the Stockton Ports in 1964, when Dalkowski posted an 8-4 record and a 2.83 earned run average, the best in his nine-year career.

Dalkowski broke into pro ball in 1957, at Kingsport, Tennessee, 23 miles from Bristol on the Tennessee–Virginia border, where Rocket Ron made history.

The night Dalkowski started his first game for the Kingsport Orioles, the movie *The Man with the Golden Arm* was playing at a local drive-in theater. The film has nothing to do with baseball, but its title was perfect for heralding the arrival of an 18-year-old phenom with a fastball so fast it was referred to as a radio pitch—you could hear it but you couldn't see it.

A movie based on the life story of pitching great Dizzy Dean was playing at a Bristol theater when Necciai fanned 27. A commentator for Mutual Broadcasting, Dizzy tipped his hat on the air to "Ron Necktie" for some "pretty fair country pitching."[4]

Bristol manager George Detore even compared "Necktie" with Dizzy, saying, "Of all the pitchers I've seen in the big leagues, Necciai more closely resembles Dean because of his long arms and his speed."[5]

Altogether, Necciai (pronounced Netch-eye) struck out 109 batters in 42⅔ innings at Bristol, giving up 10 hits and 2 earned runs for a miserly 0.42 earned run average.

By August, he was in the majors, pitching for the "Rickeydinks," the nickname for the 1952 Pittsburgh Pirates. "This is forced feeding on our part," Rickey said of the decision to bring up Necciai. "If we were a good team, I wouldn't be doing this."[6]

At 6-foot-5 and 185 pounds when he was healthy, Ron was a string bean.

"Who hung the uniform on the mound?" Pirates catcher Joe Garagiola wisecracked.

Ron was the only teenager in Organized Baseball with ulcers, inspiring the catchphrase, "Necciai jitters."

This is one of a series of *Bristol Herald Courier* photos Ron Necciai posed for at Shaw Stadium in Bristol, Virginia, after becoming the first and only pitcher in pro baseball history to strike out 27 in a nine-inning game. "Take a good look at this boy," the caption concluded. "You'll see him in the majors." *National Baseball Hall of Fame Library, Cooperstown, NY.*

Jim Waugh, an 18-year-old pitcher, was Necciai's roommate at Pittsburgh. The day before Ron made his major-league debut against the Chicago Cubs, Waugh beat them, 4-3. "I tried to tell him there was nothing to it," Waugh said. "Outwardly, he seemed kind of loose. Inwardly, it was a tense struggle for him. He didn't get any sleep the night before he pitched. And he had trouble eating. It was a battle of nerves for him."

Necciai joked about it with sportswriters who asked if he was nervous. "Who me?" he replied. "Why here it's 12 o'clock and I'm only on my third pack of cigarettes since nine this morning."[7]

The Cubs wasted no time spoiling Ron's debut, scoring five runs in the first inning that resulted in a *Pittsburgh Post-Gazette* headline reading: CUBS HOLD "NECKTIE" PARTY, 9-5.[8]

Ron lasted six innings, allowing seven earned runs and 11 hits, while walking five and striking out three. "He was shaking so bad out on the mound, he couldn't see my signals," Garagiola said.[9]

Ron told a wire service correspondent that he didn't know which way home plate was in the first inning. Later, he said, "They were determined to leave me in there long enough to either get my brains beat out so bad I'd forget it or get some faith in myself."

The next night, Ron volunteered to pitch in relief against the Cincinnati Reds. His fastball humming, he whiffed five of the 10 batters he faced. "That was the best stuff I ever had in my life," he said. "Better than the 27-strikeout game."[10]

Big innings were his undoing in his next two starts against the Cardinals and the Philadelphia Phillies. "I put three men on base and let someone hit one," he lamented.

Teammates tried keeping Necciai loose by kidding him about the poor lighting in minor-league ballparks. "Geez, Ron, those hitters couldn't see anything," they joshed. "You should've struck out everybody."

Prior to a night game in St. Louis, Pirates outfielder Gus Bell told Necciai that a fan from Bristol was looking for him and was wearing sunglasses.

"Sunglasses?" Ron asked.

"He's not used to bright lights like this in the big city," Bell said. "He's used to the lights down there where you pitched."

Necciai poked fun at the 27-strikeout game himself. "They measure light in candle power. That was the night the candles were out."

Ron often used self-deprecating humor to keep things in perspective.

"What a joke!" he said in describing his first and only win in the majors, a 4-3 decision over the Boston Braves. In eight innings, he allowed two earned runs and seven hits, and struck out one. "I should've lasted one-third of an inning. I didn't have anything. My fastball looked like a big change. Everybody was standing there looking for something to come out of a cannon."

A 1-0 loss to Cincinnati was a moral victory as he limited the Reds to six hits in seven innings and walked only three. "The hitters didn't dig in on him," Pirates catcher Clyde McCullough said. "He threw hard. His ball sailed; it sank. His curveball dropped down like raining water."

Ron lost another close one to Cincy, 4-3. In 7⅓ innings, he limited the Reds to six hits and a walk. The play of the game was a snapshot of the last-place Pirates' 111-loss season. "That was the day Brandy Davis decided to steal home," Ron said.

There were two outs in the ninth inning. The Pirates had the tying and winning runs in scoring position. Davis, a speedster who had swiped 77 bases in 80 attempts the year before in the minors, was on third. He dashed for home and was out by several feet, ending the game. "Brandy ran into the dugout, picked up the phone, and called the press box and said, 'I did that on my own.'"

Ron finished with a 1-6 won–loss record, a 7.04 earned run average, 32 walks, and 31 strikeouts in 55 innings. "We could invent ways to lose," Ron said. "If we got close, we'd figure out something."

The 1952 Pirates supplied Garagiola with all the material needed to become a humorist and Hall of Fame sportscaster. "Nobody could have written that stuff," Ron sighed. "We did everything but win ballgames."[11]

In January 1953, Ron was drafted by the U.S. Army. There was a war going on in Korea, and a lot of ballplayers had to give up baseball for the military. The food Ron ate in the army put him in the hospital for most of the three months he lasted. His ulcers started to bleed. When he returned to Pittsburgh in April 1953, after receiving a medical discharge, he was down to 150 pounds. Doctors told him to take it easy. They didn't want him to touch a baseball until he was bigger and stronger.

While throwing in practice, he felt a pain in his shoulder. "It was a sharp pain. My arm swelled. I had no strength. That was the first sore arm I ever had in my life. Imagine. One sore arm and it lasted forever."

How good was Rocket Ron?

"Best pitching prospect I ever saw," Garagiola said. "I never saw a young pitcher come up with a better arm—a more whippy, fluid, rhythmic arm. He could throw a sidearm curveball, a sidearm fastball, and he had as good an overhand curve as I ever saw. He would've been as big a winner as ever picked up a baseball had he not been hurt."

Rickey was widely criticized for rushing the development of Necciai and other youngsters in the Pirates organization. "I don't think he was rushed at all," Garagiola said. "I would've brought him up because we weren't going anywhere, and he had a major-league arm. Let's find out what he can do."

Ron agreed.

> Mr. Rickey did what he thought was best for everybody at the time. It's just an occupational hazard. Race drivers, they drive into walls. Pitchers, they hurt their arms.
>
> When the season ended, I had long talks with Mr. Rickey. He asked me if I felt I'd been pushed too far, too fast. I never thought so. If I belonged there, I might as well find out now rather than blow around six, eight, 10 years in the minor leagues. I really felt I was going to be all right.

Ron paused as he reflected on his career. "Some people win, some people lose. I happened to be a loser, that's all."

History is much kinder to Rocket Ron, his record in the majors a footnote to the 27-strikeout game that will never be matched. "There's no way I could ever buy what that game did for me. It's a fantastic trivia question. You can get rich in bars."

You can also get drunk in bars. And Steve Dalkowski did that all too often, earning a reputation for drinking almost as legendary as his fastball.

"He was a hard thrower and a hard liver," said Al Ferrara, an ex-Los Angeles Dodger who played against Dalkowski in the minors. "He could drink, and he could fire. They are not out of proportion to each other."

"He always had trouble off the field," Dunlop added. "He drank too much; he chased anything that wiggled. He was a helluva guy, but he just didn't have any self-discipline."

Dalkowski is the stuff of movies, inspiring the character Nuke Laloosh in *Bull Durham*.

Artist Ben Sakoguchi celebrated Dalkowski in a painting by pairing him with the fictional Rickie "Wild Thing" Vaughn played by Charlie Sheen in *Major League*.

In 1958, Dalkowski was taken to the Aberdeen, Maryland, Army Proving Grounds, where a military radar machine reportedly measured his fastball at 98.6 miles per hour—the same speed Bob Feller recorded in his heyday. Follow-up research revealed he was actually clocked at 88.14. But the accuracy of the machine was questionable and the results left for others to interpret and embellish. "If they measured Dalkowski today, I'm sure they'd get him at 120," Ripken remarked two decades later. [12]

Dalkowski was listed at 5-foot-11, but Dunlop insisted he was at least two inches shorter. Teammates at Stockton in 1964 called him "The Shmoo," after the cartoon character with smooth skin and the shape of a plump bowling pin with stubby legs.

Steve didn't get anyone out in his first pro start, walking four batters, while uncorking two wild pitches. He pitched again the next night, striking out one of the two hitters he retired, walking two more, and unleashing a fastball that hit Bob Beavers of the Bluefield Dodgers in the head, just above the right ear. The ball ricocheted off Beavers's helmet back over the pitcher's mound and landed near second base.

"You could hear it hit him—POW!" said Kingsport catcher Bill Massey. "The ball just zoomed away. And he went down like a bale of cotton. I didn't think he was dead because there was movement. But I actually thought he could die."

Beavers survived and continued playing baseball at the semipro level. The pitch sheared off some skin, but contrary to the myth that's still repeated, it didn't tear off his ear lobe. "I was just in the hospital overnight so it's not like I suffered all that bad."

Dalkowski went to the hospital after the game but wasn't allowed to see Beavers. "I understand he had a pretty rough time over it," Beavers said. "I wish I had got in touch with him later. I would've told him that it was just part of the game."

The beaning was cited by some as a major reason Dalkowski never made it to the majors because he was terrified of hitting someone in the head.

Kingsport was a preview of the future. He was pitching a no-hitter in one game, striking out 10 of 12 batters. He wound up losing a three-hitter

Steve Dalkowski blurred the lines between fact and legend, so moviemaker Ron Shelton went with the legend of the bullet-firing pitcher in creating the fictional Nuke LaLoosh for his classic film *Bull Durham.* "Steve was the hardest thrower ever in the history of baseball," declared Billy DeMars, one of his minor-league managers who tried to get him to control his fastball, as well as his drinking. No one succeeded, and Dalkowski never made it to the majors. *National Baseball Hall of Fame Library, Cooperstown, NY.*

and walking 21 in slightly more than seven innings. In his only win at Kingsport, another three-hitter, Dalkowski struck out 24 and walked 18. For the season, he whiffed 121 and walked 129 in 62 innings pitched. As one columnist kindly put it, "Dalkowski has a fastball equal to any in the big leagues but hasn't been properly introduced to the strike zone yet." [13]

There was a brief glimmer of hope the following spring, when Dalkowski struck out three Cincinnati batters on 12 pitches in an exhibition game at Baltimore's Memorial Stadium. It was reported later that Cincinnati manager Birdie Tebbetts threatened his players with a $100 fine if they stood close enough to swing. "I got them this far," he said, "I want to open the season with them." [14]

Steve became known as "Whiff or Walk" Dalkowski. In 1960, at Stockton in the Class C California League, his whiffs and walks were exactly the same—262. For Stockton manager Billy DeMars, that was progress. "I tried to impress upon him that even though he didn't have the greatest record (7-15), at least he brought his base on balls down even with his strikeouts."

During his three years in the majors, DeMars faced Bob Feller, the pitcher who was the benchmark for speed until Nolan Ryan came along. He managed Dalkowski at Aberdeen, South Dakota, in 1958, and Tri-Cities, Washington, in 1961. "Steve was the hardest thrower ever in the history of baseball," DeMars declared. "His fastball was unbelievably fast. He didn't know how to throw slow."

DeMars tried to get Dalkowski to throw his excellent curveball more often, but he wouldn't do it. "In his head, he wanted to throw the fastball—get it over the plate."

Everyone in the Orioles organization was trying to help him do that.

"You know, when you're talking about guys who throw hard, you have to put them in two categories," explained Paul Richards, the Orioles manager at the time. "On the one hand, you have guys who can throw hard and get the ball over the plate. Then you have a guy like Dalkowski who could throw harder than anyone I've ever seen, but you would have to give him the planet as a target, and then maybe he would miss." [15]

Nothing worked until the spring of 1962, when Clyde King, manager of the Orioles' Rochester affiliate, put a batter on both sides of the plate and had Steve throw at half-speed. He threw strikes.

Dalkowski was more likely to hit the backstop than a hitter, according to Al Ferrara. "He was up and down instead of in and out. You didn't have to worry about him hitting you too much."

Dalkowski didn't hit a single batter in 1962, at Elmira, New York, in the Class A Eastern League. He pitched a nine-inning game without walking a batter for the first time, notched a league-leading six shutouts, whiffed almost twice as many as he walked (192-114), and had the best earned run average of his career up to that point—3.04. In one stretch, he pitched 37-straight scoreless innings.

"I got him not to throw every pitch as hard as he could," said Elmira manager Earl Weaver, who would go on to lead the parent Orioles for 17 years, winning four American League pennants and a World Series title. "And he developed a slider that he could throw over the plate."

It looked like Dalkowski was finally going to make it to the big leagues in 1963. He was even pictured on a Topps baseball card along with three other rookie pitchers.

The Orioles' spring training camp in Miami was buzzing about Steve's six innings of hitless, scoreless relief pitching going into a game against the Yankees.

He struck out three of the first five Yankees he faced, including two of their biggest stars, Roger Maris and Elston Howard. The sixth batter, Phil Linz, bunted. As Steve fielded the ball, he felt something pop in his left arm. He stayed in the game and pitched to Bobby Richardson.

"My first pitch just took off high and away," Dalkowski recalled. "It's a good thing Bobby was a right-handed batter, or it would have killed him. Same thing with the second pitch."[16]

Steve was removed from the game with what was diagnosed as a pinched nerve in his left elbow. His flirtation with greatness in the majors was over. In 7⅔ innings, he allowed no runs and 1 hit, while striking out 11 and walking 5. The injury put him back in the minors.

He was playing at Elmira in June 1964, when Harry Dunlop got a call in Stockton from Harry Dalton, the Orioles' farm director.

"Do you want Dalkowski?" Dalton asked. "He got into more trouble. We're going to let him go. Everybody has given up on him."

"Yeah, I'll take him," Dunlop said.

"If he acts up or gives you any problems, you don't have to call the office," Dalton concluded. "Just release him."

* * *

Dunlop got into managing in 1958—six years after Necciai's 27-strikeout game linked them for life in the history books. He was in his fourth year as player-manager of the Stockton Ports, taking over in 1961, the year Dalkowski left town.

The first time Dunlop saw Dalkowski pitch was during batting practice at spring training with the Rochester Red Wings in 1963. He heard the loud popping sounds of a hard-throwing pitcher warming up in the bullpen to pitch batting practice but didn't recognize the short, stubby guy.

Red Wings slugger Luke Easter and the other veterans in the batting cage area cleared out when they saw him walk to the pitcher's mound. "You guys go up and hit now," one of them told a younger player. "We'll wait."

Dunlop was about to find out why Easter, a minor-league legend himself, didn't want anything to do with the pitcher. "The first pitch he throws hits the bar on top of the batting cage and bounces all over the place."

He asked a player standing nearby, "Who the hell is that?"

"That's Steve Dalkowski."

Dunlop had heard about Dalkowski's wildness—knocking out boards in backstops and ripping holes in screens behind home plate, plunking a fan buying a hot dog at a concession stand, and breaking an umpire's mask in three places, leaving him unconscious.

He was aware of the oft-repeated tale about Ted Williams, who supposedly could see the seams of a speeding baseball. Yet, after a Dalkowski bullet whizzed passed him in the batting cage, the "Splendid Splinter" said he didn't see the ball.

"There were some ridiculous stories," Dunlop said. "I'd hear them and say, 'Oh, that can't be true.' I didn't believe any of that stuff. After I saw Dalkowski throw, I thought maybe it was true."

He knew about the telephone calls other managers received in the wee hours of the morning reporting that Dalkowski was sleeping off a hangover on a lawn or in jail. Dunlop explained his decision to take Dalkowski: "As a coach and manager, you think 'Maybe I can help the guy get straightened out.' You feel that you can perhaps get more out of somebody."

One of the first things he did was alert a friend, the Stockton police chief, in case Dalkowski was found wandering the streets at night. "There might've been a couple of times his guys took Steve home. I don't know. He never told me."

Dunlop put it on the line with Steve when he arrived in Stockton: "I'm not going to check you every night to see if you get in. You're old enough and ought to be able to do that. All I want you to do is be ready to work—start every fourth or fifth day."

He ended with a warning: "If you take any of these young players with you after the games and I hear about it, you're gone."

Before he was injured, the Orioles envisioned him as a left-handed Ryne Duren, a premiere reliever in the early 1960s who, like Dalkowski, was a triple threat, with a blazing fastball, a drinking problem, and poor eyesight requiring thick glasses.

Dunlop used him as a relief pitcher the first four games. "He still threw hard, but he wasn't the 100-plus guy at that time. He had this cut fastball that they call a slider nowadays. He could throw that thing over about 70 to 80 percent of the time when he threw it."

Dunlop wanted him to throw the slider more than his fastball. "When I was catching him, if he went a couple of balls in a row, I'd call that thing and he'd throw a strike. He'd get back in the groove. He was wild. He had you moving all over the place. But he wasn't as wild as all the stories that I'd heard about him."

Dalkowski started and won four-straight games, fanning 39 and walking 15.

"He was quiet and shy," Dunlop said. "You wouldn't even know he was a ballplayer if you saw him. He was not very confident."

Dunlop always remembered Bristol manager George Detore telling him he was going to bat fourth in the lineup. Harry balked because he wasn't a power hitter, but Detore insisted he was the only guy on the club that could do the job he wanted.

"I would've jumped off a building for him," Dunlop said. "The best thing you could ever do is pump somebody up like that."

And that's what Dunlop did with Steve. "I pumped him up all the time."

He responded with career bests in wins (eight) and earned run average (2.84). He whiffed twice as many batters as he walked (141-62), won more games than he lost (8-4) for the first time, and completed seven of his 13 starts.

"Having him throw the breaking ball more than his fastball, he came around and had a helluva year," Dunlop said. "He did a good job all the time. He was no problem whatsoever—never got into any trouble."

After Steve racked up 18 strikeouts and walked one in a game he lost, Dunlop got another call from Harry Dalton.

"Hey, you really did a great job," Dalton said. "Pittsburgh is really interested in Steve. We're going to send him to Columbus."

A Pirates farm club in the International League, the Columbus Jets were led by Larry Shepard, a no-nonsense manager Dunlop knew well.

Dunlop called Dalkowski into his office to deliver the news.

> Steve, this might be the last chance you're ever going to have to get to the big leagues. Go up there and do the job. Don't get into any trouble because Larry Shepard is not going to put up with any bullshit. He's a great person. He'll do anything to help you, but if you screw up, you're done. Just do what you've done here, and you'll make it.

The deal that sent Dalkowski to the Pirates was conditional, meaning they could send him back to the Orioles if they didn't like what they saw.

Dalkowski won his first game and belted a grand-slam homer.

"The next game he was his old self," Dunlop said.

He was bombed for seven runs on eight hits and six walks in 4⅓ innings.

"After the game," Dunlop continued, "he got arrested downtown throwing rocks at street lights. I forget exactly what it was. They (the Pirates) called up and said, 'We're going to return him. We don't want to take a chance with him.'"

In 1965, the Angels acquired Dalkowski from the Orioles at the urging of Everett "Rocky" Bridges, a journeyman infielder for seven big-league teams in his second year as manager of their San Jose Bees club in the California League. Dalkowski had struck out 22 and walked only four in two of his starts against the Bees the year before. Rocky wanted to give him another shot.

"Rocky was an outstanding baseball man," said Roland Hemond, farm and scouting director for the Angels. "I didn't want to give up on Dalkowski if Rocky felt he had something left."

Dalkowski lost more games than he won at San Jose (2-3); walked more batters than he whiffed (34-33); and was no longer unhittable, as his record of 35 hits in 38 innings attests. "We gave him one more chance, but we didn't have any success with him either and that's a shame," Hemond said.

For Dalkowski, life after baseball was as hard as getting his fastball over the plate. His golden left arm was picking fruits, vegetables, and cotton in late 1974, when Larry Press, sports editor of the *Bakersfield Californian*, found him.

"Five rough years, beset with personal problems," Press wrote, summing up Dalkowski's time in Bakersfield. "He has worked in the fields around here and now is looking for work. He's not particular, but he'd like 'something better than working in the fields.' Anyone wishing to contact him should call 325-9377."[17]

A few years later, Ray Youngdahl, a former teammate and probation officer in San Mateo, California, had to go through the local sheriff's office to locate Dalkowski. He lived in a seedy hotel in Oildale, an economically depressed, crime-ridden town near Bakersfield.

"He's not going to make it," Youngdahl was advised. "All he does is drink. He's probably going to die or get himself shot and killed."

In 1961, at Tri-Cities, Billy DeMars had handpicked Ray to room with Steve and try to keep him out of trouble. "That was like trying to put a bull some place where you couldn't keep him in," Ray said.

Ray went to Bakersfield to get Steve and take him back to his home in San Mateo, a round trip of 540 miles. "He was my roommate, my buddy. I can't let him die," Ray insisted.

Steve entered an alcohol recovery program and stayed for more than a year. "We got him sober to some extent," Ray said. "He seemed to be all right."

Steve wanted to see his wife in Oildale. "We put him on a bus heading to Bakersfield," Ray explained. "First stop was San Jose. He's off. We lost him again for years."

Steve was homeless and living on the streets of Los Angeles on Christmas Eve 1992, when he entered a laundromat and asked a woman for money. She got enough information to reconnect him with his second wife, Virginia, who had moved from Bakersfield to her native Oklahoma.

A year later, Virginia suffered a stroke and died. Steve's sister, Patti Cain, decided it was time for her brother to return home to New Britain, Connecticut. "She got him home and saved his life," Youngdahl said.

In 1994, Patti put Steve in a nursing home down the road from the high school baseball field where he set a state record of 24 strikeouts in a game. He had scouts for all 16 major-league teams dreaming, unaware that his alcoholism would eventually drown his talent and make his life a nightmare.

Dalkowski was 25 years old his last go-around with Earl Weaver. "You won't live to be 33," Weaver chided him.[18]

Alcohol-induced dementia robbed Steve of many memories, but he was 79 in 2018, and still counting. He already had outlived Bo Belinsky, Steve Barber, Dave McNally, and Dean Chance, teammates who achieved the big-league stardom that eluded him.

Youngdahl visited New Britain in 2003, and got Patti's permission to take Steve to see the hometown Rock Cats play at New Britain Stadium.

"Let me have just one beer," Steve whispered to Ray as they entered the ballpark. "Just one beer."

"Are you crazy?" Ray said. "I'm not getting you close to the beer."

Steve's comeback from alcoholism has made him an even bigger legend in New Britain. "When we walked in, everybody knew who he was," Ray said.

"Steve Dalkowski was the pitching legend of all minor-league players," Dunlop said. "Everybody heard about him."

One Christmas in the early 1970s, Dunlop got a call from Steve. He could tell he was drinking because of his slurred speech.

> Harry, I just wanted to call you up and wish you and your family the greatest Christmas. You're the only person that ever treated me like a man. Everybody else treated me like I was a little kid. They were always telling me what I had to do, what I didn't have to do. You just told me what you wanted me to do and that was it. And you let me do it.

Dunlop felt good but also sad. "He was just special with his stuff. You looked at him and said, 'God, how come this guy can't make it. And then you realized why—he couldn't control himself."

But out of the ashes of his career, Dalkowski has risen to enjoy some of the glory he missed.

In 2009, he was inducted into the Shrine of the Eternals, established by the California-based Baseball Requilary to celebrate the game's pioneers, free spirits, and legends who would need a ticket to get into the National Baseball Hall of Fame at Cooperstown, New York.

Shoeless Joe Jackson and Pete Rose are in the Shrine despite the alleged gambling scandals that kept them out of Cooperstown. So is Curt Flood, who paved the way for free agency by challenging baseball's reserve clause, which had given teams almost total control of their players. Rebels Bill "Spaceman" Lee, Dock Ellis, and Jim Bouton are honored, along with such icons as Yogi Berra, Jackie Robinson, and Satchel Paige—players that left a lasting imprint on the diamond.

Two nights before his induction into the Shrine, Dalkowski threw out the ceremonial first pitch prior to a Dodgers game at Dodger Stadium. It was his first time on the mound at a major-league ballpark since 1958, at Baltimore's Memorial Stadium, when he fanned three-straight Reds batters in an exhibition game.

Steve could hear the crowd cheer as he threw the ball toward home plate. For a brief moment, he was in the big leagues.

* * *

Ron Necciai was a first baseman when he started his pro career, but by his own admission, he couldn't hit a curveball with four ironing boards. He didn't throw very hard either.

"But there was a story behind that," said George Detore, his manager at Salisbury, North Carolina, in 1950–1951, and at Bristol in 1952. "He could throw real hard, but he broke a kid's ribs pitching in high school and they never let him throw hard again."

Necciai didn't stay long in Salisbury or Shelby, North Carolina, where he appeared in one game. "It was a disaster," Ron said. "I think I walked the world."

For the record, he walked 11 batters in just three innings.

He left Shelby before the 1950 season was over and went to work at a steel mill in his hometown of Manown, Pennsylvania.

Detore got a call from the Pirates' front office wanting to know if they should release Ron. "Hell, no," he said, "bring him back to spring training next year."

Ron returned to Salisbury in 1951.

"He was just a mediocre thrower, but he had a good, long build and long arms," Detore said. "Being a scout at heart, I thought, 'Geez, someday this kid might be able to throw hard.'"

Detore spent most of his playing career in the high minors with the San Diego Padres of the Pacific Coast League. He was the Padres catcher in 1937, outhitting an 18-year-old teammate named Ted Williams by 43 points—.334 to .291.

At Salisbury in the Class D North Carolina State League, Detore's job was to spot raw talent and develop it for the Pirates. He set out to transform Ron from a thrower into a pitcher.

"There's a big difference between a thrower and pitcher," Ron explained.

> The thrower is a young kid who still has fire or, as Mr. Rickey used to call it, "The fear of God." Pitchers are the guys who have lost the fear of God, but they now have ability. They know whether the ball is going up or down, in or out. They give you three different curveballs, eight different changes of speed.

Detore literally started at ground level with Ron. He took him behind the Salisbury ballpark, gave him a rock, and told him to hit a pole. "You'd pick a rock up and unconsciously your arm goes to the natural place," Ron said. "You do it naturally. That's the proper way to throw a ball."

Detore taught Ron the fundamentals—how to stand on the mound, grip the ball, stride, and cover first base.

"To be a good pitcher, you have to be a human machine," Ron said. "You do everything with exact repetition. You hold the ball the same, stride the same, make your motion the same. Everything has to be the same. Like picking up a fork. You can do it without thinking. To be a good pitcher, you have to perfect repetition."

Ron had the speed, but he lacked a good curveball. "We couldn't figure out why I couldn't learn how to throw a curveball," he said.

At the end of one practice session, Ron called out to Detore, "Hey, Skip, how would this do?"

Detore watched Ron throw a reverse curve that exploded. "For cripes sake, that's it!" he hollered.

It was a defining moment for Detore. "From then on, I knew we really had something. He was beautifully built. He had an effortless delivery and threw straight overhand. Poetry in motion."

"I have long joints in my arm," Ron said. "I was never able to throw a curveball like everybody else. I threw what we called when I was a kid, a drop."

Detore could envision great things for Ron even though he lost his first seven games and was winless when Branch Rickey Jr. visited Salisbury on a tour of the Pirates' farm system, which he headed.

"Geez, I haven't seen much of anything," Rickey Jr. bemoaned.

"I've got a kid that you might like a little bit," Detore replied.

Detore made Rickey Jr. wait until late in the game. "I put him in with the bases loaded and nobody out, and he struck out the side. He struck out five of the six hitters he faced in the last two innings."

Rickey Jr. charged into the Salisbury dugout before the game was over to lecture Necciai. "What are you doing here?" he began. [19]

"I got a real good behind-chewing about why I was playing with such kids," Ron said.

> None of us had visions of going to the big leagues. They were so remote from where we were. I didn't know what I was doing or where I was going. When he said, "I'll put you in a league where you could make some money, go someplace, and be something," I thought, "Geez, there must be another place."

Do what Detore was telling him, win four games, and he'll go to another place, Rickey Jr. concluded.

Ron fanned 17 batters in a game and won four of his next six decisions to improve his record to 4-9 and earn a promotion to New Orleans in the Class AA Southern Association. "Won and lost records don't mean much," Rickey Jr. explained. "It's the ability in the box that counts."

At New Orleans, Ron lost five of six games and walked 42 batters in 33 innings, but Rickey Jr. maintained "anybody could tell by simply looking at him that he was a comer."[20]

In the fall of 1951, Necciai went to Deland, Florida, for what the Pirates billed as the "first postseason baseball school in history for rookies."[21]

"This was Mr. Rickey's idea," Ron said. "Give people intensive training in their weakness."

Ron focused on improving his control.

When Branch Rickey Sr. took over the Pirates in late 1950, he launched a five-year plan that defied baseball tradition and conventional logic. "Instead of bringing raw talent along slowly in the minor leagues, he embarked on a hothouse effort to raise it right at home," Marshall Smith wrote in *Life* magazine. [22]

Some folks called it "Operation Peach Fuzz." Ron was one of 12 rookies, average age 19, at Deland from towns within a 30-mile radius of the Pirates' ballpark, Forbes Field.

Fresh out of high school, the 18-year-old Harry Dunlop was at Deland to learn how to catch pop flies and gain experience catching professional pitchers.

The first time Harry caught Ron in a practice game, a fastball shot past him, permitting a runner to score from third.

The morning after every game, Rickey met with the players to critique their performance.

"He called everybody, Mister, instead of your first name," Harry said.

Rickey asked him to stand up. "When Mr. Necciai was pitching, and you had men on second and third, the ball got by you and went to the backstop and a run scored. What happened?"

"I guess I just couldn't catch the ball, Mr. Rickey."

"I know darn well that you did not just miss it," Rickey said tersely.

"Mr. Necciai, stand up. What happened?"

"Mr. Rickey, I screwed up. He called for a breaking ball and I threw a fastball."

"Thank you, Mr. Necciai. That's more like it."

Rickey used the incident to make a point with the players. "Mr. Dunlop, I appreciate you wanting to protect your pitcher, but always tell the truth. If you lie, you're never going to survive in life."

That was the beginning of a lifelong friendship between Harry and Ron. They survived the rookie camp and were invited to join the big-league club at spring training in San Bernardino, California.

Ron was both impressive and intimidating in an exhibition game against the New York Giants, blanking the defending National League champs for five innings on two hits and a walk. At one point, Ron decked the Giants' Sal Yvars with a pitch that was high and tight. Yvars got up and headed for Ron with brawny Pirates catcher Clyde McCullough in hot pursuit. "He was pretty close when McCullough grabbed him by the top of his head and pulled him over backward," Ron said.

"Let that boy alone!" McCullough warned Yvars.

The Pirates played the Cubs in New Orleans on their way back to Pittsburgh for the season opener. In a disastrous ninth inning, Ron was tagged for four runs on four hits and a walk. "I was nervous and had been losing weight," he revealed. "I was spitting blood."

He had stomach ulcers, so the Pirates' team doctor put him on a diet of cottage cheese, Melba toast, skim milk, and baby food, and sent him home for three weeks to recover. "If I had my pockets full of lead, I weighed 165—maybe," Ron lamented.

Rickey asked Ron where he wanted to go to get in shape and play again. "I told Mr. Rickey I wanted to go where Detore was."

That happened to be Bristol. "I had no idea where Bristol was or even if there was a ballclub there," Ron said.

Rickey sent him to Bristol. "I knew I wasn't going to be there very long. Once I got myself back in shape, they were going to move me to Charleston or Burlington."

With Detore and Dunlop, the team's catcher, Ron was in the right place at the right time.

"George was like a father to all of us," Dunlop said. "He'd get on your butt if you made mistakes, but he was right there to pat you on the back when you needed it."

Ron was a fierce competitor and cocky. So, the 45-year-old Detore challenged Ron during batting practice to throw the ball past him. He struggled to do it. "Just remember," Detore said, "there's always going to be somebody that's going to be better than you."

Detore instructed Harry, "His ball moves so much, let it go where it wants. Just catch the ball."

That's what he tried to do. "I probably blocked more curveballs when I was catching him than anybody I ever caught in pro ball," Harry said.

In Ron's Bristol debut, he fired a two-hit shutout and struck out 20. He whiffed 19 in his next start. Three days later, he pitched 4 innings of relief, fanning 11 consecutive batters to break a minor-league record that had been around for 42 years.

Ron was easygoing except on the days he pitched. "I was always excited. Time never went fast enough for me. You wake up in the morning and say, 'What time is it?' You can't wait for time to pass to get at it."

That was the case the evening of May 13, 1952, when he struck out 27 in a game against the first-place Welch Miners at Bristol's Shaw Stadium.

A memorandum written by Detore in 1969 tells the behind-the-scenes story.

"His ulcers were really kicking up badly, so I told him to go to the clubhouse and lie down and I would start someone else," Detore recalled.

Ron took two pills prescribed to pacify his stomach and rested.

"About 15 minutes before game time," Detore continued, "he came back to the field and said he would like to try it and see how things went. I let him warm up and had someone else hot just in case he couldn't pitch."[23]

He whiffed the first four Welch batters, but he didn't strike out everyone. There was a ground out in the second, an error in the third, a hit batsman in the fourth, and a walk in the seventh.

Going into the seventh inning, one of the Bristol players asked Detore, "Skip, you know what the hell he has done?"

"I got a pretty good idea," Detore said.

"He's got 17 strikeouts."

"That's par for the course."

"Ron wasn't one of those guys that got them out 1-2-3," Harry said. "He threw an awfully lot of pitches. There were a lot of deep counts—2-and-2, 3-and-2. His curveball was probably as good as it ever was. He just completely baffled them."

In the dugout between innings, Ron snacked. "Cottage cheese, skim milk, Melba toast. Keep something in my stomach."

Twice during the game, Detore sent pitcher Bill Bell to the mound with alkaline tablets and a glass of water.

"On a couple of occasions," Detore wrote in his memo, "I wanted to let someone else take over, but he said he would finish if it killed him."[24]

From the second inning onward, Detore had pitcher Frank Ramsay on standby in the bullpen. The first time Ramsay was told to warm up, he said, "They aren't 'smelling' him, what's the problem?"

"He's sick," Detore said.[25]

The last two innings Welch players tried to bunt the ball. They still missed.

Ron had a 7-0 lead and 20 strikeouts to start the eighth inning.

He was aware of his no-hitter because of how his teammates were acting in the dugout, but he didn't know his strikeout total even though the crowd of 1,183 was chanting the numbers as they piled up. "They always did that when I pitched," Ron said.

Harry heard the yells, too, but he was too busy trying to corral Ron's curve to pay much attention.

The first Welch batter in the ninth, pinch-hitter Frank Whitehead, hit a pop fly in foul territory near Harry at home plate. The ball fell to the ground untouched. On the next pitch, Whitehead was called out on strikes.

"Twenty-four," the fans hollered.

The play went unnoticed at the time. But in a 2008 book based on interviews with players from both teams, Whitehead and Bristol first baseman Phil Fillatrault were quoted as saying Harry intentionally let the ball drop. In fact, Fillatrault claimed he and some fans were hollering, "Drop it! Drop it!"

There's no mention of this in news accounts of the game because Dunlop said it never happened. "No way in the world did I intentionally drop that ball. I was 18 years old and trying to prove I was a ballplayer. Besides, I'm not that smart. And to set the record straight, no way was our first baseman or the fans yelling for me to drop it. I just flat missed it."

With two outs in the ninth, Welch's Bobby Hammond swung and missed at a two-strike curveball in the dirt that got past Harry, enabling Hammond to reach first base.

Harry "missed the ball that would have ended the game on purpose to get to the next man," Hammond said later.[26]

"The ball clipped the corner of the plate and bounced up over my head," Harry insisted. "I never touched the ball at all."

Ron had 26 strikeouts and a shot at 27 with Welch's Bob Kendrick stepping to the plate. He had already whiffed three times. "The ball was on you before you could get the bat off your shoulder," Kendrick said. "You just couldn't see the ball."[27]

Kendrick swung anyway and missed.

"Twenty-seven!" the fans shouted.

Ron didn't know it, but he'd just broken the all-time record of 25, set in 1941, by a pitcher who was briefly a teammate with the Pirates at spring training two months earlier—Clarence "Hooks" Iott. Not even the sportswriter covering the game for the *Bristol Herald Courier* knew for sure what Ron had done, reporting it was "possibly an all-time mark for Organized Baseball."[28]

"We didn't really realize what he had accomplished," Harry said. "Of course, the next day when everybody started calling, it kind of sunk in a little bit: 'My God you mean nobody has never done this before?' Then it became really something."

"That's when all the hullaballoo started," Ron added.

The team's office was flooded with telephone calls requesting interviews with Ron from newspapers, radio, and television stations throughout the country.

The baseball writer for the Associated Press wire service wrote that Ron "may be the Bobby Feller of the future."[29]

Ron pitched two more times for Bristol.

The first was a relief appearance. He whiffed eight of nine batters, including five in the same inning, as two of them reached base after strike-out pitches eluded Harry.

An overflow crowd of 5,800, the largest to see an Appalachian League game, showed up at Shaw Stadium for "Ron Necciai Night," to count the strikeouts their new hero piled up in his last game. Rickey Jr. was there to see for himself.

After touting Ron to his father, Rickey Jr. had watched in horror at the Deland camp seven months earlier as he walked the first two batters in a game, hit the third one in the head, and then fired a pitch two feet behind the next batter's head. Rickey Jr. was probably as nervous as his protégé, who was now a national celebrity.

"He's a miracle," Rickey Jr. said after Ron fired a two-hitter and struck out 24.[30]

Next stop for Ron was Burlington, North Carolina, in the Class B Carolina League. First, he went to Pittsburgh to get his ulcers checked out.

Joe Garagiola lauded Ron after catching him during a workout at Forbes Field but said he had one serious fault: "He wants to strike out everybody."[31]

Meanwhile, back in Bristol, Harry caught back-to-back no-hitters by Bill "The Bomber" Bell, an 18-year-old right-hander who tossed a third later in the season. "I caught three no-hitters in 14 days, and I thought, 'Boy, this is going to be good,'" Harry said. "Things went downhill after that."

Harry also was promoted to Burlington and caught Ron the two months he was there in 1952.

Necciai had a reputation to live up to as Rocket Ron, the new strikeout king of baseball. "At home, everybody came to see me win and strike out everybody. On the road, everybody came to see me get my brains knocked out. The sportswriters are there all the time, wanting to know

Ron Necciai, left, and his catcher, Harry Dunlop, were linked for life by the 27-strikeout no-hitter that made Necciai a national celebrity. They moved up to Burlington together, but Harry didn't make it to the majors until 1969, when he joined the Kansas City Royals as a coach. *Courtesy of Ron Necciai.*

about this and that. A lot of questions. It keeps the heat on you. You can't let up."

Rocket Ron picked up where he left off in Bristol, striking out 7 in 3 innings of relief and 14 in his first start.

"Necciai was under the most pressure ever put on a Carolina League pitcher," one writer observed, and proved he's "without a doubt a great performer."[32]

Pitching for a last-place team that was as terrible as the parent Pirates, Ron struck out 172 batters in 126 innings, while posting a 7-9 won–loss record and league-best 1.57 earned run average.

Ron was headed for Pittsburgh. Upon arriving at Forbes Field, Joe Garagiola ribbed Necciai, "Hey, you've been here an hour and haven't struck out anybody."[33]

Garagiola was traded to the Cubs in June 1953, and finished the 1954 season with the Giants. He lost track of Necciai.

Shortly before Ron went into the army, Rickey Sr. told him, "Don't get shot. You're going to come back and win a lot-t-t of games."

After his disastrous stint in the army, Ron was sent to Burlington to recuperate. In his first start, Ron tossed a 5-hitter and struck out 13 in a 7-inning game. He appeared in 6 games, pitching 17 innings and giving up 11 runs, 12 hits, and 18 walks. "He couldn't throw the ball," Jim Waugh said. "He lost his speed."

Ron sat out the last two months of the season with a throwing arm so sore he couldn't comb his hair with it.

He went to spring training with the Pirates in 1954, but the pain in his arm only got worse. He decided to retire. "RON (NO-HIT) NECCIAI QUITS BUCS, BASEBALL," announced a banner headline in the *Pittsburgh Post-Gazette*. "The rocket of Ron Necciai has descended," the story began.[34]

"I couldn't get anybody out," he said. "So I came home and worked in the hardware store."

Ron was sitting on the bannister of the porch in front of his mother's house in Manown when a big Chrysler whizzed past, skidded to a halt, turned around, and drove back to where he was. Stepping out of the car was Garagiola and catcher Ray Kaat, Giants teammates on their way home to St. Louis after the 1954 World Series. They had dinner with Ron and then left.

"It was kind of ironic," Garagiola said. "Here's a guy who could've been one of the biggest stars and here he was sitting on this little porch. How many cars went by not recognizing him? I was one of the lucky ones that recognized him because I saw him pitch."

Rickey Sr. didn't want to give up on Ron. "There have only been two young pitchers I was certain were destined for greatness, simply because they had the meanest fastball a batter can face," he said in 1952. "One of those boys was Dizzy Dean. The other is Ron Necciai. And Necciai is harder to hit."[35]

He persuaded Ron to try again in 1955, and he did, appearing in a combined five games at Hollywood in the PCL and Waco in the Big State League. He couldn't throw the ball hard, so he threw in the towel and went home.

As a last resort, Rickey Sr. arranged for Ron to see the orthopedic surgeon who had operated on Dean and pitcher Van Lingle Mungo for the same problem—a tear in the posterior glenoid, or rotator cuff. "It didn't work for them and it won't work for you," the surgeon said bluntly. "Go home and get yourself a job in a gas station because you're never going to pitch again."

Ron became a highly successful manufacturers' rep for hunting, fishing, and shooting equipment, eventually teaming with a partner to establish their own company, Hays, Necciai & Associates. His ulcers stopped nagging him.

Dunlop never played in the big leagues, but he coached 21 seasons for the Kansas City Royals, Chicago Cubs, Cincinnati Reds, San Diego Padres, and Florida Marlins. He worked closely with future Hall of Fame pitchers Bruce Sutter in Chicago and Tom Seaver in Cincinnati. "Ron threw as hard as anybody I've ever been around—Seaver and guys like that. His curveball was like an old-fashioned drop. It rolled off the table, almost like Sutter's split finger. He had great stuff."

Ron's 27-strikeout feat is ranked tops among the 50 most famous records in minor-league history by the National Association of Professional Baseball Leagues. "It's something that is never going to happen again," Harry said.

The game bonded Ron and Harry for life. They returned to Bristol in 1999, for the unveiling of a plaque commemorating Ron's amazing performance. The plaque is encased in a brick monument outside DeVault Stadium, less than a mile from the site of the old ballpark, Shaw Stadium.

Ron: When I'm asked which pitcher had the best stuff? The answer is easy. No doubt - you did! You made me a smart catcher when you pitched.

Joe Garagiola

"Who hung the uniform on the mound?" Pittsburgh catcher Joe Garagiola quipped after Ron Necciai joined the Pirates late in the 1952 season. Garagiola wasn't joking when he signed this photo, writing that Ron "had the best stuff" of any pitcher he caught. *Courtesy of Ron Necciai.*

Ron let others make a big deal of the game. He downplayed it.

"It was done on the lowest level," he pointed out. "It wasn't done in the big leagues."

"I had one hot night," he told others. "One hot night doesn't make a lifetime."

While signing autographs at Bristol almost a half-century later, Harry turned to Ron and asked, "How many people did we have at that game?"

Ron chuckled at the memory of all the folks who claimed their parents or cousins were there and told them about it. "There were 1,800 people at the game," he said. "But I've talked to 30,000 that were there."

A hot night might not make a lifetime, but it can last one.

NOTES

FOREWORD

1. *Los Angeles Times*, April 7, 1965, Part 3, 9 (main edition).

PREFACE

1. J. G. Taylor Spink, comp., *Official Baseball Guide—1955* (St. Louis, MO: Sporting News, 1955), 108.
2. *San Gabriel Valley (CA) Tribune*, April 26, 1997, C4.
3. *San Gabriel Valley Tribune*, April 26, 1997, C4.

INTRODUCTION

1. *Baseball Digest*, September 1963, 55.
2. *Baseball Digest*, September 1963, 56.
3. *Life*, April 5, 1948, 117.
4. *Gallup (NM) Independent*, August 18, 1959, 4.
5. *Los Angeles Mirror-News*, August 1, 1956, Part III, 2.
6. *Baseball Digest*, September 1963, 56.
7. *Bristol (VA) Herald Courier*, May 24, 1952, 6.

1. BUSHES AND BUSHERS

1. *Sporting News*, October 28, 1953, 10.

2. *Sporting News*, January 29, 1898, 4.

3. Ring Lardner, *You Know Me Al* (Richmond, VA: Westvaco Corporation, 1994), 33–34.

4. *Sporting News*, January 3, 1962, 17.

5. *Los Angeles Times*, November 7, 1912, Section III, 1.

6. "Babe Ruth Quotes," *BaseballLibrary.com*, http://www.baseballlibrary. com/baseballlibrary/ballplayers/R/Ruth_Babe.stm, accessed October 24, 2018.

7. *Los Angeles Times*, January 11, 1931, F4.

8. Notes on Smead Jolley from document dated June 17, 1955, National Baseball Hall of Fame, Cooperstown, NY, 4.

9. *Ogden (UT) Standard- Examiner*, May 1, 1956, 10.

10. Notes on Smead Jolley from document dated June 17, 1955, National Baseball Hall of Fame, Cooperstown, NY, 4.

11. *Sporting News*, January 25, 1964, 7–8.

12. *Sporting News*, March 1, 1945, 7, 10.

13. *Portsmouth (OH) Times*, May 26, 1942, 10.

14. *Hagerstown (MD) Daily Mail*, December 24, 1941, 9.

15. *Sporting News*, March 1, 1945, 7.

16. *San Gabriel Valley Tribune*, April 26, 1997, C4.

17. *San Gabriel Valley Tribune*, April 26, 1997, C4.

18. *Sports Illustrated*, March 20, 1978, 1.

19. *Lakeland (FL) Ledger*, July 6, 1978, 29.

20. *Kansas City Star*, January 22, 1973, 7.

21. *Waco (TX) News-Tribune*, June 17, 1955, 13.

22. *Pittsburgh Post-Gazette*, March 26, 1951, 19.

23. *Terre Haute (IN) Star*, April 16, 1951, 8.

2. FOLLOWING A DREAM

1. *Lubbock (TX) Morning Avalanche*, April 20, 1950, 4.

2. *Lamesa (TX) Daily Reporter*, March 23, 1950, 2.

3. *Brownsville (TX) Herald*, April 30, 1947, 7.

4. *Corsicana (TX) Daily Sun*, May 20, 1950, 8.

5. *Odessa (TX) American*, August 7, 1956, 11.

6. *Lamesa Press-Reporter*, March 19, 1978, 11.

7. *Lamesa Press-Reporter*, February 12, 1978, 9.

8. *Lamesa Press-Reporter*, August 20, 1978, 9.

9. *Lamesa Press-Reporter*, February 26, 1978, 11.

10. *Lamesa Press-Reporter*, May 21, 1978, 6.

11. *Hickory (NC) Daily Record*, February 8, 1950, 6.

12. *Fresno (CA) Bee*, March 12, 1948, 23.

13. *Hickory Daily Record*, February 8, 1950, 6.

14. *Pampa (TX) Daily News*, December 12, 1949, 4.

15. *Lamesa Press-Reporter*, May 21, 1978, 6.

16. *Lamesa Daily Reporter*, December 15, 1949, 2.

17. *Hickory Daily Record*, February 8, 1950, 6.

18. *Hickory Daily Record*, March 14, 1952, 6.

19. *High Point (NC) Enterprise*, March 13, 1952, D1.

20. *High Point Enterprise*, January 22, 1952, 13.

21. *Brooklyn (NY) Daily Eagle*, June 26, 1952, 19.

22. *Hickory Daily Record*, August 25, 1978, 5B.

23. *Lamesa Daily Reporter*, April 13, 1950, 2.

24. *Lamesa Daily Reporter*, April 14, 1950, 3.

25. *Lamesa Press-Reporter*, March 26, 1978, 9.

26. *Lubbock Evening Journal*, February 23, 1951, 9.

27. *Lubbock Avalanche Journal*, February 25, 1951, Section II, 1.

28. *Lamesa Press-Reporter*, November 12, 1978, 13.

29. *Amarillo (TX) Daily News*, February 23, 1951, 22.

30. *Lubbock Evening Journal*, February 23, 1951, 9.

31. *Lamesa Daily Reporter*, March 5, 1951, 3.

32. *Lamesa Daily Reporter*, February 25, 1951, 4.

33. *Lamesa Daily Reporter*, March 1, 1951, 4.

34. *Lamesa Daily Reporter*, March 29, 1951, 4.

35. *Sporting News*, March 28, 1951, 25.

36. *Sporting News*, April 28, 1951, 29.

37. *Abilene (TX) Reporter-News*, May 1, 1951, 9A.

38. *Abilene Reporter-News*, April 27, 1951, 6A.

39. *Abilene Reporter-News*, May 3, 1951, 12A.

40. *Amarillo Daily News*, June 5, 1951, 11.

41. *Abilene Reporter-News*, May 26, 1951, 7A.

42. *Abilene Reporter-News*, June 2, 1951, 7A.

43. *Sporting News*, December 5, 1951, 17.

44. *Lubbock Evening Journal*, July 1, 1952, Section I, 11.

45. *Big Spring (TX) Daily Herald*, March 8, 1953, 8.

46. *Lamesa Daily Reporter*, September 3, 1953, 1.

47. *Lubbock Morning Avalanche*, April 22, 1953, Section II, 6.

48. *Lubbock Morning Avalanche*, May 30, 1953, 4.

49. *Odessa American*, May 12, 1953, 5.
50. *Lamesa Daily Reporter*, May 29, 1953, 1.
51. *Lubbock Avalanche Journal*, May 31, 1953, Section II, 1.
52. *Odessa American*, June 3, 1953, 7.
53. *Odessa American*, June 7, 1953, 11.
54. *Lubbock Morning Avalanche*, July 31, 1957, Section II, 2.

3. ROUND TRIP TO NOWHERE

1. *Amarillo Daily News*, June 1, 1948, 6.
2. *Sporting News*, August 4, 1948, 34.
3. *Amarillo Daily News*, August 18, 1948, 12.
4. *Amarillo Daily News*, August 16, 1948, 2.
5. *Amarillo Globe-Times*, September 6, 1948, 12.
6. *Amarillo Daily News*, September 8, 1948, 13.
7. *Abilene Reporter-News*, July 1, 1948, 10.
8. *Amarillo Daily News*, September 8, 1948, 13.
9. Bob Rives, "Bob Crues," *Society for American Baseball Research*, http://www.sabr.org/bioproj/person/a8b82ed5, accessed October 24, 2018.
10. *Sporting News*, December 22, 1948, 23.
11. *Odessa American*, July 13, 1948, 4.
12. *Odessa American*, July 13, 1948, 4.
13. *Amarillo Daily News*, September 29, 1948, 7.
14. *Amarillo Daily News*, March 26, 1946, 4.
15. *Amarillo Globe-Times*, September 15, 1958, 11.
16. *Amarillo Globe-Times*, June 30, 1947, 6.
17. *Amarillo Daily News*, July 22, 1947, 5.
18. *Amarillo Daily News*, July 23, 1947, 6.
19. *Amarillo Daily News*, September 3, 1948, 10.
20. *Amarillo Daily News*, April 2, 1948, 8.
21. *Amarillo Daily News*, October 14, 1948, 14.
22. *Lubbock Avalanche-Journal*, March 27, 1949, Section II, 1.
23. *Amarillo Sunday News-Globe*, October 3, 1948, 18.
24. *Jackson (MS) Clarion-Ledger*, November 28, 1948, 14.
25. *Amarillo Daily News*, March 22, 1951, 11.
26. *Amarillo Daily News*, August 16, 1951, 11.
27. *Amarillo Daily News*, August 9, 1951, 8.
28. *Lubbock Morning Avalanche*, June 24, 1953, Section II, 3.
29. *Amarillo Globe-Times*, August 28, 1974, 29.
30. *Amarillo Globe-Times*, January 15, 1975, 29.

4. THE MAN WHO WORE
THE TEXACO STAR

1. *New York Times*, September 22, 2005, C19.
2. *Roswell (NM) Daily Record*, September 3, 1954, 10.
3. *Albuquerque (NM) Journal*, August 13, 1961, D3.
4. *Los Angeles Times*, August 31, 1982, Part III, 3.
5. *Amarillo Daily News*, March 18, 1949, 23.
6. *Amarillo Daily News*, March 14, 1950, 12.
7. *Amarillo Sunday News-Globe*, April 19, 1952, 17.
8. *Amarillo Sunday News-Globe*, April 19, 1952, 17.
9. *Albuquerque Journal*, April 18, 2004, D3.
10. *Artesia (NM) Advocate*, May 9, 1952, 4.
11. *Albuquerque Journal*, October 14, 1953, 18.
12. *Artesia Advocate*, August 21, 1953, 4.
13. *Artesia Advocate*, October 30, 1953, 1.
14. *Roswell Daily Record*, November 5, 1953, 8.
15. *Miami (FL) News*, April 10, 1959, 3C.
16. *Clovis (NM) News-Journal*, July 19, 1954, 5.
17. *Clovis News-Journal*, July 19, 1954, 5.
18. *Roswell Daily Record*, August 13, 1954, 10.
19. *Lubbock Evening Journal*, August 13, 1954, 8–9.
20. *Gallup Independent*, August 23, 1954, 3.
21. *Roswell Daily Record*, September 1, 1954, 10.
22. *Big Spring Herald*, September 3, 1954, 11.
23. *Artesia Advocate*, September 1, 1954, 3.
24. *Milwaukee (WI) Journal*, September 19, 1954, Sports, 1.
25. *Corsicana (TX) Daily Sun*, September 8, 1954, 7.
26. *Sports Illustrated*, September 20, 1954, 32.
27. *Carlsbad (NM) Current-Argus*, September 6, 1954, 8.
28. *Sports Illustrated*, August 31, 1998, 176.
29. Harry Turtledove, "The Star and the Rockets," *Tor.com*, http://www.tor.com/2009/11/17/the-star-and-the-rockets/, accessed October 31, 2018.
30. "The Unnatural," *X-Files*, episode no. 19, written by Chris Carter and David Duchovny, directed by Duchovny, April 25, 1999.
31. *Philadelphia Daily News*, July 3, 1996, S12.
32. *Albuquerque Journal*, September 23, 1998, B1.
33. *Daily Oklahoman* (Oklahoma City), August 30, 1998, 38.
34. Bob Rives interview with Joe Bauman, 1994.
35. *Albuquerque Journal*, September 23, 1998, B1.
36. *Santa Cruz (CA) Sentinel*, October 11, 2001, D3.

37. *Roswell Daily Record*, August 11, 2005, B1.

5. FATHER, SON, AND LITTLE LEAGUE

1. *New York Times*, August 25, 1956, 8.

2. *Carlsbad Current-Argus*, July 29, 1956, 10.

3. *St. Louis Post-Dispatch*, March 27, 1948, 6.

4. Notes from Jim McConnell interview with Tom Jordan, October 22, 1992.

5. *St. Louis Post-Dispatch*, March 27, 1948, 6.

6. Notes from Jim McConnell interview with Roy Partee, November 12, 1992.

7. *St. Louis Star and Times*, May 6, 1948, 38.

8. *El Paso (TX) Herald-Post*, July 20, 1953, 19.

9. *Roswell Daily Record*, June 14, 1956, 16.

10. *Roswell Daily Record*, June 17, 1956, 16.

11. *El Paso Herald-Post*, July 20, 1953, 19.

12. *Amarillo Globe-Times*, July 20, 1953, 13.

13. *Amarillo Daily News*, September 4, 1953, 13.

14. *Amarillo Daily News*, July 27, 1953, 4.

15. *Amarillo Daily News*, May 18, 1955, 13.

16. *Sports Illustrated*, October 1, 1956, 4.

17. *Williamsport (PA) Sun-Gazette*, August 25, 1956, 9.

18. *Sporting News*, September 5, 1956, 17.

19. *Williamsport Sun-Gazette*, August 25, 1956, 1.

20. *Roswell Daily Record*, August 27, 1956, 12.

6. THE MELLOW IRISHMAN'S
MERRY BAND OF CUBANS

1. *Odessa American*, December 9, 1998, 7D.

2. *Washington Post*, March 16, 1948, 13.

3. *Washington Post*, March 16, 1948, 13.

4. *San Angelo (TX) Standard-Times*, June 16, 1968, 4D.

5. *Big Spring Herald*, June 6, 1947, 5.

6. *Abilene Reporter-News*, June 7, 1947, 4.

7. *Paris (TX) News*, February 8, 1948, 11.

8. *Odessa American*, July 11, 1948, 11.

9. *Austin (TX) American-Statesman*, August 4, 1949, 26.

10. *Abilene Reporter-News*, March 30, 1949, 7.

11. *Odessa American*, December 9, 1998, 7D.

12. *Odessa American*, May 20, 1949, 8.

13. *Big Spring Herald*, May 7, 1950, 11.

14. Patricia Stasey Aylor, *Stealing Home* (Ballinger, TX: Ballinger Printing & Graphics, 2012), 101.

15. *San Angelo Standard-Times*, June 16, 1968, 4D.

16. *Washington Post*, July 8, 1950, 10.

17. *Chattanooga (TN) Times*, July 16, 1950, 43.

18. *Corsicana Sun*, May 26, 1950, 9.

19. *San Angelo Standard-Times*, June 16, 1968, 4D.

20. *San Angelo Standard-Times*, June 16, 1968, 4D.

21. *Wilmington (DE) Morning-News*, March 14, 1951, 31.

22. *Washington Post*, March 21, 1951, 17.

23. *Washington Post*, March 19, 1951, 11.

24. *Washington Post*, March 21, 1951, 17.

25. *Washington Post*, February 20, 1951, 17.

26. *Big Spring Herald*, July 27, 1951, 7.

27. *Vernon (TX) Daily Record*, March 13, 1951, 7.

28. *Big Spring Herald*, January 25, 1952, 11.

29. *Abilene Reporter-News*, November 4, 1952, 20.

30. *St. Louis Post-Dispatch*, March 23, 1955, 6B.

31. *San Angelo Standard-Times*, June 16, 1968, 4D.

32. *Hobbs (NM) News-Sun*, August 5, 1956, 5.

33. *Odessa American*, December 9, 1998, 7D.

34. *San Angelo Standard-Times*, March 30, 2005, 1D.

35. *Los Angeles Times*, March 29, 1991, C9.

36. *New York Times Sunday Magazine*, July 13, 2014, 18.

37. *Artesia Advocate*, August 31, 1954, 3.

38. Toby Smith, *Bush League Boys* (Albuquerque: University of New Mexico Press, 2014), 152.

39. *Big Spring Herald*, September 6, 1968, 5B.

40. Aylor, *Stealing Home*, 121.

41. *Make No Little Plans: Daniel Burnham and the American City*, documentary directed by Judith McBrien, aired nationally on PBS stations in 2010, http://www.pbs.org/programs/make-no-little-plans/.

42. Beau Tiongson, "A Real 'Field of Dreams,'" *Glen Rose (TX) Reporter*, July 31, 2012, http://www.yourglenrosetx.com/article/20120731/News/307319899, accessed October 28, 2018.

43. Tiongson, "A Real 'Field of Dreams.'"

44. *Reader's Digest*, October 1952, 10.

7. THE BOBO AND JOJO SHOW

1. *Sporting News*, May 30, 1951, 14.
2. Ogden Nash, with illustrations by C. F. Payne, *Lineup for Yesterday* (Mankato, MN: Creative Editions, 2011), 30.
3. *Washington Post*, April 1, 1942, 20.
4. *Washington Post*, August 27, 1946, 13.
5. *Sporting News*, January 27, 1954, 12.
6. *Chattanooga Times*, April 14, 1949, 21.
7. *Chattanooga Times*, March 25, 1949, 37.
8. *Las Vegas (NV) Sun*, June 21, 1968, 25.
9. *Eureka (CA) Times Standard*, April 30, 1954, 10.
10. *Chattanooga Times*, April 14, 1949, 21.
11. *Chattanooga News-Free Press*, April 12, 1949, 14.
12. *Monroe (LA) News-Star*, April 17, 1949, 9.
13. *Washington Post*, March 27, 1950, 10.
14. *St. Louis Post-Dispatch*, June 13, 1950, 22.
15. *Chattanooga Times*, March 29, 1949, 13.
16. *Chattanooga Times*, May 2, 1960, 3.
17. *Chattanooga Times*, May 2, 1960, 3.
18. *Chattanooga Times*, April 20, 1949, 17.
19. *Chattanooga Times*, May 3, 1949, 11.
20. *Chattanooga Times*, June 14, 1949, 13.
21. *Chattanooga Times*, June 14, 1949, 13.
22. *Sporting News*, November 28, 1940, 4.
23. *Chattanooga Times*, May 7, 1949, 9.
24. *Chattanooga Times*, May 21, 1949, 11.
25. *Chattanooga Times*, June 12, 1949, 43.
26. *Birmingham (AL) News*, June 7, 1949, 25.
27. *Chattanooga Times*, July 11, 1949, 9.
28. *Chattanooga Times*, May 26, 1949, 15.
29. *Chattanooga Times*, July 3, 1949, Section 4, 1.
30. *Chattanooga Times*, July 4, 1949, 1.
31. *Chattanooga Times*, July 4, 1949, 8.
32. *Memphis (TN) Commercial-Appeal*, July 14, 1949, 34.
33. *Memphis Commercial-Appeal*, July 14, 1949, 34.
34. *Chattanooga News-Free Press*, July 14, 1949, 13.
35. *Washington Post*, July 16, 1949, 10.
36. *Chattanooga Times*, March 28, 1950, 11.
37. *Beckley (WV) Post-Herald*, July 19, 1949, 6.
38. *Washington Post*, July 15, 1949, B5.

39. *Chattanooga News-Free Press*, July 14, 1949, 13.
40. *Chattanooga Times*, July 15, 1949, 17.
41. *Chattanooga News-Free Press*, July 15, 1949, 13.
42. *Washington Post*, February 27, 1950, 10.
43. *Chattanooga Times*, July 25, 1949, 9.
44. *Chattanooga Times*, August 10, 1949, 13.
45. *Chattanooga News-Free Press*, August 13, 1949, 14.
46. *Sportfolio*, July 1947, 98.
47. *Chattanooga Times*, August 29, 1949, 11.
48. *Chattanooga News-Free Press*, August 29, 1949, 10.
49. *Chattanooga Times*, December 26, 1962, 17.
50. *Chattanooga Times*, September 2, 1949, 17.
51. *Chattanooga Times*, September 8, 1949, 13.
52. *Chattanooga News-Free Press*, September 10, 1949, 1.
53. *Chattanooga Times*, March 17, 1950, 37.
54. *Chattanooga Times*, March 1, 1950, 11.
55. *Chattanooga Times*, March 28, 1950, 11.
56. *Chattanooga Times*, March 28, 1950, 11.
57. *Washington Post*, March 27, 1950, 10.
58. *Atlanta (GA) Constitution*, June 1, 1950, 29.
59. *Chattanooga News-Free Press*, April 11, 1950, 10.
60. *Nashville (TN) Banner*, April 14, 1950, A10.
61. *Chattanooga Times*, April 16, 1950, 51.
62. *Nashville Banner*, April 15, 1950, 8.
63. *Sporting News*, May 3, 1950, 39.
64. *Chattanooga Times*, May 7, 1950, 50.
65. *Chattanooga News-Free Press*, May 3, 1950, 14.
66. *Nashville Banner*, May 3, 1950, 22.
67. *Chattanooga Times*, May 7, 1950, 47.
68. *Chattanooga Times*, May 8, 1950, 11.
69. *Chattanooga News-Free Press*, May 26, 1950, 17.
70. *Chattanooga News-Free Press*, May 26, 1950, 17.
71. *Chattanooga Times*, December 26, 1962, 17.
72. *Chattanooga Times*, August 7, 1950, 11.
73. *Washington Post*, April 2, 1951, 8.
74. *Chattanooga Times*, August 3, 1950, 17.
75. *Chattanooga Times*, September 20, 1950, 17.
76. *Atlanta Constitution*, April 3, 1951, 8.
77. *Washington Post*, February 27, 1951, 13.
78. *Sporting News*, September 27, 1950, 11.
79. *Washington Post*, December 11, 1962, C1.

80. *Uniontown (PA) Evening Standard*, March 15, 1951, 30.
81. *Chattanooga Times*, March 15, 1951, 21.
82. *Washington Post*, April 2, 1951, 8.
83. *Sporting News*, April 11, 1951, 12.
84. *Birmingham News*, June 27, 1951, 26.
85. *Birmingham News*, August 12, 1951, C1.
86. *Birmingham News*, September 21, 1951, 1.
87. *Birmingham News*, October 5, 1951, 38.
88. *Tennessean (Nashville, TN)*, March 21, 1952, 49.
89. *Sporting News*, April 16, 1952, 2.
90. *Washington Post*, April 4, 1952, B3.
91. *Sporting News*, April 16, 1952, 2.
92. *Sporting News*, June 18, 1952, 16.
93. *Sporting News*, January 13, 1954, 11.
94. *Sporting News*, January 27, 1954, 12.
95. *Indiana (PA) Gazette*, September 1, 1953, 11.
96. *Chattanooga Post*, June 24, 1969, 12.
97. *Washington Post*, July 20, 1947, C2.
98. *Chattanooga News-Free Press*, April 4, 1952, 14.
99. *Sporting News*, May 24, 1945, 10.
100. *Louisville (KY) Courier-Journal*, April 19, 1947, 14.

8. "A BOY NAMED KINGSTON"

1. *New York Herald Tribune*, March 2, 1955, 24.
2. *New York Herald Tribune*, March 2, 1955, 24.
3. *Sporting News*, March 16, 1955, 15.
4. *Kansas City (MO) Star*, March 11, 1955, 32.
5. *Kansas City Times*, March 11, 1955, 34.
6. *Kansas City Star*, March 11, 1955, 32.
7. *Amarillo Globe-Times*, July 23, 1957, 11.
8. *Rochester (NY) Democrat and Chronicle*, August 17, 1963, 20.
9. *Savannah (GA) Evening Press*, September 11, 1954, 8.
10. *Council Bluffs (IA) Nonpareil*, July 9, 1950, 25.
11. *Council Bluffs Nonpareil*, July 18, 1950, 8.

9. PLAYING DRUNK

1. *Sporting News*, August 5, 1959, 9.

2. *Pantagraph (Bloomington, IL)*, March 6, 1955, 28.

3. *Pantagraph*, March 6, 1955, 28.

4. *Oregonian (Portland, OR)*, May 16, 1955, Section 2, 1–2.

5. *Oregonian*, July 28, 1955, Section 2, 1.

6. *Oregonian*, August 14, 1955, Section 2, 1.

7. *Oregonian*, January 20, 1956, Section 2, 1.

8. *Sporting News*, June 19, 1957, 29.

9. *Sporting News*, June 19, 1957, 29.

10. *Frederick (MD) News*, October 2, 1958, 6.

11. *Seattle (WA) Times*, July 7, 1960, 24.

12. Dan Raley, *Pitchers of Beer: The Story of the Seattle Rainiers* (Lincoln: University of Nebraska Press, 2011), 249.

13. Charlie Metro, with Tom Altherr, *Safe by a Mile* (Lincoln: University of Nebraska Press, 2002), 211.

14. *Seattle Times*, July 7, 1960, 24.

15. *Seattle Times*, July 7, 1960, 24.

16. *Seattle Times*, July 6, 1960, 49.

17. *Seattle Times*, July 7, 1960, 24.

18. *Seattle Times*, August 2, 1962, 30.

19. Branch Rickey, edited by John J. Monteleone, *Branch Rickey's Little Blue Book* (New York: Mountain Lion Books/Macmillan, 1995), 110.

20. Brent Kelley, *Voices from the Negro Leagues* (Jefferson, NC: McFarland, 1998), 145.

21. *Pittsburgh (PA) Courier*, August 22, 1942, 1.

22. *Pittsburgh Press*, August 21, 1942, 30.

23. *Pittsburgh Post-Gazette*, August 4, 1976, 32.

24. *Pittsburgh Post-Gazette*, July 28, 1976, 18.

25. *Pittsburgh Post-Gazette*, March 21, 1993, 49.

10. A WHIFF OF THE BIG TIME

1. George W. Hilton, *The Annotated Baseball Stories of Ring W. Lardner* (Stanford, CA: Stanford University Press, 1995), 339.

2. *Des Moines (IA) Tribune*, May 16, 1942, 6.

3. *Santa Cruz (CA) Evening News*, May 28, 1940, 7.

4. *Santa Cruz Sentinel*, August 16, 1994, A-12.

5. *San Francisco Chronicle*, April 29, 1951, 4H.
6. *Tucson (AZ) Daily Citizen*, June 18, 1950, 7.
7. *San Francisco Examiner*, July 3, 1955, 10.
8. *Oregonian*, July 19, 1950, Section 3, 1.
9. *Oregonian*, July 19, 1950, Section 3, 1.
10. *Oregonian*, August 14, 1951, Section 3, 1.
11. *Oregonian*, August 14, 1951, Section 3, 1.
12. *Oregonian*, March 27, 1951, Section 3, 1.
13. *Oregonian*, April 14, 1951, Section 3, 1–2.
14. *Santa Cruz Sentinel*, October 9, 1938, 6.
15. *Sporting News*, April 21, 1940, 9.
16. *San Francisco Examiner*, June 19, 1940, 21.
17. *San Francisco Examiner*, October 21, 1940, 15.
18. *San Francisco Examiner*, April 7, 1947, 20.
19. *San Francisco News*, March 16, 1948, 16.
20. *San Francisco Examiner*, March 15, 1948, 23.
21. *Sporting News*, April 7, 1948, 19.
22. *Sporting News*, January 1, 1947, 3.
23. *San Francisco Examiner*, March 4, 1949, 17.
24. *San Francisco Examiner*, March 5, 1949, 15.
25. *San Francisco Chronicle*, March 6, 1949, 5H.
26. *San Francisco News*, March 3, 1949, 23.
27. *San Francisco Chronicle*, March 6, 1949, 5H.
28. *San Francisco Call-Bulletin*, March 30, 1949, 20.
29. *San Francisco Call-Bulletin*, April 1, 1949, 21.
30. *San Francisco Examiner*, April 1, 1949, 30.
31. *San Francisco Call-Bulletin*, April 1, 1949, 21.
32. *Oregonian*, April 8, 1949, Section 3, 2.
33. *Oregonian*, September 1, 1955, Section 2, 16.
34. *Sacramento (CA) Union*, March 6, 1953, 8.
35. *Oregonian*, September 7, 1952, Section 2, 3.
36. *Sacramento Union*, March 6, 1953, 8.
37. *Sacramento Union*, March 10, 1953, 5.
38. *Oregonian*, March 24, 1953, Section 3, 1.
39. *Los Angeles Times*, November 5, 1954, Part 4, 1.
40. *Oregonian*, April 15, 1953, Section 3, 1.
41. *Oakland (CA) Tribune*, March 7, 1955, 29.
42. *Oakland Tribune*, January 14, 1955, 41.
43. *Oakland Tribune*, June 30, 1955, 56.
44. *Sporting News*, July 6, 1955, 8.
45. *Cincinnati (OH) Enquirer*, July 22, 1955, 29.

46. *New York Times*, July 23, 1955, 12.

47. *Cincinnati Enquirer*, July 22, 1955, 34.

48. *Cincinnati Enquirer*, July 24, 1955, 54.

49. *Cincinnati Enquirer*, August 4, 1955, 32.

50. *New York Daily News*, August 14, 1955, 26.

51. *San Francisco Chronicle*, August 8, 1955, 4H.

52. *Oregonian*, September 12, 1955, Section 2, 4.

53. *Santa Cruz Sentinel*, February 12, 1985, 9.

54. *Ukiah (CA) Daily Journal*, August 24, 1994, 6.

55. *Dave Newhouse Sports Talk Show*, KNBR Radio, San Francisco, April 1984.

11. UNWANTED

1. *Sporting News*, June 25, 1947, 1.

2. *St. Louis Star and Times*, July 20, 1949, 21.

3. *St. Louis Post-Dispatch*, December 10, 1948, 10D.

4. *Tennessean*, December 25, 1949, 17.

5. *Baseball Digest*, September 1951, 54.

6. *Chicago Sun-Times*, May 19, 1951, 25.

7. *Washington Post*, March 19, 1951, 11.

8. *Baseball Digest*, October 1950, 39.

9. *Sporting News*, August 2, 1950, 9.

10. *Pittsburgh Press*, July 22, 1950, 6.

11. *Pittsburgh Press*, July 22, 1950, 6.

12. *Pittsburgh Post-Gazette*, September 20, 1950, 20.

13. *Pittsburgh Press*, November 30, 1950, 45

14. *San Gabriel Valley Tribune*, March 22, 1993, C3.

15. *Pittsburgh Press*, May 25, 1951, 35.

16. *Sporting News*, May 30, 1951, 4.

17. *Chicago Tribune*, March 25, 1952, Part 3, 2.

18. *Chicago Tribune*, March 25, 1952, Part 3, 2.

19. *Baseball Digest*, September 1951, 51.

20. *Baseball Digest*, September 1951, 51.

21. *Baseball Digest*, September 1951, 55.

22. *Sport*, November 1949, 84.

23. *Sport*, November 1949, 84.

24. Notes from Jim McConnell interview with Bob Dillinger, March 10, 1993.

25. *Daily Journal* (Franklin, IN), April 7, 1976, 4.

26. *Lincoln (NE) Journal Star*, July 24, 1944, 9.

27. *Sporting News*, December 7, 1944, 4.

28. *Arizona Daily Star*, July 1, 1945, 15.

29. *St. Louis Post-Dispatch*, April 14, 1946, 1B, 2B.

30. William B. Mead, *Even the Browns* (Mineola, NY: Dover Publications, 2010), 141.

31. *St. Louis Post-Dispatch*, April 26, 1947, 6A.

32. *St. Louis Post-Dispatch*, May 9, 1947, 8C.

33. *Sport*, November 1949, 23, 84.

34. *Pittsburgh Press*, August 1, 1950, 27.

35. *Sporting News*, May 5, 1948, 17.

36. *Baseball Digest*, September 1951, 54.

37. *Pittsburgh Press*, February 28, 1951, 30.

38. *Sporting News*, May 12, 1948, 9.

39. *Baseball Digest*, June 1952, 67.

40. Notes from Jim McConnell interview with Red Embree, April 10, 1992.

41. *Chicago Daily Tribune*, July 15, 1952, B1.

42. *Baseball Digest*, July 1953, 9–10.

43. *Sacramento Bee*, May 26, 1955, 36.

44. *Sacramento Bee*, May 24, 1955, 28.

45. *Sacramento Bee*, May 26, 1955, 36.

46. *Sacramento Union*, May 30, 1955, 4.

47. *Baseball Digest*, September 1951, 51.

48. *Oregonian*, August 28, 1953, Section 2, 1.

49. *Sporting News*, June 15, 1955, 17.

50. *Baseball Digest*, September 1951, 53.

51. *Baseball Magazine*, August 1947, 295.

52. Notes from Jim McConnell interview with Bob Dillinger, March 10, 1993.

53. *Detroit News-Free Press*, August 6, 1995, 4D.

12. MADE FOR HOLLYWOOD

1. *Los Angeles Herald-Express*, April 24, 1952, C8.

2. *Salt Lake (UT) Tribune*, March 7, 1960, 25.

3. *Los Angeles Times*, March 25, 1955, Part IV, 1.

4. *Los Angeles Mirror*, May 21, 1955, Part III, 1.

5. *Los Angeles Mirror*, August 13, 1954, Part III, 1.

6. *Central New Jersey Home News* (New Brunswick, NJ), May 17, 1948, 14.

7. *Indianapolis News*, August 18, 1949, 18.

8. *Kingston (NY) Daily Freeman*, June 20, 1950, 12.

9. *Los Angeles Times*, June 5, 1952, Part IV, 2.

10. John Schulian, *Twilight of the Long-Ball Gods* (Lincoln: University of Nebraska Press, 2005), 13.

11. *San Francisco Call-Bulletin*, July 31, 1952, 7.

12. *Pittsburgh Post-Gazette*, April 8, 1954, 21.

13. *Sporting News*, September 9, 1953, 23.

14. *Los Angeles Mirror*, June 9, 1954, Part III, 1.

15. *Los Angeles Times*, June 15, 1954, Part IV, 1.

16. *Los Angeles Mirror*, June 14, 1954, Part III, 1.

17. *Los Angeles Mirror*, June 15, 1954, Part III, 1.

18. *Los Angeles Mirror*, August 12, 1954, Part III, 1.

19. *Los Angeles Mirror*, August 16, 1954, Part III, 3.

20. *Los Angeles Times*, August 18, 1954, Part IV, 2.

21. *Los Angeles Times*, March 26, 1955, Part III, 2.

22. *Los Angeles Times*, May 3, 1955, Part I, 33.

23. *Los Angeles Mirror*, May 21, 1955, Part III, 1.

24. *Los Angeles Mirror-News*, August 29, 1956, Part III, 1.

25. *Los Angeles Times*, August 29, 1956, Part II, 1.

26. *Seattle Times*, July 29, 1964, 29.

27. *Honolulu Star-Bulletin*, August 13, 1963, 34.

28. *Honolulu Advertiser*, May 26, 1963, C8.

29. *Honolulu Advertiser*, August 12, 1962, C1.

30. *Honolulu Star-Bulletin*, April 1, 1963, 20.

31. *Honolulu Advertiser*, March 9, 1965, B6.

32. *Honolulu Advertiser*, April 15, 1964, B7.

33. Thomas E. Van Hyning, *Puerto Rico's Winter League* (Jefferson, NC: McFarland, 1995), 120.

34. *Honolulu Advertiser*, May 10, 1989, C1

35. *Honolulu Advertiser*, May 10, 1989, C1.

36. *Honolulu Advertiser*, April 15, 1964, B7.

37. Phillip M. Hoose, *Necessities: Racial Barriers in American Sports* (New York: Random House, 1989), 92.

38. *Pittsburgh Press*, March 30, 1953, 18.

39. *Pittsburgh Press*, May 27, 1953, 44.

40. *Jet*, August 26, 1954, 54.

41. *Pittsburgh Post-Gazette*, April 14, 2013, F1.

13. A TALE OF TWO LEGENDS

1. *Pittsburgh Post-Gazette*, February 25, 1959, 27.
2. *European Stars and Stripes*, August 17, 1996, 24.
3. *Sporting News*, May 7, 1966, 39.
4. *Sports Illustrated*, June 1, 1987, 91.
5. *Sporting News*, May 21, 1952, 36.
6. *Pittsburgh Post-Gazette*, August 7, 1952, 15.
7. *Pittsburgh Press*, August 11, 1952, 15.
8. *Pittsburgh Post-Gazette*, August 11, 1952, 16.
9. *Sports Illustrated*, June 1, 1987, 92.
10. *Sports Illustrated*, June 1, 1987, 92.
11. *Pittsburgh Post-Gazette*, October 14, 1992, A11.
12. *Syracuse (NY) Post-Standard*, April 24, 1979, 19.
13. *Kingsport (TN) Times-News*, September 8, 1957, C1.
14. *Syracuse Post-Standard*, April 24, 1979, 19.
15. *Long Beach (CA) Press-Telegram*, September 6, 1974, C1.
16. *New Mexican* (Santa Fe, NM), July 6, 1979, C4.
17. *Bakersfield Californian*, September 16, 1974, 18.
18. *Baltimore Sun*, February 16, 2003, E1.
19. *High Point (NC) Enterprise*, July 23, 1951, 9.
20. *Pittsburgh Press*, October 24, 1951, 36.
21. *Pittsburgh Press*, October 19, 1951, 39.
22. *Life*, August 13, 1956, 97.
23. Memorandum written by George Detore, June 9, 1969.
24. Memorandum written by George Detore, June 9, 1969.
25. Letter from Bill Ramsay, brother of Frank, to National Baseball Hall of Fame, April 14, 1976.
26. George Stone, *Rocket Ron* (West Conshohocken, PA: Infinity Publishing, 2008), 119.
27. Stone, *Rocket Ron*, 119.
28. *Bristol Herald Courier*, May 14, 1952, 1.
29. *Kingsport Times-News*, May 18, 1952, 2D.
30. *Kingsport Times-News*, May 22, 1952, 9.
31. *Bristol Herald Courier*, May 28, 1952, 2B.
32. *Bristol Herald Courier*, June 6, 1952, 10.
33. *Pittsburgh Press*, August 9, 1952, 6.
34. *Pittsburgh Post-Gazette*, March 18, 1954, 16.
35. Branch Rickey, edited by John J. Monteleone, *Branch Rickey's Little Blue Book* (New York: Mountain Lion Books/Macmillan, 1995), 60.

BIBLIOGRAPHY

Aylor, Patricia Stasey. *Stealing Home*. Ballinger, TX: Ballinger Printing & Graphics, 2012.

Bauer, Carlos. *The Early Coast League Statistical Record, 1903–1957*. San Diego, CA: Baseball Press Books, 2004.

Dobbins, Dick. *The Grand Minor League*. Emeryville, CA: Woodford Press, 1999.

Hilton, George W. *The Annotated Baseball Stories of Ring W. Lardner*. Stanford, CA: Stanford University Press, 1995.

Hoose, Phillip M. *Necessities: Racial Barriers in American Sports*. New York: Random House, 1989.

Joyner, Ronnie, and Bill Bozman. *He Hits! He Steals! He's Bob Dillinger!* Dunkirk, MD: Pepperpot Productions, 2006.

Kelley, Brent. *Voices from the Negro Leagues*. Jefferson, NC: McFarland, 1998.

Lardner, Ring. *You Know Me Al*. Richmond, VA: Westvaco Corporation, 1994.

McConnell, Jim. *Bobo Newsom: Baseball's Traveling Man*. Jefferson, NC: McFarland, 2016.

Mead, William B. *Even the Browns*. Mineola, NY: Dover Publications, 2010.

Metro, Charlie, with Tom Altherr. *Safe by a Mile*. Lincoln: University of Nebraska Press, 2002.

Mickelson, Ed. *Out of the Park: Memoir of a Minor League Baseball All-Star*. Jefferson, NC: McFarland, 2007.

Nash, Ogden, with illustrations by C. F. Payne. *Lineup for Yesterday*. Mankato, MN: Creative Editions, 2011.

Neyer, Rob. *Rob Neyer's Big Book of Baseball Legends*. New York: Simon & Schuster, 2008.

Raley, Dan. *Pitchers of Beer: The Story of the Seattle Rainiers*. Lincoln: University of Nebraska Press, 2011.

Revel, Layton, and Luis Munoz. *Forgotten Heroes: Alfred Pinkston*. Carrollton, TX: Center for Negro League Baseball Research, 2013.

Rickey, Branch, edited by John J. Monteleone. *Branch Rickey's Little Blue Book*. New York: Mountain Lion Books/Macmillan, 1995.

Salin, Tony. *Baseball's Forgotten Heroes*. Lincolnwood, IL: Masters Press, 1999.

Schulian, John. *Twilight of the Long-Ball Gods*. Lincoln: University of Nebraska Press, 2005.

Smith, Toby. *Bush League Boys*. Albuquerque: University of New Mexico Press, 2014.

Snelling, Dennis. *A Glimpse of Fame*. Jefferson, NC: McFarland, 1993.

Stone, George. *Rocket Ron*. West Conshohocken, PA: Infinity Publishing, 2008.

Sutter, L. M. *New Mexico Baseball*. Jefferson, NC: McFarland, 2010.

Van Hyning, Thomas E. *Puerto Rico's Winter League*. Jefferson, NC: McFarland, 1995.

Veeck, Bill, with Ed Linn. *Veeck—as in Wreck: The Autobiography of Bill Veeck*. Chicago: University of Chicago Press, 2001.

INDEX

135; "KITCHY-KITCHY-KOO," 149;
Marco Polo of the Majors, 138; Nomad
of the Diamond, 138; "Old Bobo," 136;
Original Rambling Rose of Baseball,
138; Road Map, 138; Wandering
Minstrel of Baseball, 138
Nickson Hotel, 70
Nix, Ralph, Jr. "Skippy," 73, 74
Nixon, President Richard M., xv, 58
Noren, Irv, 282
Normandy, 196
North Camp Hood, Texas, 45
Notre Dame, 115
Novikoff, Lou "The Mad Russian," 4
Nuevo Laredo, Mexico, 87
NuMex refinery, 73
Nunez, Esteban "Steve," 126, 129

Oakland Oaks, 183, 232
Oakland Tribune, 227, 234; Newhouse,
Dave, 234
Oaks Park, 228
O'Brien, Johnny, 191, 192
Odendahl, Max, 96
Odessa, Texas, 16
Odessa American, 29; Peeler, Ben, 29
Odessa Oilers, 114
O'Doul, Francis "Lefty," 186, 215, 220,
221, 222; "Marble Head O'Doul," 222
Oildale, California, 304
Oklahoma City, Oklahoma, 60, 63
Oklahoma Journal, 357
Oklahoma Semipro League, 64, 79
Oklahoma State University, 60
Olbermann, Keith, 78
Old Style beer, 195
Olds Rocket 88, 78
Oldsmobile, 1, 142
Oneonta, New York, 45
Operation Peach Fuzz, 309
Optimist League, 88
Orange Crush, 64
Oregonian, 184, 185, 212, 226, 257;
Gregory, L. H., 184, 185, 212, 226, 257
Organized Baseball, xxii, 16, 23, 24, 35,
44, 48, 70, 74, 96, 97, 98, 117, 159,
162, 164, 175, 177, 182, 201, 204, 292,
312
Orsino, John, 285

Ortega, Evelio, 121
Ortiz, Oliverio "Baby," 70
Osenbaugh, Roger, 254, 257, 258
Osmond, Marie, 7
Ott, Mel, 136
Owens, Jesse, 246
Owensboro, Kentucky, 23

Pacific Coast Highway, 214
Pacific Coast League (PCL), ix, xii, xx, 2,
3, 20, 82, 94, 168, 181, 186, 190, 207,
209, 213, 218, 220, 227–228, 229, 230,
232, 233, 235, 253, 261, 263, 267, 268,
273, 276, 280, 288, 306; PCL Hall of
Fame, 288; PCL Historical Society,
288; PCL Triple Crown, xxi
Paige, Satchel, 24, 244, 306
Palys, Stan, 229
Pampa Daily News, 20; Hasse, Warren, 20
Pampa Oilers, 16, 41
Panhandle Hall of Fame, 54
Papa Joe Cambria, 111
Parker, Wes, 263–264; Brentwood, Los
Angeles, California, x; Dodgers, x; first
baseman, x; Gold Glove Award, x;
Japan, Nankai Hawks, x; University of
Southern California, x
Parnell, Mel, 255
Parr, Royse, xvi, 64–66; "pop boy," 64
Parris, Collier, 27; *Abilene Reporter-News*,
27
Partee, Roy, 93
Pascual, Camilio, 112, 120, 121; "Little
Potato," 118, 120
Pascual, Carlos "Potato" "Spud," 116–119,
122, 124
Paterson, New Jersey, xiii, 283
Pat's Slammers, 133
Patterson, Lin, xvi, 68, 96
Paul, Gabe, 228, 229
PCL. *See* Pacific Coast League
Pearl Harbor, 77
Pecos, Texas, 29
Pecos League, 108
Pecos River, xx
Pecos Sales Company, 81
Peeler, Ben, 29, 30; *Odessa American*, 29
Pelican Stadium, 150
Perez, Marcos, 287; *San Juan Star*, 287

ABOUT THE AUTHOR

Gaylon H. White is the author of *Singles and Smiles* and *The Bilko Athletic Club* and coauthor with Ransom Jackson of *Handsome Ransom Jackson: Accidental Big Leaguer*. These highly acclaimed books were published by Rowman & Littlefield.

The Los Angeles–born White graduated in 1967 from the University of Oklahoma, with a bachelor's degree in journalism and broadcasting. He was a sportswriter for the *Denver Post*, *Arizona Republic*, and *Oklahoma Journal* before working nearly 40 years for such varied companies as Hallmark Cards, Inc.; the Goodyear Tire & Rubber Company; Control Data Corporation; and Eastman Chemical Company.

At Eastman, White worked closely with industrial designers, and in 2015 the Industrial Designers Society of America selected him as one of its 50 most notable members from the past half-century.

He and his wife, Mary, live in Kingsport, Tennessee. They have three children and seven grandchildren.